Proto-Phenomenology, Language Acquisition, Orality, and Literacy

New Heidegger Research

Series Editors:

Gregory Fried, Professor of Philosophy, Boston College, USA

Richard Polt, Professor of Philosophy, Xavier University, USA

The New Heidegger Research series promotes informed and critical dialogue that breaks new philosophical ground by taking into account the full range of Heidegger's thought, as well as the enduring questions raised by his work.

Titles in the Series:

After Heidegger?
Edited by Gregory Fried and Richard Polt

Correspondence 1949–1975
Martin Heidegger, Ernst Jünger, translated by Timothy Quinn

Existential Medicine
Edited by Kevin Aho

Heidegger and Jewish Thought
Edited by Micha Brumlik and Elad Lapidot

Heidegger and the Environment
Casey Rentmeester

Heidegger and the Global Age
Edited by Antonio Cerella and Louiza Odysseos

Heidegger Becoming Phenomenological: Preferring Dilthey to Husserl, 1916–25
Robert C. Schaff

Heidegger in Russia and Eastern Europe
Edited by Jeff Love

Heidegger's Gods: An Ecofeminist Perspective
Susanne Claxton

Making Sense of Heidegger
Thomas Sheehan

Proto-Phenomenology and the Nature of Language
Lawrence J. Hatab

Heidegger in the Islamicate World
Edited by Kata Moser, Urs Gösken and Josh Michael Hayes

Time and Trauma: Thinking through Heidegger in the Thirties
Richard Polt

Contexts of Suffering: A Heideggerian Approach to Psychopathology
Kevin Aho

Heidegger's Phenomenology of Perception: An Introduction, Volume I
David Kleinberg-Levin

Confronting Heidegger: A Critical Dialogue on Politics and Philosophy
Edited by Gregory Fried

Proto-Phenomenology, Language Acquisition, Orality, and Literacy: Dwelling in Speech II
Lawrence J. Hatab

Proto-Phenomenology, Language Acquisition, Orality, and Literacy

Dwelling in Speech II

Lawrence J. Hatab

London • New York

Published by Rowman & Littlefield International Ltd.
6 Tinworth Street, London, SE11 5AL, UK
www.rowmaninternational.com

Rowman & Littlefield International Ltd. is an affiliate of Rowman & Littlefield
4501 Forbes Boulevard, Suite 200, Lanham, Maryland 20706, USA
With additional offices in Boulder, New York, Toronto (Canada), and Plymouth (UK)
www.rowman.com

Copyright © 2020 by Lawrence J. Hatab

All rights reserved. No part of this book may be reproduced in any form or by any electronic or mechanical means, including information storage and retrieval systems, without written permission from the publisher, except by a reviewer who may quote passages in a review.

British Library Cataloguing in Publication Data
A catalogue record for this book is available from the British Library

ISBN: HB 978-1-78661-398-1

Library of Congress Cataloging-in-Publication Data Available

ISBN 978-1-78661-398-1 (cloth)
ISBN 978-1-5381-4806-8 (pbk)
ISBN 978-1-78661-399-8 (electronic)

To Stephanie and Rustum

Contents

	Preface	xi
	Introduction	1
	1 Language Acquisition and Child Development	3
	2 Language Acquisition	4
	3 Oral and Written Language	5
	4 The Literate World	6
1	Proto-Phenomenology and Language: A Summary of Volume I	9
	1 Proto-Phenomenology and the Lived World	10
	2 The Personal-World	14
	3 The Environing-World	15
	4 The Social-World	22
	5 Projection	26
	6 Temporality	27
	7 Embodiment	29
	8 Disclosure and Interpretation	30
	9 Language	35
	10 Truth and Pluralism	47
2	The Child's World	55
	1 Ecstatic Dwelling	61
	2 The Personal-Social-World	64
	3 The Environing-World	79
	4 Affective Attunement	86
	5 Projection	88

	6 Temporality and History	90
	7 Embodiment	91
	8 On the Way to Language	93
3	**Language Acquisition**	**103**
	1 Natural Language	103
	2 The Phenomenological Priority of Language	105
	3 Language Learning and Dwelling	107
	4 The Personal-Social-World	115
	5 Embodiment and the Environing-World	125
	6 Temporality and History	131
	7 Differential Fitness, Development, and Truth	137
	8 Summary	143
4	**Orality and Literacy**	**151**
	1 Oral and Written Language: Two Different Worlds?	152
	2 The Alphabet and Learning How to Read and Write	155
	3 Orality in Ancient Greece	160
	4 Elements of Orality and Literacy	164
	5 Proto-Phenomenology and Literacy	179
5	**Philosophy and Literacy in the Greek World**	**187**
	1 Myth in Ancient Greece	188
	2 The Homeric World	190
	3 The Advent of Philosophy	192
	4 Plato and the Poets	195
	5 Literacy and Philosophy	198
	6 Plato and Writing	205
	7 Some Effects of Literacy in Greek Philosophy	217
6	**The Transcribed World**	**235**
	1 From Greek to Latin	237
	2 The Evolution of Literacy	241
	3 Print	245
	4 Science and the Book of Nature	249
	5 Representation and Subjectivity	253
	6 Literal and Metaphorical Language	260
	7 A Post-Literate World?	265
	8 Concluding Remarks	272
Glossary		**281**
Bibliography		**287**
Index		**305**
About the Author		**313**

Preface

Volume I of my investigation, *Proto-Phenomenology and the Nature of Language*, attempted to devise a new vocabulary and focus regarding Heidegger's phenomenology, geared toward the question of language. I tried to work *from* Heidegger's thought in my own way and with my own terminology, with a concentration on the early analysis of factical existence in *Being and Time*, of everyday embeddedness in meaningful practices and experiences—without venturing into Heidegger's larger ontological concerns. I take that groundbreaking analysis to be rich in prospects for engaging a number of standard philosophical questions: meaning, values, knowledge, selfhood, social relations, practical life, and language (among others). I was able to find some resonance with philosophical work outside the continental tradition, even with new developments in cognitive science. Yet, I wanted to maintain a core commitment to what has come to be called hermeneutical phenomenology. Accordingly, I have aimed for a wide audience, which is risky but fitting my philosophical disposition. With even further expansion, the second volume of my work is meant to supplement and fortify a proto-phenomenological approach to language by exploring areas of study that are usually not addressed in philosophy or that have not been given sufficient attention when taken up by philosophers: namely, child development, language acquisition, and the difference between oral and written language.

Some readers of Volume I have been disappointed by my relatively thin treatment of writers in the phenomenological tradition, beyond an obvious reliance on Heidegger and Merleau-Ponty. The same might hold for readers of Volume II. I want to reiterate here what was perhaps inadequately articulated in Volume I: for better or worse, my approach does not aim to properly survey continental or phenomenological writers, either to document shared treatments or attend to alternative accounts. My orientation and vocabulary have drawn mostly from Heideggerian phenomenology, but in a manner that opens pathways not duly addressed in Heidegger's work. The same can be said for much of phenomenological thought, especially when confined to its technical terminology, the engagement with its historical background, and debates among its significant authors. An admitted motive in my work is to stimulate more effective outreach to non-continental sources and disciplines outside of philosophy. For these and other reasons, I did not want to get caught up in exegetical comparisons of relevant treatments in phenomenology. This is not meant to discount the importance of such sources; I was more driven to venture forth in my own way, yet in a manner that I hope is still faithful to phenomenological philosophy.

In addition to continental treatments referenced in Volume I, there are other works that at least deserve mention because they accord well with or predate my account of proto-phenomenology. One important text I have omitted is Robert Sokolowski, *Phenomenology of the Human Person* (Cambridge: Cambridge University Press, 2008); also Jan Patočka, *The Natural World as a Philosophical Problem*, trans. Erika Abrams (Evanston, IL: Northwestern University Press, 2016). After the completion of the first volume, I came across two books that fit my approach in a number of significant ways: Andrew Inkpin, *Disclosing the World: On the Phenomenology of Language* (Cambridge, MA: MIT Press, 2016); and Charles Taylor, *The Language Animal: The Full Shape of the Human Linguistic Capacity* (Cambridge, MA: Belknap Press, 2016).[1]

This second volume includes some reiteration of material from Volume I, which will aid readers who are coming to Volume II without having read Volume I. Indeed, the first chapter is an abridged summary of the entirety of Volume I. Those familiar with the first volume can therefore skip chapter 1. I have also included a glossary of terms used in my investigation, which can be helpful for new readers.

I once again thank Richard Polt and Gregory Fried (and Sarah Campbell of Rowman & Littlefield International) for including my study in the New Heidegger Research series. Their interest in publishing work inspired by, conversant with, but not restricted to, Heidegger's thought is commendable. My investigation probably pushes this ambition to the limit, but my hope is that readers of Heidegger will recognize my analysis as a worthy extension of Heideggerian phenomenology. I particularly want to thank Richard Polt for taking the time to read my manuscript chapters and provide helpful feedback. As always, thanks to my wife Chelsy, for continuing to love and support a man who lives in a proverbial cave most of the time.

NOTE

1. Inkpin's work is an effective account of presentational disclosure in language and a "minimalist phenomenology" rooted in everyday life. He provides complementary readings of Heidegger, Merleau-Ponty, and Wittgenstein to fill out the philosophical picture undergirding his investigations. He also does well to show links with the 4E model of cognitive science. Taylor's study advances the constitutive of role of language in shaping meaningful experience of the world. He challenges descriptive, instrumental, and naturalistic models of language by way of a hermeneutical emphasis on the German Romantics Hamann, Herder, and Humboldt, along with Heidegger, Gadamer, Merleau-Ponty, and Wittgenstein. Both Inkpin and Taylor attend well to the social conditions of language, and Taylor includes an examination of language acquisition in childhood. Neither writer, however, takes up the role of literacy in traditional linguistic theories and its transformation of oral language. Another distinctive feature of my own work is the articulation and extension of an immersion-contravention-exposition dynamic drawn from Heideggerian phenomenology. Nonetheless, Inkpin and Taylor have offered impressive investigations that are a significant contribution to the growing interest in phenomenological approaches to language.

Introduction

Volume I of my investigation advanced a proto-phenomenological analysis of the lived world, followed by its application to the question of language. Much of philosophy since the Modern period has been based in the subject-object binary, largely in deference to scientific rationality, where nature is construed in objective, material terms divorced from human values, purposes, and meanings. Epistemological questions have been dominant and grounded in representational relations between the mind/brain and the external world. Cognition has typically been examined in monological terms, as transactions between an individual mind and the world, and between individual minds in communication formats. Language too has been construed as a representational relation between words, semantic meanings, and grammatical structures on the one hand, and mental states or external realities on the other hand.

A proto-phenomenological account of the lived world begins with the "first" world of normal everyday existence prior to reflective analysis and the subject-object division. Even some versions of phenomenology miss this normal domain by emphasizing cognition and abstract constructions of "consciousness" and "intentional objects." Much of human experience, however, is a matter of immersed engagement in practical and social environments, where meaningful practices such as getting dressed or having a conversation are not perceived to be relational transactions between mental states, external objects, and actions, or between mental beliefs and a communicative transfer to other minds. Rather, it is the direct and immediate space of the immersed practice itself, *there* in the environment. From this perspective, the self, other selves, and things in the world are a seamless flow of engagement. What follows is the notion of a threefold personal-social-environing-world—a single world with three interpenetrating dimensions—which is meaning-laden rather than objectified, socially shaped rather than individualized, and environmentally engaged rather than separated into internal and external spheres. Conditions of immersion are more original than reflective disengagement, but disturbances interrupt engagement and then draw attention to specific aspects of self and world, which allows space for subjective and objective angles that have animated traditional philosophical theories. The point is not that subjective, objective, and representational notions are false, but that they are derived from an original field of immersed involvement that should be rendered in more immediate, *presentational* terms. Knowledge at this more original level is better understood as practical know-how and tacit understanding, as habituated conditions of pre-reflective aptitude. Disclosure of the world is not at first an objective description or a representational relation, but a presentational field constituted by active engagement, affective attunement, and tacit know-how. The summary term I use in this account is *dwelling*, which in its verb sense indicates meaningfully inhabiting life, and in its noun sense suggests an actual environing habitat.

Proto-phenomenology focuses on language as the core of world-disclosiveness, as the circulation of language and world that is ever operative, even when we have experiences without speaking—because meaningful human "experience" traces all the way back to learning language as a child, which begins to shape how the world is engaged and understood. The phenomenological priority of language is not equivalent to linguistic idealism because language is situated in social, practical, and natural *environments*, and so not reducible to the lexical perspective of "words" alone. In any case, the world-disclosiveness of language should be understood originally in immersed, embodied, engaged, and presentational terms. Yet the "difference" between words and the world allows for descriptive articulation and a temporal, exponential expansion beyond immediate occasions of experience. Language, in sum, is the constitutive power that informs both normal understanding and then, derivatively, the many refined expositions of disciplinary knowledge. Proto-phenomenology simply calls for rational disciplines to not forget or conceal their first world. Philosophy and science, for example, as meaningful human endeavors, remain animated by energies operating in the lived world.

Such critical constraint placed upon philosophy and science can have persuasive force if one follows a phenomenological pathway, as I have done in studying Heidegger for almost fifty years. First-person attention to normal experience is the initial gateway to a proto-phenomenological account—which is not a matter of "introspection" or "consciousness" but an opening to the personal-social-environing-*world*. My hope has been that readers can follow this path and find it convincing. Yet I indicated in Volume I that *baseline* philosophical orientations do not themselves stem from inferential logistics, but rather existential bearings. That is why no core philosophical position, including mine, can ever be a slam dunk, can ever be established by demonstrative argument. Nevertheless, in the course of my career, I have come to embrace two avenues of analysis that can strengthen a proto-phenomenological account of language with a certain empirical supplement. Those avenues stem from research in (1) child development and language acquisition, and (2) the history of literacy and its alteration of oral language. The inclusion of these research areas in my approach to language is the subject of this second volume. After chapter 1, which is a condensed summary of Volume I, the book will proceed according to the following themes.

1. LANGUAGE ACQUISITION AND CHILD DEVELOPMENT

Chapter 2 will coordinate proto-phenomenological findings with stages of child development, where children first become acclimated to their world. Childhood has not been given sufficient consideration in philosophy, most likely because philosophy examines complex reflections that are not evident in a child's experience and abilities, especially in preverbal stages. Childhood has been largely ignored, downplayed, or described as a prelude to, or deficiency of, mature rational competence. Even when child development is addressed positively by philosophers, the analysis usually emphasizes reflective processes that I maintain are not exhibited in early experience and behavior. The predominance of theoretical paradigms and rationalized vocabularies has concealed much of a child's world and how it differs from adult understanding.

I argue that proto-phenomenology can best help us make sense of a child's emerging world. Attention to pre-reflective dwelling improves upon standard approaches to child development that have emphasized exclusive conditions, scientific experimentation, and theoretical models of mentality. Yet, I will address important advances in developmental psychology that can resonate with a phenomenological orientation, that has questioned many working assumptions in the field, which are diagnosed as uncritical adoptions of adult perspectives and theoretical formats drawn from the subject-object divide. In particular, I draw from so-called naturalistic studies of children in their normal environments and interactions with caregivers. There has arisen a recognition that traditional research has controlled for and presumed theoretical criteria concerning how children behave, learn, and comprehend—which screens out complex and variegated modes of dwelling in a child's experience. I will show how this revised approach to child development matches up well with proto-phenomenological findings, even though there remain some facets of the research that can be improved by more apt phenomenological attention and analysis. Significant phenomenological concepts applicable to child development include immersed dwelling, the social-world as constitutive of a child's self-development, embodiment, practical involvement with the environing-world, and affective attunement.

2. LANGUAGE ACQUISITION

Chapter 3 will establish that the same kind of complementary relationship between proto-phenomenology and developmental psychology applies to research on language acquisition, where phenomenological concepts can help focus, articulate, and revise findings concerning how language emerges in a child's world and indeed prepares that emergence long before words are first spoken. Especially relevant here are the personal-social-environing-world, immersion and imitation, joint attention, embodied practice, habituation, and temporality. What follows are a few selected topics that forecast the way in which proto-phenomenology contributes to understanding child development and language acquisition.

The important role of imitation in various linguistic, social, and behavioral circumstances in a child's life can be taken as an original condition of immersion. Mimetic behavior shows that what is "outside" in the child's environment precedes a fully formed self that is "inside," so to speak; in other words, the direction toward self-formation is first cued by absorption in environmental prompts. Indeed, psychologists speculate that an infant comes to learn about the self primarily through the emotional responses to them by others, a process that then can be looped back to allow vicarious learning about the experiences of others around them.

When children learn to talk, their world begins to open up. But the setting of child-rearing shows that language should not be understood simply as the employment of words in a lexical sense, but as a symbiotic development of the child's capacities for understanding and behavior in the midst of a prompting linguistic environment. It is clear that language is a multi-faceted environmental influence on children from their first moments of life. If language were simply a matter of communicating with words, then all the verbal behaviors we naturally engage in with infants before they learn to speak would seem to be a wasted activity. But research has shown that our instincts here are appropriate and crucial for the child's full development later on (even for brain development). This suggests that infants are exposed to a preverbal "rehearsal" of a communication nexus from the very start: in terms of facial expressions, touch, physical interactions, gestures, sounds, rhythms, intonations, emotional cues, and a host of behavioral contexts.

Research in child psychology demonstrates that language acquisition, including preverbal rehearsals, is essentially a social-world, an intersubjective process that precedes and makes possible later developments of focused individuation *out of* an original social environment, especially the pre-lexical phenomenon of joint attention, which is the somatic precondition for language learning. Even the emergence of self-consciousness can be shown to arise out of the social field of language practice. In developmental psychology, the notion of "inner speech" or "private speech"—meaning self-directed verbalization—accounts for how language is implicated in self-consciousness, as an internalization of speech that generates the capacity to become the object of one's own attention, one's own thoughts and behaviors.

With respect to language acquisition, with the host of preverbal linguistic rehearsals in play right after birth and throughout early stages of development, an important insight emerges: What happens *before* a child learns to speak shows that language is a complex constellation of practices, and is from the beginning an active, performative, affective, embodied, purposeful environing-world, which first shapes a child's sense of things. The configurations of this engaged world are further articulated when the child learns to speak and develops linguistic competence in transactions with the social environment. This kind of linguistic saturation in a child's world from the start adds more weight to a central argument advanced in this investigation: the phenomenological priority of language in world-disclosure.

Maturation surely expands horizons and develops powers and cognitive skills that traditional philosophy has emphasized and assumed to be the proper locus for understanding reality. Yet proto-phenomenology aims to situate these powers and skills in a more original environment, which attention to child development can secure as the generative origin of future human possibilities. Such an unfolding is not a periodic movement that strictly speaking leaves early stages behind. What has been called a "hybrid" or "nesting" effect shows that maturity builds *from within* its beginnings, which are *retained* in a kind of organic expansion and assimilation.

3. ORAL AND WRITTEN LANGUAGE

There is another way to strengthen the findings of proto-phenomenology: by establishing (1) the precedence of oral language as a lived world, (2) the derivative character of written language, and (3) the essential dependence of philosophy on the technology of writing and literate skills. In other words, a critique of philosophy's disengagement from the lived world should begin with the genealogical case that philosophy is made possible by reading and writing.

After children acquire speech, they then learn how to read and write—which, I hope to show, entails a momentous transformation of language and its relation to the world. Although child development has been taken up in some philosophical discussions, the difference between spoken and written language has rarely been given much attention. Yet the surest way to understand how philosophy has concealed the lived world is to recognize that philosophy is essentially a literate phenomenon, that it would not be possible in its full sense without writing, and that its typical assumptions, methods, and theoretical postulates are saturated with a literate inflection, an orientation toward the written word and its transformative effect on language. The general question occupying chapters 4–6 concerns the complex associations of written and oral communication, which helps focus the phenomenological interrogation of philosophy on behalf of a more original environment of factical speech. Chapter 4 examines the manifest differences between oral and written language, with specific attention to alphabetic script. From a developmental standpoint, there is included a discussion of how children learn to read and write.

The acquisition of speech and literacy is the historical background for any individual who might come to philosophize. Moreover, the history of philosophy itself reaches back to ancient Greece, where there is a comparable scenario, because I will argue that the advent of alphabetic writing in the Greek world was a necessary condition for the development of philosophy—especially in terms of how the first philosophers challenged the original setting of Greek culture, namely oral poetry, which will be shown to embody a phenomenological picture of the lived world. Chapter 4 concludes with articulating a set of distinctions that characterize oral and written language: sound and sight, time and space, plasticity and identity, embodiment and disembodiment, lived context and decontextualization, enchantment and disengagement, performance and reflection, narration and abstraction, tradition and innovation, and presentation and representation.

The dawn of philosophy has typically been described as a movement from the deficiencies of a more primitive mentality to the truth-bearing character of rational thinking. Yet such a progressive model is suspect, in part because of the priority of lived experience assumed in proto-phenomenology. If early Greek culture was in fact more expressive of the lived world, then the birth of traditional philosophical formulations should at least be open to interrogation if factical experience was unduly suppressed or marginalized. Chapter 5 explores this question by focusing on the oral character of epic poetry and Plato's philosophical critique of poetry. Also covered are the ways in which literacy was implicated in Greek philosophical methods and discoveries.

4. THE LITERATE WORLD

The close relationship between philosophy and literacy is much more pronounced in the modern world, because literacy in the Greek world, even in philosophy, was still caught up in oral practices to a significant degree. Chapter 6 shows how literacy more and more came to animate intellectual life in the Western world after the Greek and Roman periods. Specific factors in this development include (1) the role of learned Latin in scholarship up through the Modern period, and (2) the effects of print technology. A growing literate inflection of thought was in time implicated in the development of modern science, a representational model of knowledge, and the modern subject-object binary. After recounting the role of literacy in the differentiation of metaphorical and literal language, the chapter concludes by examining the value of literacy and the prospects for a post-literate world measured by a correlation of orality and literacy, which a proto-phenomenological philosophy of language hopes to inspire.

Chapter 1

Proto-Phenomenology and Language: A Summary of Volume I

I answer the phone and hear my father tell me, "Your mother died last night." I ask my girlfriend a question and she answers, "Yes, I will marry you." I receive a letter that says, "Your manuscript has been approved for publication." The effect of these words is an immediate disclosure of important meanings in my life, constituted by a range of comprehensions and feelings. Right away my world is altered. How is it that sounds from the mouth or marks on a page—which by themselves are nothing like things or events in the world—can be so world-disclosive in such an automatic manner? Philosophical reflection *on* language differs markedly from normal usage because now language itself becomes something to talk about. We step back from engaged linguistic milieus (like the ones I opened with) and turn elements of such scenarios into objects of investigation: sounds, words, meanings, things, thoughts, feelings, speech, speakers, and communication between speakers. With such delineations there arise questions concerning how (or whether) words can be linked to things, meanings, or thoughts, and how (or whether) different speakers can be joined in communication about things, meanings, or thoughts. The manifest differences exhibited in such elements (words and things, different minds) make it difficult to navigate or answer such questions. To a large extent, philosophical treatments of language in the West have proceeded by way of these delineations that follow from the reflective objectification of language. I will call this mode of thinking *representational*, which is evident when language is thought to "represent" or "signify" things, meanings, or thoughts; and when communication is accomplished by a transfer of representations from one speaker to another by way of verbal conveyance. Representational delineations of language, reality, and speakers have informed most of the topics and guiding questions in the philosophy of language.[1]

The representational model of language is anchored in the subject-object distinction, which was clinched in Modern philosophy, beginning with Descartes.

Here there persists a differentiation between the interior mental space of the subject and the exterior space of physical objects, a division that prompts the questions concerning the relations between thoughts and things, mind and world, and mind and other minds. The alternative approach in this investigation is anchored in the concept of *dwelling*, which is meant to capture the pre-reflective character of the lived world, which is not perceived as a subject-object transaction, but an engaged *field* of experience that precedes delineations of mind and world, understood as internal and external spheres. Along these lines, language too is a mode of dwelling, which is indicated in the examples given earlier. In such cases, I am not experiencing transactions between words and things or transfers between linguistic agents and recipients. There is simply an immediate, direct disclosure of meaning—and here it is not a matter of semantic meaning but existential meaningfulness, how such moments figure in the meaning of my life. In this respect, the "world" disclosed by language is not the brute sense of an "external world," but settings of meaningful import (as in the world of art, or people coming from different worlds). The immediate disclosive effects of language in occasions of dwelling have what I will call a *presentational* character that precedes their being re-presented as subject-object and subject-subject relations. Language at a more original level is *presenting* a meaningful world, rather than representing something in the world. Presentation will mark my use of the term *disclosure*, which names the un-covering of something in the world before it is subjected to reflective analysis.

The representational model of language depends on a host of philosophical assumptions, and so a presentational account must confront these assumptions with an alternative orientation, which amounts to a phenomenology of dwelling. A phenomenological approach aims to describe the way in which the world *appears* in lived experience, in a manner that is faithful to appearances without importing alien or inappropriate theories. A phenomenology of the lived world examines what it is like to directly engage the world in a pre-theoretical manner before it becomes an object of reflection. This *first* world is the domain of what I am calling proto-phenomenology, which is distinguished from some models of phenomenology that are still caught up in reflective or representational prejudices. What is "first" in my usage is not a matter of chronological origins, but rather the pre-reflective character of the lived world that precedes objectification (and even some formal constructions operating in phenomenology).

1. PROTO-PHENOMENOLOGY AND THE LIVED WORLD

Appearance in the lived world is not *mere* appearance hiding some "reality," but rather the emergence or showing-forth of something. Phenomenology attends to this positive sense of how things show themselves in the way they show themselves, without presuppositions that are unfaithful to phenomena. Unlike some versions of phenomenology, my approach does not begin with abstract notions of consciousness, intentionality, intuition, constitution, synthesis, qualia, or any such philosophical construct, but simply with what life is like in normal experience, in a way that would be evident to any human being. Such is the lived world we already inhabit before philosophical reflection or scientific analysis. This world is the domain of *factical* experience, and I use this word not in reference to the "factual" but the concrete embeddedness and engagement in meaningful activities that mark pre-reflective existence.[2]

The lived world is the first setting in which we find ourselves, and its proto-phenomenological analysis amounts to a kind of naturalism, not in the current philosophical sense of being grounded in the findings of natural science, but in a manner consistent with the Greek and Latin words *phusis* and *natura*, having to do with birth and emergence, and thus a "nativism" referring to the world in which we are born and raised, that which comes "naturally" to us. For much of Western philosophy, this approach would be deemed naïve, but that is why such a phenomenology is implicitly a critique of much that has transpired in philosophy. I begin with a *presumption of immanence*, which means that the world into which we are born is from a phenomenological standpoint the primary reality, and nothing in thought can be divorced from it. This world of engagement has first-order priority over any reflective construct, because all realms of thought emerge out of factical life and cannot presume a more original status.

A central feature of proto-phenomenology is its common-sense ontology. Immediate reality is life in the midst of a world of perceptible things—that is, our occupation with natural and artificial entities like animals, plants, rivers, houses, tools, cars, and so on, along with all the activities involved with these things and their significance. The presumption of immanence surely puts aside any transcendent reality beyond earthly life, but the "thingly" character of the lived world also assigns a secondary status to analytical reductions that have marked many philosophical projects, wherein the various entities in experience are bracketed in favor of ingredient components that make up or explain anything whatsoever: sense data, concepts, elements, atoms, and so on. Atomic accounts *can* have priority if the context pertains to explanatory questions ("What are things composed of?") rather than phenomenological description. In proto-phenomenology, however, the first order of being involves how we normally exist in the world. Something like scientific accounts of material composition, natural causation, or mathematical structure would pertain to subsequent (usually explanatory) orders that are emergent out of, and derived from, the lived world. A central feature of this investigation is the *coexistence* of scientific and nonscientific domains in a *contextual* manner.

All told, proto-phenomenology amounts to an *existential naturalism*, having to do with the factical meaningfulness of the world into which we are born, in which we already find ourselves before we examine it philosophically. What are the characteristics of the lived world? Therein we are embodied beings inhabiting natural and cultural environments. We have desires, needs, concerns, and interests driven by the assignments of life. We possess habits, capacities, and practical skills that enable dealings with things and other people. Aspects of the world are opened up by a host of feelings, moods, perceptions, and comprehensions. Normative guidance and a wide range of valuations function in every dimension of life. From birth on, individual existence is shaped and furthered by social relations. Everyone is born into a world not of their choosing and shaped by inherited customs and traditions. And everything so far described is saturated with language usage. Finally, the factical world is finite in being temporal, ever-changing, and subject to chance, and in pressing limits on knowledge, agency, achievement, and well-being—all consummated by the ultimate limit of death. In all, the lived world is embodied, environed, meaningful, active, capacious, felt, understood, social, inherited, and finite. I assume that the elements here described are evident to anyone and would cut across all human cultures, with obvious differences in how these common features are specified.

With the presumption of immanence there is nothing more original than the lived world. So, whatever the character and findings of philosophy and science, these disciplines have necessarily arisen out of this first world. In much of the Western tradition, the relationship between philosophical thinking and factical life involved a corrective or progressive narrative—that there is something essentially problematic about the lived world, and that rational thought will either liberate us from its defects or perfect us by overcoming its confused, disordered, unenlightened condition. The remedial task of philosophy, especially since the modern period, has assumed the following: the authority of theoretical reason; the appeal to stable foundations that can ground and govern thinking; the standard of indefeasibility that can survive doubt and disputation; the division of mind and world into a thinking subject and external objects; and the construal of "nature" as the sphere of material things devoid of purposes and values. Each of these assumptions finds the lived world falling short, which accounts for the remedial attitude of traditional philosophy. I aim to turn things around by arguing for the priority of factical life, not only as our first world but also as a region of truth that cannot be dismissed or set aside in philosophical thinking.

The presumption of immanence entails that human beings fully belong in the world and that factical life has ontological and veridical primacy on its own terms and cannot be set aside or thought to require rationalized explanation to be intelligible. In this analysis, the lived world is gathered around the term *dwelling*, which captures in its verb sense active living and in its noun sense the natural and cultural environments in which we live. The features of dwelling will allow a more situated philosophical vocabulary and expose the shortcomings in much of traditional philosophical language. Human dwelling *inhabits* the world in an irreducible and inextricable manner, a "field" concept that precedes the dichotomy of subject and object, of reflective consciousness and external things. Dwelling "in" the world is not like spatial location, but more like being "in love" or "in pain." A phenomenological account of dwelling cannot begin with, or be limited to, the third-person standpoint. It begins with the first-person standpoint and what it is like to actively engage in the affairs of life, before such engagement is subjected to reflective analysis. Here, of course, we confront the difficulty of attending reflectively (as I am now) to pre-reflective experience, which runs up against the circular problem of immanence, namely how philosophy can adequately describe a lived world that is already in play *before* philosophy aims to interrogate it.

1.1. Indicative Concepts

Phenomenological reflection on the pre-reflective world will employ what I call *indicative* concepts. As concepts they gather the sense of lived experience, but primarily in concrete, performative terms rather than abstract, constative terms. As "indicative" concepts, they simply *point* to factical experience for their realization. In this way, phenomenological concepts are nominal in nature, as verbal experiments in sense-making that simply *show* rather than define, that are not meant to satisfy traditional conceptual criteria presumed to govern or ground thinking (definitions, universals, essences, necessary, and sufficient conditions). Rather than *giving* sense to inchoate experience, indicative concepts are meant to gather the already implicit sense of factical dwelling. That is why ostensive exemplification can be appropriate in the operation of proto-phenomenological concepts. Much of traditional philosophy has focused on concepts as formal entities unto themselves, apart from an indicative function. Indicative concepts, on the other hand, are simply nominal notions showing phenomenological regions of life that are not "objects" of investigation but *ways* of engaging the world. The success or failure of indicative concepts will be measured, not by theoretical principles or rules of inference, but by whether or not they resonate (with readers) in opening up the lived world. One way to highlight the indicative character of this investigation is that it honors the circularity of immanence. It does not propose to "explain" or even propose "transcendental conditions" for dwelling in the world. It points to what is already in play and not in need of explanation or schematics in order to be intelligible. Yet, phenomenology is a philosophical advance because it uncovers the meaning and contours of the lived world in a manner that everyday existence would tend to conceal.

1.2. Ecstatic Dwelling

I begin a proto-phenomenological account by characterizing pre-reflective experience as *ecstatic*. I use this word in connection with the ancient Greek word *ekstasis*, literally "standing-outside," and carrying a meaning of absorbed captivation. Ecstatic experience involves an *immersion* in activity that is not experienced as conscious reflection on a "self" relating to an external action scene; there is simply the *doing*, an absorbed involvement in the world without being self-conscious about it. The "standing-out" connotation is meant to capture immersion *in an environment*, in something outside the self and not simply a psychological state. In dwelling, we inhabit the world as a familiar extension of ourselves; we know our way around, so to speak. Naturally, there are unfamiliar elements of experience and in extreme cases familiarity can be utterly undone. But human life could never function well or prosper without a bedrock of comprehension and customary practices that fit us for coping with the world and pursuing what we care about. Since dwelling and world are coextensive, I repeat that "world" is understood not as the external world in the brute sense of objective surroundings, but as a horizon of meaningfulness or a context of concern, as indicated in something like "He lost his whole world when she died." So, when "world" is used in this investigation, it pertains to milieus of existential meaning and not simply "objective reality." A world of meaning is phenomenologically prior to objectivity in the strict sense because even objectification must be meaningful (e.g., as a preferred path to knowledge). The notion of world can be articulated in three ways: the personal-world, the environing-world, and the social-world.[3] It is important to stipulate that these constructions amount to one world with three dimensions, that each dimension is correlative with the others in a reciprocal network, and that no one dimension can be understood apart from the others.

2. THE PERSONAL-WORLD

The personal-world pertains to human selves, but not in terms of abstract models of selfhood or identity that are typical in philosophical discussions (consciousness, thinking subject, intentional subject) but rather the personal life that each of us leads, what it is like to live in the world from an individual standpoint, which is expressed in first-person language, which is a grammatical indication that experience is *mine*. In this way, the self is not a "what" but a *who*, pertaining to how one is engaged in life experiences and narratives.

The personal-world does not connote something intrinsically selfish or egoistic, and it is not reducible to something purely individual or introspective; it simply involves how the world *matters* to each of us, how everything we do is something we care about, even if what we care about is overcoming the ego, changing the world, or proclaiming the meaninglessness of existence. So, statements like "I am a scientist," or "I want to help you," or "I am working against injustice" (as uttered in real-life circumstances) are all expressions of the personal-world.

Proto-phenomenology itself begins with attention to first-person orientations that open up the meaningfulness of the lived world, which is suppressed or concealed if the "impersonal" third-person standpoint is assumed to be the starting-point and baseline foundation for philosophical investigation. But it must be stressed that the personal-world is not something merely subjective because it simply initiates a phenomenological method of inquiry and is by no means a restriction to individual selfhood conceived as something isolated from the wider world. Accordingly, the first-person standpoint in phenomenology cannot merely be a matter of introspective mental states, of intentional consciousness, of beliefs and desires related to actions in the world, but rather indicative attention to ecstatic immersion in *fields* of action. That is why each personal-world is inextricably caught up in the environing-world and social-world.

3. THE ENVIRONING-WORLD

The environing-world names the range of natural, social, and cultural milieus in which the self is situated, and which present the affordances that make human action and practices possible in an *ecological* network. *Ecology* is a word pertaining to environmental structures and is derived from the Greek word *oikos*, meaning home or dwelling. An "affordance" is an ecological concept referring to a correlated possibility-for-action, which cannot be understood solely in terms of the environment or the action alone. So, the ground as an affordance is a possibility for walking. A phenomenological ecology cannot begin with discrete regions of agents and external surroundings, but rather the field-concept of meaning-laden ecstatic immersion. Practical dealings with the environment are a good place to start.

3.1. Immersion and Exposition

I draw a distinction between engaged *immersion* and disengaged *exposition*, the latter term meant to capture occasions when we do experience entities as "objects," as outlying things to be observed and examined rather than put to use in practical tasks. Here the word ex-position is meant to suggest the "positioning" of a thing "apart" from the self and immersed practice. Immersion does not exhibit such delineations. The phenomenon of usage, in its performative sense, cannot be understood sufficiently by way of exposited descriptions of a user, an instrument, and the activity; we must begin with an *indicative* concept of use, with what it is like *to be using* an instrument in a non-reflective manner. When absorbed in writing, I am not explicitly conscious of my hand as such or my pen as an object bearing properties, or even the larger purpose of my writing; these things are recessed in the immersed practice. Such activity is not empty or aimless; it is intelligent in being saturated with meaning and purposefulness, though in a tacit manner. Skilled practices exhibit *circumspection*, or knowing one's way around the practice field and understanding its implications; also *capaciousness*, or knowing how to do something, a practical intelligence that is not overtly characterized as mental states or propositional forms (knowing-that); it is fully exhibited *in* the practice without having to be articulated. Reflective analyses and inferences do not fit the smooth, automatic performance of skilled activity.

3.2. Exposition and Contravention

An explicit awareness of intentions and external conditions usually arises when there is some disturbance in the practice. If my pen runs out of ink or feels uncomfortable after a while, it becomes *exposited* as a thing with properties. The disturbance turns my attention to relevant aspects of the pen (the tip, ink supply, weight) that are recessed in the activity of writing. I also attend to the purposeful background of the practice in the face of obstacles (I cannot finish writing until I get a refill or another pen). Common reactions to a disturbance (being annoyed or frustrated) *show* the implicitly purposeful character of the practice, so that meaningfulness is intrinsic to the activity, in a way that would not be the case for a robotic writing device that broke down, which would simply stop working. Annoyance presupposes that a disturbance has interfered with something that matters, that is infused with existential import.

What follows is that the meaningfulness of a practice is caught up with an awareness of finitude and limits. As living beings, we are needful of conditions to survive and prosper; yet such conditions can fail or be lacking, which accounts for the natural fragility of life. Practical disturbances specify something that pervades human comportment, namely that meaning is structurally related to some negative condition of privation or deprivation. The indicative concept I assign to disturbances and limit conditions is *contravention*, in the sense of something that comes (*venire*) to disrupt (*contra*) meaningful immersion. Contravention can be shown in matters of breakdown, resistance, obstacles, mistakes, absence, lack, loss, danger, surprise, disorder, and unusual or unfamiliar occurrences. In any case, it is contravention that prompts the shift from ecstatic immersion to exposition. The unfolding of exposition out of immersion helps situate the subject-object distinction in this phenomenological account. With respect to the notions of mental beliefs and external objects, *both* are exposited out of a prior field of ecstatic immersion—when we become conscious of intentions and their settings in the midst of some contravention.

In a broad sense, exposition gives rise to a prevailing tendency in philosophy and other forms of analysis, namely *reification*, a framing of discrete "entities" marked off from other entities, relations, and activities. Proto-phenomenology has less to do with "entities" than with *ways* of acting and living that elude reification and discrete delineations, which are hard to articulate except in an indicative manner. Indicative concepts afford a sense of "being" that is more verb-oriented than noun-based, that can apply to temporal, historical, and social phenomena—which are fully real but not amenable to standards of object-designation, fixed form, individuation, or constant presence. Hence we can legitimately talk of phenomena such as "being educated" or "being a parent." Exposited reification cannot be the first or last word with factical phenomena.

Most patterns and dealings in life can be experienced in an immersed manner. One can even be absorbed in one's culture, job, or social roles in different ways and degrees. The point is that immersion need not suggest a psychological feeling of *fusion* with something, but simply non-reflexive performance without directed attention. Exposition of these kinds of absorption can arise from different types of contravention, at times from outside incursions, at other times from internal malfunction or discomfiture. In any case, a break with expectations or conduciveness can prompt the exposition of any immersed activity and its significance. In addition, immersion and exposition can be exhibited in varying degrees. So, it is not a matter of simply proposing sheer absorption or reflective disengagement alone in mutual exclusion; they can overlap in different proportions. It must be stressed that immersion and exposition are both fully real conditions, which are shown and marked in the *shifts* between the two perspectives. From a phenomenological standpoint, however, exposition is derived from immersion by way of contravention, by some interference with the flow of the practice-field.

3.3. Everyday Exposition

The meaningful and purposeful background of practices is retained in everyday exposition because attention to environmental conditions stems from caring about the project at hand and how to resolve a disturbance. In ordinary exposition, we are not likely to think in terms of abstract categories like "representations" and "objects." In everyday life, we remain involved in particular circumstances, such as my writing project. Modern philosophical models have been wedded to scientific objectivity, which is a sophisticated extension of ordinary exposition that does indeed require drawing back from common sense practices and learning highly abstract conversions of natural things into disengaged "material objects." The everyday exposition of a malfunctioning tool is still embedded in its specific features and role in a meaningful task. Such normal experience is put aside in scientific thinking, in order to discover universal and measurable features of entities as such, independent of value or use—where a broken tool that interrupts my fixing something now becomes an "object" bearing "properties" and subject to natural laws. Scientific disengagement and its modern philosophical legacy can uncover genuine truth about the natural world—for instance, a causal account of how a tool came to break—but not exclusive truth. As a specific *context* of discovery, scientific constructions should not be taken as dispositive of all philosophical questions or the full nature of human action. If a box is "too heavy" to lift, I can respond by looking for someone to help me or perhaps get a dolly. Scientific thematization disregards this existential horizon by way of conversion into measurable elements of mass, weight, and gravitational force, an explanatory order *derived* from factical settings through procedures of abstraction, quantification, and causal reckoning—but no longer *attentive* to the meaning of such settings (too heavy to lift). Everyday exposition shows a kind of *factical* reflection wherein we think about specific concerns, survey possibilities, or examine elements of our needs and activities. Here the word "exposition" captures the familiar connotation of articulating the aspects and meaning of a practice. Yet, this is something different from *philosophical* reflection about knowledge, mental faculties, ontological properties, and so on. But it helps show how philosophical examination is not an alien invader but an extension and modification of ordinary exposition.

Objective descriptions and talk of mental states are not invalid, but attention to pre-reflective practices that do not exhibit a transaction between beliefs and external conditions shows the difficulty in subject-object models of cognition. In response, such modeling could appeal to unconscious representations or inferences that are intrinsic to the practice, but this comes across as phenomenologically suspect. Yet, what about learning new practices or confronting unfamiliar situations? In cases of, say, learning a new language or how to play the piano, there seems to be a clear sense of reflective distance apart from the practice and a kind of division between mental states and external conditions: That word *Welt* is the German word for my word *world*; that note on the page refers to this key that I must remember to hit with this finger, and so forth. This quite rightly involves distinct spaces of exposited reflection and objectification (because of the contravening effects of having to learn an unfamiliar practice). Yet even here ecstatic immersion is not canceled out because such learning milieus bank on other skills and familiarities that make the learning possible: I already understand what words and notation are, how to follow instructions, how to converse, how to use relevant devices such as books and pencils, and so on—a background of immersion that is usually neither noticed (unless something gets in the way) nor thematized in the learning environment. Such capacities and many more can be traced all the way back to childhood, when we were first outfitted for engaging the world. In addition, when a new practice has been mastered it becomes a non-reflective, skillful competency, which is to say it becomes the immersion of "second nature," where one can speak the language or play the piano without overt rules, reflective distance, bilocation, or analytical dissection. An important point emerges here: the immersed character of second nature shows that the relationship between immersion and exposition can be *bidirectional*. The reflective posture of learning skills can evolve into new modes of smooth, automatic practice. Second nature is an essential element of dwelling, because it points to the ubiquity of habits in both everyday life and highly refined activities. Habits involve learned routines and skills that, once mastered, settle into an instinctive facility that no longer requires conscious direction and that usually operates without explicit awareness (unless some contravention occurs).

3.4. The Scope and Importance of Exposition

Immersion has a certain phenomenological priority because exposition emerges out of contraventions to ecstatic engagement. Yet exposition is no less real in its world-disclosive function; nor does it carry any deficiency compared to immersion (unless it leads to philosophical alienation from the lived world). Indeed, immersion can involve deficiencies that exposition could repair. As indicated, one can be immersed in one's social and cultural environment—in an unreflective manner that can host a range of impediments to improved or advanced understanding. Thoughtless absorption is a precondition for undue biases, prejudice, and blockage of new possibilities at all levels of personal, social, and cultural life; also for superficial beliefs that conceal the richness and complexity of natural or cultural phenomena. So immersion, in addition to being phenomenologically basic, is problematic when it confines, constrains, or diminishes human understanding. It is surely these questionable elements of immersion that spawned the traditional philosophical preference for reflective thinking. Yet, a reflective standpoint also generated epistemological models and methods that proto-phenomenology aims to interrogate and limit. The positive role that exposition plays in opening up what immersion can conceal does not alter the phenomenological priority of factical engagement that much of philosophy has concealed.

3.5. Representation

The notion of representation is a prevailing concept in contemporary philosophy of mind, cognitive science, and linguistics. Representations involve various mental objects (beliefs, concepts, percepts, rules, structures, images) and their referential function, which then brings questions concerning the relation between thoughts, intentions, brain states, or words and corresponding aspects of the world. Representational theories work with the categories of reference (denotation), meaning (connotation), and objects of reference. The most basic questions involve how representational relations obtain (how thoughts, words, or brain states match up with their objects), how representations can be assessed, and how representations in one mind can be communicated to another mind.

In proto-phenomenology, ecstatic immersion is not a representational relation but a *presentational* immediacy. Yet, there is an intelligence in pre-reflective behavior, for which representational explanations are neither necessary nor sufficient conditions. Such explanations are not useless; they can be accounted for as expositional derivations from engaged immersion, and they can prepare new occasions of immersion, as indicated earlier in the learning of practices that become second nature, which shows a bidirectional relation between exposition and immersion. Yet, immersed practices *in performance* do not exhibit a representational character, and so the only recourse for representational theories would be something like unconscious representation, which is hard to fathom phenomenologically. The field-character of dwelling dissolves the baseline problem of how mental or neurological representations can "match up" with their objects (immersion simply *is* the coalescence of self and world). With that problem set aside, representational orientations can be allowed to perform whatever legitimate function they might serve—for instance, an articulation of learning environments or causal explanations of human processes in physiological terms. Beyond the mind-world relation, there are any number of representational functions that signify or denote entities, structures, and activities: photographs, gauges, maps, diagrams, road signs, turn signals, and so on. Given all this, especially the fact that representation is a natural consequence of the immersion-exposition dynamic, my analysis cannot be called anti-representational; it simply claims that representational accounts should yield philosophical priority to phenomenological descriptions of the lived world and ecstatic dwelling.

The prioritization of representational thinking may be due to the very posture of advanced philosophical thinking, which is a highly reflective departure from factical life and which is then prone to presuming the same for all human comportments, in the manner of mental structures applied to the external world. Yet this can be called the *philosopher's fallacy*, borrowing from what Dewey named the "psychologist's fallacy," which is the "confusion of experience as it is to the one experiencing [it] with what the psychologist makes out of it with his reflective analysis."[4] My use of indicative concepts is meant to avoid this fallacy and pay heed to factical experience in its pre-expositional, immersed character.

3.6. Know-How

Capacious practical immersion applies to the distinction between knowing-how and knowing-that, between practical ability and propositional knowledge (in cognitive science this distinction is sometimes rendered as procedural knowledge and declarative knowledge). There is an ongoing debate between intellectualism and anti-intellectualism, concerning respectively whether know-how is governed by, or separable from, propositional knowledge. My phenomenological account certainly would not side with intellectualism because propositional knowledge pertains to exposition and not ecstatic immersion. Yet my approach is not anti-intellectualist in a strict sense, because many forms of cognition can be implicit in, and exposited from, engaged practices; and learning environments can involve an array of propositional, factual, and representational aspects involved in skill acquisition. But when such aspects become recessed in the manner of second-nature habits, an intellectualist reduction to propositional knowledge is incongruous with the phenomenology of immersion.

3.7. The Scope of Proto-Phenomenology

One advantage of proto-phenomenology is its comprehensiveness, because it can incorporate and account for an objective mode of being as a derivative, disengaged exposition out of engaged, purposeful practice. Subject-object frameworks have a difficult task in accounting for pre-reflective practice (if it is treated at all). As indicated before, in using my pen, properties and self-consciousness are recessed. I normally do not experience writing as the mental formation of an intention that is transferred to bodily actions joined with external conditions judged to fit my intention—I simply pick up the pen and write. Another mark of comprehensiveness is the capacity to articulate engaged elements that usually go unnoticed in highly reflective activities as well. Even advanced domains of scientific knowledge cannot be divorced from the tacit competencies of scientific work (laboratory skills and normal practical habits). Indeed, science has its own environing-world that stands *between* scientific thinking and its results. Institutional settings, experimental scenarios, and various instruments are a kind of "mid-world" that is necessary for scientific findings but that is often recessed and usually not thematized in accounts of science. In addition, a full picture of science cannot be separated from the meaningfulness of the scientific enterprise itself, especially the dispositional drive to find natural explanations and the satisfaction experienced in solving problems or discovering new facts. The *background* of science shows its own personal-social-environing-world, its own range of habits and skills, an immersion-exposition dynamic, and activities saturated with purposes and cognitive/methodological norms.

3.8. Meaning and Value

The environing-world cannot be construed in brute objective terms because its practice-fields are in the main intrinsically purposeful. Human practices serve aims and needs; they are *for the sake of* meaningful projects large and small. The existential importance of practical projects shapes a network of preferences, requirements, and satisfactions that issue estimations of practical and moral value, of what counts as worth doing or doing well. The *direct* (immersed) meaningfulness of the personal-environing-world shows that values and purposes are not "added on" to external circumstances as some kind of mental injection. Contrary to the fact-value/is-ought divide that took shape in modern science—where the natural world is value-free, without purpose, and independent of human interests—in factical experience the world is meaning-laden, so that from a phenomenological standpoint, values and purposes have a kind of being in the world and not simply in the subject, since the subject-object dichotomy is derived from a more original field of enveloping significance. Even nature, understood as an environing-world, is not simply a set of physical entities and forces, but settings of significance in terms of weather, seasons, daylight, nightfall, food, resources, habitation, wilderness, generation, destruction, beauty, fearsomeness, and so on. Human beings *dwell* in a meaningful world. Indeed, the environing-world, as a surrounding *place* of inhabitance, precludes human understanding of the lived world being reduced to any kind of subjectivism, even in sophisticated senses of idealism, constructivism, representationalism, or intentionalism. We dwell *in* the environing-world. We are *thrust* into it from birth and cannot help but engage with it and care about it.

4. THE SOCIAL-WORLD

The modern conception of the self has mostly been individual-based. The disengagement of reflection divides the self not only from its environment but also from other selves. A common view has taken social relations as a second-order sphere compared to the original immediacy of self-consciousness. Social arrangements and formats are understood as constituted by, or reducible to, individual conditions and interests. The lived world suggests something different, a "social self," where correlations with other selves are more original than strict individuation. The experience of social relations is not factically perceived as an inside-out conjunction of erstwhile interior selves. Others are just as much a part of my environing-world as the practical mileus discussed earlier; and there is a similar kind of ecstatic immersion wherein I am absorbed in joint engagements without an explicit division into separate selves. Normally, I do not launch myself into social relations from the standpoint of a discrete self-consciousness. I simply dwell with others in innumerable co-concerns and interactions that occupy most of my (non-philosophical) life. Under normal circumstances, the first-person and second-person perspectives are co-original in human comprehension. Unlike representational theories of communication—where the problem of other minds can find a foothold—joint engagement shows that we always already understand each other *as* minded beings in a shared enterprise, as intelligent collaborators in some meaningful endeavor. Accordingly, disagreements and disparities are *contraventions* of a default sense of mutual cohabitation. Joint engagement is evident at all levels of social interaction and is most refined in organized activities such as team sports and dance, where the flow of performance is an irreducible blend of reciprocal comprehension and capacity.

The social-world does not entail an utterly uniform set of understandings across the board, where individual members of the community see the world in the same way. Individual differences in experience and comprehension persist, but there must be significant overlap in a shared world for human life to develop and function. Even a sense of individual identity—who one is, one's personal-world—cannot be separated from other persons and how one is engaged by them. The writings of Rousseau and Hegel initiated an understanding that *recognition* is essential to self-awareness and self-estimation, such that self-regard is interwoven with how we are regarded by and related to others in social and practical milieus. Self-development and self-realization cannot be achieved apart from a host of intersubjective processes, affordances, and challenges. This is not to deny individuality, or distinctions between one's self and others, or the reality of introspection and self-consciousness; it is only to propose an ecstatic, intersecting social milieu that is more original than the individualized model of a conscious self.

The summary point is this: the social-world is not some addendum to the personal-world; the former is only analytically distinct from the latter. Every personal-world is at the same time a social-world, in which other human beings are *experienced* as persons like ourselves and *engaged* as co-inhabitants of a concernful world. Only when introspective self-consciousness is presumed to be the starting point for selfhood is understanding other selves taken to be a "mind-reading" project, where understanding other minds must be constructed in a series of inferences. Yet from early in life, humans become habituated in ways of being that *from the start* are socially charged and expressive of shared existential interest—and thereby originally "co-minded."

4.1. Empathy

One avenue to understanding the social structure of selfhood and the ecstatic character of social experience is the phenomenon of empathy. Empathy is a disposition that can be called an ecstatic dwelling with another person's weal and woe, an affective sense of another's circumstance that can involve positive and negative conditions—which thus includes both feeling the misfortune of others (as in sympathy or compassion) and enjoying their good fortune. In any case, empathy is most clearly comprehended in its vicarious character, where one feels the condition of another person without directly undergoing that condition—so I can feel happiness at someone's success when I myself am not in a like situation, and I can feel sorrow at someone's misfortune when my life is going well. Empathy is therefore an affective response that is more fitting of another person's situation than one's own. Some capacity for empathy seems to be normal for human beings (an incapacity for empathy is a central characteristic of so-called sociopaths). Mature empathy should be understood as a multidimensional blend of affective, cognitive, and participatory elements. Yet affective empathy seems to be developmentally primal and the precondition for acquiring the other elements. Most important, empathy appears to be natural to the human condition, rather than simply a cultural construct that is foisted upon the self. More on this is in chapter 2.

Empathy is a vivid example of ecstatic immersion in the social-world. Here the relational character of the self is not simply environmental in a situational sense, but a psychological enlargement of the self, a dwelling-with-others that feels their fate with engaged attunement. Analogous to the phenomenology of practical immersion that undermines the notion of representational/inferential processes, empathy shows moments when we simply are joined with another person's fate, a kind of emotional contagion that "comes over" us (which at times can even be an unwanted disturbance). Here we do not take in external data, process it as misfortune, trigger our memory bank, and then transfer it out to the other person—the joint affect simply happens. We are existentially *with* others in cohabitive caring.

Empathy, understood as a genuine capacity for shared concern and an enlargement of the self, obviously has ethical implications in challenging psychological egoism, wherein self-interest is the full horizon of selfhood and other-regarding dispositions and measures are called into question, or intelligible only if translated into self-regarding benefits. Other persons are not simply there in my environment; we are co-engaged with a common world of needs, interests, successes, and failures, which saturates the ways in which human beings interact with each other. This is why interpersonal relations are so much more complex and proscribed than thing-relations (using a tool does not carry the normative concerns that attach to dealing with persons). We owe something to the interests of other persons, which can modify how we interact with them. Such is the domain of ethics, which can benefit from a proto-phenomenological analysis because empathy and the social-world allow release from a reductive individualism or egoism that would render the notion of moral obligation to others problematic from the start. The personal-social-world, which exhibits value-laden environments, shows that ethical norms are an intrinsic part of human existence, in such a way that moral skepticism cannot get off the ground.

4.2. Socialization and Individuation

The personal-world and the social-world are still one world. It is impossible for an individual human being to develop as such apart from a social environment, which is clearly evident with child development. Socialization requires common patterns of behavior, understanding, and valuation. The transmission of cultural meanings and orientations "incorporate" individuals into wider congregations of significance and purpose. Yet individual differences persist, if only from the standpoint of being distinct biological organisms. The personal-social-world includes the ongoing possibility of divergence and disparity, including the mutual understanding of the meaning of this element of life. The tension between individuation and socialization plays out in the stress between common arrangements and deviation, which can be disruptive but sometimes for the better, as in occasions of productive innovation. In any case, the tensional structure of the personal-social-world shows that human culture is not utterly uniform or static through time (which is one reason why the social-world is not consonant with social determinism). The social-world cannot and should not be separated from individual deviation, given the importance of innovation, diversity, and critique. What is often called *authenticity* pertains to different ways in which individual persons find their distinctive paths in life that are no longer defined simply by conventional patterns and expectations. At any rate, the personal-social-world is animated by a dialectic of reciprocal contraventions, which (1) regulate individual energies for the sake of common purposes and (2) challenge communal constraints for the sake of novel possibilities.

5. PROJECTION

The ecological character of the social-environing-world includes *projection*, which is meant to capture the sense of being thrown or cast into something, as in a projectile or a film projected upon a screen. Projection involves being caught up in circumstances not of one's own choosing or making. Even circumstances that do involve choice can be a projection when their aspects and norms are already in place before we enter them. Projection specifies something intrinsic to the tripartite world structure we have examined: that selfhood is not a self-constituted phenomenon; the personal-world cannot be understood apart from the social-environing-world. Most of the meanings in factical life are a matter of projection, or already there in natural, social, and cultural environments that shape possibilities in advance of our initiation, so that we are projected *into* these milieus, especially the many cultural patterns, norms, and institutions that take us up from birth and shape us to maturity. As adults, we continue to dwell within these cultural parameters that are not of our own making—even if one such parameter calls on us to find our own way.

There are passive and active forms of projection, the former excluding any initiating choice and the latter involving choice. Examples of the passive type are being a biological son, daughter, or sibling; also the place or country where one is born and raised. Active forms of projection include friendships, occupations, and marriage, which involve the choice of initiation, but *into* milieus that receive us with already constituted domains—into the measures of, say, being a friend, a physician, a husband—which are rarely if ever up for grabs or radically defeasible. Both passive and active forms of projection require individual (adult) appropriation and enactment, and so they cannot be modes of absolute domination or robotic compliance. Allowing for variations across cultures, we can say that being a son, a parent, a professor, or a citizen is neither a strictly active nor passive endeavor but a mix of interests, actions, and decisions *in the midst of* expectations, obligations, and responsibilities. We can borrow from the grammatical form of the middle voice, which was more widely used in ancient Greek than in modern languages. The middle voice would apply to circumstances in which I am actively participating in something not of my own making or control, as in "I am being educated." Projection, therefore, involves middle voice practices and forms of life. And the ambiguity of such a construction is well attested in the complicated demands and orchestrations of factical existence, wherein it is often hard to find clear, discrete sites of determination in the self or outside forces. Here we approach a richer account of affordances, of worldly conditions understood not simply as extant entities but interactive affiliations between an organism and its environment (e.g., the ground as an affordance for walking and a tool as an affordance for making something). The generative function of human affordances has been called their "scaffolding" effect, how they support, enable, and further human comprehension, behavior, and practical ability. Scaffolding can be found in environmental, technological, and social conditions that show an individual self to be anything but a self-contained or fully autonomous entity. The human self should be understood as a dynamically extended and ecological being.

6. TEMPORALITY

The lived world is essentially temporal, which is a primary indication of finitude in the sense that we are stretched between birth and death, and experience is not a purely fixed condition but rather a process of movement. Traditional philosophy has analyzed time as a series of now-points, where the governing concept is the now-as-present, so that the past is no-longer-now and the future is not-yet-now. Since the course of time therefore seems to involve negation and nonbeing, the question of what time "is" has been an enduring puzzle. But lived temporality can be shown to sidestep this problem. We dwell in a temporal, narrative condition; we experience time as a looping intersection of time dimensions, as a coming to presence out of the future and shaped by the past. The "absences" of the future and past have a *presence* in anticipation and recollection. In this way, human experience is *extended* into the future and past; it is presently engaged with future possibilities enabled and prompted by past orientations.

Factical temporality cannot be captured by a formal conception of time that measures change with quantified units, as in the case of clock time. There are lived senses of time that simply indicate imprecise moments and spans of meaningful experience, as in the following: it is time to go; it was a time of peace; I have no time now; daytime; harvest time; having a good time, and so on. Quantified time itself arises out of lived concerns because it serves them in valuable ways by coordinating accounts and activities through a standardized measure; yet it cannot apply universally to all senses of temporality with which human beings live. The association of temporality with meaning is essential for distinguishing factical time from abstract conceptions that screen out existential import. The future and the past are a yet-to-be and a no-longer that *matter*, such that the future can be exciting or worrisome and the past can be celebrated or regretted.

There is a certain priority of the future in lived time. We are always presently occupied with the coming-forth of life. Even the past comes forth in a way because memories are occurrences that arise and come to us. The meaning-laden character of human experience and activity is usually for the sake of some purpose or aim, some forward-looking bearing that can be implicit and yet brought to attention in the face of contravention. Accordingly, what lies ahead in the future is animating current concerns. Thus, life is continually occupied with a not-yet, something yet to come. But the future is not on that account non-existent or separate from the present and past. Future possibilities are prepared by present capacities and concerns that are shaped in the past. And factical presence is never "the present," or the "now," because it is a movement, a circulation of the future and the past with a looping figure-eight structure; it is both retentive and protentive (as recollection and anticipation), laden with the past and pregnant with the future. The futurial character of temporality exhibits an intrinsic openness in human existence, in that as long as we exist, we are marked by *possibility* rather than full actuality, which from an existential standpoint allows for a sense of human freedom. At the same time, the figure-eight structure of temporality not only undermines a strict determinism but also the radical freedom of an autonomous self. Engaging the future is always prepared by past bearings and constrained by projected circumstances in the present environment. Yet degrees of freedom are evident because the present-future dimension includes adjustments of inheritance in the light of current contravening conditions, at times to the point of innovation or reformation.

The futurial structure of the past can be illustrated by the temporal arc of memory and habit. Neuroscience has shown that the function of procedural memory is not primarily to "record" the past but to shape the (present) anticipation of the future, as capacious preparation for action, which is triggered by the coming tasks of life. The same kind of circulating figure-eight structure can be found in habits that function as readiness for future action. And this temporal structure can operate in a tacit manner, without conscious awareness or explication. In general, then, we never really live in the "now," and the past is not gone, and the openness of the future is not wide open. Individual human beings cannot be understood apart from their past cultural inheritance and current meanings have a temporal shape in being forward-looking concerns and possibilities shaped by traditional bearings.

6.1. History

The existential content of temporality is history, which involves the specific narratives, concerns, and projects that animate living endeavors, in other words the course of meaningful cultural events in time. History is not simply given in the past, because an interest in the past is not purely antiquarian but rather attention to its value for present life and its future aims. History therefore shares the figure-eight structure of temporality, which should be kept in mind when studying the past to avoid the trap of interpreting a previous age solely in terms of what happened afterward and how it pointed toward future developments. In the past, the future was yet to be determined, and that indeterminacy was part of a past culture's own (then present) concerns. Nevertheless, lines from the past to our own time are extremely important in grasping the rich complexity of current concepts, principles, or ideals. Generational transmission through the ages gives our ideas a historical density that cannot be ignored if their saliency and import are to be well understood. When we study the Greeks, for example, we study ourselves. That said, studying the past cannot be construed as a straightforward discovery of a historical period "as it really was" on its own terms, independent of current lenses that affect how historical questions are posed, what the terms of analysis will be, and what aspects will be selected or emphasized.

7. EMBODIMENT

The presumption of immanence and proto-phenomenological analysis show that human life is essentially embodied, that the elements of dwelling have a somatic base. Not only does this rule out metaphysical dualism, but also a reductive physicalism, because a phenomenology of embodied life is analytically distinct from strictly physical descriptions. The *lived body* (identified in the work of Merleau-Ponty) is different from the objectified body, which marks the disciplines of biology and physiology (and even everyday expositional attention to the body). The lived body is an embodied-world that reiterates the personal-social-environing-world and the full array of structures therein, especially ecstatic immersion, engaged practices, habits, and know-how. With my example of writing with a pen, I *am* my body in performance, which is thoroughly absorbed in a tangible environment outside my skin. Here embodiment is a *field* of action. As in all cases of immersion, contravention will prompt exposited attention to aspects of the environment and the agent body (a tool can be the wrong size for my hand or cause discomfort). Exposition can range from ordinary attention to refined examination, all the way to physiology. But the lived body should be understood *indicatively* in engaged, pre-expositional terms. It may even be that the phenomenon of practical immersion—where specific attention to physical properties and conditions as such is *recessed*—allows for intimations of "nonphysical" dimensions. The body-in-action, as it were, is "invisible" as an exposited object.

7.1. Place and Space

Human embodiment opens up an existential approach to space. As opposed to abstract conceptions such as points, lines, figure, dimension, and mass, a lived sense of space stems from the environing-world and can be better grasped as a sense of *place*, of meaning-laden locations and locales, such as home, field, land, sea, sky, temple, market, neighborhood, city, wilderness, and so on. Many spatial designations arise from the perspective of the human body and positions in the environment: left, right, above, below, here, there, near, far, and so forth. Such designations are originally imprecise indications of location that stem from dwelling in places.

To summarize the discussion of space and time, spatial and temporal comprehension in the lived world are context-dependent and indicative of specific meanings, while abstract scientific concepts of space and time are context-independent (apart from the context of scientific investigation itself), and meant to apply uniformly to any and all cases. Generalized conceptions of "objective" space and time are perspective-free and cannot give any help in understanding perspectival senses of temporality and place, as in "soon," "later," "earlier," "here," and "there." Lived time and space come first and allow the derivation of abstract time and space by way of expositional disengagement from factual contexts and perspectives. The derivative character of such abstract concepts does not rob them of their descriptive and predictive power, only their exclusivity. Lived senses of time and space are the setting out of which abstract concepts can emerge, and the former exhibit their own intelligibility in being indicative, communicable, and workable in less precise but fully functional ways. Moreover, the ecological character of factical time and space—embedded in worldly circumstances—offers relief from the question of whether time and space are "real" or only ideational constructs. Lived time and space are not simply mental frameworks but ways of dwelling in the world.

8. DISCLOSURE AND INTERPRETATION

The chapter thus far has offered a sketch of how a proto-phenomenological analysis attends to the factical background of reflective thinking, the immanent dwelling in a meaningful world that (1) is always already in play and thus precludes justification, (2) precedes the subject-object distinction, (3) makes possible familiar philosophical categories by way of a contravention-exposition dynamic, and (4) unsettles traditional standards in being embodied, environed, enactive, social, projected, inherited, temporal, and finite. Next for consideration is how human beings open up, and are open to, their environments, how the world is disclosed in factical life. Disclosure names the ways in which we engage and comprehend what the world is like and how it manifests itself. Four basic avenues of disclosure will be examined in this and the next section: affective attunement, tacit intimation, interpretation, and language.

8.1. Affective Attunement

Much in the world can be revealed by emotions and moods, which should be distinguished from "feelings" that are more focused in the self (e.g., pain and hunger). Emotion (e.g., fear) is more focused than the atmospheric character of mood (e.g., anxiety and boredom), which is often the constitutive setting for an emotion. Affect in this discussion is meant to span the range of moods, emotions, and feelings, especially since each of these can be interwoven with the others. Affect is a matter of existential *disposition* rather than mere cognition. Yet affect need not be the absence of cognition; it can attune us to the world in an illuminating manner. Emotions can be intentional in that they are *about* something in the world, often in informative ways (e.g., legitimate fear in dangerous circumstances). Appropriate access to the world is not always a matter of strict cognition. Of course, emotions can lead us astray, but it would be wrong to think that knowledge is utterly without affect or mood (consider the role of curiosity in cognition). Research in neurobiology has shown that emotion can play a key role in high-order thinking, and that rationality cannot function well without emotional input. From an evolutionary standpoint and in general terms, emotion is central to *evaluating* situations as relevant to existential concerns; and without such evaluation, cognition would lack the capacity for a good deal of situational intelligence. The world-disclosive character of affective attunement is more evident when "world" is construed as contexts of meaning—not mere cognition but existential meaningfulness, how and why things matter.

8.2. Intimation

Another element of disclosure is *intimation*, and this term is meant to capture the tacit familiarity and background comprehension that mark much of the environing-world discussed in section 3. Intimation is a kind of "peripheral" understanding that is different from more focused cognition (ideas and beliefs). It implies the "intimacy" of ecstatic immersion, and yet it can be articulated by exposition (so it is not non-cognitive in the strict sense). Intimation is also shown in know-how, the tacit import entailed by an activity or practice, and generally the background understanding of the meaning of a project, which sets up foreground as-indicators that pick out elements and conditions relevant to the task at hand. Background-foreground indications also pertain to general areas of inquiry, such as history and mathematics, whose different orientations will call for different ways in which, say, numbers function. Intimation is also shown in the meaning-laden and immersed character of lived experience, such as the immediate recognition of a friend at a party without having to process any perceptual data. Finally, intimation brings up an essential feature of the lived world, its *correlational scope*. In various contexts of meaning, there are extensive networks of relationships that figure in the significance of things and activities, usually in a recessed and tacit manner: as in a classroom, the range of relations implicated in a whiteboard, marker, lecturing, students, the history and goals of education, and the kaleidoscope of lives that have prepared and that will be touched by the force of learning. The correlational scope of the lived world in fact is an immense set of connections and effects that is comprehensive of everything that matters in life, in such a manner that piecemeal analyses can never be the last word.

8.3. Interpretation

A phenomenology of the lived world shows that no inquiry can begin from scratch, since it is saturated with prior modes of understanding and engagement that are *already* in place before inquiry. Part of this saturation is the historical inheritance that shapes us from the start in childhood. All of this can go without notice because of its tacit character, but it speaks against the "view from nowhere," the notion that knowledge can proceed from an unadulterated starting-point or achieve purely objective results independent of human involvement and historical influences. We have noted that phenomenology attends to appearances without alien presuppositions. Yet one presupposition often found in traditional philosophy is that one can engage the question of knowledge from a presuppositionless standpoint. Proto-phenomenology shows that thought is always already contoured by a host of prior conditions.

Contrary to the Cartesian ideal of a transparent, self-grounding starting-point in the rational subject, the inquiring self is already shaped by its world and historical inheritance before reflective interrogation. The absence of an unmediated starting-point means that understanding the world is a matter of *interpretation*, not in the sense of "mere" interpretation, but rather two baseline hermeneutical provisions: (1) an explication of something implicit, and (2) a particular perspective that sets up one mode of access among other possible modes. The first sense of interpretation is what proto-phenomenology is all about, an attempt to articulate the pre-reflective background of disclosure. The second sense of interpretation involves different possible orientations toward the world, which reiterates the previous discussion of as-indicators, of how a particular background sets up the way in which phenomena are engaged.

This brings us to the notion of hermeneutical pluralism. Contrary to reductive models of knowledge, there are many possible perspectives on the world that can be appropriate *in context*. Interpretive pluralism can be tracked in terms of (1) *interrogative diversity*, where different kinds of questions—concerning causality, quantity, values, art, ethics, history, practical tasks, social relations, individual desires, and so on—call for different responses shaped by the contours and implications of the respective questions, and (2) *phenomenological diversity*, where different types of phenomena—living and nonliving things, artifacts and natural objects, physical bodies and activities, actual and possible conditions, social roles, thinking, feeling, speaking, and so on—call for different kinds of analysis. Pluralism rules out reductionism, which assumes that all questions can be traced to, or judged by, one form of inquiry and its manner of response, or one sphere of being.

Given the two baseline senses of interpretation—phenomenological explication and perspectival pluralism—there is also an *enactive* sense of interpretation that pertains to the ways in which the world is actively engaged in the different pathways of understanding. Enactive interpretation can be grasped first in the orchestration of various orientations on things, the shifting between perspectives on given phenomena or circumstances—for instance, the shift between factual and evaluative descriptions. Such is the *selective* character of interpretation that focuses attention on a particular perspective according to its relevance, which screens out other perspectives. Second, whatever orientation might be in place, there is the actual engagement of emerging possibilities of analysis set up by that orientation's criteria, methods, and capacities—for instance, the developing *course* of factual or evaluative accounts in the midst of complex scenarios or contending treatments (as in actual scientific research and ethical deliberation).

8.4. Reductive Naturalism

One form of reductionism in contemporary philosophy is the naturalistic assumption that answers to philosophical questions must be based on findings in natural science. The mind-body question, for example, has been dominated by versions of physicalism, especially informed by brain physiology; and the field of cognitive science addresses a wide range of philosophical questions by way of burgeoning developments in neuroscience and brain mapping. In some respects, it is wrong to think that cognitive science and proto-phenomenology are mutually exclusive. Brain research and phenomenology can supplement each other in a number of ways (as I will show further). But interpretive pluralism rules out the notion that physiological facts could provide a sufficient account of human thought and experience.

Much of contemporary philosophy is preoccupied with causal accounts of thought, perception, and action. I can accept answering causal questions with scientific facts about human physical systems. But I want to maintain a distinction between causal explanation and phenomenological description, where the former represents a highly refined form of exposition. If the question concerns, say, the biological cause of an experience of worry, I would be satisfied with a physiological account. But if such an interrogative context assumes an explanatory reduction, such that worry is nothing more than physical processes in the body, that is another matter. What *causes* a feeling in physiological terms cannot suffice for answering the question of what a feeling *is* in the full sense, its meaning and character in lived experience—which is the domain of phenomenology. Here I am confining the notion of causality to standard scientific accounts of physical processes in terms of constant conjunction, regularity, or probability, all gauged by the standard of repeatability and predictability. I therefore do not want to say that "reasons" can be causes. Reasons can explain why I am worried, but this would occupy a dimension phenomenologically distinct from a causal explanation of what produces this feeling in my brain. Reasons satisfy communicative expectations addressing *why* people do what they do, while causes are better reserved for explaining *how* things in the world operate in the way they do.

The personal-social-environing-world is a realm of meaningfulness that cannot be captured by physiological or neurological findings—which can suffice for causal explanations but not for lived concerns and interests (which bring us to scientific orientations in the first place). Dwelling in the world eludes purely physical descriptions. If I am "in love," it makes no sense to say that love is "in" my brain, or that my brain is in love. My brain cannot love any more than it can walk. Reductive physicalism amounts to a category mistake, or the mereological fallacy, where some horizon of life is reduced to objective aspects, thereby missing the full horizon of meaning. Being in love pertains to *persons* in a social-*world*; and meanings such as this call for articulation in phenomenological terms, rather than a reduction to physical properties. A neurological reduction cannot account for familiar senses of agency that are intrinsic to the personal-world, especially the sense of gathering experience into a coalescing whole ("my" writing project), which then shapes experience along the lines of "planning," "willing," "effort," and so on. Such psychological phenomena perform a narrational and expressive role in factical life that neurological descriptions cannot supply. Proto-phenomenology is not a denial of, or a substitution for, causal explanations—I have no doubt that without my brain and its neurological processes I could not be in love—but rather an appeal for descriptive pluralism, where the mental and the physical indicate different dimensions of *natural life*, in light of what I have called existential naturalism, which thus is nothing like metaphysical dualism or theism.

8.5. Embodied Cognition

We have established embodiment as an essential condition of the lived world. Merleau-Ponty was the progenitor of attention to the lived body and how it shapes world-disclosive comprehension and sets the stage for advanced levels of cognition. In cognitive science, the notion of embodied cognition—which is part of the so-called 4E model of cognition, as embodied, embedded, extended, and enactive—pursues research programs that can coordinate with phenomenological findings. Embodied cognition involves the ways in which functions of the body and its dealings with the environment—which are distinct from the brain—contribute to cognitive processing, both causally and constitutively. Such an orientation challenges the reliance of traditional cognitive science on neural representations and the assumption that the brain is the exclusive site of cognition.

The enormous store of metaphors in human thinking that are drawn from embodied experience—having to do with structures, spatial relations and movements, visual, aural, and tactile images, illumination, and concealment—cannot be taken as merely a set of comparisons or ornaments. From a developmental standpoint, at least, but beyond that as well, such metaphors are really the lifeblood of thinking and comprehension. Indeed, research shows that cognition is better understood as a brain-body-world nexus that includes physical abilities and sensorimotor circuits. Thus when we hold a belief, put a thought aside, construct a theory, get to the bottom of things, or so forth, it may be that such uses are not *merely* metaphors that express mental states, because in factical life, cognition and bodily engagement go hand in hand. Accordingly, such metaphors would not have to jump some fundamental gap between (physical) doing and (mental) knowing. The biography of thinking begins with and extends from the somatic intelligence of navigating physical environments. Bodily metaphors, then, are inevitable episodes in the story of cognition. We will have more to say on this in coming discussions.

9. LANGUAGE

The most important vehicle of disclosure is language. In my analysis, the emphasis is on natural language, which is the language into which we are born, the language we learn as children and come to speak normally, our "mother tongue." A proto-phenomenology of natural language cannot be grounded in signification theories, where words are simply signs for things in the world or ideas in the mind. Language should be understood first as a mode of dwelling—indeed as the most extensive mode—where we inhabit language as the opening up and articulation of meaning. All other elements of dwelling are given voice in language. A phenomenological examination must begin with factical language, with meaningful speech practices and exchanges in the midst of the personal-social-environing-world. As such, language is not primarily an individual faculty but *public communicative practice*, a shared environment that exhibits an ecstatic condition of engaged immersion, which only derivatively can be exposited into objective conditions such as words, signs, semantic meanings, and grammatical structures. Originally the self is absorbed in a communication network of *talk*, which is a talking *about* the world and its meaning *with* other persons. Just as we can be absorbed in using an instrument without conscious reflection, we are usually engaged in speech about the world without reflective attention to words, intentions, reference, and so forth.

9.1. The Phenomenological Priority of Language

My position is that language is at the heart of human dwelling, that language is the opening up of the world and the precondition for thought. Language cannot be grasped simply as object-designation, or the representation of things or thoughts, or the conveyance of meaning, because any such theory draws from a host of notions already presented in language. To think that the world is a set of nonlinguistic things or events that are designated by words is to overlook the fact that "thing" is a word—as are "event," "world," "is," "a," and so on. The very idea of language as a set of words or signs is exposited from the speech-world in which we dwell before any explanatory or reflective project. It can be said that language *presents* the world before anything (including language) can be re-presented. From this standpoint, there is "nothing" outside of language, at least in the following sense: What can one *say* about a nonlinguistic foundation of language, or something prior to language? Put positively, from a phenomenological standpoint, the world is disclosed through language. This is not to countenance something like linguistic idealism. With proto-phenomenology, we *inhabit* a world; it is not produced or even "constructed" by us as language speakers. There is an extra-linguistic world that must be presumed, because speech is first and foremost immersed in practices navigating an environing-world and not simply a set of linguistic signs. Moreover, there are many constraints (environmental, practical, and social) that limit and check what can be said. Yet even what is "other" than, or "limiting" language has been *expressed* as such and thus rendered comprehensible. Language does not produce the world but it has a certain priority in being the window to the world, without which the meaningfulness of the world would not open up. A dramatic example is the case of Helen Keller, who tells of how the meaning of things was hidden from her until she was finally able to access language and communication through the sense of touch. One might object to the priority of language advanced here: Are there not experiences and activities in which language is not operating, as in, say, enjoying a sunset? Yes, but to have a human "experience" of something—something meaningful that can be articulated as such—presupposes a wealth of prior understandings that go all the way back to childhood and the learning of language (which will be dealt with in the next two chapters).

Language exhibits all the elements of the lived world; indeed, it is the articulated disclosure of that world (which is the sphere of interpretation). Language encompasses the full structure of the personal-social-environing-world, in that each of us is an *individual* speaker communicating *with* others *about* the world—which is mirrored grammatically in first, second, and third person usage. Moreover, language itself is an environment in which we dwell; it is a meaning-laden activity and capacity that usually goes unnoticed (*as* such an articulated phenomenon) in everyday life. The most basic and original form of language is face-to-face talk in the course of factical existence, which primarily concerns engaged dealings with the environing-social-world. Normally, we dwell in speech—in the manner of ecstatic immersion—which is a field of conversing-about-the-world, wherein descriptions and meanings are experienced directly without self-conscious reflection about "words" in relation to "things" and "speakers." Not only does speech concern engaged practices, speech itself is an engaged practice. Not only does speech concern capacious know-how and habituated activities, speech itself is a capacious habit (assuming normal linguistic competency), which *as* such goes unnoticed and recedes in favor of what is being disclosed in speech.

Like all forms of immersion, the ecstatic speech-world can shift into exposition in the face of contravention, which then draws attention to specific facets of this ecological field—wherein we become attentive to explicit elements such as the meaning of words or the correlations of words and things (ranging from everyday exposition and interrogation all the way to linguistic theories). Within this field of speech, there is also a bidirectional relation between immersion and exposition, in a manner equivalent to the discussion in section 3 about learning to play the piano. In learning new uses of language or a new language altogether, analytical distinctions and steps initiate a process that can evolve into second-nature capability.

As in the lived world generally, speech practices are meaning-laden, saturated with the concerns, purposes, and possibilities directly indicated in face-to-face conversations. The semantic meaning of words is not the same thing as the factical meaningfulness of words engaged in real-life circumstances. The semantic meaning of the word "love" is not the same as hearing "I don't love you anymore." A comparable abstract distance is shown in all the expositional analyses of linguistics, in formal constructions such as propositions, grammatical functions, signification, and syntax. In lived speech, existential meaning is the immediate inhabited force of language, and not simply a matter of "reference," "expression," or "transmission." In both the production and reception of spoken language, words are not mere conveyors of pre-linguistic meaning and thought; they *present* meaning in a direct manner.

9.2. The Personal-Social-Environing-World of Speech

Language as a personal-world indicates the first-person experience of speaking and listening in a meaningful environment of speech. Yet language readily illustrates the inseparability and reciprocity of the personal and social worlds. Most linguistic theories seem restricted to individual occasions of speech and their meaning, thus following a monological perspective. But the primacy of face-to-face speech means that solitary utterances are derived from the more original dialogical field of speaking-listening-responding—of communicating. The *addressive* character of language shows that linguistic meaning should not be reduced to the intentions of individual speakers. Communication is more than just an exchange of words and their meaning. It is a social-world that is intimated as such by participants. Conversations presume a communicative purpose and tacit meanings in the course of talking; even contraventions in immersed exchanges (disagreements or misunderstandings) are jointly recognized as such, as an intrinsic part of conversational practice.

The personal-social-speech-world exhibits the dynamic tension between individuation and socialization discussed in section 4. The social bedrock of language is never free from individual inflections, from personal variations and idiosyncrasies all the way to creative innovations. Although communication is the core of language, it is rarely achieved without remainder, excess, or disparity. The shared character of a linguistic world does not entail strictly uniform or identical meanings, but significant overlap must be in place if language is to function at all. Although language, in its acquisition and practice, requires a presumption of common usage, this does not entail some store of precise and stable meanings to which all individual utterances can be referred. Given different contexts and personal perspectives, speech as a form of address must be flexible, variable, and porous, because meaning is rarely fixed and communication is not always isomorphic. To our consternation at times, meaning is not an individual possession or protectorate; it involves intersecting collaborative achievements and movements in a social dynamic of elaboration, sometimes in contravening ways. Perhaps that is why linguistic theories have tended toward monological models; with dialogical address as a baseline phenomenon, language exceeds anyone's control. Even with such excess, communication is the central function of natural language, but in a manner that exceeds another kind of control, namely reflective governance. In line with the immersed character of everyday speech, the conversational capacity to make sense and understand the sense of other speakers is normally a habituated skill, which is enacted in an immediate and spontaneous way, and which precedes exposition into conversational components or overt rules. This skill includes enactive interpretation shown in the shifts between diverse settings of speech. The capacity to engage in conversations is more a matter of tacit intimation than conscious direction.

Face-to-face communication is not simply a social-world. It includes the environing-world in a triangular structure of addressive talk *about* something or some circumstance in life. Speech in this respect is usually not refined theoretical reflection; it is discourse within engaged joint activity in a given context. Linguistic "usage" is much more than the abstract notion of "speech acts" because it is speech in the midst of, and for the sake of, actual practices with other people. This wider perspective does include performative elements of speech, but also the various embodied behaviors that figure in face-to-face conversation (gesture, eye-gaze, nodding, pointing, etc.). The language-world in a fuller sense should be understood along the lines of factical dwelling, as an ecological field of action. Human speech in a focused sense is a specific practice, of course, but it is also embedded in, and informed by, active engagements with the world and other people.

The practical sphere of language as a tripartite personal-social-environing-world can be gathered in the phenomenon of joint attention (a triangular structure experienced and understood as a shared engagement with the world), which seems unique to humans, and which from a developmental standpoint precedes and makes possible language acquisition in children. Infants at an early stage exhibit shared attention and behavior, which can follow the attentive behavior of others (their gaze or pointing) as well as direct someone's attention (holding something up or pointing). Such social processes are more original than language in a specific "lexical" sense but they prepare, and seem to be intrinsically geared toward, the triangular structure of language as a joint engagement with the world. It should be noted that the precedence of such processes is another check on linguistic idealism.

The field-character of the speech-world is a holistic structure that cannot be properly understood in a piecemeal manner; it therefore blends or correlates particular elements of language that have been emphasized by different linguistic theories—in ways that exclude, diminish, or sidestep other elements. A proto-phenomenological account exhibits a triangulated field in which individual speech acts, social forces, communication, and the environing-world all coalesce in a disclosive network. Most theories of language have a representational bias that focuses on specific facets of the linguistic field: (1) reference, having to do with the relation between words/speech acts and reality; (2) meaning, regarding either semantic meaning or the intention of a speaker; (3) communication, understood as transactions between individual speakers; and (4) linguistic structures that govern reference, meaning, and communication. The holistic character of language is such that none of these elements can be prioritized or understood apart from the others. Even "analyzing" the field simply in terms of the exposited elements working together misses the blended character of immersed face-to-face speech in factical settings.

9.3. Language and Temporality

Language and temporality are coextensive and reciprocally correlated. Language itself is temporal as a flowing process of speech; and it is time-structured grammatically in past, present, and future verb tenses, including the looping intersections indicated in complex verb constructions ("Tomorrow we will have been married twenty years"). The correlation goes deeper when we consider temporality not simply as a rough sense of time dimensions, which can be evident in animal experience, but as the rich, detailed sense of meaningful time, of past, present, and future dimensions of concrete life, of its concerns and possibilities—where the virtual worlds of the past and future are intertwined with the lived present. In this respect, temporality is made possible and informed by language, which shapes the narrative character of experience and tells the stories of human existence.

There is also a constitutive sense in which language gives temporality its dimensional scope, by giving presence (in words) to the "absences" of past and future events. This will receive some discussion in section 9.6, but here I focus on memory, the precondition for meaningful temporal experience. In section 6, it was noted how functional memory is not primarily recording the past but coding and preparing future actions, as exemplified in habits. In this way, memory is part of the figure-eight structure of temporality, of forward-looking possibilities enacted with capacities readied by the past. There is evidence from neuroscience and social science that functional memory is made possible by language, which affords virtual reconstructions of past experience that are selective and comprehensive retentions rather than a mere rewind, and that serve as programmatic preparation for present and future actions. And it is language acquisition that allows children to develop episodic and autobiographical memory, a narrative structure of experience, and generally the sense of finding oneself in time, of being an extended self that is projected in temporal dimensions.

9.4. Language and Representation

The distinction between ecstatic immersion and disengaged exposition helps illuminate how certain objective models of language are derived from a more original ecological base. It is common to begin an examination of language with lexical entities such as words, utterances, and sentences, which can then be analyzed in terms of meaning, reference, and structure. In philosophy, truth is commonly associated with "propositions" as truth bearers, which is a formal conception of sentences that sets up the schematic relationship between assertions and states of affairs in the world. My argument is not that these linguistic, logical, and psychological models are invalid, but that they are not sufficient for understanding language or truth. As in the case of learning a second language, the steps of translation in early stages do show that representational notions of meaning and reference are intelligible in an explicit manner. Yet the learning process requires immersion in an acquired language as the precondition for translation. And developed fluency in a new language reiterates immersion when it comes to second-nature proficiency. Thus, representational and propositional models have a derivative status because a focus on dwelling shows that with such models, language is exposited out of a prior dimension of ecstatic speech.

Language (historically and for each of us personally) is originally a matter of face-to-face speech, of communicative practice in the midst of factical concerns. Such proto-speech is a mode of ecstatic immersion in conversations that are not experienced as a transactional exchange of discrete elements between separate agents—of beliefs transported by words out to recipients who process these conveyors into beliefs, the result of which is communication—but rather immediate *presentations* of meanings in the triangular structure of the personal-social-environing-world. In normal everyday conversations among competent speakers, there is a smoothly functioning interaction that is absorbed in the disclosive power of speech—most clearly if the conversation concerns directly present circumstances, but also in conversations about distant or past and future affairs. In any case, the effects of face-to-face speech can be automatic, vivid, and striking, and therefore world-disclosive in a manner comparable to direct experiences. Some examples: "Your child was in an accident," "The war is over." "Your book has won an award." Such examples must be considered indicatively, as actually occurring in real life—wherein "Your child was in an accident" is not a "proposition" (a formal placeholder for any utterance) and not the subject of a "propositional attitude," but a momentous disclosure of your world, the fate of your child.

Representational theories of language—including exposited notions of words, meanings, sentences, syntax, and "coding" processes between speakers and listeners—face a number of explanatory difficulties: not only accounting for how representations and codes connect with the world but also making sense of spontaneous capacities for immediate comprehension and production of language, especially the so-called creative aspect of language usage, where individual speakers (including children) are not bound by inputs or guidance because they can go on with their own unique occasions of speech, which is a case of enactive interpretation. Also problematic is accounting for implicit intimations of coherence and correlational scope, as well as the interpretive capacity to directly discern what kinds of speech are appropriate for different contexts and circumstances. Research has shown that all such capacities are better construed as functions of ecological, social, and temporal intelligences (all usually in concert)—which is consonant with a proto-phenomenological account. Such macro-level intelligences involve intimations of discrete thinghood, relative location, and directional movement (ecological intelligence), other persons as minded agents and the difference between the mere utterance of a speaker and what a speaker means (social intelligence), and lastly the temporal differences between spoken utterances and referenced events, along with flexible shifting between temporal perspectives in one's own speech and the speech of others, so that the meaning of verb tenses is grasped automatically (temporal intelligence).

9.5. Language and Embodiment

Language in factical life is originally face-to-face speech, and in this setting, embodiment plays an essential role—not in the sense of explaining language by way of physiological, neurological, or organic causes (although such domains can be contextually relevant), but the *lived* body that engages in communicative practices. It is here that a phenomenology of gesture, facial expression, and sound enters the picture. The idea of "body language" is familiar, especially how the body can communicate in a nonverbal manner, sometimes in subtle ways that can belie verbal expression (e.g., tightly folded arms giving away animosity or apprehension). There is even a deeper sense in which corporeal expression is intrinsic to lived speech, which will be developed in coming discussions of language acquisition, orality, and literacy. For now, we can note the importance of gesture, facial expression, and sound *in* verbal communication, in a manner that cannot really be called "nonverbal" but rather *sub*-verbal. Such corporeal elements are often thought to be, at best, peripheral to language, but they seem to be intertwined with speech in a constitutive manner. In general terms, gesture and speech are naturally synchronous and co-expressive, in the sense that a gesture is neither redundant nor merely ornamental to speech. Rather, gesture is functionally correlated with linguistic meaning, often facilitating and enhancing the comprehension of speech.

Another embodied feature of speech is its sonic character, usually called intonation. Sound here is not simply the conveyance of spoken words; it is the fusion of sound and words in the manner of *voice*, as distinct from sounds like grunts or moans and the expressive calls and cries made by animals. Human language is at once sound and sense, where utterances are saturated with meaning in factical speech. Intonation involves a host of sonic elements that figure in meaningful expression: tone, pitch, tempo, rhythm, emphasis, accent, volume, and even pauses and silences. Intonation is primarily implicated in the expression of emotion and degrees of intensity. Tone, pitch, and volume can express pleasure, excitement, anger, and various resonances linked to different contexts. One result of considering gesture and sound is that face-to-face speech is *at once* a visual and aural phenomenon. This helps reinforce the ecological character of language as a material presence *there* in one's world, in which one can be ecstatically immersed. The sights and sounds of language together embody this environment.

9.6. Differential Fitness

In line with the analysis thus far, I offer a concept that can gather the nature of language in a way that can inform much of what has been said and what is to come: *differential fitness*. Language is fitness in the manner of non-reflective communicative disclosure as heretofore analyzed. In this sense, language and its social-situational environment "fit" each other, not in the sense of representational correspondence but more akin to the way hand and glove fit each other. Think of a conversation with someone teaching you how to fix something, answering questions and guiding your actions as you work along. Here there is bidirectional flow and triangular attention, where speech, activity, and things in the environment coalesce as a seamless field of operation. The fitness of language should not be taken as a stable identity or fixture of meaning because speech is shaped by and manifests the temporal movements, contextual shifts, and contravening factors. Language fitness simply denotes the normal course of life wherein our speaking, behaving, and environing-world are blended as a correlative presentational field and *presumed* to be reciprocally conjoined, where speech and world fit together.

The differential character of language stems from considering the phonic (and graphic) nature of words as such. Here we notice the general semiotic difference between spoken words and what is spoken about. Even with the fitness of language, a differential element is implicit in both diachronic and synchronic ways. Out of the immediate disclosive power of fitness, the sustained capacity to speak allows the retention of words—*and their existential meaning*—in the *absence* of their referents, a capacity that seems to be unique to humans. In this way, the "non-being" of the past and future can have a *presence* in speech because of semiotic difference as such, although this is not thematized explicitly in oral language. In any case, the world-disclosive force of language does not need a direct reference in the immediate environment to evince genuine disclosive force. With such possibilities, language offers a function of crucial significance: the capacity to extend disclosure beyond first-hand experience, which opens a boundless scope of comprehension for the otherwise constrained access of individuals and groups solely within their own sphere of experience.

Semiotic difference also makes possible a range of intellectual functions that are the building blocks of knowledge, such as generality spanning a set of particular uses, ranging from indicative concepts to scientific classification. Other capacities include: analogical thinking; following inferences; hierarchical classification; describing hypothetical circumstances; learning and using symbolic constructions without direct reference; learning and constructing new terminology; counterfactual thinking; a recursive dynamic of lexical recombinations, insertions, revisions, and extensions; and transmitting cultural codes to the next generation for an extension of possibilities. Most basic in all this is the capacity for relational thinking, which opens up an enormous store of comprehension and extended knowledge, and which appears to be a distinctive mark of human intelligence. Causal thinking is a signature consequence of understanding differential relations because grasping a causal sequence involves traversing temporal dimensions, wherein a present effect is structurally related to past patterns and future repetitions (as distinct from one-off coincidental correlations). Relational thinking also allows for "conceptual blending," which opens new spaces for cognition by juxtaposing different events or lines of thought for the purpose of comparison, contrast, or synthesis.

The differential fitness of language is a correlative whole, where difference and fitness cannot be separated, although they can be distinguished in analysis. Yet the fitness of language must have a certain priority. Difference is understood *in* language, and language is first an environment in which we dwell and find ourselves, which is most clear when we take child development into account, where we first become linguistically out-fitted for the world. Without fitness, difference would not emerge, as something *other* than immediate reference. Yet without the differential force of language *implicit* in all its moments, the fitness of language would not be capable of extension, responsive flexibility, and innovation.

9.7. Language and Thought

Before the so-called linguistic turn, the primary focus of Modern philosophy was cognition and thought, notably illustrated in Kant's shift from "reality" to how the rational mind thinks; also in 19th-century debates about the nature of logic, particularly the laws governing thought. From this perspective, language is simply a vehicle for expressing thought. Since the early 20th century, many developments in analytic and continental philosophy have challenged the notion that thought can be understood apart from, or prior to, language. Two main questions arise from these developments, and they have been the focus of much research in cognitive science, linguistics, psychology, and philosophy of mind. The first question concerns whether language is constitutive of thought in the sense that human cognition is fundamentally informed by, and does not precede, linguistic operations. The second question follows from the first. If language to a significant degree is constitutive of thought, does the cross-cultural diversity of language systems mean that the world is understood in different ways? If so, that would imply linguistic relativism (or determinism).

My adherence to the phenomenological priority of language seems to fit the notion that language is constitutive of thought and that thinking is a kind of internalized speech, or at least is informed by language in a developmental sense. Similarly, my emphasis on pluralism might open the door for linguistic relativism. What I hope to establish, however, is that most research on these questions is driven by representational assumptions and expositional analyses of language and thought. A phenomenology of dwelling and its ecological account of language will allow different pathways that can address these questions without siding with either pole of the research debate: on the one hand, that thought is somehow different from, and more original than, language; and on the other hand, that different languages imply different forms of thought and different worlds. Although I maintain that language informs an understanding of reality, the lived world allows for much overlap between different linguistic systems. Both sides of the debate emphasize exposited approaches to linguistic formats and cognitive structures, which misses insights drawn from immersion in factical environments. An indicative approach to non-exposited dimensions of speech practices can open space between so-called communicative and constitutive models of language, where the latter takes language to be productive of thought and the former takes language to be simply expressive of non-linguistic cognition.

I maintain that thinking and factical language can be distinguished phenomenologically but not separated in any strong sense. Language, especially in developmental terms, shapes in different ways most of what thinking indicates. Yet since language is embedded in a social-environing-*world*, the ecological structure of speech rules out a reductive linguistic idealism; and whatever thinking is taken to mean, it cannot entail a reductive psychologism or confinement to introspective "mental states." Dwelling in speech presupposes an embodied, enactive, public, tangible practice-field that exceeds, and makes possible, the supposed interior space of thinking. For this argument to gain any traction, language cannot be restricted to exposited lexical tokens and thought cannot simply entail an exposited sphere of beliefs, concepts, representations, or rules. Both language and thought must be housed in the lived world. That is why something like a "propositional attitude" cannot do justice to the intertwinement of language and thinking in my analysis.

Although thinking and speaking, thought and language, are correlative in this investigation, that does not entail their *identity*, especially when considered expositionally. We can certainly distinguish ideas and words or beliefs and speech. But the lived world shows occasions of practical intelligence that exhibit neither overt uses of language nor abstract cognitive processes. Moreover, not everything in the human mind is specifically linguistic—and "mind" here is used in an indicative manner to simply point out familiar non-discursive mental phenomena, such as imagination, recollection, and anticipation. Such phenomena can be called "pictures" in the loose sense of introspective attention to virtual experiences, events, or circumstances. We can add affective and reflective occasions to fill out a recognizable sense of "internal" mental states that are distinct from overt cases of acting and speaking. Accordingly, not everything in human understanding is a matter of language in the exposed sense of *verbal tokens*. This sidesteps a common (and loaded) way of depicting the constitutive theory of language in a strictly lexical and representational manner, so that a thought about, say, electrons can only be entertained by activating a representation of the *word* "electron." The factical relationship of language and disclosive understanding cannot be reduced to mere verbalization. To move from non-verbalized occasions to a cognitive domain of thought apart from language (as in some theories) bypasses crucial developmental factors in the history of every human person. The same could be said for the proposal of psychological domains apart from language. The fact that we can articulate occasions in such domains does not support the notion that language simply gives expression to these occasions. From early in life, human beings are incorporated into a world of meanings and abilities that take shape in the triangular dynamic of joint dwelling in speech. A basic question that looms in the background of this discussion is this: What could be said of someone's mind or thought or even selfhood who was not exposed to language as a child? Some testimony to the depth of this question is given by Helen Keller, who was deaf, blind, and mute until she was able to access language through the sense of touch:

> Before my teacher came to me, I did not know that I am. I lived in a world that was no-world. I cannot hope to describe adequately that unconscious, yet conscious time of nothingness. I did not know that I knew aught, or that I lived or acted or desired. I had neither will nor intellect. I was carried along to objects and acts by a certain blind natural impetus. . . . When I learned the meaning of "I" and "me" and found that I was something, I began to think. Then consciousness first existed for me.[5]

The ecological practice-field of language acquisition, along with mature immersion in speech practices, shows that even overt occasions of language cannot be adequately described simply by way of exposited verbal tokens, namely "words." That is why non-verbal occasions do not necessarily stand apart from language in a fuller sense. In the research addressing the language-thought relation, a significant limitation—on both sides of the debate—is that language and thought are almost always understood in expositional and representational terms, which colors the questions, experimental procedures, and findings in such studies. Much can be learned from these investigations but many implied philosophical questions would be better served by the indicative character of phenomenological concepts.

What is evident in some of this research is that thought and language should not be segregated from each other, because such a divisional scheme shapes experimental projects and tempts the search for a grounding function on either side of the ledger. There are many basic biological powers that precede and make possible linguistic ability, and that continue to play a role after the ability is acquired, which will be discussed further in chapter 3. But language does not simply arise out of basic biological conditions; it exponentially expands and extends those conditions in ways that exceed and transform them into world-disclosive powers. I would call this development a "nesting" effect that builds from the core out in an assimilating manner; but even here the metaphor misleads because the layers in question are only evident as such *because* of the disclosive function of language. In any case, however the research in question is interpreted, a proto-phenomenological account of immersion and second nature is needed to provide the counterweight of a holistic field to correct for representational assumptions that continue to guide most of the research and its interpretive conclusions. Language should not be confined to the representational notion of "words," nor should thought be restricted to cognition apart from verbalization. Both should be incorporated into their "world," their ecological field of enactment. Indeed, it is helpful that some research points in this direction, albeit without the help of appropriate phenomenological concepts.

10. TRUTH AND PLURALISM

A philosophical treatment of the lived world and language calls for an account of how the question of truth can be treated in a phenomenological analysis. If we confine the discussion of truth to matters of language, the ecstatic immersion that is characteristic of communicative speech practices allows the notion of *presentational* truth, as distinguished from representational models (e.g., the "correspondence" of propositions and states of affairs, which follows from presuming the subject-object binary). Presentational truth can be applied to a host of aptly disclosed conditions that are not experienced as a bridging of discrete spheres, and that do not or need not involve procedures of justification. Nevertheless, such a discussion will have to show what "apt disclosure" means, since truth is conceptually juxtaposed against "untruth" (error or deception) in any human culture and from the start of any person's development as a language speaker. Presentational truth can be understood from a number of angles. Consider someone helping me repair something, where what is said is immediately presumed as duly disclosive (absent some contravention) without justification. Much of ordinary utterance and conversation is presumed to be disclosive in a similar way. Only a hyper-skepticism would toy with a standard that required justification for any and all utterances before genuine truth conditions could be satisfied. Such a standard is not only impractical but unrealistic in a substantive sense when considering how language functions in everyday life.

Presentational truth involves the default assumption of disclosiveness that marks much of human discourse in the manner of tacit *trust*. Indeed, the word *truth* is etymologically connected with trust by way of the word *troth*, pertaining to faith in a pledge, as in betrothal. Trust by definition is not a matter of certainty or justification but rather a kind of faith, as in trust that someone will be "true" to their word; but it is not blind faith because degrees of trust*worthiness* must be in the mix, at least implicitly. Outside of philosophical analysis, the default trust in truth is not usually a conscious or deliberate comportment; we simply are normally predisposed to take speech as sincere and disclosive. In fact, a specific awareness or articulation of trust usually unfolds when the possibility of violating trust is intimated. The stronger the trust, the less it is voiced or put in view. The deep background of trust in truth is a matter of tacit immersion, not theoretical exposition or inferential application of beliefs. Yet trust should not be taken as simply an attitude devoid of rationality. Aligning trust with presentational truth speaks to the myriad ways in which reasoning relies on a tacit background of trust. It is hard to imagine human life functioning well without such an implicit predisposition of trust in presentational truth. Of course, deception is a common phenomenon in human communication, but it is driven by contextual and specific motivational conditions—and it relies on normal veridical trust for its prospects of success. Truth is the default expectation in human speech. Veridical trust is also implicated in the extensive role that testimony plays in knowledge, where deference to disciplinary findings, expertise, and presumed authority compensates for the absence or impossibility of first-hand engagement. The trust in testimony shows the interpersonal, even intergenerational structure of a good deal of knowledge; it also udercuts a monological epistemology and a baseline notion of rational autonomy, self-sufficiency, or self-constitution.

Contraventions can disturb trust and open up the problem of truth and untruth, as well as space for representational conceptions of truth—where presentational immediacy is exposited as a partition of the language-world correlation into distinct spheres of propositions and states of affairs. Recalling the concept of differential fitness, it is the fitness of language that bestows presentational truth, and the differential element allows for the possibility of untruth, a disjunction between what is said and what is the case (whether it be error, distortion, or deception), especially concerning the diachronic distance of past and future conditions. In any case, a default presentational trust in truth would seem to be a necessary condition for the normal course of life. Except in extreme circumstances, skepticism could not serve well as a first-order disposition.

Presentational truth does not rule out or replace representational truth, but it names a more original dimension that can cover more ground and dissolve some of the puzzles attached to representational formats. Presentational truth can address the complex tacit background of a correspondence relation, and the ecstatic character of presentational immersion can sidestep puzzles pertaining to how something like a linguistic proposition can "match" something in the world, or how a mental state can "represent" an external state of affairs. Since such binaries arise as an exposition out of an original condition of ecological dwelling, the puzzle is such only if we take representational relations as the exclusive model for thinking about truth. In most direct experiences and everyday speech practices, the theoretical problem of correspondence does not arise; language can be immediately disclosive. The ecological character of dwelling shows that *before* language and world are divided by exposition, they already coalesce in ecstatic speech practices, where they do not need to be bridged.

The matter of untruth most clearly prompts the distinction between statements and states of affairs, due to a "misfit" of what is said and what is the case. Yet such differentiation can still be seen to emerge out of a prior field of linguistic immersion; and real-life matters of untruth arise from contraventions, such as doubt, that prompt expositional attention to the possible divergence of what is said from what is the case. Expositional differentiation is derived from, and does not override, the undifferentiated field of ecstatic immersion. The mistake is taking expositional contexts, where something like representation can make sense, as the grounding model for linguistic activity—thus presuming that language as such must be grounded in representational relations. Accordingly, there are ways to talk about truth as *fitting discourse* without assuming a binary representational division between subjects and objects. Outside of philosophical theories of truth, in the normal course of life, the very *issue* of truth and untruth does not arise until contraventions disturb the tacit trust in presentational truth.

10.1. Settings of Truth

A phenomenological approach to questions about truth would begin with how truth functions in the lived world and its existential conditions. First of all, truth must exhibit some sense of authority in its differentiation from untruth and its allowance of judgment—to provide a robust response to radical versions of skepticism, subjectivism, relativism, conventionalism, or constructivism. Yet second, truth cannot be a purely objective matter because truth must first *matter*, we must care about it; and truth serves the meanings and interests that constitute factical life. Third, the finite character of the lived world and the vicissitudes of natural language call for an orientation toward truth that permits its authoritative sense without a requirement of indefeasibility or strict certainty. Fourth, truth should not be taken as uniform because it can function in different ways and in different interpretive *settings*—in science, history, ethics, politics, religion, technology, art, and so on. A setting for truth is a hermeneutical perspective that "sets up" a manner of inquiry or engagement—like a scene setting in the theater—and that sets out the as-indicators marking the modes of enactive interpretation. Different settings stem from different contexts of meaning—causal explanation, understanding the past, evaluative concerns, instrumental tasks, social roles, practical engagements, artistic endeavors—which issue truth conditions or norms that can open up the world in ways appropriate to the specific setting. Given the ecological character of factical comportment, different perspectives on the world can track different ways in which an *environment* is opened up, which is therefore not a reduction to human constructs but a responsiveness to the environment at hand. Perspectival responsiveness is different from radical relativism (where all perspectives have equal authority) and it can even allow a modest realism that is different from strict objectivism.

How can a pluralistic conception of truth issue a sense of warrant? As long as we assume a contextual focus that appropriately gathers different discourses, we can rest with an orchestration of such interpretive contexts without the need for reducing different kinds of disclosure to one form, as in the case of scientism, where only scientific descriptions are said to provide decisive truth. Contextualism reiterates the interrogative and phenomenological pluralism discussed in section 8.3. Whatever the context, what would be the exposited features of truthful discourse? I offer the following *inhabitive* truth conditions, namely measures that shore up different ways of dwelling in the world: (1) *Responsive fit*. In line with the fitness-character of language, truth is fitting for phenomena, in that what we say is responsive to what is going on and where the world (in its full phenomenological sense) is responsive to what we say. Such co-responding suggests something like the correspondence theory but without its theoretical baggage or a restriction to certain kinds of claims (factual description or object designation). Responsive fit simply calls for being "true" to phenomena by attending carefully and thoroughly to matters at hand and avoiding omissions, distortions, or confusion with different kinds of phenomena. Responsiveness also implies a disposition of openness to phenomena, of letting things show themselves and being wary of prejudgment. (2) *Reliability*. Truth has a continuity that is not utterly unstable, instantaneous, or unrepeatable; we can go on with it. This is not to be confused with eternal truth or absolute certainty. (3) *Workability*. Truth is effective, it renders us fit to engage and navigate the world successfully. The pragmatic theory of truth applies here, but we would not want to say that truth is only a matter of practical utility or problem-solving. (4) *Agreement*. Truth is shareable and communicable, rather than mere subjective opinion. This is not to say that agreement is sufficient for truth (fitness and workability show that truth cannot be merely conventional), or that seamless unanimity could or should be the aim of thought. (5) *Consociation*. Given the importance of upbringing, inheritance, trust, and corroboration, truth is a cooperative, socially structured endeavor rather than a monological construction. (6) *Sense*. Truth gathers experience into a shape that allows understanding, orientation, and familiarity, where things make sense. Veridical sense in this respect is not a rigid, systematic structure or a single governing order.

In line with this analysis, "untruth" would involve failures or diminishments of inhabitive truth conditions. Suppositions of truth can generate or encounter contraventions, and that is when critique is possible, both synchronically and diachronically—the latter meaning that over time something taken as true might no longer exhibit fitness, reliability, or workability, owing to changing conditions or new findings. Such contravening circumstances can bring about innovation or even revolution, in everything from social movements to science.

The set of truth conditions sketched earlier shows in a rough manner how truth can be both one and many. The unity of truth here is certainly not the kind sought in traditional concepts of one kind of truth or a single universal standard. The conditions simply show a range of features or functions that any claim to truth would satisfy. But the range is such that it could fit different ways of engaging the world, in science, ethics, art, and other settings. The word *truth*, then, can cut across different settings as a focal term with an indicative function, rather than a single standard with a regulating function. The indicative meaning of truth would simply point to different modes of *appropriate disclosure*.

Inhabitive truth conditions open up the validity of pluralism when a certain setting or context can lose its manner of appropriate disclosure if subjected to undue assessment from another setting or context—which would go against the interrogative and phenomenological diversity outlined in section 8.3. For instance, if the interrogative context is causal explanation in the sphere of physical entities, then natural science is appropriate; all six truth conditions can be met, and spiritual or mentalistic notions would be out of place. But if such a setting is presumed to be universally applicable, what can follow is a physicalistic explanation for anything that pertains to human life. Then we run into truth-conditional failure in a shifting context—neurological descriptions of my brain states at the time of composing this sentence would not be able to convey its meaning (thus violating responsive fitness and workability). Not every engagement with the world is a matter of physical causation. Say that I have a brain tumor and my surgeon is showing me its location on an MRI. "There it is," he says, "and we will be able to remove it safely. Don't worry." I say, "OK, but I am still really afraid for some reason." He points to another location on the MRI and says, "Here's why you're afraid; that's where fear is produced." This would be a startling response (violating fitness and sense) and I am quite sure that it would not arise in a situation like this. We continually orchestrate and navigate different phenomenological contexts (in enactive interpretation) and there are times when certain philosophical notions make for "false moves" in factical situations. Accordingly, untruth can be shown both within settings and between settings when there is an undue incursion from one setting to another (e.g., "creation science," where the intimation of something supernatural violates all the conditions of truth in natural science).

With respect to an account of phenomena, we can ask about its truth in terms of the following questions: Is it fitting, reliable, and workable? Is there agreement and sense? Is it contextually appropriate? Then various answers regarding truth and untruth can be worked out. Moreover, truth will often be a complex matter, since the six conditions are inter-relatable and many areas of thought involve a combination or orchestration of different settings and contexts. Think of a murder trial, for instance, with an array of empirical, conceptual, normative, scientific, psychological, and historical factors that can be brought to bear. The different settings involved here overlap in being gathered by the meaning and purpose of a trial. And the shifts of enactive interpretation (e.g., between normative, empirical, and psychological settings) are typically automatic, without a need for explanation or transitional steps. In any case, being "true" to phenomena will often require polyvocal complexity, which can be suppressed by a preference for univocal or unmitigated accounts. A true history of the American Civil War, for example, calls for a wide range of perspectives. Indeed, the truth of something like war requires an existential depth that perhaps only literature or poetry can provide.

Now that this chapter has sketched the features of proto-phenomenology and its application to the nature of language, the next two chapters will show how dwelling in speech first takes shape in child development and language acquisition.

NOTES

1. In this chapter, for the sake of economy, I omit almost all of the scholarly references found in Volume I.

2. Phenomenology, as understood by Husserl, was a "transcendental" project providing necessary, a priori conditions for the possibility of experience and knowledge, which therefore was not simply an empirical or descriptive enterprise. Natural experience and the engaged world are "bracketed" in order to discover "pure" phenomena in consciousness that can provide cognitive grounding and justification. Proto-phenomenology opens up what is *already* at work in normal experience; so it is transcendental only in a very loose sense, without a justificatory program. The goal is not to lay out stable "conditions for the possibility" of experience and knowledge, but rather the *actual* conditions of factical life that call for explication, not validation.

3. I use hyphenation in world designations as a graphic reminder of the field-character of the lived world.

4. *The Philosophy of John Dewey*, ed. J. J. McDermott (Chicago, IL: The University of Chicago Press, 1981), 165.

5. *The World I Live In* (New York: NYRB Classics, 2004), 113, 117.

Chapter 2

The Child's World

We are all big babies—thrown into the world by our birth and usually thrown out with the bath water by philosophy. Childhood and child-rearing have not been given sufficient consideration in philosophy, likely because philosophy engages in complex conceptual reflections and articulations that are not evident in a child's abilities and experiences. Childhood has usually been ignored, downplayed, or retrospectively described as a nascent prelude to, or deficiency of, mature rational competence. For Aristotle, children are incomplete human beings, a potential ready to be actualized. He minimized their capacity for understanding the world, but he also recognized the importance of instilling habits that prepare mature functioning, especially in ethics. For Hobbes, given the ideal of mature reason in his contractarian model, children are inferior beings more in the state of nature, and they are in a position of strict servitude with respect to parental authority. Descartes took childhood to be ruled by the body's appetites and sense perceptions, which helps explain the difficulty of arriving at mature powers of rational knowledge. Even adult beliefs are not as "unclouded and firm as they should have been if we had had the full use of our reason from the moment of our birth, and if we had always been guided by it alone."[1] Locke's empiricism offered that children have no cognitive understanding at the beginnings of life—a tabula rasa that is written upon by experience. For Kant, children (and wives) are the property of the male parent, although they have rights against abuse. Lacking rational freedom, children do not have full personhood and so they have less importance than adults (e.g., the death of a child is less significant). Witness Kant's famous definition of enlightenment as rational deliverance from "self-imposed immaturity." With Mill's strong liberty principle, children represent the limit of that measure, since they do not have mature reasoning. Here Mill shares a modern conception of childhood as a primitive state of naïveté that requires paternalistic control for their own good.

Even when child development is addressed positively in philosophical work, the framework of analysis is usually biased in favor of reflective processes that I submit are not exhibited in early experience and behavior—such as a child's "concept" of this or that, or "theory" about this or that. The predominance of theoretical paradigms and expositional vocabulary has produced much distortion of a child's world and its relation to adult understanding. Some 20th century philosophers, however, show affinities with proto-phenomenology and its pre-theoretical approach to childhood—namely that the experience of a child is not simply a deficiency to be filled in but an original environment that is not an absence but the *beginnings* of the human condition, which are not entirely left behind in maturity. Accordingly, attention to childhood learning can show the shortcomings in many philosophical assumptions, not only concerning childhood but adult experience as well—for instance, assumptions about representational thinking, subject-object divisions, the primacy of theoretical reason, and essentialist theories of meaning. Philosophers who complement proto-phenomenology include Dewey, Wittgenstein, and Merleau-Ponty.[2]

Before the 20th century, philosophical thinking about childhood was for the most part based on either presumed theories or conventional cultural beliefs. The scientific study of child development did not fully bloom until early parts of the 20th century.[3] Significant theories of child development include: maturationalist theory (Arnold Gesell), which emphasizes psychological development over environmental influences; behaviorist theory (Watson, Skinner), which assumes the child to be a blank slate that is shaped by environmental forces; psychoanalytic theory (Freud, Erikson), which focuses on psycho-sexual development, abnormal behavior, and the resolution of conflicting emotional states; cognitive development theory (Piaget), which emphasizes mental stages in a child's active exploration and manipulation of the environment; socio-cultural theory (Vygotsky), which stresses social dynamics and interactive learning; and bio-ecological systems theory (Bronfenbrenner), which focuses on overlapping familial, community, and cultural systems that affect a child's development.

Although proto-phenomenology can draw from some of these theories, I believe it is particularly qualified to help make sense of a child's experience and development, especially in early stages. Indicative concepts drawn from pre-reflective dwelling provide an orientation that can improve upon standard theories, which have emphasized exclusive conditions or scientific suppositions. There are recent trends in developmental psychology, however, that can accord with a phenomenological approach, since they have called into question many standard assumptions in the field that depend upon the uncritical imposition of adult perspectives, representational constructions, and theoretical vocabulary drawn from the subject-object divide. What is most helpful is a turn to so-called naturalistic studies of children in their actual environments and interactions with caregivers. Such a shift stems from a recognition that traditional research protocols and testing methods have controlled for and presumed theoretical criteria about cognition, behavior, and learning that screen out complex and variegated factical elements in a child's world. Such circumstances in natural settings, which have been recognized and thematized in the new research, match up well with proto-phenomenological findings: ecstatic dwelling, the personal-social-environing-world, the immersion-contravention-exposition dynamic, intimation, know-how, habit, second nature, projection, temporality, embodiment, and enactive interpretation. Especially pertinent is the "experiential child" approach in the work of Katherine Nelson, which challenges "theory-theories" and emphasizes the social/ecological engagements of the child's development in terms more attentive to factical experiences in their actual milieus.[4] Yet it must be said that even in this new research, there often persists an uncritical deployment of representational and epistemological assumptions that proto-phenomenology can critique—to the betterment of the research, in my view.

The predominance of reflective paradigms has concealed significant elements of a child's world and their relation to adult experience. Despite the obvious importance of advanced rational capacities, the fact that such abilities have a history in an individual's life, that they emerged out of, and often in tension with, other quite different comportments, suggests that child development should be of pressing interest to philosophy. Indeed, from the standpoint of this investigation, an examination of the child's world provides a robust groundwork for a phenomenological approach to philosophical questions. For instance, child development will help illuminate how human life is temporal and historical in a special sense: namely, the intersection of personal, social, and cultural history in the milieu of child-rearing—since the raising of children is always informed by the historical influences upon caregivers and teachers, along with their forward-looking hopes and expectations for children under their charge.

One way to grasp the philosophical import of this developmental milieu is to consider the radical implications of Aristotle's claim that knowledge is marked by the capacity to teach, rather than mere experience (*Metaphysics* 981b8ff). Teaching requires comprehension of the full range of factors and processes that build cognition, not simply experience or knowledge alone. What I find interesting in this remark is that the longstanding philosophical stipulation that knowledge must somehow exceed mere experience is expressed not in terms of some transcendent source or "pure" faculty of a priori cognition, but rather the *practical* setting of pedagogical inculcation, which simultaneously preserves and creates cultural phenomena by "leading" someone (*educere*) toward acquiring the knowledge and skills that have shaped the lives of predecessors. Education is the lifeblood of culture, which survives the passage of time through the shaping of children. It is notable that the Greek word for education, *paideia*, which also denotes the idea of culture and learned accomplishments generally, is derived from *pais*, the word for child; so, with *paideia*, the Greeks named an intrinsic relationship between children, education, and culture. The point is that knowledge and human life generally could not be sustained apart from the regenerating field of child-rearing.

This investigation limits its discussion to what can be shown in child development studies from a contemporary Western perspective. The very notion of childhood is a hermeneutical concept that is not uniform across cultures and historical periods.[5] In the West, in fact, until the 17th century, there was no emphasis on childhood as a special, separate stage of life. Children were seen more as small adults on their way to maturation, and they usually mingled with the adult world and its activities, rather than an environment unique to their own age. Over time, there have been many changes in how children are perceived and how their roles and needs are understood: the variable takes on discipline, freedom, control, and management; seeing children as needing either protection from the wider world or exposure to some of that world as a preparation for life; how child labor has been regarded in different eras; and how today the lives of children are filled with scheduled activities, unlike more self-generated play and experience in times past.

The very idea of "stages" in child development first emerged in late 19th-century research. In the 20th century, the notion of adolescence, as a distinct stage between dependence and maturity, took shape for the first time, and it has been a major factor in modern life. Yet with all the variations and different conceptions of childhood, we need not slip into strictly relativistic or conventionalist assumptions. The lived world offers some baseline common elements of human existence; and given the ecological and historical features of a proto-phenomenological analysis, cultural differences or changes in perceptions of childhood need not be taken as arbitrary constructions but rather responses to different circumstances or environments that can call forth and actualize different natural capacities, which is made possible by the adaptable plasticity of the human condition.

Before proceeding, a central question must be addressed: Can there be a phenomenology of early childhood? Volume I confronted the problem of how pre-reflective experience can be addressed by philosophical reflection; indicative concepts were posed as the solution. Such concepts point to first-person engagement in factical life—not introspective attention to "mental states" but what it is like to dwell in world *environments*. Yet childhood is a special problem because (1) we cannot access first-person experience of our early life as infants and toddlers, since memory does not extend that far back, and (2) children at the earliest stages cannot verbally relay their experiences to us. I assume such early periods to be a condition of immersed engagement without reflective self-awareness or exposition, which are powers that fully take shape with the emergence of language. Pre-linguistic infancy is a remarkable "absence of presence," which is different from the time before we were born. We all *were* that presence, we were *there*, but it is concealed to us as first-hand self-awareness.

How then can we come to understand early childhood experience? Philosophy and science are constituted by exposed articulation of mature experience, which hides the way in which exposition and reflection themselves emerge out of the original immanence of infancy and pre-linguistic experience—stages that are hard to fathom from an adult perspective and thus almost irresistibly interpreted through the lens of reflective exposition. Accordingly, early child development has been retrofitted with more familiar (mature) capacities, so that we imagine a child's "mind" or "concepts" or "theories," primitive though they may be. Such retrofitting, however, conceals how language (especially literacy) shapes such an account of pre-linguistic experience. That concealment is owned up to and acknowledged in a proto-phenomenological analysis, which I think is best able to make sense of a child's world.

Despite the lack of direct access to early childhood experience, proto-phenomenological concepts can be disclosive because they are not grounded in "mental states" but rather ways of being in the world: immersed, embodied activities in meaning-laden environments marked by fluctuations of pleasure and pain, success and failure, freedom and constraint. Existential naturalism and ecstatic dwelling well fit naturalistic observation of child behavior without theoretical presuppositions or experimental controls. Just as the adult lived world is a field of tacit meanings and interactive behaviors that need not be grounded in mental states, we need not "read" an infant's "mind" to know when significant dispositions or bearings are in play. A child's joy or distress is fully disclosed *there* in her behavior, her world. So, if a phenomenological sense of ecstatic dwelling and ecological embeddedness are cogent for occasions of immersed adult experience, that sense can easily be extended to a child's circumstances, with the advantage of being more apt for that world than most assumptions in child development theories. Indicative concepts are not a matter of causal explanation or theoretical confirmation, but simply a pointing to what is *shown* in a child's behavior, environment, and social relations.[6]

An examination of childhood is essential for both proto-phenomenology and human self-understanding. First, the circularity that marks *interpretation* is grounded in child-rearing. Before we reflect on the world or ourselves, there are already operating habits, meanings, and orientations that enable us to navigate the world and that cannot be fully put aside. Unlike philosophical notions of "a priori" categories that ground knowledge, the existential "already" involves factical bearings that animate and make possible all human enterprises, including rational knowledge. Such bearings are not sophisticated cognitive faculties but modes of dwelling that originate in how we are raised and enculturated from the first moments of life. Second, it is obvious that human persons are the temporal/historical product of their early environments. Yet I hope to show that this is not simply a temporal sequence of changes. Human development is not strictly speaking a passage *from* early stages *to* later outcomes in a linear process that supersedes initial periods or leaves them behind. Early stages make subsequent outcomes possible and they remain active in dynamic interaction with later capacities throughout the lifespan.[7] Development runs *through* early stages to maturity in a nested, assimilating manner that sustains beginnings in the looping figure-eight structure of temporality. Who we are, and what we may become, cannot be separated from how we began. Such developmental loops work against perfectionist biases, wherein childhood can be assessed as a regrettable lack or delay of rational powers and autonomy, which is passed through the sooner the better.[8] One of the virtues of studying child development in a temporal/historical manner is that early conditions of dependency prompt us to ask whether "autonomy" in a strict sense ever can or should mark adult selfhood.[9] Even at the child's level, however, dependency is not a matter of developmental determinism because temporal openness and tensions in the personal-social-world preclude outcomes being fully fixed by environments. But for both children and adults, the ecological character of world-involvement precludes freedom being construed as radical autonomy. In summation, the cognitive, perceptual, practical, and linguistic powers that mark human maturity emerge out of the primal engaged immersion of childhood. The environment of childhood and its launch of mature capacities is such that it recedes into the background of adult experience in the manner of second nature. This background cannot be reduced to any foreground exposition, but an indicative approach can compensate for the circularity of immanence at work here.

Proto-phenomenology argues that philosophy cannot be grounded in abstract categories, refined perspectives of objectivity, or rigorous projects of justification; rather, it must begin with the meaning-laden lived world and its common-sense ontology—with what is already in place before philosophical reflection. Phenomenology calls for non-remedial attention to this domain of facticity. The "precedence" of the lived world is evident when we consider child-rearing, which is saturated with "folk" understanding and existential meanings that hardly seem optional, bracketable, or defeasible. One cannot imagine raising children in the light of certain questions that are commonly deemed mandatory for philosophy: moral skepticism, external world skepticism, Gettier problems, substance attribution, personal identity, material constitution, relativism, and so on. It is not that such questions are unimportant, but the way these philosophical problems are constructed or addressed is usually dismissive of "ordinary" features of life that are essential for getting philosophers to the venture of posing such questions in the first place.[10] If I am a parent, there is a real child out there in the world, who is the same child I dealt with yesterday, who is not a bundle of impressions, who calls for my obligatory care, and who guarantees my not being a brain in a vat.

1. ECSTATIC DWELLING

Proto-phenomenology stems from a presumption of immanence and assumes an existential naturalism, which is to say that the world we are born into and find ourselves in is the primary reality; and its factual features are the first order of consideration. Before reflective analysis, we are already engaging the world in a practical manner. The origin of all such engagement is our birth and development as children. It seems sensible to regard this early world as ecstatic immersion, but the predominance of representational and cognitive assumptions is such that childhood experience is usually understood as early occasions of concept formation, theory testing, or information processing based in a child's "mind." Much of cognitive science since the 1950s has taken knowledge to be analogous to digital computation, which however has nothing to do with existential meaning in the lived world, especially the circumstances of a developing, desiring organism.[11] Research on child development has usually been shaped by such theoretical assumptions, in such a way that experimental protocols distort or omit wider and richer domains of a child's experience—precisely because these domains do not fit presumed cognitive functions. Experiments are typically pitched as testing a stipulated type of cognition; and they proceed according to a piecemeal set of specific skills and short-term occasions that block out the wider temporal structure and situated contexts of a child's normal environment. That is why such experiments can mis-measure competence when compared with naturalistic studies. Too often, experiments are preoccupied with *what* a child knows, without attention to *how* and *in what circumstances* a child comes to learn.[12] A standard methodological tenet in traditional research is that controlled experiments are needed to screen out variables and contingencies that might infect results. But these "infections" are such only in light of the need for analytic precision and closure, not the actual existential character of factical life, which simply *is* variable, contingent, spontaneous, and erratic.

As indicated earlier, naturalistic studies of child development fit a phenomenological posture because they stem from suspicion about theoretical bias and experimental distortion of a child's world.[13] What is called for is observation of children in their normal circumstances outside a laboratory. In this manner, it is easier to recognize and study the spontaneous activities and behaviors of children in interaction with caregivers (not researchers). With such natural observation, phenomenological concepts assumed in this investigation are more likely to be manifest: children are engaged in embodied exchanges with their physical and interpersonal environments; a child's world is a practice-field that is meaning-laden, socially prompted, interactively guided, and affectively charged.

Perhaps the signal error committed by traditional theories of child development is what Dewey called the "psychologist's fallacy," which in the present context assumes that a child's experience is governed in some way by the same mental processes adults follow (I have argued that even elements of adult experience have been analyzed in this fallacious manner). Many development theories assume representational structures in a child's early learning and even picture children as proto-scientists enacting primitive hypothesizing, testing, and confirmation in navigating their environment.[14] Some of the questionable assumptions that are challenged by proto-phenomenology and new research in the field include: (1) that basic cognitive systems are a constant from childhood to adulthood (language acquisition and literacy will render this assumption suspect); (2) that core modules of knowledge are inborn and manifest themselves in early infancy; and (3) that some context-independent framework is needed to sort out, organize, and schematize the various aspects of a child's experience.

The primary orientation spawning such theoretical assumptions is a focus on the child as an individual mental agent, following the subject-object binary so prevalent in modern thought. What is missing is the generative and scaffolding force of physical, cultural, and social environments—plus a child's ecstatic immersion in such milieus. Childhood "knowledge" is much less an interior process and more the development of tacit habits, intimations, and situated know-how. Children learn in behavioral and instructional formats into which they are *projected* and in which they are immersed. Contrary to the typical model of internal processing, child development is primarily an outside-in dynamic with an ecstatic structure that later gets "internalized" only after language acquisition.[15] A child's world, therefore, is a circulating field that *draws out* behavioral and meaning-laden responses, which are animated by immediate needs and their affordances.

1.1. Wonder

A child's world is mainly driven by affective attunement rather than "cognition" in the strict sense. Pleasure, pain, and appetites are surely central to early experience. But I have argued that affect also includes more subtle phenomena such as curiosity, which brings our attention to something obvious in a child's bearing from the outset: wonder. Plato and Aristotle claimed that philosophy begins with wonder, with a sense of strangeness in familiar things or a perplexity that prompts a questioning spirit. We may not know directly the character of infant experience, but we easily notice their transfixed stare and excited delight at simply witnessing and participating in the world. Animals display many intelligent capacities, but what seems different about human children is a primal *interest* in things and in their own developing skills, seemingly for their own sake beyond mere utilitarian functions or desire satisfaction.[16] Such primal wonder is a dawning of the human world, which is not simply an array of objectively present things but rather a world that *matters*, that draws our interest and curiosity.[17]

1.2. Immersion and Contravention

Childhood wonder seems to be an original condition of ecstatic immersion, an absorbed fascination with what is *there* in the environment. In addition to this primal orientation, a phenomenological account of immersion can address the beginnings of human awareness by way of the correlation of immersion, contravention, and exposition, although the latter term from the child's standpoint is better reserved for later stages of articulation. To whatever degree infants have been familiarized with their surroundings, they will usually give more focused and sustained attention when something contravenes normal occasions. Child development research in fact has commonly deployed this phenomenon in experiments testing an infant's comprehension of how the world works. Extended "looking time" indicates response to an anomaly, which can imply an understanding of, say, object permanence, motion, or gravity when scenes have been arranged to violate or suspend ordinary patterns. In this way, habituation and dehabituation can reveal early instances of infant comprehension.[18] Yet too often such findings are couched in terms of an infant's "concepts" or "theories," when it would be more apt to take the plasticity of habituation and basic forms of embodied intimation as indicative of a "field" phenomenon rather than a "mental state."[19] Nevertheless, such patterns of infant attention are evidence at very early stages of the correlation between immersion, contravention, and meaningful disclosure established by proto-phenomenology. Exposition in a specific sense emerges later in language development, but an infant's natural engagement with disturbances to familiarity shows at least in behavioral terms a primitive preparation for coming processes of disclosure.

Once children pass through infancy, they begin to encounter the full sense in which contravention functions in development—how limits, restrictions, and mistakes figure in learning to navigate and manipulate their environment.

The familiar idea of learning by doing includes the dynamics of trial and error.[20] Even in learning to walk, a child's body will instinctively adjust its balance in conjunction with the experience of falling. All sorts of play activities also teach skills in the wake of constraints and mishaps. Social and linguistic training proceeds in part by pointing out and correcting mistakes. Here begins the vexing but productive process of facing and learning from limits, which of course continues throughout life.

Early childhood validates both the primacy of immersion and the concurrent experience of disclosive and generative contravention. Such phenomena indicate a continuity in human development all the way back to infancy—not in the sense of common cognitive structures, as some theories propose, but basic existential bearings of meaningful engagement, embodied intimation, practical abilities, and modes of disclosure that launch everything to come. One reason why such things may not come into view in research—beyond theoretical biases concerning what to look for—is that they have receded into the background to such a degree as to escape notice, especially since research capacities themselves rely on a tacit reservoir of skills, habits, and competencies that allow such sophisticated bearings to develop in the first place: perceptual habits, manual skills, social and practical norms, a narrative sense, linguistic abilities, and more go all the way back to childhood and they have a scaffolding effect in the acquisition and maintenance of refined mature powers, especially modes of "cognition" that are unduly retrofitted to early childhood in most research.[21] Proto-phenomenology is able to address *both* the continuity of human development *and* the shifts to transformative powers such as language and literacy—in the manner of a nesting effect that builds hybrid skills in an assimilating process *through* earlier abilities, not a linear passage that leaves prior stages behind.[22] This is why indicative concepts in phenomenology can apply to both childhood and adult experience.

2. THE PERSONAL-SOCIAL-WORLD

When analyzing the tripartite personal-social-environing-world in Volume I, I gave more extensive treatment of the environing-world in order to establish basic phenomenological concepts pertaining to the self's engagement with its environment, concepts that would then be in place for further consideration of the personal and social world—with the proviso that the three worlds are still one world with three interpenetrating elements. In a discussion of child development, there is reason to give proportionally more extensive treatment of the personal-social-world, particularly because social forces are the more crucial environment for the care, nurturing, and unfolding of a child's early life. Adults can engage their environment on their own; but with very young children, this world is almost completely shaped by the protection, guidance, and prompting of caregivers.

2.1. Nature and Nurture

In Volume I (141–143), I distinguished between the *natural*, the *cultural*, and the *arbitrary*, in order to avoid the false choice between nature understood as invariant essence (the "nature" of something) and culture understood as arbitrary variance. Alternatively, the natural can refer to what is intrinsically self-manifesting (e.g., organic growth), the arbitrary can denote what is merely conventional or externally superimposed (e.g., etiquette), and the cultural can be located in between these polarities rather than on one side or the other. Thus, the cultural can exhibit natural *potentialities* that require environmental instigation for their actualization, as in the case of language. Environmental variations will then make for different manifestations of a natural capacity. So, the natural and the cultural can be released from the distinction between invariance and arbitrary differences, now understood as the distinction between an intrinsic capacity and modified enactment.

That is why the nature-nurture binary with respect to children does not hold up under scrutiny. The consensus in most research is that a child's development is neither genetically determined nor wholly constructed by the environment, but rather an intersection of genetic endowments, natural propensities, and nurturing stimuli.[23] Moreover, the "second nature" of developed habits and skills stems from a confluence of nature and culture that cannot be reduced to either brute facts or arbitrary superimpositions. The intersection of nature and nurture is not even clearly delineable into two discrete cooperating spheres: the womb is a contributing environment for the biological development of the fetus, and an infant's behavior will influence how caregivers in the social environment respond to the child (and vice versa).[24]

The reciprocal effects of nature and nurture cannot be sufficiently understood in a third-person objective manner. What should be emphasized are the existential *meanings* at work for both caregivers (their hopes, concerns, and interests) and infants (their experiences and affective responses) that drive the interactive dynamic, which is mutual immersion in a lived world.[25] Added to this on the caregiver side are the contraventions that prompt expositional attention to problems in a child's circumstances and responses (which are more on the "nature" side of the equation). Herein is the dawning of a child's "personal" world, which nevertheless is utterly dependent on the affordances of nurturing. A child's world would be nothing without a supportive and instructive social environment, which shows at the inception level why the personal and social worlds are still one world, a reciprocal circulation of individual and collective energies. It should be noted that child development is no less a mode of adult development, especially with a first child, where becoming a parent involves a dramatic new set of obligations, burdens, possibilities, and achievements that are surely transformative, even a revision of one's own sense of self.[26] In this way, children give birth to their parents in an existential, contextual sense. With child-rearing, there is an indivisible world of shared meaning and development.[27]

2.2. Imitation

The role of imitation in various social and behavioral circumstances in a child's life can be taken as a perfect illustration of ecstatic immersion. Mimetic response shows that what is "outside" in the child's environment precedes a fully formed self that is "inside," so to speak. Children may need to be shown what to imitate, but not how to imitate.[28] A natural mimetic capacity in children indicates that the direction toward self-formation is first cued by absorption in environmental prompts. Evidence for the ecstatic character of imitation can be found in the phenomenon of "invisible imitation," wherein infants mimic with a part of the body such as the face that is not visible to the infant. Piaget had suggested that such a capacity requires the development of a "body schema" around the age of 8–12 months. But there are displays of this mimetic capacity right after birth, as with tongue protrusion. This early capacity suggests an immediate outward immersion that need not require some inner formed sense directed outward.[29] Early imitation is not actually a deliberate "copying" of external behavior because it dwells in an undivided co-being and we-feeling in infancy, followed by a kind of animistic participation at the toddler stage.[30]

What is particularly revealing in child development, then, is "motor mimicry," which is essential to an extensive range of learning experiences. Motor mimicry is a kind of empathic embodiment in which, for example, we spontaneously wince at other people's pain, smile at their delight, recoil at their peril, ape their movements, and so forth. Such behavior has been generally perceived as a puzzle in traditional psychology.[31] Why is it done, especially when we ourselves are not undergoing the movements? It seems that the role of motor mimicry in early childhood provides an answer, and ecstatic immersion greatly enhances an understanding of such behaviors. Mimetic response, especially in a child's early face-to-face engagements, would seem to be a fundamentally ecstatic phenomenon. In spontaneous mimicry, we can presume, as noted earlier, that the "outside" comes first and is productive of the child's "internal" states. Indeed, psychologists speculate that an infant comes to learn about the self primarily through the emotional responses of others, a process that then can be looped back to allow vicarious learning about the experiences of others around them.[32]

Imitation at the earliest stages of human development is a social dynamic of reciprocal effects. Caregivers reproduce and encourage an infant's cooing, smiling, and babbling, which sets up interactive behaviors that extend to all levels of instruction and training to come—and that is an experientially *shared* endeavor apparently unique to human beings.[33] What also seems missing in animal imitation is (1) an infant's uncoached *interest* in this shared activity of reproduction, and (2) a child's apparent comprehension that more specified instances of imitated behaviors are purposeful.[34] In the second year, children expand mimetic sense with their grasp of goal-oriented practices. After observing someone fail to perform a task like taking something apart, a child can spontaneously repeat the task and get the result. If the same circumstance involves a robot, however, a child will not try to duplicate the action—which seems to indicate a natural intimation of meaning-laden behavior in human beings.[35] In summation, imitation in children is essential for incorporation into cultural meanings and the possibility of language acquisition. As Nelson says:

> Imitation by infants and toddlers is a ubiquitous tool, a model of adopting cultural means and ends, and of fitting in the surrounding social world, as well as a way of mastering the affordances of artifacts. Imitation does not *cause* language or culture, but it is a necessary enabling condition.[36]

2.3. Joint Attention

The coalescence of selves in the personal-social-world is well illustrated in the phenomenon of "joint attention," which is the subject of a growing field of research in different disciplines (philosophy of mind, psychology, cognitive science, neuroscience, child development, and ethology), the findings of which show that human mentality is an intrinsically social phenomenon, beginning in childhood but in maturity as well.[37] Natural capacities such as gaze following, pointing, and communicative looks are interpersonal, reciprocal functions that show a triangular structure of different persons inhabiting a common focus on something in the world. Pointing seems to be specific to human experience (if you point for a primate, it will regard your finger rather than the target of pointing); and it exhibits an inter-subjective structure because when infants point, they look back at adults to see if they notice it too—a ubiquitous feature of child behavior called "social referencing."[38] The triangular shape of pointing is a matter of pointing *to* something in the world *for* someone else's attention (either to share an experience or elicit information). Especially in early development, a shared experience of embodied attention is the *starting point* for coming to understand aspects of the world and their significance. In this context, it is noteworthy that the impairment of autism involves certain barriers to joint attention.[39] Accordingly, under normal circumstances, the first-person and second-person perspectives are co-original in human comprehension.

Both developmentally and performatively, a shared world—exemplified by imitation and joint attention—*precedes* the attribution of perceptual and cognitive states to discrete individual minds.[40] As we have noted, right from birth, newborns display a capacity to imitate sounds, gestures, and behaviors, a fluid and integrated natural endowment that launches the full range of human linguistic, cognitive, and practical powers.[41] The ecstatic immersion characterizing early imitation shows that the social environment prepares and makes possible an individual child's propensities to engage the world. An infant's natural capacity for joint attention—the earliest stages of the threefold personal-social-environing-world—prepares and makes possible the instructional dynamic of learning new skills, especially when it comes to language acquisition.[42]

Infants can instinctively follow the attentive behavior of others (their gaze or pointing) as well as direct someone else's attention (holding something up, or pointing, or offering something). With such occasions, there seems to be an implicit understanding of joint attention *as* a shared activity that is mutually interesting. Such engaged co-disclosure is a social, embodied, practical milieu that is "intelligent" and more original than later developments of individual "mentality." That is why the notion that a child (or an adult) needs a "theory of mind" in order to understand the mentality of others is suspect—and in any case *too late* to capture the primal intelligence of joint attention.

Some treatments of joint attention remain wedded to representational and transactional models in accounting for a shared network. Other approaches, however, are more faithful to a social-world phenomenology by stressing an immediacy and embeddedness in shared attention, rather than some kind of referential process—so that joint attention is better rendered as joint *engagement*. Unlike representational transactions—where the problem of other minds might still find a foothold—joint engagement shows that we always already understand each other *as* "co-minded" beings in a common enterprise, as intelligent collaborators in a factical endeavor. Accordingly, disagreements and disparities are *contraventions* of a default sense of mutual cohabitation. Joint engagement is evident at all levels of social interaction and is most refined in organized activities such as team sports and dance, where the flow of performance is an irreducible blend of reciprocal comprehension and capacity.[43]

A productive ability for joint attention seems to emerge in children at eight to nine months of age.[44] Here an infant will follow a mother's gaze when it shifts to a new object. Before that period of development, an infant will attend either to the mother or the object but not the triangular interaction of infant-mother-object. At this earlier stage, the mother's engagement with the infant is primary, not her attention to something in the world. When the infant becomes mobile, there arises an awareness of *divided* attention between the infant's and the mother's engagement with things beyond the mother-infant relation. Therein begins the expanding discovery of things in the world and how different perspectives on things obtain in such discovery. Joint attention is the precursor to joint activity, where the parent and child will engage with some object or bodily behavior, usually rituals of play in the beginning and moving toward purposeful dealings and manipulations (e.g., putting a toy together). At first, children are passively dependent on adults to initiate, structure, and enact joint behavior, which has a scaffolding effect on the child's ability to participate and comprehend what is going on. By the latter half of the first year, a child can initiate and manage basic features of a joint venture. By the end of the second year, a child will become more of an active partner, displaying some independence and creativity in the course of performance.[45]

2.4. Individuation

The dependence of newborns on their nurturing environment is clear evidence for seamless correlations in the personal-social-world, at least in developmental terms. Proto-phenomenology argues for such correlations in adult experience as well, so that an "autonomous self" is a non-starter in absolute substantive terms when seeking to understand human life. Yet with adult experience, the personal-social-world presupposes a distinction between individuated selfhood and social forces (and also allows for relative senses of autonomy in ethical and political contexts). The question at hand concerns when and in what sense individual selfhood is evident in early stages of child development.

Newborns are obviously individual organisms and we can presume their own specific experiences right from birth. But if "selfhood" implies an individuated *sense* of distinction from the surrounding world and other selves, we have to be cautious in assigning selfhood early on—including corollary terms such as a child's "mind" or "intentions." As shown in Volume I, phenomenological displays of personal selfhood are indicated in first-person utterances and their existential significance. Indeed, my analysis aims to show that a clear sense of individuated self-consciousness in children first takes shape with language acquisition—which is one reason why memories of childhood are lacking before that threshold. Yet phenomenological attention to non-reflexive, ecstatic immersion and ecological "fields" is still able to address early childhood experience with a loose sense of a child's "self" that is not defined by later features of maturation, but rather displayed in active engagements with a social-environing-world. So, we can see and surmise in an indicative manner what is going on with children *in their behavior*, without additional suppositions about their "mental states."[46]

Merleau-Ponty argued that a discernible sense of selfhood and otherness is something that develops in time and is not given originally in early stages of a child's life.[47] He interpreted neonatal imitation in a manner consistent with ecstatic immersion, as a mode of "affective sympathy," a process of contagion prompted by what is "outside" in the environment rather than some kind of schematic comprehension in an infant's consciousness.[48] After ground-breaking research on neonatal imitation in the 1970s, some phenomenologists questioned Merleau-Ponty's account, arguing that imitation presupposes some kind of primitive self-other awareness from the start.[49] But my analysis favors Merleau-Ponty's treatment, although an indicative approach can find a balance between the two positions.[50] The very facts of imitation can surely lend themselves to a self-other framework: an infant's own attention to outside behavior prompts a bodily response in kind. We can easily exposit these facts by way of self-other intimations in the infant, especially because sheer non-differentiation seems so incongruous with the sequential course of imitation. Yet I have argued that even adult experience in immersed conditions does not fit strict self-other differentiation. Adult cases can be *exposited* as self-other relations, and we can do the same for infant experience. But for infants themselves, there is no expositional process. It would seem more apt to say that infant imitation is pure immersion, a field phenomenon exhibiting a visceral sense of embodied know-how and intimation, which precedes the possibility of exposition into clear delineations of selfhood and world. Even though we can readily notice a tacit prelude to self-other awareness, ecstatic immersion seems to be the more appropriate description. It could be said that the looking-time phenomenon—where an infant gives sustained attention to an unusual occurrence—offers a kind of *inarticulate* exposition prompted by contravention, although without any specified features beyond the infant's focused regard.

How and when does more manifest self-other differentiation emerge in children? The event of birth could be called the first carnal sense of individuation, of separation from the womb. The first weeks of life involve biological functions adjusting to this new environment, in a mostly passive dependency without any self-other awareness or perceptual discrimination.[51] Research shows a number of stages in the development of specific self-awareness, the dynamics of which, it should be said, are not *lost* in adult self-awareness.[52] Although the earliest condition of neonates lacks distinct self-other demarcation, a certain embodied distinction is implicit in imitation episodes and the experience of touch. By the second month, the reaction of smiling at interactive play is evident, which suggests the instinctive pleasure of joint behavior. By four months, reaching for things implies a situated sense of eye-hand-thing conjunction. At five to six months, once infants are familiar with their own mirror image, looking-time attention to the novelty of another infant's image is displayed, which indicates a default focal awareness of the infant's own body. By eighteen months, on seeing themselves in a mirror, infants will reach for a mark put on their body in order to touch or remove it, suggesting a specific recognition of their own body as such. At two to three years of age, children can display embarrassment at social recognition. By the fourth year, if children see themselves on television and are asked who it is, most will give the first-person answer, "Me." In the next chapter, the crucial role of language in the development of self-awareness will be examined.

At early stages, infants are not aware of their own agency as such. The attention, reaction, and prompting of caregivers provide the first occasions of quasi-selfhood in being the "focal center" of attention from others in the midst of shared embodiment.[53] It is also becoming evident how interactive play contributes to self-development in improvised co-ordinations with others acting out narratives of engagement with the outside world.[54] All told, it should be clear that early self-development fits the tripartite structure of the personal-social-environing-world assumed in this investigation. None of us begins life as some isolated atomic "self"—and indeed, such correlated dimensions of worldhood remain manifest in adult experience.

In Volume I, the discussion of truth was connected with a disposition of trust, in order to thematize a direct sense of presentational truth that precedes representational structures. Unless subject to contravention, veridical trust is a default condition of disclosure and comprehension, especially with regard to the extensive role of testimony. Such trust is also implicated in how we experience things in normal perception. In developmental terms, this kind of perceptual trust is first at work in the triangular structure of joint attention and imitation. A child's early orientation toward the world depends upon the reception and incorporation of meaningful practices in shared activity.[55] Children do not *articulate* a trusting disposition, but their very bearing must be a reliance on socially transmitted disclosure of how the world is and how to deal with it. In this early period, the "truth" of things must be presupposed as the ready reliability of a culturally charged practical environment. Such a setting can be fathomed as the original sphere of "objectivity" in that it exceeds the child's own perspective and shapes it according to ecological conditions, affordances, and established practices—keeping in mind that this kind of objectivity is not "value free" but rather saturated with existential meaningfulness.

In addition to such exogenous forces that figure in a child's self-development, there is an important stage that launches the process of individuation out of earlier conditions of immersion, a stage that dramatically illustrates the proto-phenomenological correlation of contravention and exposited disclosure, namely separation anxiety.[56] Human attachments and negative experiences of separation from attachments occur throughout human life in various forms and contexts: losses of, or threats to, possessions, things, people, habits, beliefs, possibilities, environments, or roles; encounters with something different, novel, strange, or unfamiliar.[57] Despite the difficulties and distress that can accompany such experiences, human growth and development are impossible without separating from certain attachments and confronting new situations—so that facing anxieties is essential to human development.[58] Particularly emblematic is the role of separation anxiety in early childhood. Acute separation anxiety usually occurs around eight to ten months of age, typically in the context of parental separation and object absence. Such anxiety alters the earlier, more undifferentiated bond with caregivers and things. For this reason, separation experiences are correlated with the course of individuation, of (1) coming to experience oneself *as* distinct from erstwhile attachments to persons and things *by way of* their absence, and (2) feeling the *importance* of such persons and things on account of their absence.[59] In phenomenological terms, then, it can be said that separation anxiety is a double movement of contravention-and-disclosure; it is not a fully negative phenomenon because its affective force helps sharpen a child's experience of itself and its world (of feeling the import of things and being the bearer of that import), thus enriching experience and fostering growth.[60] The process of early separation and individuation is less a cognitive-perceptual phenomenon and more an emotional-motivational phenomenon.[61] Additionally, around the third year, mostly facilitated by language development, children develop a sense of object constancy, that absent things can still exist; and in such a context, memory and anticipation help mollify anxiety and promote a toleration of separation.[62]

Healthy child-rearing involves a balance of love and setting limits, which on the child's side is experienced as a fluctuation between the satisfaction and frustration of interests. Individuation prompted by separation will then involve a certain internalization of that fluctuating balance initially shaped in the care environment.[63] In other words, part of human development involves confronting finite limits in the environment, learning to tolerate such limits, and negotiating various co-ordinations between self and others, interests and frustrations, and presences and absences—co-ordinations that can hold off extremes in either direction. A life without estrangements and losses would be a life without meaning and growth. Yet too much estrangement can lead to disintegration, trauma, incapacitation, or even excessive attachment as a refuge from negative experiences. The value of such balancing acts is borne out by developmental psychology.[64] In early life, experiences of loss and responses to separation are an index to a child's adjustments later in life. Too much care and too little care are both detrimental. Over-protectiveness stifles growth and resiliency. Parental neglect, withdrawal, or abuse can produce excessive separation that makes coping with loss even harder, which explains the irony that it is often more difficult for children to leave abusive homes.[65] Early experiences of acute insecurity or deprivation make toleration of loss more burdensome and can also spawn excessive self-regard and hyper-attachment to compensate for looming stress and anxiety. Children who experience acute emotional conflict and stress are more likely to develop rigid, polarized thinking for psychic protection. Children in more stable emotional environments are more apt to fathom intellectual complexity and ambiguity.[66]

A child's world is both alluring and anxiety-ridden, a conjunction correlated in such a way that children can discover new vistas and capacities through contraventions of familiarity. A sign of a child's natural openness to anxiety is the fascination with scary scenarios in stories and pretend play.[67] Most children have an impulse for risk-taking, the danger of which is concealed because of their lack of experience; yet the impulse is worthy in general terms as a precondition for experimental ventures in life. A child's openness to the world obviously brings with it possible threats to well-being; but with the exception of extreme cases, children can be resilient in the face of negative experiences. We should be cautious with familiar worries about the effects of loss or witnessing violence. These days, grief counseling and trauma therapy seem to be on hand as a matter of course, as opposed to targeting manifest cases of disturbance. Such indiscriminate counseling can even be self-fulfilling by creating tribulation by suggestion.[68]

2.5. Ethics and Child-Rearing

In Volume I, ethics was examined in terms of a pre-reflective normative background that is always already in play before philosophical reflection on ethical questions. That background is best understood as initially an inheritance of nurturing effects early in life. It is not that the background is immune to interrogation or revision, but it stands as a necessary condition of ethical existence that cannot be ignored in moral philosophy (as Aristotle recognized). A look at child development can help articulate the nature and function of a pre-reflective normative background, and proto-phenomenological concepts are well suited to such articulation with respect to a child's world.

From a practical standpoint, the raising of children illustrates the beginning of a socialization-individuation dynamic. As we have seen, the social-world is crucial in the self-development of a child, but not to the point of sheer dominance. Children from early on are recognized as distinct personalities and they are expected to become self-directing agents to one degree or another. Individuation involves a tension between the personal-world of the child and the social-world (as parents know all too well). That tension is inevitable and even desirable if cultural transmission is to be inflected with differentiation and variation rather than mere duplication. In any case, the tensional dynamic of socialization and individuation is precisely where ethical norms take shape.[69]

Childhood and social development show that early stages of life are neither amoral nor pre-moral because they are saturated with norms, values, and goods.[70] Such spheres of ethical emergence can be roughly organized around the importance of freedom, responsiveness to others, and situated limits—a triad that echoes the structure of the personal-social-environing-world. To begin, freedom can be understood as a good in the child's world, in terms of the many bearings and behaviors stemming from a child's needs, interests, and desires. Such occasions, however, are often restricted by the social and natural environment; accordingly, children experience from the start indigenous limits and obstacles to their freedom. In this regard, a range of alternating elements are ethically relevant for a child's actualization of potentials in a finite world: alternations of pleasure and pain, satisfaction and frustration, gain and loss, success and failure, safety and risk, excitement and boredom, and familiarity and strangeness. The most ethically significant limit to a child's freedom is presented in the social-world. Manifestations of freedom encounter friction with the freedom of others and with various role and power relations in the social milieu, particularly child-parent, sibling, and peer relations. Here children learn the complex normative permutations of socialization in relation to individual freedom: such things as sharing, cooperating, turn-taking, reciprocity, fairness, and respecting property. On a more affective level, children are regularly exposed to ethical scenarios of cruelty and kindness, hurting and helping, self-interest and concern for others.

A consideration of normative elements in a child's environing-world overlaps significantly with the social-world, one example being the value and importance of a child's practical dealings with things: the cultivation of various skills, habits, and performances in a host of making, doing, and playing scenarios. We can also consider how correlations of a child's behavior and the environment exhibit the dyad of nature and nurture in ethical development. Here we notice two ways in which the concept of ecstatic dwelling is relevant. First, the relation between a child's nature and the environment seems to be a fluid, reciprocal correlation that embodies the holistic structure of immersed engagement. Second, we have seen how imitation in social and behavioral development shows that what is ecstatically *there* in a child's environment precedes a fully formed "internal" mentality. The movement toward self-formation is first prompted by absorption in ecological settings. The social-environing-world is productive of ethical development as a web of enculturating forces: reward and punishment, praise and blame, modeling, prompting, and exhortation. Evidence of this formative nexus is shown when children exhibit spontaneous social referencing, by looking to others to get their bearings in social practices.[71] Children also become oriented to various arenas of power and authority in their world, and concurrently with occasions of obedience and disobedience, compliance and resistance.

The three ethical spheres in the personal-social-environing-world become more variegated, complex, and intricate as children become more individuated, especially in the course of language development. In line with what we have established about language generally, the acquisition of speech begins to open and articulate a child's ethical-world, beginning with such basic utterances as *yes* and *no*, *nice* and *mean*, *good* and *bad*, in the context of early behaviors. A child's linguistic development permits giving a presence to the absences of past and future, thus enriching the capacities of memory, anticipation, and imagining different possibilities. Such temporal alterability is essential for the possibility of moral instruction, of instilling a sense of the differential element in every *ought* and *ought not*. At the same time, to the chagrin of most parents, the cultivation of linguistic ability and alterability enhances the child's resources for resistance (the verbal creativity of a child in trouble is often astounding). So, language development permits both the convergences of socialization and the divergences of individuation.

Language development, individuation, and socialization also exhibit early manifestations of social practices that have always been the life-blood of ethics. Children display an innate capacity for various rituals of question and answer, reason-giving, negotiation, reciprocation, and modification in the context of ethical situations. Role-playing, pretend play, and storytelling are also an important part of developing a child's ethical sense.[72] All such practices suggest an early facility for ethical appropriation in a social setting, as opposed to sheer rote learning or mechanical conditioning—and so children seem to be budding ethical thinkers from early on. Moral development is neither pure cultural transmission nor a child's own self-construction; it is a child's re-construction and re-creation of inherited cultural meanings.[73]

The point of this discussion is to spotlight the complex network of goods, values, and norms that are intrinsic to a child's environment and growth from the start, the array of meaningful practices and relationships that shape an early ethical bearing in a pre-reflective manner. Moral theories can be said to draw on such a milieu in a more reflective manner. But the modern bias of subject-centered reason is challenged by a proto-phenomenological look at human development, which shows that before we think about morality, we are already ethically situated and projected. Since various ethical forces come to shape the self in the first place, then the modern theoretical tendency to ground ethics in self-reflection requires an originating "self" that in many respects is a fictional object. A similar critique can be leveled against philosophical challenges to truth in ethics, as in the case of moral skepticism, fictionalism, or the error theory. Volume I tried to bring flexibility and plurality to the question of truth, rather than exclusive reliance on truth standards that are difficult to meet in the ethical sphere. Although there is much to question in ethical matters, one is hard-pressed to imagine parents being sincere moral skeptics when raising their children.

The various permutations within and between normative spheres in a child's world illustrate the complexities and tensions that are intrinsic to an ethical environment. Parents and children are readily aware of the commingling of diverse and competing goods that are not amenable to neat organization or clear resolution. Parents, for instance, experience the tension between (1) permitting, even encouraging a child's freedom to explore the world and activate interests, and (2) worrying about the dangers, risks, and sufferings that the world can visit upon an advancing child. There is also the tension of wanting a child to develop both a healthy self-regard and a concern for others. There is no formula or guidebook that can suffice in such settings. Raising children is at best an attentive experiment marked by a blend of instruction, encouragement, protection, joy, hope, and anxiety. Children, too, come to experience the difficult confluence of goods in their world. From early on, they have a natural interest in the value of freedom and desire satisfaction. They also need no help in recognizing unfair treatment—when, say, another child might get a larger piece of cake. But they also understand in a rough way that fairness should be reciprocal, and yet fairness to others might block or limit their own freedom and desire satisfaction. Children experience this tension as a perplexing yet compelling feature of the social world, which is simply there as a mode of projection that cannot be overridden.

Consider the stress between individuation and socialization in another register. Children normally display tendencies of assertiveness, resistance, aggressiveness, pride, and possessiveness that surely can be problematic for the cultivation of pro-social dispositions. Norms in the social-world continually check such tendencies in various ways. Even with the force of such restrictions, however, children exhibit a ready interest in testing the limits of norms, often with a sense of excitement. Despite the difficulties here, it is important to recognize the significant role that a child's resistance plays in individuation and development. An utterly obedient child would likely develop into a feeble adult, if at all. The contraventions exhibited in childhood resistance, especially in the infamous "no" stage, are an essential ingredient in a child's growth. As Hegel and Nietzsche have indicated on a larger scale, there is no individuation without some degree of conflicted differentiation from others. The child's "no" is in part a carving out of its own space. Yet this generative conflict *remains* a social phenomenon, not an atomic condition, because without the force of norms, there would be nothing to resist. Short of violence—which implies an impulse to eliminate or disable a conflicting party—disputation regarding socio-cultural possibilities is not an anti-social phenomenon, and harmonious homogeneity is not the only sign of social order.[74] In any case, a child's resistance is essential for individuated self-development, as a simultaneous freeing-from and freeing-for, even a kind of play that invites the world to be an oppositional force for the sake of expanded discovery. Early disobedience is more existential than moral, more a looking in different directions than a deliberate flouting of norms.[75] Recognizing the generative role of resistance can prompt a selective strategy of proportionate discipline rather than dominance or knee-jerk rectification in every case.[76]

Both parents and children learn that the complex tensions of an ethical environment cannot be fully managed or regulated from the standpoint of rigid guidelines or systematic order. The best that can be achieved is an ongoing balancing act of negotiation, orchestration, and experimentation. Such contingent modes of coping with the fluid intricacy of the social-world continue to mark ethical bearings beyond the milieu of child-rearing. Mature ethical life involves refinements and modulations of that original milieu, especially concerning correlations of self-regard and responsiveness to others, freedom and responsibility, appropriation and authority, development and limits—a dynamic that exceeds the strict taxonomies and directives that have animated many moral theories.

2.6. Empathy and Ethical Development

In Volume I, empathy was examined as an ecstatic fellow-feeling, a vicarious sharing of another person's fortune or misfortune—a direct, non-inferential immersion that spotlights the joint structure of the personal-social-world, and that provides a precondition for pro-social ethical possibilities. Empathy seems to be natural to the human condition, although contingent on a number of factors that make it far from regular or universally expressed. Nevertheless, developmental psychology can help articulate the issues involved and address a number of existential questions: How is it that we come to care about others? How does caring get blocked? How might caring be nourished?[77]

Face-to-face play between parents and infants (at two to three months) entails the sharing of emotion and develops an affective attunement that may be the precursor to later empathic responses. At ten to twelve months, babies begin to sense the emotional meaning of facial expressions, and this begins their social development, which soon exhibits a capacity to respond vicariously to emotional expressions and behaviors. Some cases: a nine-month-old becomes overwhelmed at the distress of other infants; a fourteen-month-old sees another infant crying and she begins to cry and looks to her mother; a fifteen-month-old is arguing with another child, who begins to cry, and the first child leaves to fetch a teddy bear for the crying child. Empathic experience seems to emerge in stages and in a manner that makes an assumption of mere "conditioning" problematic. In the first year, prior to self-other differentiation, infants experience "empathic distress," wherein the distress of another person causes one's own feeling of distress (an infant crying at the sound of another infant crying). Such contagion would seem to be a developmental base that makes later empathic displays possible. In the second year, with self-other differentiation, children can respond empathically to the distress of another person that they recognize is not their own. At two to three years, children learn more clearly that the feelings of others belong to *them*, and this actually enhances responsiveness to their cues. With the learning of language, empathy can relate to more complex emotions and can be aroused by the mere recounting of an absent person's misfortune. Children in later years can begin to empathically generalize about groups or grasp larger life situations and their meanings. In maturity, a broadened understanding of life and its complexities can modify empathy in various ways.

It seems that empathic responses are biologically coded, yet a child's environment can influence whether it flourishes or withers. In addition to prosocial dispositions, empathy appears to be implicated in a wide range of social behaviors and attitudes: self-awareness, communication skills, and social understanding. It is important to note that empathy should not be understood as unidirectional from either side of the self and other persons; it is developmentally bi-directional, *inter*personal rather than *intra*personal. It is not simply an "out to" or an "into" or even a mere "with," but a reciprocal co-presencing that prefigures a significant range of intersubjective processes. Empathic responses that a young child receives from others are both a factor in the self-formation *of* the child and a reinforcement of the child's empathic responses *to* others throughout development. The point is that the individual self from early on has *relational* capacities and needs in addition to mere biological drives and the dictates of pleasure and pain.[78]

Research suggests that a "transference" model of empathy presuming a self-based trajectory "into" another person is reductively flawed.[79] It seems to be a genuinely ecstatic phenomenon. At the same time, the development of empathic concern appears to be a confluence of instinctive predispositions and environmental influences. A number of factors enhance the development of empathy: a secure, nurturing, affectionate environment (which diminishes excessive self-concern); modeling and identification; inductive socialization (e.g., the golden rule); and opportunities for helping behaviors and their reinforcement. It must be emphasized that the need for a nurturing environment is not a challenge to empathy being "natural" (no less than with language development). Early instances of empathy in children suggest that it is not simply a cultural construction or the result of social conditioning. Deprived environments, however, show that empathy is neither automatic nor easily sustainable under adverse conditions; it is possible for empathy to be diminished, concealed, or lost. Yet there is some relief from citations of exceptions or extreme cases (the occurrence of radical selfishness in circumstances of acute deprivation) presumed to invalidate the naturalness of empathy, as though invariance or permanence were necessary conditions for something being natural. Empathy is a natural *potentiality* that is poised to be actualized by appropriate ecological affordances. In any case, empathy as a natural capacity in both adults and children provides not only telling evidence for genuine prosocial dispositions that can animate ethics, but also vivid illustration of how the extra-individual structure of the social-world manifests itself experientially.

3. THE ENVIRONING-WORLD

The social-world initially has the most direct and extensive effect on young children, but the environing-world is no less important. In addition to the obvious need for stable and non-threatening physical conditions in immediate domains, infants will begin to navigate and manipulate their concrete surroundings, which is essential for subsequent perceptual, cognitive, and practical development. Conditions of radical isolation, as in the case of feral children discussed in Volume I, show how crucial the social-world is for a child's development; but cases of deprivation and confinement, as in Romanian orphanages uncovered in the 1980s, add the requirement of a child's engagement with the environing-world to prepare future abilities and even sensory comprehension.[80] These unfortunate children exhibited significant social, emotional, cognitive, and physical impairment, as well as a diminished capacity for normal perception, as exemplified by one case, Rudy: he displayed little affect, eye contact, or interest in others; he had focusing problems and suffered from sensory overload; he could not navigate the environment in relation to his body; and he could not distinguish shapes with his hands.

In normal conditions, young children exist as embodied immersion in their physical environment—not sealed up in some inner consciousness beholding an external world. Contraventions of comfort will cause a disturbed reaction, but otherwise non-attentive immersion is a given. I mean this in a sense that holds for adults as well. When I am seated in my office chair, I am normally not consciously aware of its pressure on my body or the tactile feeling of sitting in a chair. The same holds for the ground when I am walking and countless other sensorimotor circumstances.[81] With adults, contraventions will allow expositional attention, but all human beings have a baseline carnal immersion that is more pervasive and less qualified in infancy.

The point of this initial treatment of normal and abnormal conditions of ecological experience at the beginning of life is to demonstrate (1) how essential the social-environing-world is to human development, and (2) how non-reflective immersion is continued and sustained as a tacit background in adult life as well, which is the ever-present precondition for advanced human disclosive powers—and which, precisely because of its tacit character, usually goes unnoticed or gets retrofitted *with* those advanced powers in most philosophical discussions.

3.1. Locomotion

Children begin to crawl between seven to nine months of age. Such locomotion and the coming venture of learning to walk are significant factors in a child's separation from early social bonding and an impulse to explore surrounding environments, which facilitates the expansion of capacities and interests—a burgeoning independence that surely is a mixed blessing for parents. Domain-specific theories of development emphasize the solipsistic standpoint of a child's cognitive processing of new data in this stage by way of discrete modules and core concepts that had been operating from the start. Development of the neuromuscular system would be the only new factor at this point, which would simply extend the range of data. New approaches challenge such theories in a way that is consistent with the ecological structure of the personal-social-environing-world, which disrupts targeting a child's "mental states" as the primary progenitor of learning. Emerging comprehension at this stage is more an embodied sensory-behavioral complex than "cognition," and it unfolds as a multidimensional and context-dependent process.[82]

Locomotion opens up new modes of experience that were unavailable earlier and that are not simply discrete internal domains of cognition but rather mixed venues of ecological interaction, which allow qualitative changes in an infant's world: for instance, social and emotional development, awareness of self-movement, distance perception, spatial comprehension techniques, and the search for hidden objects. Joint attention expands beyond the immediate proximity of parent and infant prior to locomotion. Now children initiate discovery on their own, but continuous social referencing sustains the triadic structure of joint engagement. Locomotion also alters socio-emotional behavior, where children become more willful in seeking their freedom, but also more intense in displays of attachment behavior.

Two things need to be emphasized in our discussion. First, development at this stage is an integrated correlation of individual, social, and environmental factors, which is more a dynamic-systematic-existential lived world than simply a series of cognitive and practical skills centered in a child's mind or behavior. The child is ecstatically extended in a fluid, blended, and reciprocal network of ecological affordances. Second, cultural differences matter a great deal in how such early stages of development unfold, especially because the dramatic new conditions that obtain in children venturing forth in the world can elicit different degrees of management and allowance: from rigid control, to orchestrated scaffolding, to hands-off approaches.[83] American children over the past decades have been hyper-managed to an extraordinary degree. No longer set loose outdoors to play with peers on their own, children today are enveloped by organized activities designed and overseen by adults, with little time for undetermined, self-directed play and discovery.[84]

3.2. Trial and Error

Contraventions of immersed conditions allow exposited explication of the tacit meaning and purpose of a practice. In addition to this disclosive function of contravention, I have previously noted the way negative limits are constitutive of meaningfulness in a finite existence, in that positive features of life, such as success, health, and gain, are structurally related to their privation, namely failure, illness, and loss—not just semantically or conceptually, but in the factical experience and import of such occasions. I also discussed how contravention can generate immediate disclosive effects in an ongoing activity, as in the case of direct learning through mistakes. Earlier in this chapter I mentioned how the familiar notion of learning by doing includes learning by failing, and how young children develop their capacities caught up with impediments and miscues. Everything from walking to social norms are learned by experiments of trial and error—*in the midst of* active engagement. In addition to satisfaction of needs and desires, such experiments initiate the meaning- and value-laden character of factical life that is sustained through maturity, particularly with respect to achieving something important that can go wrong or falter. The enjoyment of achievement and frustration at faltering is a package deal that children inhabit as they begin to move through the world. The difficult task of learning to tolerate, even appreciate, this mix of achievement and limits can better get off the ground if children are exposed to a well-balanced social environment that neither over-praises success nor over-criticizes failure. There are also extremes that can befall children as they grow older, if success is under-acknowledged or downplayed (for fear that children will not try their best) or if failure is minimized or even commended on a par with success (for fear that children will be traumatized by coming up short).

In any case, child development involves a wide array of limit-infused learning and achievement scenarios, which generate skills, abilities, and behaviors that are saturated with norms and values pertaining to proper function in practical, social, and ethical spheres. The ecological and experimental character of these learning processes rehearses a point made about improvisation in Volume I, namely that an improvised activity in the midst of altered or shifting conditions in the field of practice disturbs a model of cognition limited to internal mental constructs of representations, intentions, rules, or inferences. Spontaneous improvisation is better rendered as an ecstatic field-phenomenon with reciprocal feedback between agent and environment. Child learning milieus of trial and error are even more apt to embody such a reciprocal field, as opposed to the common mentalistic attribution of children testing their "theories" about the external world.

3.3. Habit and Know-How

We have seen that habits operate not in the manner of instinctive first-nature, but second-nature, which is to say learned capacities that settle into non-reflective immersion without conscious direction. Habits follow the figure-eight structure of temporality, as an acquired readiness for future action; they also embody the background intimation of know-how and tacit understanding, which (absent contravention) need not be explained, articulated, or guided by rules. Habits indicate the scope of routine behaviors that function without explicit attention and that form an essential foundation of life, because otherwise we would have to deliberately guide and monitor every move we make in the world. Habits are situationally cued by context, they operate according to a minimally conscious procedural memory, and they are *implicitly* intentional and motivational in character (rather than mere stimulus-response formats).[85] Tacit habits embody what is called "automaticity," the immediate processing of one's environment without self-conscious attention, which issues a host of cognitive, behavioral, and motivational effects.[86] In much of the tradition, habit has been downplayed and even denigrated for purportedly being blind, mechanical, and thoughtless. But the notion of capacious second nature allows us to see habit as spontaneous engagement with the world in a meaningful and intelligent manner.[87] The automatic immersion of habits should not be identified with mindless instinct or involuntary routines because they are meaning-laden and have to be learned. Habits occupy the full range of human capacities in practical, social, ethical, artistic, and intellectual domains. Even though learned and registered by repetition, habits are not bound by past conditions but rather open for coming occasions.[88] Skilled habits (e.g., in athletics) can be responsive, flexible, and creative. Altogether, habits enable multiple ways of comprehending and navigating the world, and they endow the capacity for human self-expression.[89] Finally, habits are not rigidly ingrained because with contraventions they can be modified or changed.

A good number of background habits begin in childhood, many of which usually lack self-conscious awareness: walking, talking, reading, writing, behavioral norms, manual skills, and practical routines. The protophenomenological argument for the priority of immersion receives its best evidence with those nonconscious engagements that reach all the way back to the beginning of life. The more refined skills developed in maturity rely on a reservoir of these older habits, so that adult capacities exhibit a nested assimilation of capacities *along with* and *made possible by* more basic habits acquired in early years—not simply a linear sequence of stages.

Child development in many ways is nothing but habit formation, where children go through the arduous (but natural) process of learning by doing and faltering and re-doing—in the acquisition of capacities for coping with the social-environing-world, which confronts a child with many limits, contraventions, and challenges that must be overcome in the learning process.[90] Children early on need a lot of help and guidance in navigating different contexts of practical life, and trust in the propriety of that guidance is essential for the confidence and willingness to learn (here begins the association of truth with trust). This nascent scenario offers further support for challenging mentalistic and cognitivist theories of development with an alternative framework of projection and correlational scope. A child's "mind" (in an indicative sense) is surely involved, but the wider picture should render children "extended" into their *world* of facilitating affordances that offer the scaffolding function necessary for learning the absorbed habits of living. It should be said that even the best research I am relying on can fall prey to mentalistic biases, which phenomenology can help interrogate. Nelson, for example, in challenging cognitivist theories on behalf of a pragmatic, experiential approach, still finds herself deploying a "subconscious" version of representations and concepts to articulate early childhood, confiding that "we cannot do without some such terms for subconscious mental processes, even at the earliest stages of postnatal existence."[91] I would disagree, unless such terms were used in a strictly indicative manner.

In a general sense, capacious practice applies to the distinction between knowing-how and knowing-that, the latter referring to propositional knowledge and mental representation. The immersion of habitual behavior, in everything from walking to highly skilled performance, cannot be properly understood by way of exposited formats of representational relations. Yet the bi-directionality of immersion and exposition shows that propositional forms can reflectively re-describe immersed activity and also help prepare the development of new habits that evolve into ecstatic practices. Nevertheless, reflective exposition, whether in everyday or philosophical terms, is derived from a bedrock of habitual enactment and is neither a necessary nor a sufficient condition for automatic performance. That bedrock of habits is launched in childhood, where learning is a result of direct imitation or ecologically situated trial and error. Immersed know-how is the more apt designation for most of what transpires in a child's world, rather than a child's mental deployment of propositional knowledge. We can indicatively talk of a child's "intelligence," but as an environmentally responsive practical aptitude, which can also be assigned to animals—and this is crucial for avoiding the anthropocentric *segregation* of animal life from human comportments. Basic embodied skills and habitual behaviors common to animals and humans are anything but blind and mechanical; they are functions of an "animate organism" engaged in meaningful life-serving activity, the *exposited* features of which are not consciously accessed but spontaneously enacted. The simplest levels of this intelligent animation in humans have been inherited from childhood and have become so tacit as to easily escape philosophical attention.[92]

Surely caregivers give a lot of thought to their dealings with children, and so cognitive reflection will always be indirectly part of a child's environment. But at the earliest stages, children themselves have no expositional involvement in their learning (as an adult would in acquiring a new skill). A child might pause before acting, seemingly "considering" what to do. But we should be careful about exporting introspective mentality here. In the next chapter, I will argue that internalized "thinking" takes shape only after the acquisition of language. Yet even there I will show how words like "think" and "know" are first learned in practical settings and different conversational contexts, rather than an introspective grasp or employment of abstract "concepts." New research fits such a practical ecological framework (despite questionable talk of childhood concepts and representations) by showing how children learn first by way of behavioral, observable, external scenarios, as well as non-optional instructions from caregivers—all of which follows Vygotsky's "outside-inside" principle of development.[93]

One reason why childhood experience has been misconstrued by way of advanced conceptions and mental categories can ironically be attributed to the extensive range of habitual dispositions. There are *mental* habits, which become so ingrained that we become immersed in them as fixed lenses, so that everything gets examined through them.[94] Proto-phenomenology amounts to an alert about questionable habits of mind that miss factical experience; and it aims to pose contravening questions that might spawn new habits of indicative exposition.

3.4. Play

Childhood play from the earliest stages is a crucial ingredient in development, and it well fits phenomenological concepts of ecstatic engagement, enactive interpretation, and improvisation, which challenge internalized models of cognition and even brain-centric explanations of thought and behavior. Play in adult terms might be called the intrinsic enjoyment of structured activity that in itself is not directed at any larger purpose. Childhood play, however, is not simply leisure activity because it helps construct a child's cognitive, affective, social, and practical intelligence. Early infant play is not structured but simply spontaneous manipulation and engagement with toys and other objects. Later forms of play become more structured and animated by narratives: dressing a doll, pretend cooking and eating, driving a car, building and taking things apart, and so on. Such play has to do with sense-pleasure, action-meanings, and rudimentary skills, a kind of world-making driven by an affective-behavioral-engagement nexus, not simply a cognition or processing of "objects." Such play is also fully "serious" as enactive interpretation and creative discovery, not simply pretense or fantasy.[95]

Traditional theories have surmised the operation of "symbolic representation" in structured and narrative play. But recent research has cast doubt on this supposition.[96] Up to three years of age, children do not readily distinguish between "pretend" play and the "real world." Ecstatic immersion in play as something fully real seems to be more to the point. A child does not equate a toy car with the family car, but the toy does not "represent" a car, it is a *version* of the real thing. Children at that age cannot associate a small model of a room with features of the real room. The "model" is something in its own right. Play is more a form of "externalizing" meaning and function, comparable to the way in which imitation operates. Active relations between self and world are a field-phenomenon and play is a way of establishing the field, in a way that mere observation or perception on the part of a child could not generate. Externalization is also a path toward shared meaning, even in early solitary play because a parent's regard is noticed and occasional intervention is appreciated if something goes awry. The early play of siblings or peers in the same vicinity is usually solitary but parallel in notice. Associative play is haphazard but can spill over between players if something becomes contagious. Cooperative play involves sharing a common enterprise. Never stress-free, this stage of play nevertheless prepares the complex reciprocal relationships of interactive endeavors and their social dynamics.[97]

The externalizing effects of play should not be taken as an outward "expression" of a child's internal mental states or representations, but as an ecological *constitution* of meaningful scenarios and engagements, which first take shape as an ecstatic presentation, *there in the world* as an embodied nexus of the child's activity and play objects.[98] We have no evidence of mental representations in a young child's psyche apart from the presentational field of a child's immersed experience.[99] Memories and later instances of expositional representation can be derived from the factical field of play but they are not the origin of a child's early engagement. It can also be said that childhood play initiates what I have called enactive interpretation, namely the ongoing exploration and iteration of a meaningful setting or context. However haphazard at first, a child's manipulations and serialization of events indicate a primal sense of participation in nonrandom episodes of significance (dressing a doll, racing a car) that are affectively charged and instigated by the child's direction.

4. AFFECTIVE ATTUNEMENT

Proto-phenomenology has established that world-disclosure is not simply a cognitive process, that feelings, emotions, and moods are disclosive of how the world matters and issues existential import. Even the most refined scientific knowledge, as a human enterprise, stems from and is fueled by dispositions of curiosity, interest, aspiration, and desire. Only computers would count as affect-free cognition, not human scientists. Of course, affect cannot be sufficient in the pursuit of knowledge and it can easily derail that pursuit, but knowledge without feelings of significance would not excite the desire to pursue it.

It seems clear that in early life, the world of children is saturated with affect, with how the world bears on their needs and interests—and such affective attunement can be called sufficiently disclosive of that world's narrow scope. Distress at hunger or pain is not simply an expression of an internal psychic state but proper signals to caregivers about real conditions that need attention, which is the earliest version of the correlative structure of disclosive communication that will reach full articulation with the emergence of language. In any case, young children experience the world as meaning-laden in a felt manner: as attractive-repulsive, satisfying-unsatisfying, helpful-harmful, pleasurable-painful. Such early experience cannot adequately be described as a "perception" of "objects," which is an exposited construction far down the road in cognitive development; it is better rendered as an ecstatic, affect-saturated experience in which self and world are not differentiated as separate spheres with incommensurate properties (feelings and objects).[100] At the start, infant behaviors—such as body movements and vision focus—are geared toward attachment relations with the mother; the behavior is not a matter of early "knowing" but rather stimulating and attracting parental care.[101]

The child's early world is an intertwinement of feeling, behavior, and an affording environment. That is why Piaget called the period of two to seven years of age a kind of animism.[102] Animism is the belief that natural or artificial things have life-like and intentional qualities. A child can easily see a doll or a toy car in animistic terms (as enjoying or wanting something) or call an object that causes pain "mean." A parent can exploit this by saying that the TV is tired and needs to be turned off. Piaget saw animism as part of the "egocentric" stage, where children see everything through their own lens of interests and feelings, where they cannot distinguish the feelings of others from their own, or objects as such from an affect-relation.

There is some truth in this rendition, but it is still caught up in the expositional distinction of subject and object. Surely children at this stage are yet to see things and other persons in their own light, as not reducible to their own experience of them. Calling this period "egocentric," however, misses the ecstatic structure of immersed engagement. Cultures, too, have been designated as animistic, and such "primitive" beliefs have been named "anthropomorphic," wherein human qualities are projected onto things in the world. Yet egocentrism and human-centrism in this regard presume a subject-object dyad that is not applicable to either early childhood or primitive cultures, both of which can be better described as pre-rational or pre-objective, not in a developmental sense loaded on the side of reason and objectivity, but in a disclosive sense that sees the world *as* meaning-laden and affect-saturated, even in a kind of "objective" manner *in* the world itself.[103] The point here need not be that young children and primitives are "correctly" perceiving the world as animated (so that a toy really is happy or a stone really is a spirit), but that meaningfulness cannot simply be explained as an internal subjective state or merely a human estimation. There is something *ecstatic* in early childhood and primitive culture that is reiterated in adult and modern experience in some respects as well, which has been presumed in this investigation. Being immersed in an experience of natural beauty, for example, in phenomenological terms is world-disclosive, not a subjective projection (as many a theory holds). In some sense, young children, primitives, and modern adults are projected *into* the world when immersion obtains. As Merleau-Ponty has said, a young child's "egocentrism" might aptly indicate that adult "objectivity" is yet to be developed, but this does not mean that children are enclosed in their consciousness and live only within themselves; rather, "it is to practice an unmeasured objectivity," which is what I call ecstatic immersion.[104]

Beginning around six years of age, children develop a more "realistic" outlook on the world, which is not along the lines of philosophical realism and objectivity. It simply involves a growing sense of things and persons as having their own aspects distinct from the child's experience of them. This stage is still constituted by meaning-laden elements of involvement and concern, not "objectivity."[105] Even though this later stage remains affectively charged, part of "reality" now involves negotiating the frequent disconnects between affective interests (feelings and desires) and the world's own course (which exhibits contraventions, other people's desires, and the unavailability or intransigence of things). Rather than call this a movement beyond egocentrism, I would call it an expansion into a multi-faceted finite existence that can both further and impede individual interests.

4.1. Affect and Interpersonal Development

A good part of an infant's growing self-awareness is mediated by reciprocal interactions with caregivers. Whatever affective attunement might be exhibited in young children, it is expanded and refined by co-affective relations.[106] An interpersonal sharing of affective experience cannot be a matter of mere imitation or mirroring because it is more than just behavior; it involves an awareness of the existential meaning of the experience *for* the other person. When infants are around nine months of age, mothers instinctively shift from imitative reactions to intimations of co-affectivity, of being partners with infants in their emotional experience. A mother will react to a child's excitement, for example, with her own vocalizations, gestures, and bodily movements, which augment or articulate the infant's behavior—thereby exhibiting joint specificity rather than mere duplication. Co-affective attunement therefore shares the meaningful feelings that animate behavior, not simply the behavior.

Shared affective attunement between infants and caregivers can be characterized by its intensity, temporality (beat, rhythm, duration), and shape (bodily gestures or actions). Research documents the following about such interpersonal exchanges: attunement is cross-modal, where a certain type of behavior will prompt a different mode (a child's vocalization will prompt a facial expression, and vice versa); intensity seems to be the most common match; mothers report that sharing the experience was the sole motivation; the processes of conjoining behavior are automatic and immersed for mothers; sharing is motivated in infants, because an unreciprocated expression brings some distress. In general terms, the importance of co-affective attunement is that infants learn about feelings being shareable with other persons and about being conjoined with a wider social-world. The reciprocal dynamic here is more than just a shared exchange, however, because feedback and stimulation from caregivers is productive of a child's self-discovery and self-expression as well.

5. PROJECTION

Projection involves modes of existence *into* which we are cast, which are not self-constructed or initiated—including active forms that receive our chosen entry with conditions and norms already in place, which thereby operate in a middle-voice manner, with our *participating* within governing guidelines (an example would be enrolling in a university). Middle-voice projection illuminates the dynamic generative aspects of the personal-social-environing-world, those ecological forces that not only support but also help develop a person's capacity to engage the world, how someone *becomes* a social and practical agent. Here we find a richer sense of affordances, of interactive affiliations between agents and their environment (e.g., a tool as an affordance for making something, or civic services as affordances for public enterprises). Such is the "scaffolding" effect of affordances, how they support, enable, and further factical life. Accordingly, the human self is not fully self-activating or autonomous, but rather a dynamically extended and ecological being.[107]

Projection in many ways defines the life of young children. Birth is the original projection: we are delivered into the world without consent or intent. Then we meet many socio-cultural parameters, practices, norms, and institutions that take us up from birth and bring us to maturity. Early life is entirely passive projection, but we should recall the bi-directional relation between children and their social environment: child and caregiver reciprocally shape how care proceeds day-to-day. In any case, young children encounter a constellation of constraints and affordances that launch development that are not optional and that establish specific features of their biographies: organic and biological constitution; bodily features; the geographical, domestic, and socio-economic environment; the social-cultural-linguistic environment; family dynamics; the histories of caregivers—and finally the contingencies affecting how this developmental nexus unfolds.[108] For everyone at this stage, none of it is a matter of free choice. With maturation, the temporal openness of human selfhood can modify or alter an inheritance, but our early projected life cannot be completely undone and is rarely without some effect.

As children develop past the earliest stages, more active middle-voice forms of projection take shape: in the learning of various practical and social skills, tasks, and especially linguistic ability. Despite the projected character of instruction sources, the learning process is best served by a cooperative balance between adult and child rather than more controlled techniques—a balance that better meets the field-character of the personal-social-world. Here social and practical affordances offer a scaffolding effect that keeps children engaged and enhances their learning by doing. Some theories have called middle-voice projection the "zone of proximal development," which pertains to the temporal arc of how future capacities are best drawn from current abilities within cooperative instruction. Such a zone must be understood in its "medial" character, as a process *in between* self-regulation and regulation by others, activity and passivity, potentiality and actuality, and guidance and independence—a process that begins in social space before being "internalized" as habituated second nature. The medial nature of this zone of proximal development prompts different analyses and techniques than would an over-emphasis on the child or the instruction. Accordingly, learning scenarios should be neither too easy nor too difficult, so that success and failure can be properly scaled to facilitate growth.[109]

5.1. The Advent of Interpretation

Proto-phenomenology has established that the human world cannot be understood in strictly objective terms; it is interpretation all the way down. Child-rearing helps clarify what this hermeneutic circle means. Human beings are always interpreting their world, but in some ways, they are also *interpreted* beings. Projected conditions in early stages of development shape the ways in which children will grow up and engage life. Everything the child encounters will provide interpreted bearings. Even physical surroundings will be interpretive as modes of artifice, constructed environments geared toward various human needs, interests, and prospects (taken *as* shelter, clothing, food, and settings for hygiene, eating, sleeping, learning, making, and entertainment). The immersion of children in their projected milieus and influences shows how human beings cannot help but be saturated with interpretation.

6. TEMPORALITY AND HISTORY

The temporality of childhood is surely a crucial instance of "becoming," since very little of human personhood "is" established early on and must develop over time.[110] But the phenomenology of temporality is more than mere becoming because it displays the figure-eight looping intersections of past, present, and future rather than mere linear movement—so that the "absences" of past and future have a "presence" in this structure, as recollection and anticipation. Explicit awareness of temporal dimensions does not emerge in a child's experience until the acquisition of language, which will be argued in the next chapter. But an *implicit* figure-eight structure does operate in functional or procedural memory. Functional memory in an unexposited sense is not a specific recall of past events but a readiness for the anticipation and execution of future actions—a capacious preparation for coming activity that is most evident in habits.[111]

In early childhood, memory is strictly functional in a figure-eight manner, which is a matter of embodied routines rather than the processing of information.[112] Here memory is implicit rather than articulated or representational, and it decays fairly quickly if an action is not replayed. Such memory registers in patterns of *meaningful* activity pertaining to scripts of enjoyment (songs and games) everyday rituals (eating, dressing, bathing), and mimetic interaction. Early memory operates in ecstatic practices of shared import, and so it indicates the first registers of the personal-social-environing-world. The temporal arc of a child's existence is literally a mode of emergent *development* rather than the unfolding and reiteration of stable formats of cognition (assumed in much of cognitive science). This dynamic will be explored later in discussions of language acquisition and formal education in reading and writing.

The *historical* content of temporality adds cultural specification to a child's developing inheritance. Parents and caregivers bring their own histories and cultural assumptions to the raising of children. Accordingly, a child is shaped by traces of history and is readied to carry it forward. Family histories and larger horizons of social/political history give young children constitutive bearings for engaging the world, as opposed to the impossible prospect of waiting for them to explore options with experimental freedom. Later in life such freedom is warranted but even early on, cultural transmission is rarely immune to some kind of variation by children as *constituents* in their history.

This investigation has emphasized the future-character of temporality because the openness of possibility is ever at work in human existence, no matter what actuality has been achieved in the past or present. Childhood is surely the most acute period of possibility, with a wide-open future and minimal actuality. Even with strong assumptions about what is or should be possible for children, prediction or control is far from secured. There is surely a consensus about what children generally need to support their development—provisions for adequate care, safety, nourishment, organic health, guidance, and stimulation—but a child's specific personality and pathways in life cannot be dictated in advance. The openness of possibility may be diminished as actualities accrue in maturity, but childhood remains the most original domain of indeterminacy that is never fully eclipsed as long as we live.[113] In Hannah Arendt's terms, human existence is characterized by "natality," a biocultural concept that indicates first of all the event of birth, which is always the appearance of some new being in the world, and thereafter the continuing emergence of novel or unexpected occasions of experience and expression borne by the freedom of human action.[114] Accordingly, the implication of "birth" in the concept of "nature" (from the Greek *phusis* and Latin *natura*) can gather the fact that human nature from the beginning is a matter of giving birth again and again until death closes all possibilities.

7. EMBODIMENT

This study has covered the central role that embodiment plays in dwelling and world-disclosure, which challenges mentalistic theories of cognition and even brain-centric assumptions in cognitive science. The lived body is not an "object" but the "bodying-forth" of corporeal practices and interactions with the surrounding world of other bodies, artifacts, and physical nature. In adult experience, indicative descriptions of mentality are valid with respect to internalized self-awareness and the grammar of psychological language.

But since we have called into question comparable mental ascriptions for young children, animate embodiment seems to be the core character of early life. All the treatments so far in this chapter have presupposed the child's body engaging with other bodies, things in the vicinity, and the immediate terrain—particularly by way of imitation, habit formation, and know-how. A child's world is through and through an incarnate world.

When children come to "know" the world, they begin with socially guided activities in tangible settings, so that interaction with other bodies is essential at this stage. Disclosive understanding here is not a mind-to-mind relation but a reciprocal distribution between co-participants in practical contexts—something that also holds for embodied cognition throughout life.[115] Even a consideration of perception in young children follows this line of analysis. Perception cannot be understood simply in terms of sense organs or neurological processes, but in an ecological manner accounting for various ways in which a child's sensorimotor functions are intertwined with the physical environment to form intimations of what the world is like. This is a *systems* analysis that shows perception to involve reciprocal correlations within a child's embodied activities in the midst of environmental affordances and effects.[116] Controlled experiments of isolated perception tasks can overlook and miss the holistic structure of this perception system, as well as its contextual flexibility in a child's everyday circumstances.

Some sense of self in children is certainly implicit in their exchanges with other bodies, but this is a sensori-tactile mode of awareness, not an introspective psychological state.[117] Indeed, touch is crucial for early self-awareness of a child's own body and contact with the world. In Volume I, touch was noted as an important but under-examined sense.[118] Touch is paradigmatic for understanding ecstatic immediacy because it has no "distance" from its environment, owing to direct contact and the joint reciprocity of the touching and the thing being touched. Touch also exemplifies direct perception without representational mediation. Although the hand is the most prominent locus of touch, the entire body is a single tactile organ, which provides its own ecstatic disclosure in terms of sensing the elements, temperature, affordances, position, relative location, movement, safety, and pain. Manual touch plays a significant role in a child's perceptual and cognitive learning, often correlated with other senses. And we have come to know how important parental touch and bodily contact are for a child's emotional and social development.[119] In any case, touch, especially in infancy, is the most direct and comprehensively contiguous mode of immersion in the world, which provides so many tangible bearings for early experiences of meaningful involvement.

This chapter has examined the various elements of a child's early life before the acquisition of language, which fits proto-phenomenological accounts of the personal-social-environing-world and absorption in meaning-laden practices. A child's engagement with this world is not a matter of "mentality" but embodied aptitude—where imitation, joint attention, locomotion, habit, memory, gesture, and play establish the early contours of dwelling. Contrary to some theories that construe these early developments in modular terms as select and discrete cognitive skills, all the features named earlier operate in a correlative and intertwined network.[120]

8. ON THE WAY TO LANGUAGE

The complementary relationship between proto-phenomenology and developmental psychology also applies to the study of language acquisition. Indicative concepts can help focus, articulate, and revise research findings concerning how language emerges in a child's world and in fact prepares that emergence long before words are first spoken by children. Especially relevant here are the social-world, ecstatic immersion, imitation, joint attention, embodied practice, habituation, and projection. The conditions established in this chapter are not simply prior to language acquisition but essentially provisional for it.

It is no wonder that a child's first words are such a momentous occasion. When children learn to talk, their world begins to open up and they start to develop in ways that far exceed pre-linguistic conditions. It is notable that the word *infant* comes from a Latin term meaning *incapable of speech*. Such incapacity, of course, is not a sheer absence but an anticipation; and *naming* infancy as lacking speech shows how central linguistic capacity is to human existence. Such anticipation is not strictly speaking pre-linguistic but a working preparation *for* the emergence of language. Our account of speech as ecological embodiment helps explain how this is so.

The setting of child-rearing reveals that language should not be understood simply as the meaning and use of words, but as the symbiotic development of a child's capacities for understanding and behavior in the midst of a prompting linguistic environment. It is evident that language is a multi-faceted environmental influence on children from their first moments of life, even in utero. If language were simply a matter of communicating with words, then all the verbal behaviors that we naturally engage in with infants before they learn to speak could seem to be wasted activity. If we assume that language is simply the co-intentional communication of mental states apart from ecological embodiment, then early "child directed speech" seems premature at best because it is bereft of conversational exchanges.[121] But research has shown that our instinct to engage in child directed speech is appropriate and crucial for linguistic development later on, even for brain development.[122] This suggests that infants are exposed to a preverbal "rehearsal" of a complex linguistic environing-world from the very start: in terms of facial expressions, touch, physical interactions, gestures, sounds, rhythms, intonations, emotional cues, and a host of behavioral contexts.[123] We should also note that a melodic, high-pitched, slower pattern of speech directed toward infants (sometimes called "motherese") seems instinctive and universal across cultures, and that such tonal patterns communicate basic affective meanings and prepare a child's incorporation of the sounds and gestures intrinsic to speech. The sing-song style of this kind of communication draws an infant's attention more readily than normal patterns of speech.[124] Indeed, fetuses in the last trimester can register auditory stimuli from the surrounding world, particularly melody contours in music and speech. Newborns prefer their mother's voice and they intimate the emotional cues of intonation. Sensitivity to pitch intervals allows them to enjoy music and the tonal structures of speech. Even crying patterns mimic melodic shapes of the natural language spoken in their environment.[125] It may be that the musicality of speech—which animates the common cultural forms of poetry and song—is not a mere ornament, but rather a primal sensuous register of language beginning in the earliest periods of communication and expression (more on this in coming discussions).

All told, the pre-lexical stage of a child's life is still saturated with language because (1) the language-world of caregivers continually shapes how infants are treated, and (2) an infant is exposed to the somatic-sonic-affective forces of speech from the first moments of life. The social-interactive structure of such forces is essential for later development because children do not learn language simply by hearing people speak; they must be actively engaged with others in factical settings of speech. Young children, for instance, will not pick up language simply by being exposed to it on television.[126] Pre-verbal rehearsals of child directed speech lay the groundwork for the interactive dynamic of language acquisition. The phenomenological priority of language advanced in this investigation receives more support and cogency when we realize how linguistic effects extend all the way back in our biographies even before we learn to talk.

NOTES

1. *The Philosophical Writings of Descartes* I, trans. John Cottingham, Robert Stoothoff, and Dugald Murdoch (Cambridge: Cambridge University Press, 1985), 117.

2. For analysis, see Maughn Gregory and David Granger, "John Dewey on Philosophy and Childhood, *Education and Culture* 28, no. 2 (2012): 1–25; Meredith Williams, "The Significance of Learning in Wittgenstein's Later Philosophy," *Canadian Journal of Philosophy* 24, no. 2 (June 1994): 173–204; and Talia Welsh, *The Child as*

Natural Phenomenologist: Primal and Primary Experience in Merleau-Ponty's Psychology (Evanston, IL: Northwestern University Press, 2013). Merleau-Ponty gave the most sustained attention to child development. See his volume, *Child Psychology and Pedagogy: The Sorbonne Lectures 1949–1952*, trans. Talia Welsh (Evanston, IL: Northwestern University Press, 2010). Heidegger did not give much attention to childhood, but for an application of his phenomenology to this question, see my "Dasein, the Early Years: Heideggerian Reflections on Childhood," *International Philosophical Quarterly* 54, no. 4 (December 2014): 379–391. For a study of child and human development that accords well with Heidegger's thought, see Bernard J. Boelen, *Personal Maturity: The Existential Dimension* (New York: Seabury, 1978), especially Chapters 2–3.

3. For an excellent critical survey of standard theories, see R. Murray Thomas, *Comparing Theories of Child Development*, 5th edition (Belmont, CA: Wadsworth, 2000).

4. See Katherine Nelson, *Young Minds in Social Worlds: Experience, Meaning, and Memory* (Cambridge, MA: Harvard University Press, 2007). I will be drawing on Nelson's work in coming discussions.

5. See Hugh Cunningham, *Children and Childhood in Western Society since 1500*, Second Edition (New York: Routledge, 2005); also, Steven Mintz, "Why the History of Childhood Matters," *The Journal of the History of Childhood and Youth* 5, no. 1 (Winter 2002): 15–28.

6. An important work that aims to guide adults into the lived world of children is Eva M. Simms, *The Child in the World: Embodiment, Time, and Language in Early Childhood* (Detroit, MI: Wayne State University Press, 2008).

7. Daniel N. Stern, *The Interpersonal World of the Infant* (New York: Basic Books, 2000), xi–xii and Chap. 8.

8. Sarah Hannan, "Why Childhood Is Bad for Children," *Journal of Applied Philosophy* 35, S1 (February 2018): 11–28.

9. See Anna Mae Duane, ed., *The Children's Table: Childhood Studies and the Humanities* (Athens, GA: University of Georgia Press, 2013).

10. For some current work on phenomenology and developmental psychology, see David Morris, "Rethinking Development," which is an introduction to a special issue of *Phenomenology and the Cognitive Sciences* 16, no. 4 (September 2017): 565–569.

11. See Nelson, *Young Minds in Social Worlds*, Chap. 2. For a proto-phenomenological critique of AI that takes up such questions, see Volume I of this investigation, 98–102, 159–161. For the primacy of desire over "belief" formation, see Asbjørn Steglich-Petersen and John Michael, "Why Desire Reasoning Is Developmentally Prior to Belief Reasoning," *Mind and Language* 30, no. 5 (November 2015): 526–549.

12. Nelson, *Young Minds in Social Worlds*, 255–260.

13. Some of what follows is drawn from Nelson, *Young Minds in Social Worlds*, Chap. 1. Nelson's work challenges theoretical, representational, and scientific biases in a manner close to my approach. Yet there still is some cognitivist distortion in working with the idea of "concepts" to depict a child's understanding of the world (221–223, among other places).

14. See, for example, Alison Gopnick, Andrew N. Meltzoff, and Patricia K. Kuhl, *The Scientist in the Crib: Minds, Brains, and How Children Learn* (New York: William Morrow, 1999).

15. Such outside-in modeling was developed by Lev Vygotsky. See *Thought and Language*, trans. Alex Kozulin (Cambridge, MA: MIT Press, 1986); also John A. Bargh, "Bypassing the Will: Toward Demystifying the Nonconscious Control of Social Behavior," in *The New Unconscious*, eds. Ran R, Hassin, James S. Uleman, and John A. Bargh (Oxford University Press, 2005), 37–58.

16. See Boelen, *Personal Maturity*, 6–7.

17. For an examination of childhood wonder that aims to supplement Heideggerian phenomenology, see Gail Soffer, "Phenomenology with a Hammer: Theory or Practice," *Continental Philosophy Review* 32, no. 4 (October 1999): 379–393. See also Jean François Lyotard, *Why Philosophize?*, trans. Andrew Brown (London: Polity Press, 2013). Lyotard compares philosophy to a child's disposition of wonder and openness to meaning-formation, rather than a condition of mature mastery.

18. See Lisa M. Oakes, "Using Habituation of Looking Time to Assess Mental Processes in Infancy," *Journal of Cognition and Development* 11, no. 3 (2010): 255–268.

19. See Gregor Schöner and Esther Thelan, "Using Dynamic Field Theory to Rethink Infant Habituation," *Psychological Review* 113, no. 2 (April 2006): 273–299.

20. See Andrea R. English, *Discontinuity in Learning: Dewey, Herbart, and Education as Transformation* (Cambridge: Cambridge University Press, 2013).

21. See Nelson, *Young Minds in Social Worlds*, 245–249.

22. Nelson discusses the work of Merlin Donald and his notion of a "hybrid mind" in *Young Minds in Social Worlds*, Chap. 2. See Merlin Donald, *Origins of the Modern Mind* (Cambridge, MA: Harvard University Press, 1991); also Katherine Nelson, *Language in Cognitive Development: The Emergence of the Mediated Mind* (Cambridge: Cambridge University Press, 1996). As Bernard Boelen puts it, maturity is a continuing dialogue with early development, not a "perfection" that supersedes earlier periods (*Personal Maturity*, ix).

23. See James Tabery, *Beyond Versus: The Struggle to Understand the Interaction of Nature and Nurture* (Cambridge, MA: MIT Press, 2014); also Michael Rutter, *Genes and Behavior: Nature-Nurture Interplay Explained* (Malden, MA: Blackwell, 2006); also Arnold Sameroff, "A Unified Theory of Development: A Dialectic Integration of Nature-Nurture," *Child Development* 81, no. 1 (January/February 2010): 6–22.

24. See Daniel N. Stern, *The First Relationship: Infant and Mother* (Cambridge, MA: Harvard University Press, 2004). From the standpoint of moral development, see Elliot Turiel, Melanie Killen, and Charles C. Helwig, "Morality: Its Structure, Function, and Vagaries," in *The Emergence of Morality in Young Children*, ed. Jerome Kagan and Sharon Lamb (University of Chicago Press, 1987), Chap. 4.

25. Nelson, *Young Minds in Social Worlds*, 250 and throughout.

26. See David Kennedy, "Parent, Child, Alterity, Dialogue," *Philosophy Today* 45, no. 1 (Spring 2001): 33–42.

27. See Nelson, *Young Minds in Social Worlds*, 8–17.

28. According to Aristotle, imitation (*mimēsis*) is a natural capacity beginning in childhood, and human beings have an advantage over other animals because they are the most mimetic and learn first by means of imitation (*Poetics* 1448b5ff).

29. See Andrew Meltzoff and M.Keith Moore, "Imitation of Facial and Manual Gestures by Human Neonates," *Science* 198 (1977): 75–78, and "Newborn Infants Imitate Adult Facial Gestures," *Child Development* 54 (1983): 702–709.

30. Boelen, *Personal Maturity*, 42.

31. Nancy Eisenberg and Janet Strayer, eds., *Empathy and Its Development* (Cambridge: Cambridge University Press, 1987), 322–23.

32. Ibid., 136.

33. Nelson, *Young Minds in Social Worlds*, 75ff.

34. See Ellen Fridland and Richard Moore, "Imitation Reconsidered," *Philosophical Psychology* 28, no. 6 (2015): 856–880.

35. Nelson, *Young Minds in Social Worlds*, 95.

36. Ibid.

37. See *Joint Attention: New Developments in Psychology, Philosophy of Mind, and Social Neuroscience*, ed. Axel Seemann (Cambridge, MA: MIT Press, 2011), from which some of my remarks are taken. See also Chris Moore and Philip Dunham, eds. *Joint Attention: Its Origins and Role in Development* (New York: Psychology Press, 2015).

38. See Daniel N. Stern, *The Interpersonal World of the Infant: A View from Psychoanalysis and Developmental Psychology* (New York: Basic Books, 1985) and Jerome Bruner, *Acts of Meaning* (Cambridge, MA: Harvard University Press, 1990).

39. See Inge Schietecatte et al., "Exploring the Nature of Joint Attention Impairment in Young Children with Autism Spectrum Disorder: Associated Social and Cognitive Skills," *Journal of Autism and Developmental Disorders* 42, no. 1 (January 2012): 1–12.

40. For a treatment of "mindsharing" that aims to resolve the debate of whether self-consciousness or mindreading comes first in development, see James M. Dow, "Mindreading, Mindsharing, and the Origins of Self-Consciousness," *Philosophical Topics* 40, no. 2 (Fall 2012): 39–70.

41. See Andrew Meltzoff and Rebecca Williamson, "Imitation: Social, Cognitive, and Theoretical Perspectives," *Oxford Handbook of Developmental Psychology*, Vol. 1, ed. P. R. Zelazo (Oxford University Press, 2013), 651–682.

42. See Michael Tomasello, *The Cultural Origins of Human Communication* (Cambridge, MA: Harvard University Press, 1999), especially Chaps. 3–4.

43. For a discussion of dance in this vein, see Maxine Sheets-Johnstone, "From Movement to Dance," *Phenomenology and the Cognitive Sciences* 11, no. 1 (March 2012): 39–57.

44. Nelson, *Young Minds in Social Worlds*, 76–78, on which I rely in what follows. Nelson's laudable account of imitation, shared meaning, and joint attention subverts her notion of a child's "private mind," which is meant to indicate what a child's own inner psychic experience might be like (249–250).

45. Celia A. Brownell, "Early Developments in Joint Action," *The Review of Philosophy and Psychology* 2, no. 2 (June 2011): 193–211.

46. I do not mean to align here with the scientific theory of behaviorism, which would discount much of what I am calling the personal-world.

47. See especially "The Child's Relations with Others," in *Child Psychology and Pedagogy*, 241–315.

48. For research on neonatal capacity for "sympathetic" bodily coordination with others that compares with Merleau-Ponty's findings, see Colwyn Trevarthen, "What Is It Like to Be a Person Who Knows Nothing? Defining the Active Intersubjective Mind of a Newborn Human Being," *Infant and Child Development* 20 (2011): 119–135. Nevertheless, the discussion is framed in terms of an infant's "mental capacities."

49. See, for example, Shaun Gallagher and Andrew Meltzoff, "The Earliest Sense of Self and Others: Merleau-Ponty and Recent Development Studies," *Philosophical Psychology* 9, no. 2 (1996): 211–233.

50. For discussions of the research and a defense of Merleau-Ponty's take on the matter, see Talia Welsh, "Do Neonates Display Innate Self-Awareness? Why Neonatal Imitation Fails to Provide Sufficient Grounds for Innate Self- and Other-Awareness," *Philosophical Psychology* 19, no. 2 (April 2006): 221–238; and Shiloh Whitney, "Affects, Images, and Childlike Perception: Self-Other Difference in Merleau-Ponty's Sorbonne Lectures," *Phaenex* 7, no. 2 (Fall/Winter 2012): 185–211.

51. Boelen, *Personal Maturity*, 16–17, 20–21.

52. I rely on Philippe Rochat, "Five Levels of Self-Awareness as They Unfold Early in Life," *Consciousness and Cognition* 12, no. 4 (2003): 717–731; also Nelson, *Young Minds in Social Worlds*, 105–107.

53. See Stephen Langfur, "The You-I Event: On the Genesis of Self-Awareness," *Phenomenology and the Cognitive Sciences* 12, no. 4 (December 2013): 769–790.

54. See E. Jayne White, "Bringing Dialogism to Bear in the Early Years," *International Journal of Early Childhood* 47, no. 2 (August 2015): 213–216.

55. For a discussion in the context of Merleau-Ponty's work, see Susan Bredlau, "On Perception and Trust: Merleau-Ponty and the Emotional Significance of Our Relations with Others," *Continental Philosophy Review*, DOI: 10.1007/s11007-016-9367-3 (May 2016).

56. This discussion is taken from my article, "Dasein, the Early Years," in which I linked child development with Heidegger's conception of anxiety figuring in the meaning of being.

57. Most of what follows is drawn from Jonathan Bloom-Feshbach and Sally Bloom-Feshbach, eds., *The Psychology of Separation and Loss* (San Francisco, CA: Jossey-Bass Publishers, 1987).

58. Ibid., 2–3.

59. Ibid., 8ff.

60. Ibid., 97. See also Boelen, *Personal Maturity*, 27ff.

61. *The Psychology of Separation and Loss*, 22.

62. Ibid., 17.

63. Ibid., 8ff.

64. Ibid., 42ff.

65. Ibid., 44.

66. See Merleau-Ponty, "The Child's Relations with Others," 242–43.
67. Boelen, *Personal Maturity*, 39–40.
68. See Michael Yapko, *Suggestions of Abuse* (New York: Simon & Schuster, 2009).
69. What follows is drawn from my book, *Ethics and Finitude: Heideggerian Contributions to Moral Philosophy* (Lanham, MD: Rowman & Littlefield, 2000), Chap. 3.
70. See Jerome Kagan and Sharon Lamb, eds., *The Emergence of Morality in Young Children* (Chicago: The University of Chicago Press, 1987).
71. Robert M. Emde, William F. Johnson, and M. Ann Easterbrooks, "The Do's and Don'ts of Early Moral Development," in *The Emergence of Morality in Young Children*, Chap. 5.
72. See Judy Dunn, "The Beginnings of Moral Understanding," in *The Emergence of Morality in Young Children*, Chap. 2. For the role of narratives in ethical development, see Susan Verducci, "Narratives in Ethics of Education," *Studies in Philosophy and Education* 33, no. 6 (November 2014): 575–585.
73. See Carolyn Pope Edwards, "Culture and the Construction of Moral Values," in *The Emergence of Morality in Young Children*, Chap. 3.
74. I have tried to work through this notion with respect to democratic politics in *A Nietzschean Defense of Democracy: An Experiment in Postmodern Politics* (Chicago, IL: Open Court, 1990).
75. See Boelen, *Personal Maturity*, 27–30, 33.
76. Ibid., 34ff.
77. See Eisenberg and Strayer, eds., *Empathy and Its Development*, from which most of what follows is drawn.
78. Inattention to relational needs is a significant flaw in many theories of child development. See Arne J. Vetlesen, *Perception, Empathy, and Judgment: An Inquiry into the Preconditions of Moral Performance* (University Park, PA: Pennsylvania State University Press, 1994), 252–271.
79. Eisenberg and Strayer, eds. *Empathy and Its Development*, 138. The rest of the paragraph is drawn from this text.
80. I rely on Eva-Maria Simms, "Chiasm and Hyperdialectic: Re-conceptualizing Sensory Deprivation in Infancy, *Phenomenology and the Cognitive Sciences* 16, no. 4 (September 2017): 637–648.
81. Volume I briefly discussed the sense of touch and its immediate ecstatic character (62).
82. See Nelson, *Young Minds in Social Worlds*, 67–69, 79–81, on which I rely in what follows.
83. Ibid., 104–105.
84. See Eva M. Simms, *The Child in the World*, Chap. 8 and "Children's Lived Space in the Inner City: Geographical and Political Aspects of the Psychology of Place," *The Humanistic Psychologist* 36, no. 1 (January 2008): 72–89.
85. See David T. Neal, Wendy Wood, and Jeffrey M. Quinn, "Habits—A Repeat Performance," *Current Directions in Psychological Science* 15, no. 4 (August 2006): 198–202.

86. See John A. Bargh and Erin L. Williams, "The Automaticity of Social Life," *Current Directions in Psychological Science* 15, no. 1 (February 2006): 1–4.

87. For a general discussion, see Tom Sparrow and Adam Hutchinson, *A History of Habit: From Aristotle to Bourdieu* (Lanham, MD: Lexington Books, 2014).

88. For a discussion in terms of Merleau-Ponty's thought, see Maria Talero, "Merleau-Ponty and the Bodily Subject of Learning," *International Philosophical Quarterly* 46, no. 2 (June 2006): 191–203. For Merleau-Ponty on habit, see *Phenomenology of Perception*, 164ff. For Aristotle on ethical virtue as habit and second nature, see *Nicomachean Ethics* 1103a14ff.

89. See James McGuirk, "Phenomenological Considerations of Habit: Reason, Knowing, and Self-Presence in Habitual Action," *Phenomenology and Mind* 6 (2014): 112–121.

90. For a Wittgensteinian take on child learning in this respect, see José María Ariso, "Learning to Believe: Challenges in Children's Acquisition of a World-Picture in Wittgenstein's *On Certainty*," *Studies in Philosophy of Education* 34, no. 3 (May 2015): 311–325.

91. Nelson, *Young Minds in Social Worlds*, 116.

92. For an excellent analysis of the animate organism as a dynamic "tactile-kinesthetic body," which even phenomenologists have missed, see Maxine Sheets-Johnstone, "On the Origin, Nature, and Genesis of Habit," *Phenomenology and Mind* 6 (2014): 77–89.

93. See Bargh, "Bypassing the Will: Toward Demystifying the Nonconscious Control of Social Behavior," *The New Unconscious*, 37–58, especially 50–51.

94. I owe this wonderful point to Sheets-Johnstone, "On the Origin, Nature, and Genesis of Habit," 80–83.

95. See Boelen, *Personal Maturity*, 25, 46–49, 51–53.

96. What follows relies on Nelson, *Young Minds in Social Worlds*, 97–104.

97. Boelen, *Personal Maturity*, 51–52.

98. See Nelson, *Young Minds in Social Worlds*, 251–252, 261–262.

99. Neural representations are even less evident, as argued in Volume I (94–95), because from any standpoint, it is hard to understand how a neurological event in the brain "represents" anything. Nelson claims that the child's *action* is a representation (261), but that seems to be a residue of mental representation as something psychological rather than active and ecological.

100. Boelen, *Personal Maturity*, 23–24.

101. Nelson, *Young Minds in Social Worlds*, 62–64.

102. See Jean Piaget, *Sociological Studies*, ed. Leslie Smith (New York: Routledge, 1995), Chap. 8.

103. I have argued in past work that "anthropomorphic" models of "primitive" thinking are freighted with rationalistic and cultural biases. This is not to discount the importance and validity of rational/scientific thought, only its universal application. See my *Myth and Philosophy: A Contest of Truths* (Chicago: Open Court, 1990).

104. See Merleau-Ponty, *Texts and Dialogues: On Philosophy, Politics, and Culture*, eds. Hugh J. Silverman and J. Barry Jr., trans. Forest Williams (Atlantic Highlands, NJ: Humanities Press, 1996), 74–84.

105. Boelen, *Personal Maturity*, 42–43.
106. This section is drawn from research found in Stern, *The Interpersonal World of the Infant*, Chap. 7. Happily, Stern calls emotional relations "affective attunement," and his research largely fits well with my analysis. His account, however, is marred by an undue reliance on representation, the "internal" character of affect, and a questionable interpretation of empathy.
107. For an account from the standpoint of cognitive psychology, see Anna Estany and Sergio Martinez, "Scaffolding and Affordances as Integrative Concepts in the Cognitive Sciences," *Philosophical Psychology* 27, no. 1 (February 2014): 98–111.
108. Nelson, *Young Minds in Social Worlds*, 17–21.
109. See Andrey I. Podolskiy, "Zone of Proximal Development," *Encyclopedia of the Sciences of Learning*, ed. Norbert M. Seel (New York: Springer, 2012): 3485–3487; and Manual Fernádez et al., "Re-Conceptualizing 'Scaffolding' and the Zone of Proximal Development in the Context of Symmetrical Collaborative Learning," *Journal of Classroom Interaction* 50, no. 1 (2015): 54–72.
110. Nelson, *Young Minds in Social* Worlds, 59–66.
111. See Moshe Bar, "The Proactive Brain: Memory for Predictions," *Philosophical Transactions: Biology and Philosophy* 364, no. 1521 (May 2009): 1235–1243; Philip Gerrans and David Sander, "Feeling the Future: Prospects for a Theory of Implicit Prospection," *Biology and Philosophy* 29, no. 5 (September 2014): 699–710; and Katherine Nelson, "The Psychological and Social Origins of Autobiographical Memory," *Psychological Science* 4, no. 1 (January 1993): 7–14.
112. Nelson, *Young Minds in Social Worlds*, 88–92, 251–252, on which I rely in what follows.
113. See Donald A. Landes, "Language Development: Paradoxical Trajectories in Merleau-Ponty, Simonden, and Bergson," *Phenomenology and the Cognitive Sciences* 16, no. 4 (September 2017): 597–607.
114. See Hannah Arendt, *The Human Condition* (Chicago: The University of Chicago Press, 1958).
115. See Gün R. Semin and Eliot R. Smith, "Socially Situated Cognition in Perspective," *Social Cognition* 31, no. 2 (2013): 125–146.
116. For a seminal account, see Eleanor J. Gibson, *An Odyssey in Learning and Perception* (Cambridge, MA: MIT Press, 1994).
117. See Rochat, "Five Levels of Self-Awareness as They Unfold Early in Life."
118. See Matthew Fulkerson, *The First Sense: A Philosophical Study of Human Touch* (Cambridge, MA: MIT Press, 2014) and Zdravko Radman, ed., *The Hand: An Organ of the Mind, What the Manual Tells the Mental* (Cambridge, MA: MIT Press, 2013), from which some of my remarks are drawn.
119. See Tiffany Field, *Touch* (Cambridge, MA: MIT Press, 2014).
120. Nelson, *Young Minds in Social Worlds*, 116.
121. Steven Pinker, *The Language Instinct* (London: Penguin, 1994), 40.
122. See Marcia Baringa, "New Insights into How Babies Learn Language," *Science* 277, no. 5326 (August 1997): 641; also Steffen Borge, "Talking to Infants: A Gricean Perspective," *American Philosophical Quarterly* 50, no. 4 (October 2013): 423–428, on which I rely for some parts of this discussion.

123. See Jerome Bruner, *Child's Talk: Learning to Use Language* (New York: Norton, 1983), Chap. 2.

124. See Catherine E. Laing, "Here's Why 'Baby Talk' Is Good for Your Baby," *The Conversation* (November 2016); also Nelson, *Young Minds in Social Worlds*, 118–119.

125. See Birgit Mampe et al., "Newborns' Cry Melody Is Shaped by Their Native Language," *Current Biology* 19, no. 23 (December 2009): 1994–1997; see also Nelson, *Young Minds in Social Worlds*, 69–70.

126. Eve V. Clark, *First Language Acquisition* (Cambridge: Cambridge University Press, 2003), 28; and Mark C. Baker, *The Atoms of Language* (New York: Basic Books, 2001), 224–225.

Chapter 3

Language Acquisition

1. NATURAL LANGUAGE

A phenomenology of language begins with natural language, the domain of factical speech in which we are born and raised.[1] An examination of language acquisition is the obvious starting point for understanding how language *becomes* a natural capacity that does not require reflective attention all the way down. Moreover, the meaning-laden character of natural language learning fulfills what is meant by existential naturalism, and the precedence of its world-forming effects embodies the presumption of immanence—namely that for all of us, "reality" is first and foremost a matter of dwelling in a speech-world, outside of which there is no "world," understood as disclosive horizons of meaning. Language acquisition also presupposes and registers a common-sense ontology of involvement with perceptible things, persons, and action scenarios, which fit and prompt the linguistic expression of nouns, adjectives, verbs, adverbs, articles, prepositions, and so on. But the early learning of language does not proceed according to grammatical formats as such, which themselves are expositional abstractions derived from actual usage in practical contexts. A child's reception and production of words, phrases, and sentences are better understood as focal indications that guide and shape ecstatic performance in meaningful circumstances.[2]

In general terms, language acquisition provides support for proto-phenomenology by turning attention to how the lived world first takes shape in human experience. Because of this inceptual vantage point—where the world-forming power of speech is most readily in view—a phenomenological analysis of language can benefit from the more "empirical" contributions afforded by developmental research, by which I mean evidence of language *in the making*, before the rich articulations of philosophy are in place, which are far advanced from, and thereby prone to concealing, that inceptual terrain.[3]

1.1. Nature and Nurture

The domain of natural language brings us again to the nature-nurture debate. Owing to expositional reification, strict lines are often drawn between nature and nurture, between what is "innate" in a child's makeup and what is "learned" as a result of environmental effects—where a weighted grounding in one side or the other is assumed to be the theoretical task. In linguistics, the divide is sometimes taken to be a choice between (1) a Chomsky-inspired conception of an inborn universal grammar or "Language Acquisition Device" that is simply triggered by outside prompts, and (2) a quasi-relativistic conception of cultural transmission that fully constitutes the infusion of language and thought in a child's experience. I indicated that the consensus in most research is that both nature and nurture contribute to the development of a child; but it is important to stress that this is a fluid, reciprocal correlation rather than simply the co-contribution of two discrete domains. The same applies to language acquisition, which is the most telling example of an intertwinement of nature and nurture.[4]

Genetically and biologically, children are not blank slates; they are hardwired to develop language, but this endowment is better conceived as a natural capacity or readiness that requires a stimulating environment for its actualization. More on the nature side of the ledger, we noted in chapter 2 a number of indigenous pre-linguistic capacities that prepare and make possible language development; and that presuppose embodied, perceptual, practical, and social aptitudes—which early on display the "field" character of the lived world.[5] Such preverbal capacities include: (1) pattern recognition in perceptual experiences, communicative gestures, and speech expressions; (2) imitation, wherein social prompting comes first before a child's own performance; (3) comprehension of relations in events and behaviors; (4) object orientations, locations, and uses; (5) spatial intimations (up-down, front-back, inside-outside); (6) figure-ground perception of things as wholes distinct from their parts and movements; and (7) awareness of communicative intent, as shown in joint attention and mimetic role reversal. All such capacities and their function in language learning require the practical engagement of *usage* in active settings of factical life and social behavior, not the mental processing of data, an application of concepts, or operations governed by idealized theories of language.[6] Nothing in this learning domain supports a clear grounding in either nature or nurture alone, but rather a dynamic intersection of reciprocal effects.[7]

Even with the mutual correlation of nature and nurture, the social-cultural-linguistic environment is of crucial necessity for early self-development, for the actualization of whatever potential capacity children may harbor in their nature. Without the social-language-world, very little of human life could emerge and flourish. Strong evidence for this can be found in Helen Keller's testimony cited in chapter 2; likewise, the cases of feral children (found in the wild and deprived of human contact) discussed in Volume I, the summary assessment of which can be put as follows: none of the children could speak; they did not respond attentively to human speech; they had much difficulty learning language and could not develop beyond rudimentary forms; they were at first socially unresponsive to other humans; they seemed to lack overt memory, self-awareness, and temporal dimensions beyond the immediate present; in many respects, the children were more animal than human.[8] Such findings call into question many traditional assumptions about human nature, especially cognitive nativism, individualism, and the modern ideal of autonomy and self-sufficiency.[9] In any case, I want to say that language acquisition is the dawning of "human nature" and its world-disclosive powers. In that emerging world, most proto-phenomenological concepts advanced in this investigation are exhibited and receive their biographical launch when children begin to talk and communicate.

2. THE PHENOMENOLOGICAL PRIORITY OF LANGUAGE

The phenomenological priority of language means that any theory or explanation of language presupposes an already functioning linguistic world, that no exposition of language can *fully* put language in view as an object of examination. Language presents the primal disclosure of a meaningful world (keeping in mind that inhabiting a language-world is not a matter of linguistic idealism). Even non-verbalized "experiences" are not divorced from language if they are meaningful and articulable. Enculturation into "human experience" goes all the way back to childhood and the acquisition of language, as this chapter aims to demonstrate.

The phenomenological priority of language can be sharpened even further when we consider the role that language plays even in pre-verbal stages of development from the earliest moments of life. First in an indirect manner, the language-world of caregivers shapes every mode of engagement with infants—of how, why, and when to administer care, of understanding, recognizing, and serving a child's needs, of preparing a child's future prospects. In a more direct manner, we have noted how newborns from the start are exposed to the somatic and sonic elements of language—facial expressions, bodily interactions, gestures, intonation, pitch, rhythm, affective cues—in the midst of various factical contexts. Of particular importance is a natural communicative impulse exhibited by infants that is a precondition for the social structure of language. Parents and infants will instinctively respond to each other's facial expressions in kind to share affective occasions. Infants seem to have an intrinsic interest in, and need for, such communication because withholding a facial response to a child's initiative will cause distress.[10] This early setting helps illuminate a point I made in Volume I (118), that communication is a wider phenomenon than the lexical features of language because it covers a host of embodied, enactive powers that are pre-linguistic and that even overlap with animal communication. Language, however, extends communication into the transformative dimension of interpretive understanding. But embodied modes of communication continue to play an active role in human speech.

In early stages of development, caregivers are in a way interpreting the behavior of infants for them (crying as an indication of distress that calls for attention). In more advanced stages before the advent of speech, parents continue that hermeneutical engagement together with now more focused and deliberate verbal associations, especially in terms of purposive behavior: *You want to get down from the chair? Here we go!* Research in child psychology demonstrates that language acquisition, including preverbal rehearsals, is essentially an inter-subjective dynamic that precedes and makes possible later processes of focused individuation *out of* an original social nexus. Here, we recall the phenomenon of pointing as a precursor to language development, which exhibits the triangular structure of joint attention and social referencing (when infants point, they look back at adults to see if they notice it too). Such is the pre-lexical domain of somatic and social habits that are a precondition for language learning.[11]

Facial and bodily gestures provide a prelude to linguistic communication in an ecstatic, ecological manner. Children intimate a range of meanings when caregivers smile, look surprised, frown, comfort, caress, or impede a behavior. Children themselves initiate meaningful gestures, such as holding up their arms in order to be picked up.[12] Between the babbling stage and the first spoken words, infants are able to grasp speech-gesture combinations and their temporal correlations.[13] Within the ecological nexus of a child's pre-linguistic world, by the end of the first year, many verbal expressions of caregivers register meaning for children before they learn to speak. Personal names and words like *no, yes, stop, very good, come here,* and *bye-bye* come to be grasped in their practical-behavioral contexts.[14] Simple requests, such as *Give me the ball*, can be carried out. This is not a matter of understanding the lexical meaning of words or the mental intentions of caregivers; rather, children intimate the meaning of shared practical contexts in an ecstatic manner, *there* in the world.

It is evident that a somatic-sonic-social ecology shapes a child's development from birth; and this pre-verbal period is far from nonlinguistic because it prepares and makes possible the acquisition of language. Indeed, an infant's brain from early on encodes the sonic patterns and structures of speech in a manner comparable to adult comprehension.[15] When children come to babble, oral expression is given its first raw form. When babbling patterns are joined with reciprocating mimicry from caregivers, there begins a significant precursor to shared speech. Infant attention is biased toward the sounds of human speech, and the degree to which caregivers direct their speech to infants in reciprocal patterns has a significant impact on the range and quality of a child's language development later on.[16]

The generative domain sketched in this section not only shows how thoroughgoing language is in human development, it also spotlights how language cannot be understood simply in terms of verbal tokens or propositions because it is grounded in a factical, practical, embodied *world*. The "lexical" elements of language (words, sentences, and their semantics) emerge out of pre-lexical elements of embodied meaning—in a process I have called nested assimilation, which carries early capacities forward rather than leaving them behind. Such erstwhile factors make the lexical elements possible and, in most respects, recede into the background in a tacit manner.

3. LANGUAGE LEARNING AND DWELLING

At this point, it would be helpful to sketch the stages of language acquisition, beginning around the first year. Here I quote Eve Clark:

> As children learn to talk, they go through a series of stages, beginning with infancy when they are unable to converse and do not yet understand any language. They go from babbling at 7 to 10 months old, to producing their first recognizable words 6 to 12 months later. Then, within a few months, they combine words and gestures, and produce their first word combinations around age 2. This is followed by the production of ever more complex, adult-like utterances, as they become active participants in conversation, taking turns and making appropriate contributions. They begin to use language for a larger array of functions—telling stories, explaining how a toy works, persuading a friend to do something, or giving someone directions for how to get somewhere. Between age 1 and age 6, children acquire extensive skills in using language and sound quite adult-like much of the time. By around age 10 to 12, they have mastered many complex constructions, a good deal more vocabulary, and many uses of language.[17]

The task at hand is to examine the early stages of language learning as modes of dwelling in speech. In this investigation, the concept of dwelling has functioned as a more original mode of existence that precedes and makes possible subject-object and mind-world distinctions, which have been unduly emphasized in philosophy and child psychology. Dwelling in speech specifies an ecstatic immersion in the world-disclosive power of language, which has been concealed by representational theories. Adult dwelling in speech regularly alternates with expositional reflection. Early language acquisition in children, however, is exclusively a matter of immersion, with reflective modes emerging gradually in the course of a child's psychological and linguistic development. Such original dwelling in speech serves to support two central proto-phenomenological findings: (1) the priority of immersion over exposition; and (2) the world-disclosive priority of language over "thought" and even "experience." I have argued that non-verbalized meaningful experiences are made possible by the historical effects of language on possible engagements with the world. It is not only the articulability of non-verbalized experience that counts here because early language acquisition *generates* the meaningful shaping of experience in the first place—a formative reservoir that becomes a tacit background for future postures of "thought" and "experience." The dawning of language in children is not simply word usage but the assimilation of language-inflected practices and bi-directional interpretation between children and caregivers. The recession of language effects into a tacit background is easier to grasp once language is taken beyond a mere lexical dimension to include embodied practices and habituation. Coming discussions will develop this proviso further.

3.1. Meaning-Laden Enactment

No one doubts that learning language in childhood is essential for human development. Theories of learning, however, are marred by the same suppositions governing most linguistic theories. Debates between nativist and environmental models respectively turn on whether (1) some universal inborn linguistic framework is simply triggered by contingent occasions of language learning or (2) language has no grounding in a priori structures but is fully inculcated externally by a learning environment. Both approaches, however, emphasize objective structures or lexical systems and sustain a subject-object binary with internal or external sources of language usage—which in either case takes a child's mental representations as the proving ground for language acquisition. Proto-phenomenology emphasizes what is missing or suppressed in this debate: that language learning is animated by (1) the mutual intersection of nature and nurture; (2) factical situations laden with existential meaning; (3) embodied practices; and (4) the reciprocal triangulation of children, caregivers, and physical environments. A child's "mind" in strict terms is neither the spark nor the recipient of language learning, which is better rendered as ecstatic enactment in ecological contexts of meaning. Following Wittgenstein, linguistic meaning is not something expressed by, or planted in, a child's mental states because it is first and foremost learned by externalized *usage* in contexts of social practice. Meaning in this discussion is not simply semantic meaning, information, or abstract codes of cognition, but rather the existential import of experiential episodes bearing on a child's well-being.[18]

No less than in a phenomenological account of language use in adults, early language acquisition is even more fundamentally a matter of active dwelling in a meaningful world. And here too any expositional account of referential relations between words and things or words and mental states is derived from a more original intertwinement of speech, conversation, action, and environmental settings.[19] We have noted in this investigation how typical theoretical problems in the philosophy of language—skepticism, representational linkage, relativism, universalism—can be resolved or dissolved in the light of ecstatic dwelling; indeed, many such problems cannot even get off the ground when the focus is factical life. That disconnect is even more evident in the context of language acquisition. When children are learning to speak in interpersonal settings or practical dealings with things, skeptical questions concerning language-reality relations or theoretical questions about how communication transpires between the minds of parents and children would (I hazard a guess) never arise. Co-ordinations of purpose and action, mutual understanding, and measures of successful usage are a matter of course and presumed to be at work in learning scenarios. I might be skeptical about a child's ability to put a toy back together, but not about the communicative field that could address the task at hand. Although difficulties and contraventions are always part of the learning process, the very point of such scenarios is intimated by all involved: how to aptly engage with others and the world by gathering the powers of speech.

I reiterate that this investigation does not question representational and expositional aspects of language, only their exclusivity in foundational terms. Even childhood language acquisition can elicit representational distinctions between words and the world: as in correcting a child's naming efforts or learning words in a picture book. My point has been that any such circumstance banks not only on the effects of language from the first moments of life but also on the background intimations of meaning by all parties: children understand that they can make mistakes and will be helped out; they grasp the point and purpose of sitting down with a parent to read a picture book; and all involved take the learning of language to be capacious, interesting, and important.

Volume I engaged the distinction between nature and convention in the setting of European explorers confronting indigenous inhabitants of the New World (142–143). Whatever linguistic and cultural differences there may have been, *that* the world of the two peoples was informed by their language is not an artificial convention. In addition, overlapping elements of dwelling in a lived world would allow the two peoples to grasp common features that could bridge different forms of language—along with a lot of gesturing and sensing the point of embodied behaviors. The two groups would not only intimate a mutual language-laden world, they would also be moved by an *interest* in working out communicative translation. At this level, there is a common human bond that can elicit reciprocal engagement (at least in non-violent occasions). Such primal attraction to the disclosive power of speech also animates shared networks in early language acquisition. Children and caregivers are both driven by an interest in the dawning of world-disclosure when children begin to speak.

Research has shown that childhood learning cannot adequately be understood in narrow terms of reference, mental states, utterances, rules, and grammatical patterns. The full scope of a child's organic life in a meaningful world must be taken into account: perception skills, affects, motor systems, and active engagement.[20] So, when children hear *Give me the cup*; *Isn't this fun? Let's put our shoes on*; *No cookie now . . . after we eat lunch*; *Show me where it hurts*; *Good job!*, it is too early to say that they are learning "concepts" of exchange, entertainment, containment, time, location, and praise, or that they are learning how to use nouns, verbs, and exclamations. Rather, they are learning how to disclose the meaning of activities and circumstances in immediate factual terms—as *embedded* in these scenarios, but also extendable in comparable ways with further experience and habituation. It should be noted that even research on language capabilities in primates raised in the human world can be impeded by faulty assumptions about language use: the kinds of testing employed can miss or overlook the practical and contextual settings that informed how these primates have been engaged by and with humans from the start.[21]

The meaning-laden character of language acquisition includes a range of normative elements that saturate a child's upbringing. Practical norms involve ways of dealing with the external world: cultivating skills in everyday tasks of eating, dressing, and playing, among others. Ethical norms also go all the way down in child-rearing, from the values and precepts governing parental care to all the behavioral and social norms children have to learn—ultimately facilitated and extended by language. Linguistic norms themselves are especially significant in upbringing, since children have to accord with speech conventions to foster communication. At early stages, training is not at a formal grammatical level, but rather the sonic level of guiding a child's

Language Acquisition 111

pronunciation and usage (*not mouses, honey, mice*)—in the midst of factical circumstances and immediate experiences, not abstract rules. Here a dialectic of sense and nonsense moves children along in finding their path, sometimes in amusing and creative ways. At this level, nonsense is not really a violation of sense because it is part of sounding out what works in the raw beginnings of speech.

Language development construed as a mode of dwelling—ecstatic immersion in meaningful practices situated in the social-environing-world—improves upon most theories of language acquisition that conceal the contours of dwelling. Happily, as I have indicated, some new research models are more consonant with a proto-phenomenological approach.[22] With naturalistic observation of children in their home environment, language usage is more fluid and reciprocally interactive than the tasks posed in laboratory settings, which are often isolated episodes of verbal designation in artificial scenarios meant to screen for specific cognitive skills. Such task protocols usually presuppose that childhood mentality is a mode of hypothesis testing—and accordingly, the experiments tend to issue self-fulfilling results. With factical usage in home situations, children are not applying ready-made theories; rather, they are aiming to accord their verbal expressions with those of caregivers in the exterior spaces of practical engagement. Moreover, a child's comprehension of the "mentality" of other people is not the execution of a "theory of mind" that infers the intentions of people implied by their behavior—a common explanatory tool in child development theories—because intelligence is exhibited *in* behavior and intentions are revealed *by* the speech of others.[23]

Traditional research assumes it is examining a child's "knowledge," without recognizing its own *interpretive* slant on what counts as knowledge—usually geared toward monological processing and discrete modules of cognition specified in singular tasks. Naturalistic observation shows that children learn language in the midst of social guidance, in wider spans of correlational scope and temporal extension, in mixed perspectives, and especially in pragmatic scenarios. Too often experiments focus on narrow occasions of a performance isolated from the scope of influences in a child's previous experience of familial and cultural stimulation. It is possible to gear experimental protocols to address this richer factical environment, but that requires a revision of what is meant by "cognition," which will disrupt many standard assumptions. What in past research would be deemed anecdotal, peripheral, naïve, ambiguous, imprecise, or irregular would now be indicative of the natural setting of language learning. Accordingly, inquiry would be directed less toward theoretical importation and more toward the actual phenomenology of a child's speech-world.

3.2. Words as Focal Indications

In Volume I (14–16), the notion of indicative concepts opened up the everyday use of words as proto-concepts, which do not unify or define particulars but rather span a range of uses that make sense *in* usage, not by way of formal classification. A competent speaker of English knows how to use words like *tree*, *friend*, *know*, and *good* without having gone through advanced procedures of collection and division. That is why students can be perplexed when asked philosophical questions like "What is friendship?" Knowing how to use the word *friend* means that it already has indicative sense because it *points* to recognizable instances of use. I called this pointing function the *focal meaning* of proto-concepts, which is like the hub of a wheel from which spokes radiate without being reduced to a common form. I have objected to talk of a child's "concepts" because for one thing, it is rarely specified what this means, although usually it seems to designate a mental state, representation, or category, which are more suited to sophisticated rational schematics than a child's practical intelligence. What I have called proto-concepts would be more apt, although any use of the word "concept" is likely to invite distortion. In any case, I am motivated to approach language learning in children by way of the focal meaning of words, wherein speech is disclosive through assimilating usage in specific contexts, which is registered for further usage by functional memory and habit formation.[24] Children come to comprehend words like *clothes*, *food*, and *toys* in direct experiences and collaborative usage. Such words are proto-conceptual in being extendable and collective, but they are not yet well understood as superordinate terms of inclusion, which organize lexical instances rather than concrete things. So young children will understand *pick up your toys* better than *a doll is a toy*. Comprehension of more abstract rather than pragmatic or functional concepts is usually delayed until primary school years.

It is true that many words are used with children in a somewhat representational manner: *"What is that?" "A cat." "That's right!"* And quasi-classification procedures can unfold when children misuse words: *"Doggie!" "No, that's a cat"*—but even here differences and similarities are gathered in rough perceptual patterns, not definitional schemes. Object-designation can indeed apply to learning words like *cat*, *tree*, and *bed*, but it is not well suited for a child's learning and use of words like *know*, *understand*, and *think*, which have a refined future in philosophy to be sure, but such constructs to come usually get unduly retrofitted to early language acquisition by philosophers. Child development specialists themselves get caught up in converting verbs like "know" into "knowledge" and explaining a child's use of *know* as a representation of the "mental state" of *knowledge—*and *I don't know* as a representation of *ignorance*.[25] Philosophers and scientists typically look for abstract concepts that can stabilize and fix the meaning of words. Yet language in factical life has a plasticity that follows shifting contexts and dialogical structures embodied in conversational speech—in all, an immersed fieldwork that is not amenable to representational formats, definitional precision, or abstract formalization. Language learning in childhood is the early launch of existential meanings that call for indicative specificity if we are to understand their non-representational and dialogical modes of "cognition."

If one asks a child, *Do you know what this is?*, an answer is more an expression of familiarity (or unfamiliarity) with an immediate experience than a transmission of an interior mental state. An answer of *I don't know* is not a reference to a psychological state of ignorance but a conversational expression of an impasse—actually a child is more likely to utter *I dunno*, which is simply a direct and ritualized conversational response in a shared endeavor that could just as easily be communicated by shrugging the shoulders.[26] When you ask a child, *What do you want for lunch?*, it is not uncommon to get no immediate response. We might picture the child mentally pondering different "objects" of "desire," unable to decide, or simply unwilling to say. It is more likely, however, that the child really has nothing "in mind" because there is nothing really *in view*. Parents can learn to put the question in a more concrete, disjunctive manner: *Do you want a peanut butter sandwich or a hot dog?* Even then, there might be hesitation. The most likely successful though impractical query would involve putting actual food choices on the table and asking, *Which one do you want?* The point is that young children have not yet developed expositional reflection; they do not tour the theater of their minds for cognitive states or affective dispositions; they are immersed in a social-environing-world. Accordingly, when children engage or use words like *know, understand, think, want,* and *feel*, they are discovering and expressing disclosive bearings *in their environments*. Words having to do with "cognition" are a matter of familiarity, acquaintance, and competence, not epistemological rubrics pertaining to belief formation and justification. Conversational practices in specific contexts of behavior and external dealings are the factical indications of a child's developing intelligence—not forming and displaying internal modes of cognition. Indeed, what the narrow notion of "mental processing" misses in early language acquisition is the largely passive *projection* of children into established norms of speech-and-behavior blends that are more an imperative than a psychological selection or choice.[27]

To finish this section's sketch of factical language learning, I reiterate a point made in chapter 1, that an object-designation model of language misses the full range of words that figure in the meaning of sentences (including the sentences describing language as a designation of objects in the world)—not only nouns and verbs but also adjectives, adverbs, conjunctions, prepositions, articles, affirmations, and negations. Children do learn words in piecemeal references to objects and actions, but even before the advent of speech they have been acclimated to a range of expressions, gestures, and tonalities that pertain to emotional, interpersonal, and existential elements of life: *Aren't you cute! Isn't this fun? Stop! Come here! Look at the kitty! Let me help you.* When children do learn to speak, they become familiar with the wide array of words that shape world-disclosive talk—not as "grammar" in a formal sense but implicated in behavioral relations with persons and things in their environment: *yes, no, good, bad, in, out, close, far, fast, slow, and, but, a, the, I, we, you, me, is,* and so forth. All such word usage is shaped by, and comes to further shape, the lived world; and it is ever joined with gesture and tonality to constitute speech as embodied enactment.

Many theories of linguistic development emphasize object naming and the execution of a child's innate store of pre-linguistic concepts that find expression in word learning, which fits communicative theories based in universal cognitive codes that are simply triggered by language acquisition. But such theoretical commitments are disrupted by empirical research and naturalistic approaches that are more in line with proto-phenomenology.[28] Early vocabularies are rich in non-object indications having to do with places, actions, events, emotions, and attitudes. Word learning and usage also exhibit flexibility and frequent overextension, which is inconsistent with universal conceptual mapping in communicative theories. Social-pragmatic models are more in accord with the evident conditions of children appropriating *different* contexts of usage that *adjust* to adult guidance. It is not a matter of a child's "mind" awaiting prompts for expressive display; it is a child's engagement with a social-environing-*world* that helps shape the possibilities of meaningful experience. Ecstatic immersion is more an extended dimension of fitting in with joint practices than an inside-out procedure of expressing concepts with words. And the "cognition" involved is not a matter of universal concepts but the development of *shared* meanings that (1) distribute across a range of different uses, (2) gather those uses for repeatable usage, and (3) allow for individual inflections.

We turn next to detail the social forces that figure in language acquisition. Children learn to speak in face-to-face conversation, which guides not only what to talk about but when and how to converse, along with interactive patterns such as turn-taking—all in the embodied setting of joint attention. The correlational scope of conversations shows that learning cannot be adequately described in terms of isolated words, phrases, sentences, or individual utterances. Mere semantic meaning and formal linguistics do not capture the social-situational contexts that generate the first contours of dwelling in speech, which should be understood primarily as an interactive *process* rather than an exposited *product*.[29]

4. THE PERSONAL-SOCIAL-WORLD

In this section, I develop further the ways in which language acquisition requires social interaction in the midst of meaning-laden practices, which blend a child's needs with the cultural inheritance of caregivers. It would seem evident to anyone that language development is a social process, since that is the way it unfolds in parent-child scenarios. But a proto-phenomenological perspective aims to demonstrate how common theoretical assumptions in philosophy and linguistics—especially individualistic, monological, and mentalistic models of selfhood—buckle under the weight of this "obvious" fact. Feral children are surely individual beings, but their social-linguistic deficits indicate that *human* nature cannot fully emerge in isolation from a social-world. In addition, early development stages show how phenomenological attention to immersed, embodied engagement is better able to address language acquisition than exposition-based theories that emphasize lexical semantics, grammar, and mental representation. Finally, in this section, I will argue that the development of a child's individuated selfhood is informed by a socially structured language.

4.1. The Social Origins of Language Development

Linguistic categories of semantics and syntax are expositional constructions that miss the pragmatic and interactive milieus occupying infants and parents, which are essential background conditions for language acquisition.[30] Long-standing debates between environmental and nativist theories (think of Skinner and Chomsky) should be exchanged for a pragmatic-social-interactive model that interweaves a child's pre-linguistic intimations of meaning with the affordances and scaffolding effects provided by caregivers. When language first emerges, parents will much less correct a child's grammar than *share* speech acts serving a child's needs, aims, and activities. It is capaciousness that counts more than linguistic form.[31] Rather than a choice between external conditioning and an internal/a priori Language Acquisition Device, speech development should be understood as a personal-social-world, as a Language Acquisition Support System, where joint engagements build from pre-linguistic comprehension and behavioral routines to predictable scripting patterns that fine-tune and expand communicative possibilities in a shared environment.[32] The lexical elements of speech are made possible and furthered by natural capacities of transactional behavior, joint attention, goal-directed activity, accepting assistance, and predicting outcomes—capacities that young children display with interest and excitement.[33] Supplementing most of these processes is a child's innate capacity for imitation, which entails ecstatic immersion in behavioral prompts in the midst of verbal stimulation. Mimetic speech is an indigenous power exhibited by children in developing their word usage.[34] All told, language development is (1) a reciprocal correlation of social guidance and natural propensities, and (2) an intersecting field of bi-directional effects between verbal articulation and social-practical engagement.

We have already sketched how play figures in child development. Even before the emergence of speech, early forms of play between infants and parents establish communicative rituals of shared meanings that prepare children for the advent of language—especially because of child directed speech from parents in the course of play.[35] The familiar game of peekaboo has a narrative-communicative structure that illustrates focused formats for sharing meaningful behavior. A child's natural delight in something like peekaboo might be called a nascent phenomenology, an interest in the concealment-and-appearance of a human face. Early games of disappearance and reappearance—for instance, hiding and showing a toy clown—engage appearances informed by anticipation and completion, wherein a parent's melodic speech registers the linguistic cadence of such experiences for the infant: *Here he goes! Where is he? He's gone! He's coming! Here he is!* In stages, the child will want to grab the clown, then aim to initiate the hiding and revealing. Infants will offer vocalized sounds that punctuate the ritual and that are placeholders for later utterances such as *Gone!* and *Bye-bye!* In all, children early on enjoy such primal occasions of structured experience, scripted communication, and agency roles. It is important to keep in mind the essential contribution of caregiver language in pre-linguistic play. The scaffolding effect is shown in "handover" patterns with children after formats are established, and in "give and take" games informed by interactive intimations of meaningful behavior.[36]

Other forms of pre-linguistic communicative patterns involve early occasions of joint attention (well established by the second month) animated by caregiver intonations that attract infant interest: *What's that? Look! See what I have?*[37] At six to seven months, children begin reaching, taking, and exchanging; and at ten months, they begin their own pointing gestures. Picture book reading, along with games of "where" and "what," initiate conversation patterns of question and answer, which imply a purposeful aim for disclosive expression. Most early occasions focus on whole things and their aspects, followed by growing attention to actions. Here begins the articulation of world-disclosure operating in nouns, adjectives, and verbs. It is normal for infant vocalization and babbling to accompany such occasions, which at first are simply encouraged but in time are "corrected" by caregivers to prompt word formation. Once children begin to talk, they can proceed on their own, without a need for prompting. Toward the second year, as children launch into speech, conversations with caregivers become a "negotiation" to draw out competency in the following sense: Parents assume that children have something worthy to say and are on their way to effective speech, a path that needs guidance and tuning (rather than simply correcting mistakes). Such conversational scaffolding is something that never entirely disappears, even in maturity—thus the error of monological conceptions of language.[38] Children intimate parental guidance in conversations and respond in the manner of reciprocal partnership.[39]

Important elements of meaning-formation in the midst of social scaffolding can be highlighted in the development of requesting.[40] Request displays imply a sense of meaningful interest, purpose, and assistance. Beginning around the end of the first year, indicative reference expands to requests directed at caregivers: for objects and support of action, or as invitations to share an activity. Here begins conversational exchange geared toward a child's possibilities, whether attaining things desired or executing aims (possibilities sometimes blocked by due contravention from caregivers). Requesting begins as babbled vocalization and develops with verbal expression. Certain intimations of meaning are shown when, for example, children ask for a toy to be assembled or fixed; with a ready response, children can wait with some patience, which implies comprehension of a purposeful process that takes time.

All the occasions discussed in this section afford children a growing comprehension of things, activities, agency, spatial and temporal understanding, aims, means, receipt, achievement, and reliance on others.[41] The emergence of speech in such scenarios cannot be confined to semantic or grammatical development; it must include an embodied, practical, social-environing-world. Children are not simply applying innate or learned linguistic rules or formats; language emerges by way of ecstatic immersion in meaning-laden circumstances. This is why young children cannot be deemed ego-centric in a strict sense. If they were truly sealed up in an interior bubble, none of the processes that figure in language acquisition could actually work. Children from the start are ecological beings. To be sure, young children are driven by many "self-regarding" needs and displays. But they are social beings even before they are socialized by cultural norms. In any case, the social-world *includes* the personal-world, which in early childhood is embodied by a child's particular aspects and behaviors. A more focused sense of personality and conscious self-awareness is made possible by further stages of dwelling in speech.

4.2. Self-Development and Language

Chapter 1 sketched the ways in which language is constitutive of thought, including the contours of selfhood. I asked if any such conditions would be possible if someone were not exposed to language as a child. An answer in the negative would not abide "communicative" theories, wherein language is simply expressive of non-linguistic thought. Some evidence for the constitutive of role of language in the emergence of selfhood was given in Helen Keller's dramatic claim that before she had access to language, she existed in a nebulous "no-world" that lacked a sense of consciousness and self-awareness.[42] It seems evident that conscious selfhood is a later development in childhood—at the very least because we lack memories of the first years of life. Some research supports the idea that self-awareness occurs only after the advent of language—indeed *by way of* speech processes. Although my investigation relies on a distinction between phenomenological description and causal accounts in physiological terms, the role of language in child development allows for a quasi-causal empirical perspective—where self-awareness follows the internalization of speech—which offers a plausible explanation for how selfhood emerges, without relying on theories that reduce any discussion of conscious mentality to physiological causes. In other words, it is a child's *experience with speech practices* that prepares self-awareness.

Research inspired by the work of Lev Vygotsky supports a social/ecological account of how a child develops an individuated sense of self—an outside-in process whereby the social-world of speech becomes internalized.

> A central hypothesis in Vygotsky's theory of development is that higher psychological functions, such as planning, voluntary attention, and strategic memory, have social origins. In response to both nativist and naïve environmentalist theories, Vygotsky proposed that higher cognitive functions are neither innate nor simply learned from the caregiving environment. Rather, he believed that children gradually construct in collaboration with adults or more capable peers, functional levels of organization that will appear later in individual functioning and cognitive development. Thus, a major task for Vygotskian researchers is to specify and document how the transfer or appropriation from interpersonal collaboration to intrapersonal functioning occurs.[43]

We have seen that fully immersed experience is not self-conscious. A kind of expositional "distance" between, say, observer and observed is required for self-awareness *of* observation and *of* the self as observer. In Vygotsky-inspired developmental psychology, a child's route to the expositional distance of self-consciousness is accomplished through "inner speech," which allows children to become the object of their own attention, of their own thoughts and behavior.[44] The movement from a child's immersion in the speech-world to inner speech is mediated by what is called "private speech," which simply means self-directed verbalization, audibly talking to oneself.[45] Private speech is not an interior domain but the replication of socially endowed speech in the midst of activity when no one else is directly involved.[46] It is important to stress that such a development is derived from the original social milieu of language, so that self-awareness arises from the *reproduction* of social formats by way of self-directed language. There is also neurophysiological evidence mapping the processes here described.[47]

Private speech in young children (talking to themselves in task performance) has often been met with concern by parents; and Piaget had taken it to be a stage of ego-centrism. But Vygotsky initiated the dismissal of this scheme by arguing that private speech is essential for cognitive and behavioral development, because here the child takes over the regulative role of the social world. Language begins as collaborative tasking and conversational guidance from caregivers; private speech is a redirection of this milieu toward independent functioning. In isolation from others, the self-reproduction of care-giving utterances provides an audible presence that is at once individuated and socialized, where children become more reflexively aware of this hybrid presence as their own, as self-activated.[48] Self-awareness in this respect is derived from the social-speech-world: cognitive and behavioral capacities begin in a social-linguistic network; private speech initiates a process that over time leads to the internalization of these capacities that now can operate "silently," as it were, by way of inner speech. To sum up, mature development, individuation, and self-consciousness are the result of an internalization of the social-linguistic environment, which is mediated by private speech becoming inner speech.[49]

After early periods of socialized speech practices, by the fifth year, children begin to fulfill the internalization process that enhances cognitive and practical skills by way of more self-initiated aims, planning, and regulation.[50] Such a process also broadens a child's experience through imagination and perspective-taking. Here language gathers its own set of possibilities, distinct from immediate occasions in the social-environing-world. Gradually the internalization of speech achieves a more automatic and tacit facility. Now the scaffolding effects of language are gathered in both social and individual performances. Private speech shifts social effects to solitary occasions; inner speech expands a child's possibilities, which then interact with the guidance of caregivers in negotiated episodes of expression, problem solving, and practical tasks. It is important to note that the mediation of private speech is central to these developments, because performance at early stages succeeds more when a child verbalizes while acting, rather than not verbalizing.[51] In any case, the circular movement of social and individual scaffolding effects in speech underscores (1) the constitutive role of language in world-disclosure, and (2) the joint structure of the personal-social-world. Now we can give specific attention to how a child's personal-world unfolds in the midst of social environments.

4.3. Personal Development

In line with an ecological phenomenology, a Vygotskian model of development shows that the experience of young children is mediated by social relations, cultural norms, language, and artifacts in the environment.[52] The emergence of human capacities and attributes would not be possible apart from this scaffolding nexus. An ecological conception of mediation, however, cannot overlook the immediacy of a child's own direct experience in this network, which is not a passive receptacle but a participant in the midst of social and cultural influences.[53] The second nature of a child's own habituation is the only proving ground for socio-cultural mediation; and as was seen in chapter 2, no shaping influences are separable from the individuated responses of children, often in modes of resistance that call for negotiation. Even early in life, the personal-social-world is a reciprocal correlation of, and tension between, socialization and individuation.

When mediating influences on children are going smoothly, we can picture a joint condition of co-immersion. Yet the contraventions exhibited in a child's mistakes, misbehaviors, or rejections bring on an expositional orientation for both caregivers and children. In pre-linguistic stages, a child's "exposition" is more behavioral than verbal. But as language skills develop, the expositional dialogue between parent and child is launched, which of course is a difficult and challenging orchestration of young desires and social constraints. Conversations often involve parental interrogation of the child's interests, with answers affording a recursive effect that helps shape or expand a child's self-understanding.

As we saw in chapter 2, childhood resistance is intrinsic to the individuation process, and so a hyper-controlled environment is not conducive for healthy growth. The same can be said for over-permissiveness. A child's immediate experiences and reactions can be called a kind of creative individuation; but the affordances, scaffolding, and constraints of social norms allow for creative *production* rather than mere anomalous deviance. To be sure, parents are never immune to worries about future outcomes in the face of certain divergent behaviors or dispositions in their children. But childhood is the prototype of an open future, and the best one can do is avoid disciplinary and permissive extremes—and hope for the best. In any case, communicative articulation in language is the vehicle for a child's self-understanding and self-expression, which otherwise would lack disclosive detail, comprehension by other persons, and whatever modulations shared disclosure might require or bring to light. In early stages of psychological development, an emotional irruption can be managed somewhat by the request "Use your words," which can mollify the intensity of feeling with more focused attention on the problem and a possible resolution opened up by dialogue. Such articulation can help both children and caregivers come to terms with the implications of forceful experiences beyond their immediate ignition. Thus begins the power of verbal narration to incorporate experiences into a "world," a context of meaning that extends the child into responsive possibilities. What comes to be called "thought" making sense of "experience" is shown in these early episodes to be "meaning gathered in speech."

To conclude, language is essential for the self-development of children, the advent of their personal-world. Speech is first shaped in a social-practical environment, which begins to be individuated by way of private speech. Then inner speech allows more focused individuation, which begins to forge a child's own perspectives and possibilities, but which continues to be guided and indeed furthered by the constraints and feedback of social dialogue. All told, the "personality" of children is shaped by meaningful invocations of language, which include narrative formats that shape a child's memories, imaginations, and affective attunements. The temporal and ecological structure of self-formation continues in maturity, but the contours of child development offer more focused attention on why human selfhood is a complex circulation of temporal dimensions, social influences, and individual inflections. At any rate, personality—understood as a narrational "who" rather than a "what"—embodies the intricate situated openness of human selfhood, understood in the following way: (1) no present moment in life can be isolated from traces of the past and an undetermined future; and (2) an intersecting personal-social-environing-world shows that no precise formative base of selfhood can be located in the individual, social, or environmental elements alone, even in an "aggregation" of these domains because their reciprocal feedback and tensional dynamic undermine any settled description.

4.4. Some Philosophical Implications

Our analysis of self-development by way of language acquisition can bear well on some philosophical questions addressed in Volume I: skepticism, the meaning of consciousness, the nature of the conscious mind, the mind-body question, and the nature of communication. First of all, radical skepticism about the existence of the external world and other minds (and even proposed solutions such as a "theory of mind" that infers mentality in others) is undermined by the phenomenology of ecological engagement in factical life. Immersed involvement with other persons in the world shows that we are always already dwelling in meaningful horizons of shared intelligence—so that our environment (the "world") and the intelligence of others (their "minds") cannot be put in question all the way down, on pain of undermining the very impetus to offer skeptical proposals to other persons in conversations, books, or public lectures. Our development in childhood only reinforces an ecological dissolution of skepticism. We could never *become* skeptics apart from a nurturing environment, practical engagement, and the "minds" of caregivers. Sincere radical skepticism could not be the guiding supposition of parents raising children.

Attention to child development also strengthens the phenomenological move from a monological to a dialogical model of selfhood, as well as the constitutive priority of language in self-development and world-disclosure. We have noted Helen Keller's testimony about how the world and her self-awareness emerged only after her access to language, which given her condition (being blind, deaf, and mute) had to involve the mediation of finger-spelling on her hand produced by her teacher. Here is Keller's (now linguistically informed) recollection of how language and the world first opened up for her at age seven:

> One day, while I was playing with my new doll, Miss Sullivan put my big rag doll into my lap, also spelled "d-o-l-l" and tried to make me understand that "d-o-l-l" applied to both. Earlier in the day we had had a tussle over the words "m-u-g" and "w-a-t-e-r." Miss Sullivan had tried to impress it upon me that "m-u-g" is mug and that "w-a-t-e-r" is water, but I persisted in confounding the two. In despair she had dropped the subject for the time, only to renew it at the first opportunity. I became impatient at her repeated attempts and, seizing the new doll, I dashed it upon the floor. I was keenly delighted when I felt the fragments of the broken doll at my feet. Neither sorrow nor regret followed my passionate outburst. I had not loved the doll. In the still, dark world in which I lived there was no strong sentiment of tenderness. I felt my teacher sweep the fragments to one side of the hearth, and I had a sense of satisfaction that the cause of my discomfort was removed. She brought me my hat, and I knew I was going out into the warm sunshine. This thought, if a wordless sensation may be called a thought, made me hop and skip with pleasure. We walked down the path to the well-house, attracted by the fragrance of the honeysuckle with which it was covered. Someone was drawing water and my teacher placed my hand under the spout. As the cool stream gushed over one hand she spelled into the other the word water, first slowly, then rapidly. I stood still, my whole attention fixed upon the motions of her fingers. Suddenly I felt a misty consciousness as of something forgotten—a thrill of returning thought; and somehow the mystery of language was revealed to me. I knew then that "w-a-t-e-r" meant the wonderful cool something that was flowing over my hand. That living word awakened my soul, gave it light, hope, joy, set it free! There were barriers still, it is true, but barriers that could in time be swept away. I left the well-house eager to learn. Everything had a name, and each name gave birth to a new thought. As we returned to the house every object which I touched seemed to quiver with life. That was because I saw everything with the strange, new sight that had come to me. On entering the door I remembered the doll I had broken. I felt my way to the hearth and picked up the pieces. I tried vainly to put them together. Then

my eyes filled with tears; for I realized what I had done, and for the first time I felt repentance and sorrow. I learned a great many new words that day. I do not remember what they all were; but I do know that mother, father, sister, teacher were among them—words that were to make the world blossom for me, "like Aaron's rod, with flowers." It would have been difficult to find a happier child than I was as I lay in my crib at the close of the eventful day and lived over the joys it had brought me, and for the first time longed for a new day to come.[54]

It is hard not to find this account thrilling. Normal language acquisition is gradual and woven into years of experience. Keller's age and the sudden eruption of linguistic comprehension spotlight the marvel of disclosive power in language. The finger-spelling also accentuates the material mediation required in the process of learning language: sound for normal children, visual gestures for deaf children, and touch for someone like Keller. The material medium performs the differential element in language we have emphasized. Material differentiation allows the fitness character of language—which for Keller was the felt spelling on one hand fitting the water flowing on her other hand—to be shared *between* persons, which ignites the social dynamic of language learning. Material mediation also allows fitting disclosure to be sustained in the *absence* of immediate occasions of experience, to enact all the relational effects of language (noun-adjective-verb relations, conjunction, disjunction, negation, comparison, contrast, synthesis, etc.), and to generate the recursive power of expanded articulation made possible by intra-linguistic permutations. Finally, material differentiation permits the transition from social embeddedness to private speech, to inner speech, and to unvocalized thought, a transition that shapes self-awareness, internally increases the disclosive power of language, and externally enriches social dialogue.

The material character of language driving such processes, along with the embodied practical environments implicated in language acquisition, can enhance the case made in Volume I for revising the mind-body question (207–213). Phenomenologically and grammatically, there are evident differences between mental/psychological and physical descriptions. I argued that such differences are functionally and existentially incommensurable, and yet fully ensconced in lived embodiment—and thereby neither divisible into substance dualism nor reducible to physiological causes. The course we have tracked in a child's transition from the social ecology of speech to the internalization of speech can illuminate how the differences between "mental" and "physical" perspectives can transpire in an embodied world that is fully *natural* in an existential sense. Consider talking with others about something in the environment presently occurring or in the midst of doing something in the world; here tangible sonic utterances and events are at work together. Then consider talking with others about something not directly happening;

here sonic utterances are in play along with the virtual fitness of speech. Then talking to oneself about doing something in the world; again, sonic utterances and virtual fitness. Then thinking to oneself about doing something; here sonic impact has shifted derivatively to a silent trace along with virtual fitness. Then simply thinking to oneself by way of the silent traces of speech in thought. In this sequence, we can notice the movement from perception to introspection and from physical dimensions to unextended ideation. The process is both continuous (not dualistic) and divergent by way of differentiated internalization.

Volume I argued for the incommensurability of mental and physical expressions from a phenomenological standpoint, which undermines physicalism by way of an existential naturalism that undermines substance dualism. With our discussion of the internalization of speech, we are able to show not only how such incommensurability first unfolds in human experience but also why dualistic impulses might ever arise—while also showing that such impulses must be constrained by the material origin of internalized speech.[55] The traces of language that mark the interior monologue of "thinking" are no longer wedded to the embodied speech-world, namely sonic expression, visible listeners, the tangible references of talk, and the sensorimotor organs of speech. All such "physical" elements are *effaced* in the "mental" traces of speech that characterize an interior monologue. Analogous to a recollected image of something in the world losing its erstwhile dimensions of actual extension, internalized traces of speech constitute the decisive effacement of physicality in the following way: the radical *difference* between word sounds and their worldly references becomes a complete recession of physical attention because sonic differentiation has been fully decoupled from tangible reference as a *silent* trace. Nevertheless, the *fitness* of speech retains its disclosive capacity with internalized traces.

The so-called hard problem of consciousness is difficult only because of the physicalistic assumption that conscious experience must somehow be explained causally in physiological terms. I have suggested that the question of consciousness—which should really be understood as self-consciousness rather than mere awareness—is better addressed by way of phenomenological description, not causal explanation. Here the "conscious self" is an *emergence* out of the social-speech-world, a fully natural setting that simply gets internalized—without any leap to some spiritual dimension separate from the physical world. Whatever causes might be operating in the brain, that third-person/physical/empirical perspective cannot itself articulate the meaning-laden speech process that generates self-awareness in a situated world.[56]

With respect to communication, the ecological model of the personal-social-environing-world has shown communication to be not a transmission of interior mental states conveyed by words but primarily an extended collocution of meaningful speech in practical settings. Language acquisition displays this ecological structure in an acute manner because a child's development of speech and individuation is first shaped in the midst of social, linguistic, and practical circumstances *there* in a child's world. In this context, the communicative function of language is ecstatically extended before a child develops an "interior" base of self-awareness. At that point, one might picture communication as an exchange of mental states, but even in maturity, an ecstatic dimension of communicative practice shows a certain phenomenological priority. Puzzles about communication only arise if this ecstatic dimension is concealed by expositional analysis. Communicative immersion gets interrupted by contravention when there is disagreement, misunderstanding, or deficits of articulation. Then there can arise expositional attention to meanings, capacities, modes of expression, and individual mentality. Skepticism about human communication only arises in an expositional or representational framework. A bedrock of communicative felicity is a precondition for being able to consider and communicate a skeptical posture in the first place.

Another version of skepticism concerns whether people can genuinely comprehend the meaning and character of another person's experience or state of mind. But a practical phenomenology regarding the ecological field of communication can respond in a cogent way. Often skeptical doubts about interpersonal comprehension stem from subject-object and subject-subject binaries, which I have called into question. Nevertheless, the personal-world is a real dimension of existence and there is surely a sense of inwardness in everyone's experience. Such a dimension, though originally derived from the social-world, has genuine purchase and it is common to wonder about the possibility of truly understanding another person or of being truly understood by others. Human psychology is so complex that I am comfortable saying that no person can be fully understood by others in a manner comparable to a person's own self-understanding. As I have indicated, communication is often contravened and then there arises the effort to resolve disparities or privations. An ecological and practical phenomenology can simply recognize such contravention and various degrees of resolution—along with the possibility that communication can break down and fail. Nothing in this scenario requires a notion of perfect isomorphic communication, whatever that would mean. Adequate degrees of mutual comprehension will simply be indicated by degrees of satisfaction among participants. We are in trouble if the only mark of true communication is unqualified identity or perfect accord.

5. EMBODIMENT AND THE ENVIRONING-WORLD

The environing-world is implicated in everything discussed so far, and it overlaps with the social-world in its scaffolding effects on a child's linguistic development. As established in chapter 1, the surrounding world is not originally an "object" of cognition but a meaningful practice-field of ecstatic involvement. Even more so than in adults, a young child's intelligence does not reflect a knowing "subject" but a *doing* in the midst of ecological affordances and useful artifacts—that is to say, the budding agency of know-how, which is ever caught up in lived embodiment. As such, a child's speech development is intertwined with practical dealings in an environment. In this section, I will also work with the outside-in structure of ecstatic ecology to gather the *projective* force of socio-cultural practices and norms that are already in place, *there* in a child's world to guide and shape the articulation of speech practices.

5.1. Joint Attention

We have established joint attention as the triangular relationship between one person gesturing or pointing *to* something in the environment *for* the attention of another person—which illustrates the reciprocal structure of the personal-social-environing-world, particularly in terms of a natural impulse for disclosive communication. Joint attention seems to be unique to humans and is exhibited early in life between infants and caregivers. Pointing to something for someone else's regard is prototypical and it stands as a pre-linguistic phenomenon that precedes and makes possible communication in speech.[57] Some examples of joint attention displayed by infants: (1) *sharing-attention and behavior*, such as engaging a toy with a parent; (2) *following-attention and behavior*, such as gaze following, gesture following, and imitative learning; and (3) *directing-attention and behavior*, namely imperatives (whining about something or gestures of requesting and demanding) and declaratives (pointing to something or holding something up). Early joint attention is a natural, embodied communicative nexus (a social-world), which is a precondition for language acquisition (and also a check against linguistic idealism understood in lexical terms). Indeed, even before a child's first words, the vocalizations and speech practices of caregivers are essential for attuning infant behavior *to* the shared nexus *as* conjoined in communication and blended with the infant's affective dispositions and sensorimotor activity.[58] When a child begins to speak, words take over (though not entirely) the indicative function of joint attention and embodied communication; in doing so, speech opens up and expands the meaning-laden purpose of communication by way of the differential fitness of language. Words also add a material focal point that gathers the communicative aim of joint attention by way of a perceptible bridging function.

We should say that the disclosive power of language is grounded not originally in "words" as such, but in a natural shared impulse to communicate existential import.⁵⁹ Within three to four months, infants display predictable stages of joint attention: checking to see if an adult is regarding something in the world; following adult attention to something; actively directing adult attention to something. There is a strong correlation between infant capacities for joint engagement and the coming production of language, which will launch from, and begin to articulate, a child's natural communicative impulses. It is important to stress that joint attention, for both children and caregivers, is understood *as* shareable and reciprocal, which is illustrated by the capacity for mimetic role switching displayed by infants, where they (1) understand themselves as receiving and duplicating a caregiver's agency, and (2) intimate the caregiver as a recipient of their own behavior.⁶⁰

Linguistic and developmental theories that miss the reciprocal communicative background of language acquisition will be constrained by lexical, representational, and referential notions that conceal how speech unfolds out of unique instincts for transactional communication. Animals and pre-verbal infants can understand utterances of direct reference: a dog will understand what saying "outside" means; an infant can respond to "Where's the doggy?" The comprehension of some verbal meanings precedes a child's own production of words by several months.⁶¹ It is an externalized communicative practice that is grasped here, not semantic meaning per se. Human language presupposes that the child intimates an utterance as drawing attention to something the speaker is already regarding or thinking—so that speech is a matter of *shared* attention, understood *as* such, and functioning by way of reciprocal effects. This triangular structure opens a child to the rich history of usage in a caregiver's language, which is super-added to immediate occasions of joint attention and primed for further applications (thus following the figure-eight structure of temporality). When various factical perspectives accumulate, actual perception can now be modified because immediate experiences become *layered* with social, cultural, and symbolic meaning.⁶² Here begins the shaping of "experience" by language, which in time will allow un-verbalized experiences that nevertheless are not utterly separable from language. Early on, one consequence of perspectival layering is that language opens up complex compounds, as when a child comes to understand a piece of candy as both something good to eat and a forbidden temptation. Animals and pre-verbal infants can understand one thing in different ways (as, say, benign or hurtful in different situations) but not one thing as a compound *of* different meanings.

5.2. Embodied Enactment

Embodiment and practical activity in the environing-world are the original domain of a child's experience. At the start, a child's "thinking" is not an epistemological project of concept formation, applying primitive theories, or exercising mental representations. Early intelligence is a matter of behavioral involvement with tangible settings of meaningful concern.[63] Phenomenological concepts of practical immersion, know-how, and habituation are more apt for rendering such early modes of understanding the world. Language acquisition is also caught up in this incarnate arena of active engagement. Parent-child conversations are interlaced with cross-somatic behaviors and dealings with things in the immediate vicinity, all shaped by the expression of conventional meanings that begin to articulate shared moments of disclosure.[64] Early language "usage" is not simply verbal expression or naming objects but *using* words *in* co-present circumstances of involvement, whether it be perceptual regard, affective stimulation, or practical handling.[65] Here is one sense in which early language can be called a "tool," but not in mere instrumental or referential terms; it is tool-like in being an *intersection* of human aims and affordances, an enabling vehicle that helps shape a child's commerce with things in the environment.[66]

Child-parent conversations are much more than verbal expressions and descriptions; they are carried on by the active bodies of children and caregivers casting out to their surroundings in the service of shared dealings and explorations. World disclosure is gathered by speech practices that multiply scaffolding effects in the environment, where children come to learn about things, actions, and relations by extending their bodies outward to investigate and manipulate, guided by caregiver speech. A child's early understanding is a distribution of practices and possibilities that are focused and driven by verbal exchanges. Think of playing with a shape insertion toy: *Which one? That one? Put it inside. Oh, too small! Take it out. Try another one. Yay, it fits!* This and many other activities will teach nouns, verbs, adjectives, and prepositions—not as grammatical forms but as distributed performances with things. A host of terms are learned in concrete circumstances and correlations: words like *up, down, inside, outside, big, small, slow, fast, on, under, here, there,* and so on—words that in time will be extended metaphorically in more "cognitive" ways, but that originally are not even verbal "forms" because they have a perceptible, tangible venue in material aspects and relationships.[67] So-called material engagement theory is pertinent here because it shows how cognition is extended out to and amid practical involvement with artifacts and the physical world. Adding a social-cultural-practical perspective offers rich possibilities for articulating early instances of the phenomenological concept of dwelling.[68]

My account benefits from, and can expand, the so-called 4E model of cognition—which takes intelligence to be embodied, enacted, embedded, and extended.[69] This is fully consistent with an ecological phenomenology of immersion. From the standpoint of mature experience and common philosophical assumptions, the 4E approach might be taken to fall short in seeming to conceal internal mentality. But the 4E framework can be bolstered by attention to early child development and the absence of such mentality at that stage. Here the 4E approach seems vindicated. Such notions as aim, purpose, intention, emotion, desire, and so on can be manifested not in a child's mind but in the *body*, in the *animate* body's activity, behavior, gestures, facial expressions, and vocalizations.[70] We do not have to "read" a child's "mind" because delight, need, anger, frustration, and enjoyment are fully evident in somatic displays and speech. With the child's factical living, we need not refer to internal mental states. We can understand a child's intelligence phenomenologically as embodied and enacted behaviors that are public *appearances*, which are comprehended *in* their appearance. My investigation can assist the 4E model in the following ways: attention to child development shows that inwardness is something that emerges *out of* a 4E ecology through the internalization of speech; the process of nested assimilation shows that the 4E baseline characterizing childhood is not lost entirely in adult life; and the immersion-exposition dynamic allows that traditional notions of mentality can still be indicatively useful as exposited articulations of meaningful speech.

5.3. Gesture and Sound

Gesture and sound help specify the ways in which language dwells in an embodied environment. We have noted how gesture and facial expression are intrinsic to oral speech and conversation in a manner that is sub-verbal rather than non-verbal. Pointing is one of the most basic forms of communication and it often accompanies speech in immediate circumstances. The same holds for touching. Nodding and shaking the head are familiar accents in conversation. Multiple hand and arm movements indicate spatial direction, location, rough mimicry of actions, and degrees of emphasis. So-called beat gestures display non-indicative hand and arm movements coordinated with the temporal patterns and pacing in speech. Gesturing is spontaneous and usually not self-conscious. Facial gestures are a ubiquitous and vivid component of speech, especially in expressing emotional states—particularly smiling, which is a universal indication of pleasure or happiness. Over 1000 facial displays have been detected in human conversations, 75% of which are specifically speech related. Gesture thereby anchors speech in action, embodiment, and sensuous experience.[71]

In addition to gestures closely associated with speech, many somatic movements and activities contribute to language acquisition because much of what children learn about speech is intertwined with physical involvement with things and persons in the environment: reaching, touching, tasting, using, playing, manipulating, wearing, exploring, and so on. Overall, gesture and somatic action illuminate not only the embodied elements of language but also its ecological character, the triangular coordination of face-to-face speech, and practical engagement with the surrounding world. It is hard to imagine the evolution of human language in a purely vocal mode.[72]

We have noted how sound as intonation enhances the disclosive effects of language, especially with respect to emotional register. Given the immersed and meaning-laden character of speech, an existential understanding of intonation must be distinguished from exposited treatments of sound in language. Such is the case in phonology, which analyzes the ways in which sonic and verbal patterns figure in the delivery and reception of speech. Phonology properly discloses exposited elements of sound in speech—for instance phonemes and syllables—but this is derivative of the ecstatic manner in which sound and sense are immediately *fused*—which is to say, not even "conjoined"—in ordinary speech. I do not hear "sound" that is "processed" as, say, an angry utterance; *I hear an angry voice*. The very notion of a phoneme is an exposited feature of language that by itself has no semantic meaning. In language acquisition, phonetic differentiation is central to the movement from babbling to learning the specific sonic markers of a native tongue. Yet this learning milieu cannot be understood as simply the processing of abstract phonemes, because a child is cued for pronunciation in ecological fields of engagements that are infused with factical meaning. Babbling begins around six to eight months of age, with syllabic repetitions such as *ba-ba*.[73] Children then begin to expand their repertoire by imitating the intonations and rhythms of caregiver speech. At ten to twelve months, babbling more and more begins to resemble speech, thereby generating the shift to word formation and production. Despite the arbitrary differences in word sounds across languages, there are certain background elements common to human speech at the level of inception.[74] Human infants are predisposed to pick up any possible language sound, but once the sounds of a native language are acquired, the capacity to register other sounds is tuned out. The same pattern has been found in spatial perception inflected by language. I would add certain factical needs, capacities, and circumstances that are roughly common across human cultures but that differ in their specifics.

With respect to language and embodiment in general terms, the core significance of sound and gesture in speech is evident vividly in early language acquisition. Children gather the disclosive power of speech not in their "minds," not even with their "words" lexically understood, but in their animate absorption in a meaningful world of practices and social relations, which are opened up somatically by hearing and witnessing speech in tangible contexts of doing, touching, and feeling. One consequence of recognizing the role of gesture and sound at the inception of language is that face-to-face speech is *at once* a visual, aural, and tactile phenomenon. This helps reinforce the ecological character of language as a material presence *there* in one's world, in which one can be ecstatically immersed.

5.4. Projection

As indicated in chapter 2, language for young children is generally a mode of passive projection, of non-voluntary exposure to the formative powers of speech—although we should not call this strictly passive because newborns and infants contribute pre-linguistic capacities (e.g., joint attention) that prepare language development, along with a natural *interest* in human speech and its exercise. Nevertheless, the language of caregivers stands as a projective repository that launches world-disclosive possibilities for children. Now meaning begins to be articulated in the nexus of the social-environing-world, and a natural communicative impulse is extended and expanded exponentially. The child's participation can be called a growing middle voice, which will be sharpened in later stages of self-awareness—and part of the delight in raising children is their creative uses of speech and their capacity to use words in their own way beyond occasions of training.[75] In any case, children are thrust into the rich correlational scope of language, which (1) articulates the world with socio-cultural norms governing speech, behavior, practices, and relationships, (2) gathers the history of linguistic usage that has shaped caregivers, and (3) guides a child's growth and experience as speech begins to flourish. With language use in particular, projection provides both a constraining and liberating effect. Children must fit in with conventional usage and linguistic formats, but that constraint has a scaffolding dynamic that allows the child's own developing personal-world to find its own voice, in a manner that is productively creative rather than anomalous.

The scaffolding effects of learning to speak generate two central elements of language that proto-phenomenology has emphasized: (1) its communicative and dialogical dynamic that animates the social-world and releases language beyond any particular site of control; and (2) its hermeneutical pluralism that is made possible by differential fitness, which enacts interpretive powers of recursion, metaphorical extension, and contextual flexibility. Such capacities open up a child's world beyond early stages of sensorimotor confinement and thus launch the exponential complexity of human language that far exceeds animal forms of communication.[76]

6. TEMPORALITY AND HISTORY

This investigation has argued that "time" is originally experienced as meaning-laden spans of temporal experience, which precedes the derived exposition of objective measures in clock time: "Our vacation begins tomorrow" is different from "What time is our flight?" The same for "We had a great time" versus "We were away for a week." Or "It's time to go back to work" versus "I have a meeting at 9 AM." A child's experience of time is at first nothing but lived temporality, which precedes learning how to "tell time." The figure-eight structure of temporality, where past, present, and future coalesce in current anticipations and recollections, is not well formed in early stages of development, although habit formation—the capacity for future actions readied by past practice—is an implicit temporal structure of embodied behavior early in life.

This section will show how a child's emerging comprehension of temporality—in terms of articulated memories and anticipations—takes shape after learning language and incorporating narrative structures. Yet even before the advent of speech, the temporal language-world of caregivers is formative of a child's early development. From daily routines of care to parental hopes about a child's life to come, language is at work in the environment from the start in an indicative manner. Moreover, the particular histories of caregivers, informed by the larger spans of history in their culture, come to bear on prospects for a child's future.

6.1. Language and Memory

Human memory is essential for navigating a temporal world because it anchors the flow of time with accumulated registers of experience, thereby precluding discontinuous chaos. Types of memory include: *procedural* memory, which is not overt recollection but the kind of somatic memory that generates habit and know-how; *declarative* memory, which is the retention of information about the world in piecemeal or aggregate form (knowing-that); and *episodic* memory, which is the recollection of past experiences in terms of what, when, and where.[77] In between procedural, declarative, and episodic memory are *situational* memory (perceptual, motor, and behavioral habits involved in an extended circumstance, such as playing a game) and *inter-corporeal* memory (habits dealing with interactive, coordinated, and communicative involvement with others).[78] The richest form of all is *autobiographical* memory, the broad-based gathering of one's own history, experiences, and identity, along with relevant episodic memories and their meaning.[79] In child development, procedural, situational, and inter-corporeal memories take shape in provisional form early on from infancy; but they are significantly enhanced and furthered once language is acquired. Declarative, episodic, and autobiographical memory, however, are fully constituted by the power of language, which fosters memory by way of cueing, narrative shape, shorthand indications of complex experiences, and macro-comprehension that sidesteps piecemeal description.[80] Along with behavioral research on this matter, the central role of language in memory formation can be inferred from so-called infantile amnesia, where we lack memories of life roughly before the age of three. Autobiographical memory begins to take shape around four years of age and becomes more robust at age six to seven. The evident source of these developments is the growing role of language in those later years, where the articulation of meaningful experience and self-awareness provide the soil for registering attention, retention, and anticipation.[81]

6.2. Language and Time

From infancy to toddlerhood, a child's sense of time is implicit and non-reflective because it is largely confined to procedural memory and habituation, which is not a matter of recall but a capacity that settles in by repetition in the past and sets a course for future action.[82] With scripted activities that are repeated regularly, children come to anticipate sequences in feeding, bathing, and playing routines; and they often become insistent that a specific order must be followed. Such impulses are not a matter of stubborn fixation but an instinctive need for patterns that can organize time in a meaningful and manageable way. Temporal memory early on is neither self-conscious nor representational because it involves ecstatic immersion in meaningful practices performed in public settings. The initial development of habitual practices is a matter of implicit memory, which is not "brought to mind" as a prelude to behavior because it is experienced *in* the behavior and built *from* like behaviors.[83] Here memory is not self-recognized as the child's own mentality because it is simply the background capacity for externalized action. In time, with conversational exchanges and a comparison/contrast with the memories of others, children come to recognize their memories as their own, as indications of their own "minds."[84]

Beyond the implicit temporality of habit, know-how, and more immediate experiences of anticipation and recollection in early stages of development, a child's comprehension of time is significantly expanded and focused by word usage—but it must be stressed that such usage is not a matter of "concept" formation or the measuring of time "slices," but rather factical situations of interest along with the scaffolding effect of conversations with caregivers. A child's emerging sense of time expresses, and validates the precedence of, the phenomenological contours of lived temporality advanced in this investigation: imprecise spans and stretches of meaning-laden attention, anticipation, and recollection.[85] Children experience and learn rough intimations of past, present, and future with words like *now, later, soon, after, before, tomorrow,* and *yesterday*. In early stages, such words do not register with any kind of conceptual discernment; they point to moments of meaningful occasions that are either current, delayed, or no longer present. Depending on the existential significance of these moments, a child's response will involve excitement, disappointment, hope, frustration, satisfaction, and so on: *We can read the book now. You have to go to bed soon. Have you seen that before? Mommy will be back tomorrow. We will eat ice cream after lunch. Did you enjoy the party yesterday?*

Verb uses will generally express time dimensions that children come to grasp readily, beginning around two years of age. But comprehending verb tenses at this stage is confined to local and more immediate time frames and does not extend much into the past and future.[86] Nevertheless, early verb usage prepares the figure-eight looping structure of temporality. Language learning here cannot be adequately analyzed simply in lexical, psychological, or mental terms because temporal understanding is bonded to meaningful circumstances of embodied life in a social-environing-world—all prompted and furthered by the scaffolding effects of caregiver speech.[87] Temporal words like *before* and *after* also figure in a child's budding awareness of causal relations, indicated in words such as *because* and *so*.[88] That comprehension, however, is not yet a matter of conceptual or logical thinking but an implicit sense of physical or psychological causal relations intimated *in the use* of words while *participating* in practical activities. Research that tests childhood understanding of causality will not get the best results if divorced or abstracted from factical settings.

Children do not easily grasp formal constructions of time (in clocks and calendars) until well into their school years. But the temporality of autobiographical memory takes shape readily before schooling, although it is an extended process that builds gradually from conversational stimulation offered by caregivers or older siblings.[89] Talk about previous experiences in relation to current or coming occasions helps a child develop a sense of having a past, which evolves from a more immediate "experiencing I" to a "continuing me"—and thereby children come to understand themselves as temporal beings, as living in the midst of a past and a future. Conversational modes that nurture autobiographical memory and emerging selfhood are most effective when they take a narrative form.

6.3. Narrative

A narrative is an organized plot of meaningful experiences in factical life, having to do with existential possibilities, values, tasks, aims, and purposes. Narratives are concrete stories, with particular characters in specific situations moving through a course of engagement with a temporal format. Reception of such stories is primarily a matter of affective attunement and intimation rather than rational analysis or abstract conceptualization. A narrative, in sum, depicts episodes of the lived world.[90] A simple depiction of an experience can count as a narrative, as can an account of other people's experience. From such a base, the differential fitness of language then allows fictional stories, an imagined account of experience not based on actual events. A myth, as we will see in chapter 5, is a meaningful story with cultural significance that is handed down as a traditional mode of world-formation. Storytelling can be seen as an important part of human evolution because it allows an expansion of meaningful experience beyond immediate occasions, the re-creation of human engagement in a variety of world-scenarios, which thereby provides cognitive, psychological, social, normative, and practical extensions of interpretive understanding. The temporal shape, correlational scope, and virtuality of storytelling can also figure in more fact-based depictions of events.[91]

Children from early on are predisposed to understand and enact narratives, albeit in the midst of help from caregivers and siblings.[92] A narrative sense begins with practical play (as in dressing a doll or playing doctor), which presents various cultural settings that exercise factical tasks. In early years, proto-narratives begin to take shape in conversations, which foster cultural appropriation, shared meanings, an awareness of different perspectives, and a feel for temporal dimensions. These early conversations, however, are generally confined to immediate circumstances. Stories begin to expand a child's horizons, in hearing about and imagining different worlds, novel situations, and possibilities beyond direct experience. Exposure to stories is a decisive variable in a child's linguistic and cognitive growth. Narratives not only expand a child's world, they also concentrate and spur self-development, to whatever degree a child can identify with characters in stories.

The core force of narrative stories is the portrayal of living characters going through significant and interesting circumstances of existential import—their meaning, possibilities, and challenges. Here children encounter and absorb cultural values and exemplars, but not in a mere descriptive sense because stories of enactment usually have some drama in them, where contraventions spark interest and attention: overcoming obstacles or barriers (heroic tales); the risks and challenges in value enactment (telling the truth or standing up for a friend); conflicts between desires and norms (stories about perseverance or courage); diversion from ordinary life (adventure stories) or common expectations (stories about creativity or invention); conflicting values (stories about mixed allegiances) and even rebellion. The point is that many stories expose children not only to social and cultural meanings but also to their drama of enactment in the midst of finite limits. Traditional fairytales are particularly effective here, despite some contemporary objections to their intensity. Children seem to love the "safe danger" of scary stories, and one might appreciate their lessons in an uncertain and vulnerable world.[93]

Finally, it seems evident that children engage stories in the mode of ecstatic immersion, with absorbed fascination and delight. Narratives in this sense are phenomenologically not "fiction" because young children have animistic circuits that breathe real life into them. Part of their infatuation with stories is exhibited in the call to "Read it again!" Repetition might be a chore for parents but there is evidence that repeating stories is part of a child's habituation and processing dynamic, even with respect to brain development.[94] It is noteworthy that the way children experience stories is analogous to the manner in which oral cultures transmit their narratives, which differs significantly from techniques in literate cultures. Indeed, childhood experience and understanding in general are a function of orality, where face-to-face speech in immediate circumstances is the primary environment, which lacks the abstract distance, organizational capacity, and analytical powers made possible by written texts.[95] We will explore this question in chapter 5 with discussions of myth and poetry in the early Greek world.

6.4. History

The "natural environment" of young children is a *cultural* environment constituted by human practices, symbols, artifacts, media, and technologies, along with adults who interpret experience and behavior as meaning-laden forms of life.[96] The cultural inheritance of caregivers is transmitted to children in such a way that the figure-eight structure of temporality is infused with historical content. Caregivers bring their cultural and linguistic backgrounds to bear in child-rearing, and their own futures are now melded with the coming prospects of their offspring. Children are raised to lead lives that cultural norms and practices have prepared and set in motion. Such a process involves mature bestowals to immature recipients. The historical trajectory is more evident when we realize that each mature caregiver was once an immature recipient, and so on back in time. The effects of cultural history on the present are usually implicit and unexamined, but forward-looking moments in child-rearing have reverberating traces of complex historical legacies. One of the virtues of philosophy is expositional attention to these traces because cultural life has been inflected by intellectual traditions in many ways, such that even child-rearing carries that influence: with respect to beliefs about selfhood, knowledge, ethics, and other spheres of interpretation. Proto-phenomenology might stimulate revised attention to child development in productive ways if such influences can be duly questioned. In any case, even without the help of philosophy, forward-looking traces of cultural history will be modified by recipients in their individual responses to that bestowal.

Since language informs and animates this historical trajectory, the development of speech in children involves the same traces and effects through caregiver language and its inheritance of the past. Grammar, semantic meaning, word usage, communication, phonetics, and other formal categories in linguistics are expositional abstractions that conceal factical dwelling in speech and its temporal-historical dynamic. The effects of history show that language is at once a convergence and a divergence. The transmission of language keeps it alive over time and provides the young with established cultural bearings that allow them to bear the flux of experience and fit in with various spheres of shared understanding. Before formal schooling, cultural transmission is largely restricted to interactive exchanges of meaning between a child's own experiences and the immediate effects of parents, caregivers, other adults, and siblings. When schooling begins, children are exposed to wider and deeper cultural influences from historical, institutional, and disciplinary domains. The trick in education at this level is finding ways to link a child's own meaning systems with these domains beyond the child's first-hand experience.[97] The inheritance of language and culture is not a matter of pure passive projection uninflected by the personal-world of students. The future of pedagogical transmission will usually bear contravention and revision as the young grow into their own worlds. That is why language and culture are not fixed in essentialist terms, either in form or content. Cultural language cannot be adequately understood apart from its historical past *and* future. Even with respect to the current formal and verbal character of a language, conservative hopes for stability have to face, for instance, the radical difference between Old English and modern English; also the continual alterations that arise in any generation of speakers. From a global standpoint, there can be no permanent structure or standard. Yet no local time period can do without some degree of linguistic standards, given that language is a communicative social-world. The point is that the convergence in standardization itself shifts over time. And as adults know well, new generations will typically challenge the boundaries of established speech. Teaching language to children is a retention of past usage, not as mere duplication but relaunching the norms of language inflected by new possibilities for future usage.

7. DIFFERENTIAL FITNESS, DEVELOPMENT, AND TRUTH

Language in this investigation has been understood as differential fitness, where fitness indicates the immersed co-responsiveness of speech and factical life, and differentiation highlights the semiotic distinction between words and the world, which makes possible (1) the dynamic of recursive relations within linguistic permutations (conjunction, negation, comparison, contrast, analogy, etc.), and (2) the expansion of disclosure beyond present immediacy and first-hand experience, which is driven by the sustainable virtual fitness of words. The differential aspect also issues the question of truth, namely the possibility of language either fitting or not fitting phenomena—and here arise the positive and deficient connotations of "appearance" with respect to language, because what is said can bring something to appear otherwise than its actual manifestation. All these elements of language and disclosure have their debut in a child's early acquisition of speech.

7.1. Immersion, Contravention, and Exposition

The structural dynamic of immersion, contravention, and disclosive exposition is a core focus of proto-phenomenology, and language is the most explicit and extensive form of exposition. What do I mean by explicit and extensive? Volume I (99–100) suggested that human intelligence should be understood as bio-intelligence—as the function of an animate organism with needs, desires, and vulnerabilities—in order to challenge reductive naturalism and mechanical models of behavior. Accordingly, nonhuman animals are not excluded from the domain of intelligence, particularly with respect to immersed know-how and felt perceptions of weal and woe. We have also seen how pre-linguistic human infants exhibit comparable levels of intelligence, while also displaying the unique human capacity for joint attention, which is a precondition for language acquisition. Language then opens up the world-disclosive possibilities charted by proto-phenomenology. The expositional displays of animals and pre-linguistic infants seem to be immersed modes of perceptual and behavioral responses to contravention: as in an infant's extended looking time or distressed reaction to, say, a medical examination; or an animal's response to, and attempts to escape, conditions of confinement. Such responses are implicitly meaning-laden in being felt registers of interest or disturbance; yet they remain immersed in, and limited to, immediate circumstances. Language and language-inflected experience allow exposition to be *explicative* of meaning and (by way of differential fitness) *extended* into temporal dimensions and non-immediate circumstances. Language is an openness, not to a different world, but the same world inhabited by animals and infants, much of which is simply *concealed* to them in their immersed immediacy. That is why adult humans can comprehend the meaning of an infant's or an animal's circumstance and respond accordingly—by comforting an infant while allowing the intrusion of a medical examination, or by finding a way to release an animal from confinement.

7.2. Development and Contravention

The development of children from pre-linguistic periods to various stages of language-infused disclosure is itself animated by the immersion-contravention-exposition dynamic: particularly in the emergence of individuation by way of separation anxiety, the process of learning by trial and error, the reciprocal and productive tension between individual interests and socialization, and generally the energetic stress between new possibilities and familiar settings. What must be emphasized in this dynamic process is its *dialectical* continuity, which can be articulated as follows: new stages of development retain previous stages in the manner of nested assimilation,[98] and such movements are driven by the differential fitness of language because the fitness of an earlier state is retained to some degree in a differentiated alteration, which then itself achieves a settled fitness that is likewise alterable by contravening factors, and so on. In other words, immersed fitness is not something to be overcome in human development, as though the true self were some kind of primal freedom or release from a constraining habitat. Rather, immersed fitness in a social-environing-world is an original condition that is continually modified, extended, and expanded by contravening occasions that launch new possibilities of fitness. Globally considered, this span of development cannot be reduced to any particular fitness condition, even though certain basic needs of children must be met for any viable life story to proceed. The openness of possibility is sustained as long as viable living is sustained. Yet this openness is ever enmeshed in periodic accomplishments of possibilities that keep a life from running off the rails. Thus, the course of human existence is a criss-crossing dynamic of immersion, contravention, and exposition, which is animated by the differentiated fitness of language.

A crucial element in a child's linguistic development is entry into the symbolic function of language. The notion of a "symbol" can be problematic, especially because representational models tend to be commonly deployed, but we can sketch the way in which differentiated fitness illuminates in a phenomenological manner the classic (Peircean) semiotic distinction between icon, index, and symbol.[99] An icon is a sign that is like its object, such as a painted portrait of a person. An index is a sign that simply points to instantiations, such as "this" in "this portrait." A symbol is a more complex interpretive sign, not directly of some entity in the world, but rather a nexus of linguistic indications that make up a certain concept, such as "person." A symbol is a more abstract, meaning-laden expression of culturally informed inter-lexical constructions, which often have a narrative feel. When children learn symbolic words, they move from more direct references, such as descriptive words for things or events (*the dog is running*) to recursive relations within and between words that expand understanding to networks of meaning gathered in a particular word or phrase. Consider the word "behave," which means to constrain behavior by obeying a norm given by parents—which implies a range of temporal and situational correlations. The differential force of symbols is evident in such extensions, but the meaning of a symbol would not register in a child without certain fitness features that figure in learning the term—in actual occasions of behavior and speech in which the word is used: *Don't do that! Remember what I said? Please behave!* Without the actual or virtual fitness of words at some level, the development of more complex disclosive language would not get off the ground. And when a symbolic word settles into a child's comprehension, it takes on its own fitness in being charged with immediate disclosive force.[100]

In summation, the immersion-contravention-exposition dynamic animated by the differential fitness of language offers a more responsive perspective on the reach and richness of language acquisition, more so than theories that emphasize naming, object designation, representation, and isolated or discrete modes of cognition.

7.3. Truth

My analysis has portrayed truth as originally a matter of presentational fitness and dispositional trust, whereupon contravention opens up (1) the explicit *question* of truth and falsity as a problem or a pending task of resolution, and (2) the derivational aptness of representational correspondence. The immersed character of early language acquisition and the social scaffolding required for word learning show that presentational immediacy and interpersonal trust are more prominent in a child's speech-world. Young children are predisposed to trust an adult speaker's testimony, even when it differs from their own observation. Between the ages of six and eleven, children gain skeptical vigilance about the possibility of error or deception in testimony, with competence and benevolence being the keys to earning trust.[101] The developmental predisposition of trust shows that (1) the modest realism and objectivity advanced by proto-phenomenology are the default condition for learning language; and (2) falsehood, in the sense of error or deception, is a derivative contravention of presentational trust. The background function of trust can be called "incorrigible" in the sense of being ineliminable for the factical beginnings of language acquisition.

A child's exposure to the true-false dynamic can be traced to the many ways in which *yes* and *no* operate as speech acts—even before infants begin to talk because caregivers will use these words regularly in the midst of a child's behavior. *Yes* and *no* at that point begin as vocal intonations and bodily interventions rather than semantic meaning. In any case, verbal affirmation and negation are together the primal indication of differential fitness, of possible divergence from settled description, which sets the stage for all future delineations of true and false speech.[102]

Negation is a universal feature of human language and it launches a slew of disclosive possibilities beyond immediate experience.[103] *No* and *not* are among the first words learned by children and they allow many meaningful utterances pertaining to presence and absence, acceptance and rejection. Types of negation uttered by children include refusal (*no go to bed*), nonexistence (*no more milk*), truth denial (*that not a cat*), failure or inability (*not find doll*), and epistemic negation (*I dunno*). Processing negative sentences takes longer for both adults and children, but typical research on childhood competence will test statements that are unusual or without context. If children are presented with negative statements in more familiar settings or supportive practical scenarios, their processing ability improves. Once again, the personal-social-environing-world, together with social/practical affordances and scaffolding, should be the preferred framework for examining early understanding of speech, not isolated verbal comprehension supposedly housed in a child's "mind."

The differential dynamic of distinguishing truth and non-truth, namely fitting and mis-fitting discourse in various factual settings, guides a child's disclosive capacities for engaging the world. Early instances of speech are based more on individual word and phrase usage; but in time, syntactical and grammatical enrichment will enhance world-revealing powers.[104] Such early language usage is consonant with inhabitive truth conditions sketched in chapter 1; it also displays pluralistic and enactive interpretation in readily shifting between descriptive, normative, behavioral, and practical contexts of speech.

Differential fitness pertains not only to conditions in the social-environing-world but also the personal-world and the possibility of deliberate concealment of beliefs or attitudes by way of denial or counter-claims. Here the question of truth is a matter of honesty and sincerity versus deception and lying. Lying is a universal mode of human speech and it involves a complex psycho-social dynamic. Lying is not simply saying something false because a mistake is not a lie. With lying, one is deliberately saying something false while knowing it to be false, thereby coupled with awareness of the truth (either the actual conditions or the mere fact of making something up). The motivations for lying are multi-faceted but generally in the service of some advantage in life or the avoidance of some disadvantage. Finally, in telling a lie one wants the recipient to believe it, typically banking on the plausible prospects for that reception. In other words, lying is the simultaneous violation of, and reliance on, the default trust in truth that marks the factual world of speech.

Children naturally develop the capacity to lie, but the process involved is complex and ambiguous with respect to ethical implications. We have seen that fictional play and pretending are an essential ingredient in a child's cognitive growth, as an expansion of meaning-laden scenarios beyond immediate circumstances, which is further gathered and extended by storytelling.[105] We have also noted that in early stages of life, children do not operate with clear delineations between the "real" and the "fictional" because affective attunement and immersion are predominant as an ecstatic absorption that sees the world *as* inflected by the needs and interests driving a child's experience. Accordingly, a young child's self-regard is such that "false" personal narratives or replies to interrogation are more wish-fulfilling world-constructions than "lies." So, a child's flexibility with the truth is not precisely deceit because the veridical and psychological contours of lying have not yet been shaped or sorted out.[106] Here, children in a sense are magically manipulating the world through the lens of their wishes, rather than lying in the strict sense. Early fabrications are not mis-representations but presentational powers to make something manifest that fits a child's bearings. Lying at this stage is not a moral failing because maturation will set out the veridical, psychological, and normative elements that constitute the conditions of truth-telling and deception.[107]

Another angle on the non-moral or pre-moral character of early lying episodes can be gleaned from some of the research in child development.[108] *Primary lying* emerges around age two to three, where children deliberately make false statements, without considering the mental states of listeners; *secondary lying* emerges around age four, where children intimate that listeners do not know the true state of affairs and are thus susceptible to false beliefs; *tertiary lying* emerges around age seven to eight, where children can conceal their deceit by aiming for consistency between the lie and follow-up statements. With primary lying, controlled experiments involving temptation and resistance reveal the following results, focusing on an experiment with sixty-five children, ages two to three years of age, where they were asked not to peek at a toy after the experimenter left the room.[109] Of the sixty-five, fifty-two peeked at the toy. Of the two-year-old peekers, only a quarter of them lied about it, while a majority of three-year-olds lied, increasing in frequency with the months of age. Supplemental testing showed that the younger children were more honest not because they were more ethically inclined to tell the truth but because of less-well-developed cognitive skills that figure in telling a lie: executive functioning, inhibitory control, and working memory. For each point of increase in cognitive function score, children were five times more likely to lie. So, younger children may simply have been less able to lie due to weaker cognitive skills. In any case, as we have seen, early instances of lying should not be interpreted in moral terms but in developmental terms as fitting the condition of ecstatic animism. Moreover, the emerging capacity to lie is concurrent with the growth of valuable cognitive skills. Childhood fabrication, therefore, is actually a mixed blessing. Although lying is socially and practically problematic, it is also developmentally salient and auspicious.

8. SUMMARY

This chapter has aimed to supplement a proto-phenomenological analysis of language with a comparable treatment of language acquisition, of how children come to talk and launch the world-disclosive adventure of dwelling in speech. The emergence of language in children presupposes modes of dwelling and requires the following elements for normal competence and growth: (1) a child's native potential for learning language grounded in joint attention, together with a natural interest in communicative practices; (2) a social environment of caregivers who use child-directed speech from the start of life and embrace the ongoing task of guiding language use; (3) children and caregivers immersed in embodied, enactive, and meaning-laden behaviors that gather and prompt the development of speech; and (4) the differential fitness of language that activates the temporal/historical structure of speech—which orchestrates the correlational scope and mixture of presence and absence that allow extended articulation of the lived world.

After early periods of language acquisition, children learn to read and write. This next stage is not simply a continuation of linguistic comprehension in a new medium because literacy provides and enables disclosive powers that are absent or minimized in a strictly oral environment. Literacy gives birth to the cognitive domains that have marked philosophy and other academic disciplines in their disclosive projects. Orality as such is more indicative of the lived world, which precedes and makes possible written language. The derivative status of literacy thereby underscores the proto-phenomenological interrogation of traditional assumptions about the nature of language. The history and effects of literacy in relation to speech will add a telling perspective to the philosophical task of this investigation. Although literacy issues an enormous expansion of disclosive possibilities, it also enables a concealment of the original oral constitution of language.

NOTES

1. A child can be raised in more than one language, but the emphasis here is on monolingual environments.

2. Early occasions of naming things also fit common-sense beliefs in referring to perceptible "wholes" before parts or attributes—thus undermining Quine's famous reference paradox of "gavagai" being indeterminate between "rabbit," rabbit parts, or rabbit actions. Whole noun references are the norm in early language usage. See Nelson, *Young Minds in Social Worlds*, 126–128.

3. The empirical contribution of language acquisition research is noted by Michael Tomasello, *Constructing a Language: A Usage-Based Theory of Language Acquisition* (Cambridge, MA: Harvard University Press, 2003), 328.

4. I draw from Vyvyan Evans, *The Language Myth: Why Language Is Not an Instinct* (Cambridge: Cambridge University Press, 2014), Chap. 4. See also Jill Boucher, "The Prerequisites for Language Acquisition," *Language and Thought*, eds. Peter Carruthers and Jill Boucher (Cambridge: Cambridge University Press, 1998), 55–75.

5. At this early stage, the personal-world is not articulated as it is in mature experience, but it can indicate what each child brings to enculturation, which always has some effect on how such influences transpire and shows upbringing to be anything but robotic duplication.

6. See Clark, *First Language Acquisition*, 8–9, 17–20. In linguistic research, Chomsky's model of innate universal grammar is yielding to a more ecological/practical/oral orientation. See Paul Ibbotson and Michael Tomasello, "Evidence Rebuts Chomsky's Theory of Language Learning," *Scientific American* 315, no. 5 (November 2016).

7. For a discussion of sensorimotor capacities that infants share with animals, that precede but become qualitatively transformed with language acquisition, see Volume I, 152–157. John McDowell has a point when he calls pre-linguistic infants "mere animals" before language gains them entry into the "world," into the "space of reasons." See *Mind and World* (Cambridge, MA: Harvard University Press, 1994), 9–10. Language provides a second nature beyond the first nature of animality. Yet "mere animality" hides the apparently unique preparatory forces like joint attention that render even first nature in this respect distinctively human.

8. See Adriana S. Benzaquén, *Encounters with Wild Children: Temptation and Disappointment in the Study of Human Nature* (Montreal: McGill-Queen's University Press, 2006).

9. See Nancy Yousef, "Savage or Solitary: The Wild Child and Rousseau's Man of Nature," *Journal of the History of Ideas* 62/2 (April 2001): 245–263.

10. Bruner, *Child's Talk*, 27.

11. See Chris Moore and Philip Dunham, eds., *Joint Attention: Its Origins and Role in Development* (New York: Psychology Press, 1995), Daniel N. Stern, *The Interpersonal World of the Infant* (New York: Basic Books, 1985), and Jerome Bruner, *Acts of Meaning* (Cambridge, MA: Harvard University Press, 1990). Also Daniel O. Dahlstrom, "Towards an Explanation of Language," *Proceedings of the American Catholic Philosophical Association* 84 (2011): especially 38–41.

12. Nelson, *Young Minds in Social Worlds*, 96–97.

13. Núria Esteve-Gilbert and Pilar Prieto, "Infants Temporally Coordinate Gesture-Speech Combinations before They Produce Their First Words," *Speech Communication* 57 (2014): 301–316.

14. Nelson, *Young Minds in Social Worlds*, 102–103.

15. Ghislaine Dehaene-Lambertz et al., "Nature and Nurture in Language Acquisition: Anatomical and Functional Brain-Imaging in Infants," *Trends in Neurosciences* 29, no. 7 (July 2006): 367–373.

16. See Athena Vouloumanos and Suzanne Curtin, "Foundational Tuning: How Infants' Attention to Speech Predicts Language Development," *Cognitive Science* 38, no. 8 (2014): 1675–1686; Betty Hart and Todd R. Risley, *Meaningful Differences in the Everyday Experience of Young American Children* (Baltimore, MD: Brookes Publishing Co., 1995); and Zhen Wu and Julie Gros-Louis, "Infants' Prelinguistic Communicative Acts and Maternal Responses: Relations to Linguistic Development," *First Language* 34, no. 1 (2014): 72–90.

17. Clark, *First Language Acquisition*, 16.

18. Nelson, *Young Minds in Social Worlds*, 157–163.

19. The same conditions apply to learning a second language, particularly at a young age in school. The so-called immersion technique is more successful than more formal learning of usage. Immersion has children engaging a new language in meaningful social and practical contexts that are naturally interesting and important to them. See Fred Genesee, *Learning through Two Languages: Studies in Immersion and Bilingual Education* (Belmont, CA: Wadsworth, 1987).

20. See Arthur M. Genberg and Vittorio Gallese, "Action-Based Language: A Theory of Language Acquisition, Comprehension, and Production," *Cortex* 48 (2012): 905–922, which gathers evidence from behavioral studies and the neurophysiological effects of mirror neurons.

21. Pär Segerdahl, "Humanizing Nonhumans: Ape Language Research as Critique of Metaphysics," in *Language, Ethics and Animal Life: Wittgenstein and Beyond*, eds. Niklas Forsberg et al. (New York: Bloomsbury, 2012), Chap. 1.

22. In much of what follows, I draw from Nelson, *Young Minds in Social Worlds*, 148, 230–237, 255–260.

23. Ibid., 218–221.

24. See Avner Baz, "On Going (and Getting) Nowhere with Our Words: New Skepticism about the Philosophical Method of Cases," *Philosophical Psychology* 29, no. 1 (January 2016): 64–83, on which I rely in some of what follows. I also draw from Nelson, *Young Minds in Social Worlds*, 159–161. See also Frederick E. Mosedale, "Meditations on the Origin of Philosophy," *Philosophical Investigations* 40, no. 4 (October 2017): 370–395. Both articles do well in using childhood language acquisition to challenge common philosophical assumptions about knowledge. See also Paul L. Harris et al., "'I Don't Know': Children's Early Talk about Knowledge," *Mind and Language* 32, no. 3 (June 2017): 283–307.

25. For example, see Karen Bartsch and Henry M. Wellman, *Children Talk about the Mind* (Oxford University Press, 1995).

26. Tomasello, *Constructing a Language*, 106ff.

27. See Alexander R. Luria, *The Role of Speech in the Regulation of Normal and Abnormal Behavior* (New York: Liveright Publishing Co., 1961).

28. See Nelson, *Young Minds in Social Worlds*, 130–144.

29. See Clark, *First Language Acquisition*, 6–8, 12–14.

30. Much in this discussion relies on Jerome Bruner, *Child's Talk*. Although the book is saddled with expositional and representational biases, the experimental research and pragmatic orientation fit well with the aims of my investigation. See also Claire Kramsch, ed., *Language Acquisition and Language Socialization: Ecological*

Perspectives (New York: Continuum, 2002) and Talbot J. Taylor, "Calibrating the Child for Language: Meredith Williams on a Wittgensteinian Approach to Language Socialization," *Language Sciences* 40 (November 2013): 308–320.

31. Bruner, *Child's Talk*, 18, 31–39.

32. Ibid., 18, 39–42.

33. Ibid., 26–31.

34. Aristotle claimed that words (*onomata*) are imitations (*mimēmata*) and voice (*phōnē*) is the most mimetic of all human abilities (*Rhetoric* 1404a8).

35. Bruner, *Child's Talk*, 45–55.

36. Ibid., 60–61.

37. Ibid., 70–88.

38. It is well attested in the research that the quality of a child's linguistic development is keyed directly to the quality and extent of verbal conversation in early years. Disadvantaged environments have a significant effect on later cognitive competence. See Betty Hart and Todd R. Risely, "The Early Catastrophe: The 30 Million Word Gap by Age 3," *American Educator* 27, no. 1 (Spring 2003): 4–9.

39. Nelson, *Young Minds in Social Worlds*, 128–129.

40. Bruner, *Child's Talk*, Chap. 5.

41. Ibid., 114–122.

42. See also Helen Keller, *The Story of My Life* (New York: Bantam 1998), Chaps. 5–7, especially page 52.

43. Adam Winsler et al., "The Role of Private Speech in the Transition from Collaborative to Independent Task Performance in Young Children," *Early Childhood Research Quarterly* 12 (1997): 61. See also Charles Fernyhough, "Getting Vygotskian about Theory of Mind: Mediation, Dialogue, and the Development of Social Understanding," *Developmental Review* 28, no. 2 (June 2008): 225–262, and Natalie Bulle, "Slow and Fast Thinking, Historical-Cultural Psychology and Major Trends of Modern Epistemology: Unveiling a Fundamental Convergence," *Mind and Society* 13, no. 1 (June 2014): 149–166.

44. Alain Morin, "Possible Links between Self-Awareness and Inner Speech," *Journal of Consciousness Studies* 12, no. 4–5 (2005): 115–134, on which I rely in some of what follows. Parts of this discussion appeared in my "Dasein, the Early Years," 385–386.

45. Winsler et al., "The Role of Private Speech in the Transition from Collaborative to Independent Task Performance in Young Children," 57–79, on which I also rely in this discussion.

46. So private speech is not the solipsistic "private language" critiqued by Wittgenstein. In fact, this discussion confirms his argument.

47. Ibid., 8ff.

48. See Stephen Langfur, "Cogitor Ergo Sum: The Origin of Self-Awareness in Dyadic Interaction," *Human Studies* (December 2018): 1–26. DOI: 10.1007/s10746-018-09487-y.

49. It is noteworthy that both Plato and Aristotle seemed to understand thought as internalized speech. See *Sophist* 263b, *Philebus* 38c–39a, *Phaedrus* 276a, *On Interpretation* 16b9–18, *De Anima* 427b11–14, *Nicomachean Ethics* 1139b15 and

1142b13–14. For the role of inner speech in thinking, see Ray Jackendoff, "How Language Helps Us Think," *Pragmatics and Cognition* 4, no. 1 (1996): 1–34.

50. Julie Kirkham et al., "Concurrent and Longitudinal Relationships between Development in Graphic Language and Symbolic Play Domains from the Fourth to the Fifth Year," *Infant and Child Development* 22, no. 3 (June 2013): 297–319.

51. See Winsler et al., "The Role of Private Speech in the Transition from Collaborative to Independent Task Performance in Young Children," 65ff. for examples from research. For the scaffolding power of language, see Andy Clark, "Magic Words: How Language Augments Human Computation," in *Language and Thought*, eds. Peter Carruthers and Jill Boucher (Cambridge: Cambridge University Press, 1998), 162–183, and Ray S. Jackendoff, *The Architecture of the Language Faculty* (Cambridge, MA: MIT Press, 1996).

52. See Harry Daniels, "Mediation: An Expansion of the Socio-Cultural Gaze," *History of the Human Sciences* 28, no. 2 (2015): 34–50.

53. See Vladimir P. Zinchenko, "Should the 'Postulate of Directness' Be Overcome?" *History of the Human Sciences* 28, no. 2 (2015): 51–71.

54. *The Story of My Life*, 22–24.

55. Here I rely on Drew Leder, *The Absent Body* (The University of Chicago Press, 1990), 122–125.

56. It should be noted that the word *conscious* had an early meaning of sharing knowledge with another person (see the *OED*), hence the phrase "conscious to. . . ." The same sense could apply to inner awareness as witnessing one's own thoughts, as in the phrase "conscious to oneself" (thus borrowed from the social structure of consciousness). The word *conscious* is derived from the Latin *conscientia*, meaning "knowing together," which could refer to shared knowledge, or to the joining together of different thoughts in the mind, or to self-awareness. Such meanings of *conscientia* in fact were all deployed by Descartes. See Boris Henning, "Cartesian *Conscientia*," *British Journal for the History of Philosophy* 15, no. 3 (August 2007): 455–485. The point is that a phenomenology of "consciousness" should avoid reification, either in the physicalistic requirement of physiological causes or the dualistic sense of "something" nonphysical. The historical plasticity of the word "conscious" suggests that contextual interpretation of usage can be disclosive enough without metaphysical commitments.

57. See Malinda Carpenter, Katherine Nagell, and Michael Tomasello, "Social Cognition, Joint Attention, and Communicative Competence from 9 to 15 Months of Age," *Monographs of the Society for Research in Child Development* 63, no. 4 (December 1998): 1–133, on which I rely in some of what follows. More generally, I draw from Michael Tomasello, *Origins of Human Communication* (Cambridge, MA: MIT Press, 2008), Chaps. 3–4. See also Cristina Colonessi et al., "The Relation between Pointing and Language Development: A Meta-Analysis," *Developmental Review* 30, no. 4 (December 2010): 352–366. Also Chad Engelland, *Ostension: Word Learning and the Embodied Mind* (Cambridge, MA: MIT Press, 2014), particularly Chaps. 1–2. Engelland discusses how Davidson and Searle recognize triangularity in language development, but they are unnecessarily wedded to internal intentional states as a baseline framework (4–11).

58. See Robert Storey, *Mimesis and the Human Animal: On the Biogenetic Foundations of Literary Representation* (Evanston, IL: Northwestern University Press, 1996), 74–80.

59. Michael Tomasello, "The Key Is Social Cognition," in *Language in Mind: Advances in the Study of Language and Thought*, eds. Dedre Gentner and Susan Goldin-Meadow (Cambridge, MA: MIT Press, 2003), 47–57.

60. Michael Tomasello, *The Cultural Origins of Human Communication* (Cambridge, MA: Harvard University Press, 1999), 105. For Merleau-Ponty on triangularity, reciprocity, and reversibility in bodily perception and speech, see "The Child's Relations with Others," and *The Visible and the Invisible*, ed. Claude Lefort, trans. Alphonso Lingis (Evanston, IL: Northwestern University Press, 1968). For a helpful discussion of Merleau-Ponty on this and other matters, see Engelland, *Ostension*, Chap. 4.

61. Nelson, *Young Minds in Social Worlds*, 102–103.

62. See Elizabeth S. Spelke, "What Makes Us Smart? Core Knowledge and Natural Language," in *Language in Mind*, 277–311.

63. Boelen, *Personal Maturity*, 42–46.

64. See Clark, *First Language Acquisition*, 45–50.

65. See Eve V. Clark, "Pragmatics in Acquisition," *Journal of Child Language* 41, Supplement 1 (July 2014): 105–116; also Nelson, *Young Minds in Social Worlds*, 122–25.

66. See Andy Clark, "Magic Words."

67. For the classic account of how metaphors function in human understanding, see George Lakoff and Mark Johnson, *Metaphors We Live By* (Chicago: University of Chicago Press, 2003).

68. See Georg Theiner and Chris Drain, "What's the *Matter* with Cognition? A 'Vygotskian' Perspective on Material Engagement Theory," *Phenomenology and Cognitive Sciences* 16, no. 5 (December 2017): 837–862.

69. See Anthony Chemero, *Radical Embodied Cognitive Science* (Cambridge, MA: MIT Press, 2009). I regret mis-stating the author's name in Volume I.

70. See Engelland, *Ostension*, 25. Engelland's overall study is an important contribution, especially in concentrating on the "animate body," drawing from both Aristotle and Merleau-Ponty.

71. See David McNeill, *Gesture and Thought* (Chicago: University of Chicago Press, 2005), Chaps. 1–2, and Herbert H. Clark, *Using Language* (Cambridge: Cambridge University Press, 1996), Chap. 6.

72. Tomasello, *Origins of Human Communication*, 229.

73. Clark, *First Language Acquisition*, 102–104.

74. Stephen C. Levinson, "Language and Mind: Let's Get the Issues Straight," in *Language in Mind*, Chap. 2.

75. In linguistics, this has been called "the poverty of the stimulus."

76. Tomasello, "The Key Is Social Cognition," 51–55.

77. See Stanley B. Klein and Shaun Nichols, "Memory and the Sense of Personal Identity," *Mind* 121, no. 483 (July 2012): 677–702.

78. See Sabine Koch et al., eds. *Body Memory, Metaphor, and Movement* (Amsterdam: John Benjamins, 2012), Chap. 1. See also Edward S. Casey, *Remembering: A Phenomenological Study* (Indianapolis, IN: Indiana University Press, 2009).

79. See Nelson, *Young Minds in Social Worlds*, 184–187.

80. See Andy Clark, "Magic Words: How Language Augments Human Computation," in *Language and Thought*, eds. Peter Carruthers and Jill Boucher (Cambridge: Cambridge University Press, 1998), 162–183; also, Stephen C. Levinson, "Language and Mind: Let's Get the Issues Straight!" and Daniel I. Slobin, "Language and Thought Online: Cognitive Consequences of Linguistic Relativity," in *Language in Mind*, eds. Susan Goldin-Meadow and Dedre Gentner (Cambridge, MA: MIT Press, 2003), 25–46 and 157–191, respectively. Also, Alan Baddeley, "Working Memory and Language: An Overview," *Journal of Communication Disorders* 36 (2003): 189–208, and Jarrad A. G. Lum et al., "Procedural and Declarative Memory in Children with and without Specific Language Impairment," *International Journal of Language and Communication Disorders* 45, no. 1 (2010): 96–107. Also, Janette B. Benson and Marshall H. Haith, eds., *Language, Memory, and Cognition in Infancy and Early Childhood* (New York: Academic Press, 2009), and Erica Consentino, "Self in Time and Language," *Consciousness and Cognition* 20, no. 3 (2011): 777–783.

81. See Katherine Nelson, "Emergence of Autobiographical Memory at Age 4," *Human Development* 35, no. 3 (1992): 172–177. See also Madeline J. Eacott, "Memory for the Events of Early Childhood," *Current Directions in Psychological Science* 8, no. 2 (April 1999): 46–49.

82. Nelson, *Young Minds in Social Worlds*, 89–92.

83. Ibid., 261–262.

84. Ibid., 261–264.

85. See Simms, *The Child in the World*, Chap. 6.

86. Nelson, *Young Minds in Social Worlds*, 189–190.

87. This analysis of temporality and language can be extended to spatial understanding too, as long as space is taken in existential terms pertaining to meaningful places and somatic practices: kitchen, bedroom, backyard, street, doorway, inside, outside, under, over, up, down, and so on. See Simms, *The Child in the World*, Chap. 2.

88. Nelson, *Young Minds in Social Worlds*, 154–155.

89. Ibid., 188–197.

90. For a definitive philosophical treatment of narrative, see Paul Ricoeur, *Time and Narrative*, 3 volumes, trans. Kathleen Blamey and David Pellauer (Chicago: University of Chicago Press, 1984, 1985, 1988).

91. See Brian Boyd, "The Evolution of Stories: From Mimesis to Language, from Fact to Fiction," *Wiley Inter-Disciplinary Reviews: Cognitive Science* 9, no. 1 (January/February 2018): 1–16.

92. In what follows I rely on Nelson, *Young Minds in Social Worlds*, 169–177 and Storey, *Mimesis and the Human Animal*, 80–91.

93. See Boelen, *Personal Maturity*, 39–40 and Marek Tesar et al., "Forever Young: Childhoods, Fairy Tales and Philosophy," *Global Studies of Childhood* 6, no. 2 (2016): 222–233.

94. See Jessica S. Horst et al., "Get the Story Straight: Contextual Repetition Promotes Word Learning from Storybooks," *Frontiers in Psychology* 2, no. 17 (February 2011): 1–11. See also Clark, "Magic Words: How Language Augments Human Computation"; Levinson, "Language and Mind: Let's Get the Issues Straight!"; Slobin, "Language and Thought Online: Cognitive Consequences of Linguistic

Relativity"; Alan Baddeley, "Working Memory and Language: An Overview," *Journal of Communication Disorders* 36 (2003): 189–208; Lum et al., "Procedural and Declarative Memory in Children with and without Specific Language Impairment," 96–107; Janette B. Benson and Marshall H. Haith, eds., *Language, Memory, and Cognition in Infancy and Early Childhood* (New York: Academic Press, 2009), and Erica Consentino, "Self in Time and Language," *Consciousness and Cognition* 20, no. 3 (2011): 777–783.

95. Nelson, *Young Minds in Social Worlds*, 223–225.
96. Ibid., 66, 252–254.
97. Ibid., 264–267.
98. Ibid., 244–249.
99. Ibid., 144–147, 150–153, 163–164.
100. The Greek word *sumbolon* has an interesting history. It derives from meanings having to do with joining together and coming to an agreement. A *sumbolon* was a token (e.g., a pottery shard) broken in half so that two parties could identify their association at a future time. The fact that the two parts are originally a seamless whole can speak against overly disjointed notions of symbolic language. Given a child's immersed condition in meaning formation, we could say that reflective analysis of a word like "behave" tends to "break apart" a meaning that originally is an embedded association that has direct disclosive effects.
101. See Elizabeth J. Robinson and Shiri Einav, eds., *Trust and Skepticism: Children's Selective Learning from Testimony* (New York: Psychology Press, 2014).
102. Aristotle defined truth in terms of affirmation and negation (*On Interpretation* 17a25), not simply as a logical function but mainly pertaining to speech, to *saying* that what is is and that what is not is not (*Metaphysics* 1011b25).
103. In what follows I rely on Ann E. Nordmeyer and Michael Frank, "The Role of Context in Young Children's Comprehension of Negation," *Journal of Memory and Language* 77 (November 2014): 26–39.
104. See Derek Bickerton, *Language and Species* (Chicago, IL: University of Chicago Press, 1990), 105–129.
105. From a cognitive perspective, see Deena S. Weisberg and Alison Gopnik, "Pretense, Counterfactuals, and Bayesian Causal Models: Why What Is Not Real Really Matters," *Cognitive Science* 37, no. 7 (August, 2013): 1368–1381.
106. Boelen, *Personal Maturity*, 41.
107. Donald Trump's psychopathic speed-lying is more indicative of a child's mentality than an adult's. How millions of Americans came to buy his run for the presidency is something I will never be able to understand.
108. Here I draw from Angela D. Evans and Kang Lee, "Emergence of Lying in Very Young Children," *Developmental Psychology* 49, no. 10 (2013): 1958–1963.
109. It is revealing that the authors note (on page 1958) that controls are needed to improve upon naturalistic observation of how children behave in normal, more comfortable contexts.

Chapter 4

Orality and Literacy

Volume I of this investigation offered a proto-phenomenological account of the lived world, the tacit existential background of dwelling in factical life that standard philosophical and scientific theories have missed, suppressed, or distorted. The most important background element is language, understood as dwelling in speech. Volume II in effect examines the background of this tacit background by way of three developmental and historical factors: child development, language acquisition, and literacy. The advent of language in childhood embodies in a primal manner the proposed features of the lived world, and its generative role clarifies and fortifies the phenomenological priority of factical speech. The face-to-face character of language learning is essentially an oral phenomenon. After children learn how to talk, they then learn how to read and write. Literacy then launches a momentous transformation of language and its world-disclosive powers.

Although child development has been explored in some philosophical work, the differences between spoken and written language have not received much attention. The academic study of literacy and its transformative effects on oral language began with the work of scholars in fields outside of philosophy: Marshall McLuhan (media and communication studies), Jack Goody (cultural anthropology), Walter Ong (literature), and Eric Havelock (classics).[1] Havelock's work specifically treated issues of orality and literacy in the beginnings of Greek philosophy. I maintain that the surest way to grasp how philosophy has concealed or bypassed the lived world is to recognize that philosophy is primarily a literate endeavor, that it relies on reading and writing skills, and that its typical assumptions and methods are saturated with a literate inflection, an orientation toward language modified by the technology of writing. Accordingly, a proto-phenomenological critique of traditional philosophy benefits from exploring (1) the differences between oral and written language, (2) the derived character of literacy from the more original domain of oral language, and (3) how philosophy's reliance on literacy has concealed the original oral background of language as a mode of dwelling.

The acquisition of spoken and written language is the historical background for any person who might come to take up philosophy. In addition, the story of philosophy itself runs back to ancient Greece, where there is a comparable history in the following sense: the advent of alphabetic writing in the Greek world was a necessary (though not sufficient) condition for the development of philosophy. That ancient scenario will be addressed more pointedly in chapter 5.

1. ORAL AND WRITTEN LANGUAGE: TWO DIFFERENT WORLDS?

The short answer to this question is that oral and written language are not "literally" two different worlds; they inhabit the same world as distinct but inseparable phenomena. The *distinction* points to a tension that cannot be resolved into a strict unity because *how* each form emerges and operates issues different kinds of performance. They are *inseparable* in the following sense: first, from a developmental standpoint, literacy is derived from, and dependent on, oral language;[2] second, from a philosophical standpoint, orality is derived from, and dependent on, written language. What does this mean? We (and I mean here we readers and writers) have no access to pure orality (apart from our earliest periods of childhood). The very concept of "orality" is a literate construction. A purely oral culture would not explicitly identify itself as such. Any understanding of orality *as* a phenomenon cannot help but be driven by (1) the gaze of we literates recognizing an oral culture as *lacking* literacy, and (2) the literate disciplinary skills that enable us to "study" an oral culture as a subject of investigation. Indeed, even pre-verbal and pre-literate children, even illiterate persons in our culture, cannot be said to inhabit a purely oral domain because their social-world and environing-world are saturated with the effects of literacy.

Despite the literate inflection of any examination of orality and oral cultures, it is possible to gain some understanding by (1) considering the indicative differences between oral and written language in our own experience and in the process of learning how to read and write, (2) imagining by contrast what it would be like to dwell in speech without written texts, (3) considering ethnographic research on oral cultures, and (4) consulting the special case of ancient Greece, which was originally an oral culture that *indigenously* developed a writing culture and the literate-world that launched the Western tradition.

The distinction between oral and written language is important because it opens up significant *differences* that have largely been concealed or ignored, not only in philosophy but in linguistics as well. Written language has not been an object of study in traditional linguistics because the usual assumption has been that language is originally speech, and that writing is simply the material transcription of spoken language; writing therefore tells us nothing more about language and need not be studied in its own right. Some developments in the field have challenged this assumption on the following grounds: not only is linguistics a literate discipline, but its very assumptions about the nature of "language" are inflected with a literate bias, which consequently alters the presumed precedence of spoken language.[3] The questions at hand in this investigation, therefore, are not confined to philosophy.

There are a number of ways in which the distinct, but inseparable, character of oral and written language fits my phenomenological study (the following sketches will be filled out in discussions to come). First, I have portrayed language as a dynamic of differential fitness. It is with writing that the differential element becomes *explicit*, because of the stand-alone nature of written words apart from speech acts. And the many cognitive capacities that stem from differentiation also become explicit and exponentially expanded with literacy.

Second, the explicit differential character of writing generates the construction of many philosophical questions that are resolvable by attending to their derivative departure from factical speech: questions concerning representation, correspondence, realism, constructivism, and skepticism. I argue that the very notion of a "representation" signifying "things" is a reification process made possible by the graphic presence of written words. Skepticism relies on the representational divide between subject and object, so that the linkage between mind and object or language and world can be put in question. Since speech, however, is originally immersed and embedded in its world, the problem of skepticism could not get off the ground in a strictly oral environment. Imagine a face-to-face conversation that began with doubt that spoken words could connect with external reality. This would amount to doubt about the possibility of a functional conversation that is already at work. The communicated prospect of skepticism about the possibility of communication is self-refuting.

Third, differential fitness and the variegated practice-field of language have a bearing on debates between essentialism and anti-essentialism. Writing permits a certain stability by converting the temporal passage of speech into a fixed position in space, which can prompt the notion of a fixed domain for language. Yet, as we will see, the differential element that persists in both factical speech and writing works against any essentialist impulse that graphic fixation may have served. At the same time, the fitness character of language (spoken or written) undermines anti-essentialist impulses as well, which carry their own reflective biases traceable to the detachment of written language from factical speech—as when language is conceived as a human construction, invention, or free play of signifiers. Essentialism misses the unsettled, open, differential character of language, while anti-essentialism misses the settling effects of fitness given in the world-disclosive capacity of language.

Fourth, even though writing gives birth to a representational departure from the presentational force of ecstatic speech, reading and writing themselves exhibit their own modes of immersion when they become habituated as second nature skills. The bidirectional nature of exposition and immersion allows that the acute kind of exposition found in the conversion of speech sounds into letters and assembled words eventually settles into the automatic facility of immersed reading and writing—which extends exponentially the virtual fitness of language. The bidirectionality of immersion and exposition shows how language, *spoken or written*, can dwell in a complex and fluid disclosive field. All the expositional questions and debates about the parts of language, its structures and relations (words, sounds, letters, meaning, reference, etc.) are derivative phenomena that are problematic only if they are set apart from the disclosive field and presumed to sufficiently characterize that field. The originality of orality—of face-to-face embodied speech—is not the last word on language, but it should be the first word, to wean the philosophy of language from its reliance on "legibility" and its concealment of the disclosive openness inhabited by both speech and writing.

Finally, my critique of the literate inflection of philosophy in no way ignores the enormous value of literacy in human development. Reading and writing expand the differential force of language into an explosion of disclosive power. To quote Walter Ong (discounting his "psychological" emphasis):

> Oral cultures indeed produce powerful and beautiful verbal performances of high artistic and human worth, which are no longer even possible once writing has taken possession of the psyche. Nevertheless, without writing, human consciousness cannot achieve its fuller potential, cannot produce other beautiful and powerful creations. In this sense, orality needs to produce and is destined to produce writing. Literacy . . . is absolutely necessary for the development not only of science but also of history, philosophy, explicative understanding of literature and of any art, and indeed for the explanation of language (including oral speech) itself.[4]

Literacy, especially for the academically inclined, is so pervasive and constitutive of thought that it is hard to bring its specific effects into view. That is why the contrast with orality is important for understanding the nature of language, spoken or written. In any case, we have to keep in mind that literacy is not uniformly exercised because it is acquired and deployed in different degrees: (1) *practical* literacy, namely reading and writing skills, which themselves exhibit degrees of proficiency; (2) *formal* literacy, or reflection on the structure and parts of language, as in the case of grammar; and (3) *theoretical* literacy, or reflection on the structure and nature of reality informed by literate skills, as in science and philosophy. Obviously, a philosophical examination of language such as mine is a function of theoretical literacy, but it also explores a self-exposition of literacy as such—in relation to orality—in order to issue a deeper and more circumspect understanding of language. Finally, a focus on philosophical literacy adds a further qualification, that writing is executed in different contexts and for various purposes, from shopping lists to academic texts.

2. THE ALPHABET AND LEARNING HOW TO READ AND WRITE

This investigation emphasizes writing systems in the Western tradition, specifically alphabetic script.[5] Writing in general terms is a technology and a material medium, whereby artificial graphic marks on a durable surface generate communication stemming from a conventional relation to (oral) language. A central feature of writing is its capacity to extend communication beyond face-to-face speech. Writing can be said to evolve from earlier material communication devices, such as stones indicating ownership of land, tally sticks, and tokens used for computing and recording the contents of sealed clay containers. Because of problems with the storage of tokens, they came to be impressed upon the clay before drying. There now arose a semiotic relation between the impression and the token, as distinct from the token-contents relation. This is a prelude to the indirect relation between writing and reference. Writing is not directly related to what is disclosed in speech but to speech as such, its phonic expression, which is the province of alphabetic script. Ideographic writing is more pictorial in bearing an iconic relation to something in the world and its meaning. Ideograms did evolve into more abstract relations to word units rather than iconic reference. But the word units were still limited to their specific reference to things like fish, bird, or grain. Properties, movements, events, and relations were difficult to render. It was the phonetization of script that allowed a graphic indication of *anything* that could be *said* and its disclosive possibilities, rather than a mere ostensive indication of something in the world. The alphabet is the most complete mechanism for graphic phonetization because it is the most efficient and accurate method for recording spoken language.[6]

2.1. Alphabetic Script

Writing in the West is based on the Roman alphabet, which was preceded by the Greek alphabet. The Greek alphabet was an adaptation of the Phoenician writing system, which was phonetic but limited to consonant sounds. The Greeks completed phonetization by adding vowel sounds.[7] The core distinction in alphabetic writing is between graphemes (the visual material marks) and phonemes (the sounds of speech).[8] The primary linguistic units in alphabetic script are letters (the first two letters in Greek are *alpha* and *beta*). Letters bear no iconic, pictorial, or referential relation to anything in the world other than phonic units of speech. Individual letters and their combinations are meant simply to represent not semantic meaning but the various sounds of spoken words: that is, the vowels, consonants, and syllables that make up any uttered word, phrase, or sentence. In fact, it is only by way of alphabetic script that we *understand* vowels, consonants, and syllables as such—and I will argue that the same holds for words, phrases, and sentences.

In any case, the alphabet represents an acute *exposition* of speech into sound units and their "assembly" into words—which is not the case in the automatic performance of immersed speech. The actual visual marks of the alphabet are arbitrary conventions that in themselves have no meaning other than their sonic indications. The written word t-r-e-e by itself bears no relation to an actual tree or even the semantic meaning of the word "tree." If I know how the alphabet functions in Latin, I can "read" the word *sestertius* without knowing what it means. After alphabetic script has been learned and mastered, reading and writing can become second nature, to the point of enacting the disclosive power of language apart from overt speech—owing to the virtual fitness of language apart from direct reference. This is a momentous example of the bi-directional relation of exposition and immersion, of being able to *dwell* in written language after the expositional reconstruction of speech by way of an alphabet. When I read "Your manuscript has been accepted for publication," there is an immediate disclosure of meaning without any attention to the expositional findings in this section concerning letters, sounds, and so forth. When reading and writing become second nature, we can easily forget the laborious linguistic transformation involved in learning the lexical shift to alphabetic script. The facility with literacy conceals the eclipsing of orality and allows the expositional error of reverse engineering language as an assembly of phonemes, syllables, words, sentences, and so on—which are orthographic constructions transferred back into speech.

2.2. How Children Learn Reading and Writing

Learning how to read begins with memorizing letters of the alphabet and their various phonetic features, along with the recognition and building of sounded words from these letters. Although speech acquisition is an effortful and extended process, it is "natural" in the sense of a child's predisposition to learn speech as a communicative project and the natural settings, behaviors, and social relations that figure in speech development. The arbitrary character of written letters, the gap between their visual markings and phonetic indications, and the expositional "construction" of written words from graphemes and phonemes makes the acquisition of literacy an almost wholly "unnatural" process with special difficulties—generally because of the abstract semiotic divide between graphic letters and the factical speech-world. Nevertheless, natural speech remains in play as the generative background for the new learning scenarios that launch literacy. Moreover, the plasticity of the human organism is such that in time literate skills can develop into new habits, where reading and writing become second nature. Yet the pre-literate world of children is primarily an oral domain, where understanding the world is the result of immediate face-to-face speech practices, a participatory nexus of involvements in a social-environing-world.[9]

From a neurological standpoint, unlike the predisposition for speech, the brain is not predisposed to read. There is a difference between the speaking brain and the reading brain, which involves a transition from phonological processing to visual processing.[10] Across all languages, reading begins as a phonological project (reading aloud), with neural structures that govern spoken language playing a primary role. As expertise develops, the visual cortex becomes increasingly active (in what is called the VWFA, the visual word form area). In this way, learning to read involves a shift from phonetic to visual processing, but in a continuous manner because the written word that is *seen* is derived from, and retains the trace of, what is *heard* in the spoken word, which is why reading aloud is a requirement at the beginning; silent reading is a later development of internalization, analogous to the internalization of speech discussed in chapter 3. Reading aloud, however, seems to be a universal prerequisite for the development of silent reading.[11] Even with silent reading, the oral factor is not utterly absent. There is neurological evidence of phonological codes being activated when a written text is processed visually.[12]

Learning letters at first is an acute expositional/representational process of constructing word recognition. The association with meaningful speech is always in the background, however, which is why reading and writing in time retrieve the meaning-laden flow of language that characterizes the speech-world. The visualization of letters at first is unlike normal visual processing of whole entities, but as reading skill increases, whole words are processed in the normal fashion.[13] In fact, it is only with written language that children come to understand what a "word" is. Pre-literate children have a tacit functional intimation of discrete words, if only in producing and receiving one-word utterances. But a specific comprehension of a word as a discrete unit of language emerges only with the advent of reading and writing, which is why non-literate cultures do not have an *explicit* designation for what we call "words."[14]

Writing is a thoroughly cultural construct, an artifact with little grounding in natural experience, which is why learning to read carries special difficulties. Nevertheless, the world into which a child is born is filled with the effects of literacy, especially regarding (literate) parents in their own development, but also in the environment proper: books, magazines, computer screens, menus, shopping lists, which young children continually witness people engaging in meaningful episodes of language use. In other words, before they learn how to read, children intimate the *point* of reading and writing, as a way of activating language apart from direct speech. That intimation is particularly prompted when parents read stories to children or share the reading of picture books.

Research also shows that before children actually learn how to process written letters and words—the "content" of reading, so to speak—they understand the "form" of writing and reading as distinct modalities.[15] This is especially the case with writing, because children are usually given drawing devices to leave graphic markings and scribblings long before they learn how to read. Young children can (1) distinguish writing from drawing, albeit in a primitive manner, (2) comprehend the notion of letter strings, word strings, and word separation, (3) generally grasp the difference between writing and other notation systems, (4) understand different genres and contexts of writing (e.g., narration and description), and (5) intimate in a rough fashion a referential relationship between graphic markings and things. All of this precedes, and makes possible, the explicit understanding of the link between graphic lettering and speech sounds, which takes time and launches the specific venture of literacy as a potent new mode of communication.[16]

Learning how to read involves a number of skills that enrich a child's understanding of language and its disclosive function. Literate capacities and growth unfold in the following ways: *phonological* development, understanding the sounds that make up words; *orthographic* development, how written words represent oral language; *semantic* and *pragmatic* development, how the meaning of words in factical circumstances and practices facilitates the decoding of written words; *syntactic* development, how grammatical forms and structure enable words to build sentences, paragraphs, and stories; and *morphological* development, how words are formed from smaller roots and units of meaning, such as un-dress-ed. As Wolf explains:

> Together, all these developments quicken the early recognition of a word's parts, foster more facile decoding and spelling, and enhance the child's understanding of known and unknown words. The more a child is exposed to written words, the greater his or her implicit and explicit understanding of all language.[17]

The orthographic comprehension that comes with reading and writing actually affects how spoken language is experienced and processed.[18] Emerging literacy enhances (1) the way language contributes to working memory, (2) the phonological-auditory processing of spoken language, (3) semantic/grammatical categorization, and (4) the ability to focus and analyze explicit phonological properties. Reading affects neurological networks having to do with oral language, native speech, and sentence processing. Evidence such as this accentuates the extent to which literacy influences a language, even its oral elements, which shows further why "pure orality" is absent in a literate culture.

Reading development is fostered and enhanced by various conditions and practices, among which are: shared reading scenarios; a loving and supportive environment; exposure to stories, which extend affective attunement and expand horizons of experience; alliteration and rhyming schemes; and reading aloud. The more a child is exposed to these circumstances from early on, the more will future performance be improved. As children gain proficiency in reading habits, a growing automaticity generates a ready ability to quickly digest and combine a host of disclosive capacities: metaphor, inference, analogy, affective import, and experiential knowledge. Such facility and acceleration significantly expand a child's linguistic, cognitive, and emotional growth.

It is important to note the influence of pre-literate oral stages on a child's life, not only for acquiring literacy but for overall development. The obvious value of reading and writing in our culture has brought on accelerated approaches to childhood learning that may not always be optimal.[19] The oral speech-world has its own salience and cannot be understood as simply a "pre-literate" domain. Children can receive enhanced vocabulary comprehension when listening to stories rather than reading them. Some contemporary preschool programs emphasize reading and scripted instruction tasks, along with formal measures of performance; but such programs can be too early for readiness and can even impede or delay development. There can arise a de-emphasis on conversational skills of speaking, listening, and responding—which are a natural part of cognitive development and less amenable to formalized testing. Finland has school programs that rank among the best, yet formal reading instruction is delayed until age seven, before which teacher-child and child-child relationships are the focus. The reading and writing skills to come may actually be enhanced with such focused attention on the social-speech-world.

Learning how to read alters the visual cortex of the brain in a way that enables the eventual perception of a written word as a "whole," taking in its form (and meaning) without going through piecemeal phonetic coding. Proto-phenomenology has emphasized a common-sense ontology, where we normally engage things like trees holistically, as opposed to the exposed atomic, elemental, or data constructions familiar to scientific and philosophical analysis. Learning how to read and write, however, requires an expositional starting point of phonetic and graphic assembly (still in the midst of immersed factical life that supports such a learning process), which then through habituation establishes new "objects" of perception (words) that can be absorbed as unfragmented wholes. With that, procedural memory helps develop the skill of reading sentences in a fluid manner, without the hesitation of connecting words one at a time.[20]

We have discussed the figure-eight temporality of understanding speech with acute procedural memory, where the retention of passing words, along with the tacit anticipation of words to come, allows a running "presentation" of meaningful discourse in an otherwise temporal "excess" of the no-longer and not-yet. A comparable looping structure of before/here/after in a spacial-temporal sense operates in the fluid course of reading sentences. Our eyes perform minute movements (saccades) and pauses (fixations) that enable the processing of meaningful word strings, along with peripheral vision that allows anticipatory perception of several letters ahead of our fixed visual focus—all of this generating the automatic flow of immersed reading.

3. ORALITY IN ANCIENT GREECE

Alphabetic writing was constructed and came into use in the Greek world most likely in the early 8th century BCE.[21] Examining this world is ideal for differentiating orality and literacy because writing was introduced indigenously, not brought into the culture as an established system from an outside source. Consequently, the Greeks went through transitions from oral modes of culture to literate modes, and those transitions can be telling for coming to understand the different orientations.[22] Chapter 5 will detail how literacy was a factor in the advent of philosophy. Part of that advent was a critique of poetry, which was originally a purely oral phenomenon. Orality and literacy, therefore, were in that context at odds with respect to cultural authority. This tension is the mirror image of my phenomenological project, which is a critique of traditional philosophy for missing what is meant by dwelling in speech, which is best indicated in face-to-face oral language. Moreover, ethnographic and linguistic research has been able to draw out features of pre-literate Greek culture from early poetry, especially Homeric epics, because much in these texts reflect an oral culture. Such characteristics in Homer's poetry turn out to display a good deal of what proto-phenomenology has advanced concerning the lived world. Accordingly, there is a kind of looping trajectory in my overall study because it challenges traditional philosophy on behalf of the lived world, which marked the oral culture of early Greek poetry, which was challenged by Greek philosophy on behalf of new intellectual powers made possible by literacy. That story will be developed in the next chapter. In this section of the current chapter, I will sketch how Homeric poetry and oral culture fit features of the lived world described by protophenomenology. This discussion will provide bearings for the next section, which will sort out the different elements of orality and literacy.

3.1. Oral Poetry in the Greek World

The first great literature in the Western tradition was Homer's epic poetry, the *Iliad* and the *Odyssey*, composed roughly around the late 8th to 7th centuries BCE.[23] The so-called Homeric question concerns whether there actually was a single poet named Homer or whether the name simply gathers multiple authors. In any case, the written texts we have are a stellar artistic achievement and their content is expressive of the early Greek world before the emergence of philosophy. Another facet of the Homeric question concerns the written version in relation to an earlier oral period before the advent of the alphabet: whether Homer was the writer or simply an oral source of the written text inscribed by others. Dismissal of an oral origin by some stemmed from doubts that such impressive literature could be composed by anyone who was illiterate. The American classicist Milman Parry (1902–1935) broke new ground by studying oral traditions in comparison with Homeric texts and showing how an oral culture could in fact engender much of what is found in Homer and that most formal and stylistic features of the written epics can be linked to a preliterate oral domain. Parry's thesis inspired later work that included research on existing oral traditions in Eastern Europe and Africa, which further supported the idea that Homer's poetry stemmed from preliterate sources.[24] An interesting element in this story is that the main impetus behind the creation and early use of the alphabet in Greece likely was not to serve mercantile or utilitarian interests, but to write down and record oral performances of epic poetry.[25] Nevertheless, it is hard to imagine that the inscription of the poetry had no effect at all on its composition. In view of research on all these matters, there are a few summary conclusions we can draw with some degree of confidence: (1) Homeric poetry is reflective of an earlier oral tradition; (2) the written texts we have were probably not the result of sheer dictation or recording; and (3) some effects of literacy were likely operative in the composition of extant Homeric texts.[26] The inscription of epic poetry in the form we possess was probably the co-creation of poet, scribe, and collector.[27]

Before examining oral elements in Homer's epics, their status and character as poetry should be noted. The *Iliad* and the *Odyssey* cannot simply be called "literature" in a modern sense because in the Greek tradition, they were world-forming and culturally authoritative as foundational texts, providing constitutive bearings for religious, social, ethical, and practical concerns.[28] Greek religion was radically pluralistic and spread among various cult domains associated with particular deities and sacred forces—which were esoteric in the sense that cult practices were not to be revealed to outsiders. Epic poetry was performed by traveling bards to audiences in public settings, and so Homer's stories provided a kind of collective culture that all Greeks could share. Moreover, the epics are significant for my purposes *as* a mode of poetry, because cultural bearings were presented as a lived world, as narratives involving particular characters in specific dramatic circumstances that are not a matter of abstract principles or transcendent sources, but rather factical existence and natural life—even with respect to the deities portrayed in the texts. More of this will be developed in the next chapter.

What can be said of the oral character of Greek poetry?[29] In general terms, it can be described in line with our phenomenological account of face-to-face speech in the lived world—but adding poetry's production of world-disclosive cultural bearings. Compared to the modern academic circumstance of reading and interpreting poetry, oral poetry differed in content, form, production, presentation, and reception. It offered meaning-laden narratives of factical life pertaining to war, work, family, religion, social relations, political norms, and heroic exploits—with an overall didactic purpose amid its pleasures as entertainment. The regular word for poetry was *mousikē*, which indicated the conjunction of words and music, where performance was sung or accompanied by music. The poet's embodied gestures were also part of the presentation. The relation between poet and audience was intimate, with rapt attention and reactions that often cued the poet's manner and course of delivery. Altogether, Greek poetry generated an immersed, embodied social-world of disclosive speech.[30]

Along with the temporal movement of performance as such, Greek poetry had an historical structure in its presentational function. Narratives usually involved traditional myths about a paradigmatic past that gave birth to current cultural meanings. This was not "history" in the modern sense but reaching back to a "time immemorial" depicting the origins of present forms of life. In the absence of written texts, this historical reach was meant to sustain a *memory* of origins that can both shape the present and be passed on to future generations. Accordingly, in an oral culture, memory was the only form of retention and preservation for both the poet and the audience. Homer's epic poems began with invoking the Muses, who are the "daughters of Memory" and who bestow to the poet and audience cultural knowledge along with the pleasures of song.[31] The "truth" of poetry is not a matter of factual accuracy but rather presentational disclosure of cultural bearings.[32] The root meaning of the Greek word for truth, *alētheia*, is un-concealment. Concealment here can refer to forgetting, which points to the veridical function of memory in oral poetry.[33] The opposite of truth in this sense is not falsehood but a concealed or lost "world."[34] Historical unconcealment in epic poetry was very different from chronological conceptions of a bygone past. Poetic evocation of the past—in performance—involved complex temporal loops of a past brought to life in the recurrent presencing of an original event.[35]

The invocation of the Muses was an invitation for them to "tell" the story or inspire the poet to transmit the story. Consequently, "authorship" is ambiguous in oral poetry because it cannot be centered in a poet's conscious mind; it is caught up in sacred sources exceeding human production. Hesiod's *Theogony* (1–108) begins with a depiction of the poet's dependence on the Muses, along with the social setting of poetic performance and its effects on cognition and emotion. The Muses, who once breathed into the poet a divine voice, are asked to join him in song, to celebrate the past and foretell the future. The Muses gladden the spirit of Zeus when they sing and the cares of mortals are forgotten in the thrall of poetry. People honor the poet like a god because of his wisdom in singing *of* the gods and *through* a divine power. It is important to highlight the sacred and historical elements of Greek poetry because they show that human beings are not the full source of meaning; they are *projected* into a world that is already shaped by an immemorial past and infused with forces beyond human construction and control.

Despite the projected character of oral poetry, individual poets were not helpless conduits. They participated in production because performance was not based on some canonical Ur-text. Traditional tales had their basic outlines but each performance allowed for improvisation within those boundaries, with modifications often prompted by the poet sensing an audience's particular reactions and inclinations. Homer's epics were not written down in full until around the 6th century BCE. Before that, there likely were sporadic and piecemeal inscriptions of the poetry, but probably only as an aid for oral delivery. In any case, even the full written text was almost always read aloud to an audience, even in the classical period. The aural character of language persisted as the focal point in cultural production.

One last remark about Homeric epics. About 40% of the texts involves speeches given in the story, often in song performances that illustrate the social-psychological setting of oral poetry.[36] The *Odyssey* is replete with occasions of song, especially in Book 8, where Odysseus enchants his audience with a long tale of his exploits, which continues through to Book 12. Emotional impact and empathic responses from the audience are often depicted; Odysseus himself weeps more than once when hearing a sad story. In the *Iliad*, even the great warrior Achilles engages in the rapture of poetic singing (9.186–9.189). Throughout these accounts of poetic performance, divine sources and powers are acknowledged and celebrated. Particularly with the *Odyssey*, we witness a tale that is much about tale-telling—and therein a certain reflexive posture in the text, although in a thoroughly embedded manner, rather than a reflection *on* poetry.

4. ELEMENTS OF ORALITY AND LITERACY

In this section, I will cull from relevant research a sketch of the elements of oral and written language, at each point in a contrasting manner. This will prepare a discussion of how literacy is operative in philosophy and transformative of orality. The next chapter will explore how Greek philosophy was implicitly shaped by literate skills and explicitly positioned itself as a challenge to oral poetry and its worldview. Accordingly, some of the elements treated in this section will receive further coverage in the next chapter. With the contrasted picture of orality and literacy outlined here, it should be kept in mind that the features of orality do show their traces in oral aspects of a literate culture, aspects that fit well the phenomenology of dwelling in speech.

4.1. Sound and Sight

Orality is obviously an aural phenomenon, the sonic character of spoken language that is experienced as something heard. Writing converts speech into a visual object inscribed on a perceptible medium. Yet oral language in the manner of face-to-face speech is not simply a matter of hearing because a number of visual elements figure in the embodied nature of conversation: gesture, posture, and facial expression. When speech is experienced in an immersed manner, the aural and visual aspects are really a single "blended" perception that is not exposited as a "combination" of sound and sight. Nevertheless, writing permits the *lexical* visibility of language, which serves a host of discoveries that at best are only implicit in orality. One important example is the very notion of a "word" as a linguistic unit.[37] In normal speech, there are no acoustic cues that isolate the beginning and end of individual words because it flows as a continuous stream of sound (think of what an unfamiliar language sounds like when it is spoken). In oral speech, it is contextual use and intimated meaning that allow understanding of "words" as they proceed; even a one-word utterance is not isolated from its conversational circumstance. In normal speech, words are "shingled" together in a sonic flow. It is alphabetic script that forces attention on words as sonic "units" to be assembled with letters. Then the graphic object clearly shows the "boundaries" of individual words. This expositional focus makes possible an *explicit* analysis of language as a set of lexical relations.

4.2. Time and Space

Orality is exclusively temporal and a continual flow of appearing and disappearing.[38] Physical things have their kind of permanence and we can keep something from moving by confining it. The sounding of speech, however, cannot be stopped without losing it; absent the flow of words there would be silence or continuous noise if a particular sound were sustained. Orality is therefore a domain of becoming rather than static being. The only way to preserve or "store" language in an oral culture is through memory, which is always subject to the limit of forgetfulness. That is why oral poetry involved mnemonic devices that would prompt impact and recall: rhythmic and sonic patterns, epithets, formulaic settings, repetition, alliteration, and assonance, among others.[39]

Since speech in the lived world is correlated with practical tasks and performative contexts, an oral culture sees language as a mode of action rather than a referential relation to "things" or "thoughts." Such a dynamic perspective accounts for the notion in oral societies that words can evince power over things or persons.[40] In that respect, language has not yet been isolated from ways of being in the world; it displays speech-acts in the strictest sense and cannot be objectified as reified tokens that attach to experience.

Vision affords sustained attention to stable entities and a kind of pinpoint focus. Sound is not only ephemeral in its passage, it also has an "enveloping" quality that is less focal when engaged, especially when its source is not in view—but even when the source is perceived, the sound as such is more encompassing than ostensive. Writing allows the spacialization of language, which converts the flow of speech into a stable visual object. Even though writing proceeds temporally when read, the words remain in their fixed location. Writing is a mode of storage that need not rely on memory, thus providing a permanence that arrests the flow of speech and supersedes the possibility of forgetting. The transmission of tradition is no longer memorial but set for perpetual access by recorded documents.

Visual objectification through writing, therefore, allows a *fixed focal point* that opens up new possibilities for engaging language and subsequent powers of thought: (1) when words are no longer subject to becoming, they can *be there* right before one's eyes and *remain there* even when not perceived; (2) the stability of a "text" permits a range of analytical opportunities that are hard to execute, if not absent, in orality; (3) oral cultures have no sense of words as "tags," "labels," or "fixtures" since they cannot be located as visual objects,[41] while writing permits the momentous occasion for understanding language as *representation*, as re-presenting the world through the differentiated focus of written words. These three possibilities, among others, will be developed further in due course.

4.3. Plasticity and Identity

Speech in factical life is pluralistic and flexible, shifting in different contexts and generally plastic in execution. Although for communicative purposes language involves certain constraints and regularity, actual occasions of speech by individuals is a matter of improvisation, of personal inflections that are spontaneously responsive to the changing course of circumstances throughout any given span of time. Oral poetry was never sheer creation de novo because it was confined to traditional mythical and narrative outlines. Each performance, however, would involve modifications within a traditional framework because of the contingency and fallibility of memory, variations in audience reaction, and different settings encountered by traveling bards. In oral cultures, repeat performances have sometimes been presumed to be identical, but empirical research has shown otherwise. Indeed, forgetting, misremembering, or modifying would seem to be detectable in a decisive way only by means of a written record.[42] What might seem "identical" in an oral culture is likely a rough sense of sameness in the manner of approximation, as in "You told me the same story last month," which is different from two copies of the same written story.

Writing allows a text to remain the same exact text throughout time and different occasions of reading. It is only with written texts that a number of familiar notions could arise, especially when compared with oral poetry. Consider authorship, which as we have noted is ambiguous and even undecidable, given the idea of divine inspiration and multiple performances by different singers. With the production of a physical text, an author's signature can be affixed, identified, and duly regarded as such. The same holds for the authenticity of a text. With writing comes the possibility of a "canonical" version of a story that can stand as the proper reference through the ages, as against unauthorized revision; also the notion of a "correct" text, as in the case of so-called critical editions.[43] The very idea of a plagiarized or corrupted text would not be possible in an oral culture; it would not even arise as an issue.

4.4. Embodiment and Disembodiment

Orality, in its face-to-face character, is a display of embodied speech and reception, given the communicative function of gesture, facial expression, tonality, rhythm, volume, and emphasis. Such is the domain of the lived body in immersed exchanges, wherein an exposited focus on physical aspects as such recedes or is not specified in presentational discourse, which simply *is* incarnate speech. Writing converts spoken language into "disembodied" alphabetic lines that do not "speak" to the reader in a strict sense. The embodied elements of speech, once recognized, show the error in the definition of writing as simply the transcription of spoken language—given all that is left out or concealed in scripted reproduction.[44]

The evolution of writing techniques has issued various attempts to compensate for the silencing of sub-verbal effects that animate the sounding of speech. The graphic insertion of accent marks, punctuation, and other notations have been introduced to capture certain sonic features of speech such as rhythm and emphasis. The transition to silent reading, however, has contributed significantly to the effacement of embodied expression in written language. In the previous chapter, I suggested that the internalization of speech plays a central role in the phenomenology of a "mental" dimension distinct from physical descriptions. The disembodied character of written language, I believe, accentuates such a process even more, particularly with silent reading. The relation between literacy and an interiorized self—which opens space for a sense of mentality—will be explored in upcoming discussions.

The difference between a written text and live speech first prepared a distinction that we literates take for granted: that between a text per se and its meaning. Such a notion became evident in the context of ancient Greek theater, wherein a written script was meant to be performed by actors before a live audience. Theater in this sense occupies a middle position between a written text and oral performance. The same script could issue different enactments and receptions owing to variations in live performance and audience reception. The *way* a line is delivered or heard can alter its meaning.[45] I had first-hand experience of this when I co-directed a performance of Euripides' *The Bacchae*. A central controversy in this play is whether the character of Dionysus is benign or malevolent, protagonist or antagonist in relation to the other main character, Pentheus. We aimed for a mixed interpretation, although leaning toward protagonist. In any case, it became very clear in rehearsals that the decisive variable in advancing our interpretation was *how* lines were voiced by the actors. The play could really go either way.

In the face of this new perspective evident in theater production, Greek thinkers began to conceive of language in new ways. Unlike oral poets, actors repeat a line exactly as written. But since the repeated lines come from a graphic script and not a human voice that might be imitated, actors inevitably inflect the performance with their own bodies, voices, and intentions. Just as musical notation cannot perform a piece by itself, a written script alone cannot issue its performance, or even its meaning in that sense.[46] Subsequently, Greek thinking was able to discern a difference between what a text "says" and what it "means."[47] Here is Socrates referring to Homer's poetry:

> You have to understand his meaning (*dianoia*) and not merely his words (*epē*). In fact, one could not be a good rhapsode unless one understood the things said by the poet. For a rhapsode must be an interpreter (*hermēnea*) of the poet's meaning to the listeners. (*Ion* 530c)[48]

Here we have a distinction between linguistic expression *simpliciter* and interpretation—and thus between "words" per se and their (now evident) "mental" significance and appropriation (analogous to an actor's contribution). That prepares the advent of representational thinking by way of a signification theory of language, where words are now "signs" for things or mental states.

4.5. Lived Context and Decontextualization

Orality is embedded not only in face-to-face speech but also multiple situational and practical settings. With writing, graphic separability from factical occasions of speech amounts to a decontextualization of language in formal terms. Writing can articulate contextual details but alphabetic script as such is detached from the immediate practical environments that animate speech. Such decontextualization can open up abstract generalities that are not evident or functional in lived experience. In Volume I, contextual pluralism was illustrated with the example of a tree (80ff.). A tree can be interpreted in different ways, as a scientific object, a physical thing with properties, a material resource, an obstacle for a road builder, a thing of beauty, among other perspectives. Any such as-indicator can be appropriately disclosive in a given context, and none of them presents the "real" tree in an absolute sense, and this constraint holds even for a scientific account. Science is hermeneutically appropriate for certain explanatory purposes, but the refined procedures of science must filter out many *real* ways of engaging trees before the supposed "real" tree is given to us. The word *tree* can span the different interpretations and thus gather them together, but in an indicative manner that points to the contextual uses without positing some universal or unified meaning that all uses are grounded in or have in common.

Later, I will develop in more detail how the decontextualization of writing permits the construction of abstract concepts apart from the evident plurality of speech practices. Certain definitional and classification procedures that are familiar in literate societies are largely absent in oral cultures.[49] There is much intelligence in oral societies, but more in line with indicative intimation than disengaged classification. The meaning of words in an oral culture is not given simply with other words (as in a dictionary), but in practical settings of embodied speech, which deliver their own specific contextual sense, as shown in these examples from ethnological research with non-literate subjects: if shown a geometrical circle, it would be named *plate* or *moon*, and a square would be called *mirror* or *door*; a collection consisting of a hatchet, saw, hammer, and log would not be separated into categories of tool and non-tool but gathered together as like things because of their *practical* linkage (tools and materials); if asked to explain what a tree is, an answer given was,

"Why should I? Everyone knows what a tree is. They don't need me telling them." Here is exhibited indicative understanding that is not abstracted from factical life.

When non-literates are tested for their comprehension of syllogistic reasoning, they seem alienated from the notion of logical validity—that is, the formal features of inference set apart from the content and truth of statements.[50] If given the following sequence—all dogs are white/Fido is a dog / is Fido white?—a typical answer would be: "I don't know; dogs are different colors." What seems to be a failure of logical reasoning actually stems from unfamiliarity with the very idea of a "proposition" as an abstract ingredient in logical structure, regardless of its truth. In the response, the truth of the statement is paramount (surely not an irrational posture). How people come to understand logical form as such depends on processes of disengagement made possible by writing: the conversion of a meaningful statement into a logical unit of inferential relations. Interestingly, non-literates can intimate validity with the inclusion of something quite familiar, namely pretending: "Let's pretend that all dogs are white."[51]

The decontextualization of words from their normal conversational use is a precondition for logical schematics that can disambiguate, purify, or universalize a lexical meaning in the service of rational and scientific explanation or description.[52] The meaning of *and*, *or*, *not*, and *is* in formal logical terms (usually designated with abstract symbols) is different from common conversational meanings. Some examples: *and* reduced to meaning *plus*, whereas in speech it can mean *and then* or *in order to*; *or* as inclusive rather than exclusive disjunction; *is* as predication rather than its myriad uses in ordinary speech. When young children are given statements of descriptive sentences matching or mis-matching a picture, they will often answer by way of agreeing or disagreeing with the *speaker* rather than assessing the objective truth or falsity of the statement. When logical meanings are considered standard, the testing of children and non-literates can detect "irrationality" when in fact alternate forms of (oral) understanding are being exhibited. When children learn language, their "concepts" do not operate according to epistemological precepts because word usage will simply gather and track multiple factors that elude conceptual precision: the histories and perspectives of caregivers, different practical settings and conversation scenarios, instruction and correction, trial and error, and memories and anticipations. Such proto-conceptual intimations are extendable and repeatable, but they shift and diverge according to enactive interpretation. Children may not be able to "define" what a tree is but they can inhabit different uses of the word "tree." Conceptual *governance* is a different perspective made possible by graphic abstraction.

A written text also opens space for a disengaged "reader" and thus an individualized mentality separated from a more original immersion in factical environments. Here can arise a discrete sense of selfhood that in my terms is a concentration on the personal-world interiorized apart from the practical-social-environing-world. In an oral culture, a request for self-description would receive an account of performative, situational, and social settings in response. I quote Ong's discussion of Alexander Luria's research:

> A 38-year-old man, illiterate, from a mountain pasture camp was asked, "What sort of person are you, what's your character like, what are your good qualities and shortcomings? How would you describe yourself?" "I came here from Uch-Kurgan, I was very poor, and now I'm married and have children." "Are you satisfied with yourself or would you like to be different?" "It would be good if I had a little more land and could sow some wheat." Externals command attention. "And what are your shortcomings?" "This year I sowed one pood of wheat, and we're gradually fixing the shortcomings." More external situations. "Well, people are different—calm, hot-tempered, or sometimes their memory is poor. What do you think of yourself?" "We behave well—if we were bad people, no one would respect us." Self-evaluation modulated into group evaluation ("we") and then handled in terms of expected reactions from others. Another man, a peasant aged 36, asked what sort of person he was, responded with touching and humane directness: "What can I say about my own heart? How can I talk about my character? Ask others; they can tell you about me. I myself can't say anything." Judgment bears in on the individual from outside, not from within.[53]

Apparently, self-conception in an oral culture is not centered in "personal" characteristics and traits because first-person responses are intertwined with relations and behavior in the social-environing-world. That is why Homeric epithets ("X, tamer of horses," or "Y, sacker of cities") are not simply mnemonic formulas but also ecological accounts of identity.

In chapter 3, we saw how individuated self-development is afforded by language in a movement from the social-world of speech to isolated private speech and then to silent inner speech. Learning how to read and developed habits of reading significantly enhance and refine this internalization process. Letters and words are first learned through vocalization. Graphic words allow lexical retention without vocalization, which evolves into silent reading. Writing thereby accentuates a de-audibilization of language and a subsequent construction of "mental" space. Reading and writing, therefore, in both form and content, are significant generators of individualized/internalized selfhood, which illustrates again a Vygotskian outside-in model of development.[54]

4.6. Enchantment and Disengagement

Because memory is the only mode of preservation in an oral culture, language has to be "memorable." Poetry, as the primary mode of cultural transmission in the early Greek world, was not simply a contingent overlay or ornament set upon ordinary speech, because the "artistic" features of poetic language were a necessary element for registering and sustaining traditional messages. Poetic performances were able to conjure the power of ecstatic immersion and emotional force to attract and capture an audience for full disclosive effect.[55] The "draw" of oral poetry was empowered by vivid imagery, elevated language, fascinating scenarios, formulaic repetition, rhythm, alliteration, and musicality, all of which are known to be effective for attracting human sensibilities. It should be said that even ordinary spoken language in a mundane setting has its own "poetic" dimension in the "musical" patterns of modulation, rhythm, pitch, tone, accent, and emphasis—the cadences of speech that are not incidental to meaningful expression and that would be jarring if reduced to a monotone delivery with a rigidly uniform beat.

Greek oral poetry took the narrative form of storytelling rather than mere description. Stories offered a lived world of dramatic action, wherein values concerning, say, courage would not be presented as an abstract dictum or maxim, but by way of particular characters who enact courage in the midst of challenging circumstances, which can thereby portray the exigencies, risks, and sacrifices that go with being courageous (think of Achilles in the *Iliad*). We have noted that Greek poetry was sung along with musical accompaniment. Dance too was often involved. Oral poetry therefore displayed and was itself an embodied *world* energized by bio-rhythmic pleasures, factical attractions, and existential lessons that bring cultural traditions to life for an audience. Homeric poetry professed its capacity to deliver knowledge and pleasure as an inseparable package. In its oral form, without written documents, that packaging was necessary for its memorial preservation. The talent required to enact such a cultural function—and the association with sacred forces—meant that poets were favored specialists who were elevated above common citizens and honored accordingly (as Hesiod tells us early on in the *Theogony*).

Oral "publication" was thus not a permanent record but an incarnate captivation that actually lived and breathed in performance. Written publication is a detached mechanical production, wherein normally the silent "performance" of a writer is silently received by a reader in some quiet location.[56] A written document persists right before a reader's eyes, thus greatly reducing the need for poetic powers of attraction—which from an historical standpoint brought about the de-poeticized language now called "prose." In Greek developments, prose was not simply a non-poetic style of writing; in some cases, it was specifically counter-posed to poetry as superior in its disclosive function, especially in history writing. The historical arc of poetry was not a matter of recording past events with empirical accuracy, but the transmission of meanings grounded in an immemorial past for the sake of guiding the future: In *Iliad* 6.357–6.358, Helen talks to Paris of their story being sung for future audiences; Hesiod's *Theogony* tells of poets singing of things past and things to come (31–32). The writings of Herodotus, on the other hand, are a *historiē*, meaning investigative research into past events, not by way of poetic inspiration but a human account based on reliable reporting.[57] And Thucydides is direct in his departure from poetry:

> From the evidence I have presented, however, one would not go wrong in supposing that events were very much as I have set them out; and no one should prefer rather to believe the songs of the poets, who exaggerate things for artistic purposes, or the writings of the chroniclers, which are composed more to make good listening than to represent the truth, being impossible to check and having most of them won a place over time in the imaginary realm of fable (*muthos*). My findings, however, you can regard as derived from the clearest evidence available for material of this antiquity.... Perhaps the absence of the element of fable in my work may make it seem less easy on the ear; but it will have served its purpose well enough if it is judged useful by those who want to have a clear view of what happened in the past and what—the human condition being what it is—can be expected to happen again sometime in the future in similar or much the same ways. It is composed to be a possession for all time and not just a performance piece (*agōnisma*) for the moment.[58]

Philosophy in its earliest manifestations was often composed with poetic diction, but in the writings of Plato, the departure from verse began. When criticizing poets in the *Republic* (607d), Socrates says he would still allow a defense of poetry, but in prose form without meter (*aneu metrou logon*).

Prosaic writing was also caught up in reflective thinking apart from the ecstatic immersion of poetic performance. The technology of writing allows for a disengaged reader of a silent text apart from the lived world, which opens space for detached cognitive reflection on forms of language abstracted from factical concretion—in one special domain, the construction of philosophical concepts (which is why the first great philosopher, Plato, found oral poetry problematic). Although written language in the form of literature can be richly world-disclosive, its sphere of performance is mostly imagination, which is only a trace of the fully incarnate experience of oral poetry. As Havelock puts it:

> The oral audience participated not merely by listening passively and memorizing but by active participation in the language used. They clapped and danced and sang collectively, in response to the chanting of the singer.[59]

This is not the kind of thing a book can excite, not to mention a philosophy lecture (at least the ones I have attended). At any rate, the embodied enchantment of oral poetry fits well the kind of "charge" figuring in Ezra Pound's definition of great literature as "language charged with meaning."[60]

4.7. Performance and Reflection

The immersive immediacy of an oral performance, its temporal expiration, and the limits of memory block a host of reflective skills made possible by the visible stability of a written work. One can scan and revisit a text, traverse its parts at will, and thereby enact critical review of language in its own concentrated domain apart from direct uses in factical speech. This opens up attention to structures, relationships, and patterns that can reveal inconsistencies, disparities, omissions, and possible revisions. Moreover, what can now emerge is the sense of a "whole" text organized into "parts"—and herein the idea of formal structure distinct from content is drawn out of language for the first time. The earliest reference to a written text as an organic whole seems to be Plato's *Phaedrus* (264c): The writing of speeches (*logographikēn*) must avoid haphazard or arbitrary arrangement; a writer (*graphonti*) should make sure that every discourse (*panta logon*) is organized like a living body with the proper organization of parts, so that it be something "composed" (*gegrammena*). Subsequent to this kind of schematic shaping, a structural framework can be abstracted and identified as such, serving as a formal requirement for future compositions, a regimen that characterized much of the Western tradition. Aristotle's *Poetics* is the classic early example, and it should be noted that he held the formal structure of a "whole" tragedy to be the most important element of poetry, while the performed spectacle (*opsis*) was the least important (*Poetics* 1450b15–25), which only makes sense if the written text is given prominence.

Reflexive attention to a written text allows an analytical precision that is either lacking or unnecessary in face-to-face speech.[61] Written words are fixed and identified in their lexical location and so they can be revised, omitted, or added with respect to their communicative efficacy. Writing implies the absence of the author's voice, so that possible comprehension problems for readers cannot be resolved in conversation. Accordingly, good writing involves keeping a reader in mind and minimizing possible misreadings by attending carefully to how well sentences convey their meaning. Some elements of oral communication are intimated by bodily gesture and sonic inflections, which are largely missing in written texts. Altogether, written communication succeeds best when it compensates for what might be missing by offering more focused articulation and detail. Such analytical precision can even come to affect a writer's own speaking voice as well.

With writing, there arises a crucial distinction: orality in its own domain does not self-identify as "oral" language, which as noted earlier is a literate construction. Not only does speech "vanish" in each temporal occasion, it is invisible to itself as a "mode" of language. Writing converts speech into a tangible object, and this process of *reification* allows language to be understood as a *medium* of transmission.[62] Now linguistic functions can be identified as such apart from the immediacy of speech, and thereby deployed in their own right as analytical-critical-productive powers—because "disembodied" words can in effect take on a life of their own in written texts. I will focus this discussion with the example of differential fitness. With oral language, the differential element is implicit. Writing allows that element to become explicit, especially when words can be examined as such with respect to lexical relations, revisions, insertions, or re-combinations. What is important here are the intellectual skills made possible by differential dynamics, which were sketched in chapter 1. It should be evident now that such skills are in the main literate capacities, at least in the sense of being explicable in writing and thus launched deliberately as ways of deploying language (e.g., generalizing, hypothesizing, analyzing, inferring, and relational thinking).

One of the most consequential differential functions is recursion, which calls for a few remarks here because writing explicates and notably executes this linguistic capacity.[63] Recursion is a process that seems to be unique to human language and cognition.[64] Language is recursive because its differential character is a release from the constraints of extant spatial and temporal conditions—and from any occurrent linguistic formulation, which makes possible multiple reconfigurations of language *within* lexical iterations: re-combinations, insertions, and mixtures that expand understanding in unlimited ways. Time traversal and analytical revision are recursive functions that generate causal explanation, recollection, and prediction. Higher order thinking and formal constructions are recursive because here language is no longer embedded in experience; it operates within its own internal relations and possibilities, which are freed for their unique orders and constructions. Science, for instance, is recursive in revising common sense language in the direction of nomological findings. In many respects, writing is intrinsically recursive, especially when it works on itself in revisions or when it responds to other writings. In general terms, literacy has a scaffolding effect on expanding human cognition beyond immediate descriptions, conversations, recollections, and anticipations. Whether in rudimentary or refined forms, the labor of writing is itself a *process of thinking* and not simply an expression of thoughts. The challenges of writing amount to the *actualization* of potential impulses toward expression.[65] The external presence of written sentences, notes, outlines, and feedback offer a material environment outside the mind for the gathering, organizing, and revising of thought—with respect to both content and structure.[66] A finished text such as a book can be called an objective record of thought, but also a launch for thinking in the reception of readers.

4.8. Narration and Abstraction

Much of ordinary speech takes a narrative form in depicting or forecasting events, actions, and lived circumstances. As we have seen, oral poetry is effective cultural transmission because it recounts stories with sensuous imagery, specific characters, emotional force, temporal movement, and momentous scenes of concrete existence. That is why the divine in Homer is a matter of personified gods—living beings who act in the world, interact with mortals, and relate to each other in dramatic ways. The epics transmit ideals, values, and purposes usually portrayed in the exploits of particular heroes. If a story concerns "justice," it is not conveyed as an abstract principle or dictum but as a way of being in the world exemplified by the specific circumstances of a god or hero. Oral poetry was a main source of education in the Greek world, wherein the narrative particularity of poetry meant that "learning" involved the "imitation" of role models depicted in traditional stories. Consequently, learning about courage, for example, would not follow from a definition or abstract rule but an exemplary maxim, such as "Be like Achilles." Education in this sense did not promote self-examination but rather incorporation into the cultural norms displayed in oral poetry.[67]

Literacy opens up very different possibilities. As we have seen, the alphabetic lines of a written word as such present a non-sensuous, decontextualized object that is nothing like living speech or narrative situations. As I will argue in the next chapter, the written word as an "abstract" object may have generated philosophical attention to universal concepts—for instance, "justice" as such, that which makes all just actions just. In ancient Greece, literate education began with learning the abstract form of letters, followed by coming to use them in reading and writing. It needs to be said that exemplary and literate modes of education can go together, as indeed they did in the Greek world, even in the classical period. Young boys were taught to read primarily in order to memorize and orally recite poetic texts. In this way, familial, tribal, and civic values were still taught by way of oral transmission and emulation. As Protagoras is given to say in a Platonic dialogue, after the young learn how to read:

> they are given the works of good poets to read at their desks and have to learn them by heart, works that contain numerous expectations, many passages describing in glowing terms good men of old, so that the child is inspired to imitate them and become like them. (*Protagoras* 325e–326a)[68]

It was Socrates who challenged this kind of education by looking beyond familial tradition and exemplification for the universal "form" of, say, courage, which could govern all instances of courageous acts and could not be satisfied by any particular instance. Literacy, I argue, allowed for such a departure from tradition when it was no longer tied to recitation and imitation but rather open to the abstract possibilities in language enabled by writing.[69]

One way to grasp the abstract character of written graphics is to consider how a text in an unfamiliar language looks to the eye. In its own way, it could be called abstract art because it delivers no recognizable image and no help at all in understanding it linguistically. Recalling the discussion of European explorers encountering native peoples, each group in time could come to understand the other language because of overlapping elements of the lived world common across cultures—and mutual intimations of *having* a language at work in one's world. When language is written down, different languages, even those with a common script, show no overlap or common elements in graphic appearance. There may be common elements in the two linguistic worlds, but nothing like that or anything else would be discoverable simply in the written script alone. Something comparable can happen when a familiar word in one's own language can look strange when just its graphic shape is in focus. The point is that written language as such embodies an abstract form that differs from any concrete experience and that can serve the construction of abstract forms of knowledge.

It should be said that abstraction carries its own potential for bridging differences between languages, and that this very issue of cross-cultural commonality is a function of literate reflection. Yet standard models of commonality have tended toward universalization, which suppresses or conceals factical differences in culture. The "ostensive" character of *indicative* reflection takes a different approach. A word like "freedom," for example, is hard to render as an abstract universal, but an indicative focus shows that freedom *in its various uses* is contextual, embodied, embedded, enabled by affordances, infused with metaphorical extension, and primarily enactive in its meaning.[70]

4.9. Tradition and Innovation

Even though repeat poetic performances in an oral culture would issue modifications, the memorial requirement put a premium on staying within familiar and established narrative frameworks. Accordingly, orality by itself tends to be traditionalistic and inhospitable to significant variation or deviation.[71] We will see how literacy, especially in the service of philosophy, came to challenge traditionalism in the Greek world.

The relationship between literacy and tradition is a split association—in generating both stabilizing and destabilizing effects. The permanence of written documents allows cultural production to be articulated and sustained over time, transmitted long after its composition. Moreover, writing is effective for regulating and controlling social life.[72] This is especially evident in the case of written laws, which can persist indefinitely and exceed any personal decrees or memorial norms that may shape a culture. Writing also permits "registering" citizens for a social "identity" that figures in so many roles, practices, and affiliations in developed societies.

Writing allows the regulation of language itself. The plasticity of language precludes it being permanently fixed diachronically, but orality affords extensive variation of usage and dialect *synchronically* across a range of speech communities and even within a community. Writing provides a vehicle for standardizing usage and production, especially when "grammar" is organized and encoded in manuals.[73] The very idea of nouns, verbs, adjectives, tenses, and all other grammatical categories is that they are expositional constructions that may be implicit in oral usage but they are not explicated as such—speech "errors" would be noticed and corrected only in context and by enunciation, not by direction of grammatical rules. Formal regulation as an *overarching* governance of practice scenarios is only possible with the organizational "distance" of script. Indeed, the word "grammar" traces back to the Greek word *gramma*, meaning a written mark or letter, derived from *graphein*, to write or draw.[74] Dictionaries are another example of certified and regulated usage, as are formal standards for types of writing and their structure. In chapter 6, we will give more attention to writing and the standardization of language.

Despite all its regulating effects, the technology of writing also allows for openness and innovation in a number of ways. The portability of books and other written documents permits individual engagement with a text, as opposed to the social immersion of public performances in oral cultures. Even though a piece of writing is more stable than oral speech, portability separates a text from the "authorized" position of the original speaker or writer, which creates space for extended variations of interpretation—given the hermeneutical and differential character of language—especially across long stretches of time. Ironically, then, written texts both assure the maintenance of a tradition and allow for interpretive departures from an author-ized "origin." As every author knows, writing a text and being read are not always in sync. A text as a physical object greatly increases the number of engagements and thereby the possibilities of interpretive variation. A written text as such is graphically stable but its meaning is not.[75]

Compared to the specialized province of oral poets as stand-outs in their societies, writing permits expanded and more distributed possibilities of composition, and thus more individualized production apart from communal scenarios. And as we will see, the spirit of interrogation fostered by philosophical literacy can engender a *tradition* of challenging traditionalism, namely free inquiry as an ideal to be taught and encouraged. In this respect, literacy and open interrogation have usually fit well with and even inspired democratic movements, which deliberately give a political voice to individual citizens, thereby (ideally) honoring their own thinking apart from standard expectations and social hierarchies, which are forces that tend to mark non-literate cultures. At any rate, literacy launches the possibility of intellectual development beyond select domains. When children learn to read and write, they experience thoughts outside their immediate environment and they work on their own thoughts when writing compositions.[76] The recursive power of language is released for indefinite possibilities of exposure, expression, revision, and growth.

4.10. Presentation and Representation

Orality is immersed in what I have called presentational truth, especially in face-to-face conversation, action-laden speech, and poetic performance. We have noted the Greek word for truth, *alētheia*, understood as unconcealment, which fits (1) the oral requirement of preserving disclosure from the concealment of forgetfulness, and (2) the direct revelation of inspired speech granted by the Muses, which is a double negative presentation (un-concealed) that is not grounded in human consciousness or processed by the rational mind. The Muses revealed truth and knowledge to an audience through the poet (*Iliad* 2.484–2.487), including knowledge of things past, present, and future (*Theogony* 31–35). Plato himself documented the inspired character of poetry granted by the Muses, a kind of *mania*, or sacred madness that possesses the poet and cannot be a matter of cognitive construction or self-controlled composition (*Phaedrus* 245a–b).

We have also noted how the free-standing character of written graphics creates an overt distinction between "words" as such and their reference, wherein words can be construed in reified terms as entities in themselves that are "signs" for things or thoughts, something that is not evident in an oral culture, given the immediacy of presentation.[77] Writing therefore prepares the conception of language as signification and of truth as a representational relation between propositions and states of affairs. The first explicit account of such constructions is Aristotle's *On Interpretation* (1–5), where he distinguishes between spoken and written "signs" (*sēmeia*) of mental states that are "representations" (*omoiōmata*) of things in the world. The chain of signification is grounded in real things and runs as follows: things are represented in mental states, which are then represented by spoken words, which are then represented by written words. But the very notion of a sign or representation, it seems, would not be evident apart from the *perceived* difference of written words marked off against the lived world of oral language. Aristotle in this text also establishes linguistic "propositions" and "sentences" (*apophansis* and *logos*) as bearers of truth about the world. So, when we talk of mental "representations" and "propositional attitudes," we have inherited the literate transformation of language from ecstatic speech in lived experience to self-referential lexical entities.

5. PROTO-PHENOMENOLOGY AND LITERACY

The orality-literacy distinction plays a role in advancing proto-phenomenology's critique of traditional philosophical assumptions that bypass the lived world, understood as dwelling in speech. The features of orality and their expression in oral culture exhibit a speech-world that operates without standard conceptions in philosophy and linguistics. The assumptions put in question are not rejected out of hand because they can have expositional value and salience; the problem is their exclusivity and presumed primacy. Expositional and reflective constructions emerge *out of* factical immersion, and their derived character is a constraint on foundational claims. That constraint is strengthened when literacy is implicated in standard theories because its evident derivational status relative to oral language shows how the "literate mind" cannot tell the full story of human language.

Nevertheless, literacy and its philosophical legacy issue momentous disclosive capacities, which we will continue to address in coming discussions. The technology of writing enables language to be taken "off-line," apart from the lived world of speech, which creates new "objects" of investigation that figure in rational/scientific disciplines.[78] At the same time, literacy and dwelling in speech are not isolated domains. The power of habit and second nature is such that even the expositional departure of written language from orality can find its own mode of dwelling once reading and writing achieve proficiency and automaticity. Reading has its own immersed character in non-reflective occasions of engaging a written text, as suggested at the beginning of this investigation. When I read: "Your manuscript has been accepted for publication," I receive immediate world-disclosive impact that is not experienced with any of the expositional formats that have occupied philosophy and linguistics—including the alphabetic steps that figure in learning how to read and write. In other words, there is such a thing as ecstatic reading.[79] Even though writing gave birth to the notion of representation, the bi-directional relation of exposition and immersion shows that literate skills can exhibit their own presentational force.[80]

Differential fitness and the temporality of language allow for world-disclosiveness that exceeds the confinement to immediate experience. The fitness character of language retains its trace in these expanded horizons, which thereby can be called "virtual worlds." Virtuality may be different from direct experience but in certain contexts and modes of engagement, its revelatory power can be robust. The learning of speech and its virtuality is coded in human nature and becomes second nature with proficiency. Learning how to read, as we have noted, is unnatural and requires the transference of certain comprehension skills to the visual medium of written words. Yet the plasticity of human capacity is such that reading and writing can develop their own automatic facility. The material character of written language is a telling example of "extended cognition," where an extra-cranial environment not only provides affordances and scaffolding for human development, but also persists *as* a perceptible setting that launches new occasions of world-disclosive language. The engrossing power of literature aptly illustrates the immersed experience of a virtual world—with a richness and complexity that can expand horizons well beyond ordinary life.[81] The imaginative power of human intelligence is such that sensorimotor systems and embodied imagery generate a simulated absorption in virtual worlds presented by written language.[82] Whatever distortions literacy may have prompted in philosophy and linguistics, writing also delivers its own modes of ecstatic disclosure in exponentially expanded ways. I hazard to say that the reader of this book may have experienced some immersed disclosive effects in reading my sentences—until, of course, I point this outbreak the spell, so to speak. Nevertheless, as shown at the start of this investigation, such a rupture can prompt attention to the *difference* between immersion and exposition, even in the refined experience of reading a philosophy book.

NOTES

1. See Marshall McLuhan, *The Gutenberg Galaxy: The Making of Typographic Man* (Toronto: University of Toronto Press, 1962); Jack Goody and Ian Watt, "The Consequences of Literacy," *Comparative Studies in Society and History* 5, no. 3 (April, 1963): 304–345; Walter J. Ong, *The Presence of the Word: Some Prolegomena for Cultural and Religious History* (New Haven, CT: Yale University Press, 1967); and Eric A. Havelock, *Preface to Plato* (Cambridge, MA: Belknap Press, 1963). Derrida has an important take on writing in relation to philosophy, which will be addressed in chapter 5. Heidegger did not provide any extensive treatment of this question, but I believe the discussions to come in my investigation are implicit in Heidegger's phenomenology. For some specific remarks by Heidegger on how writing allows an undue objectification of language, see *Introduction to Metaphysics*, trans. Gregory Fried and Richard Polt (New Haven, CT: Yale University Press, 2014), xiv, 70–71; also, *Übungen für Anfänger Schillers Brief über die Asthetische Erziehung des Menschen*, ed. Urlich von Bülow (Marbach am Neckar: Deutsche Schillergesellschaft, 2005), 82–83.

2. The use of sign language by deaf persons, of course, is an exception. In Volume I (132–134), I discussed sign language in the context of gesture and its universal function in language. Deaf children obviously learn sign language by sight, and the

fully developed system deploys finger-spelling, which relies on literacy. We can say that oral language is the norm, and the gestural system of sign language was devised to incorporate the deaf into world-disclosive language. Although embodied gesture was likely central to the evolution of language, gesture alone is not enough to build the lexical, grammatical, and symbolic functions of a complete sign "language," which is grounded in the linguistic building blocks of meaningful "words." See Wendy Sandler, "Viva la Différence: Sign Language and Spoken Language in Language Evolution," *Language and Cognition* 5, no. 2–3 (2013): 189–203. Since finger-spelling derives from the alphabetic exposition of speech, oral language can be said to have a more original status.

3. See Florian Coulmas, *The Writing Systems of the World* (Cambridge, MA: Basil Blackwell, 1989), Chap. 14; and Per Linell, *The Written Language Bias in Linguistics: Its Nature, Origins, and Transformations* (New York: Routledge, 2005).

4. Walter J. Ong, *Orality and Literacy: The Technologizing of the Word* (New York: Routledge, 2002), 14–15.

5. In what follows I rely on Coulmas, *The Writing Systems of the World*, Chaps. 1–2. See also Barry P. Powell, *Writing: Theory and History of the Technology of Civilization* (Malden, MA: Wiley-Blackwell, 2012).

6. Eric A. Havelock, *The Muse Learns to Write: Reflections on Orality and Literacy from Antiquity to the Present* (New Haven, CT: Yale University Press, 1986), 59–62; Ong, *Orality and Literacy*, 84–91.

7. Phoenician and other Semitic scripts have been called alphabetic, but the full phonetization of the Greek alphabet is technically unique. See Powell, *Writing*, Chaps. 12–14.

8. This investigation forgoes a discussion of different script traditions and how they compare or contrast with alphabetic writing. I make no claim of "superiority" for alphabetic script; I only sketch how it has in fact affected Western thought. For a treatment of Chinese, Indian, and Semitic scripts, see Coulmas, *The Writing Systems of the World*, Chaps. 6–8 and 10.

9. See Nelson, *Young Minds in Social Worlds*, 223–225.

10. I am relying on Usha Goswami, "The Basic Processes in Reading: Insights from Neuroscience," in *The Cambridge Handbook of Literacy*, eds. David R. Olsen and Nancy Torrance (Cambridge: Cambridge University Press, 2009), 134–151.

11. Nelson, *Young Minds in Social Worlds*, 276, note 11.

12. Keith Rayner and Alexander Pollatsek, "Phonological Codes and Eye Movements in Reading," *Journal of Experimental Psychology; Learning, Memory, and Cognition* 24, no. 2 (1998), 476–497.

13. Jonathan Grainger and Thomas Hannagan, "What Is Special about Orthographic Processing?" *Written Language and Literacy* 17, no. 2 (2014): 225–252.

14. Beth Roberts, "The Evolution of the Young Child's Concept of 'Word' as a Unit of Spoken and Written Language," *Reading Research Quarterly* 27, no. 2 (Spring 1992): 124–138.

15. Liliana Tolchinsky, "The Configuration of Literacy as a Domain of Knowledge," in *The Cambridge Handbook of Literacy*, 468–486.

16. In what follows, I rely on Maryanne Wolf, *Proust and the Squid: The Story and Science of the Reading Brain* (New York: HarperCollins, 2007), Chaps. 4–6.

17. Ibid., 113. For a discussion of how contravention and exposition figure in learning how to read, see James M. Magrini, "When Praxis Breaks Down: What Heidegger's Phenomenology Contributes to Understanding Miscues and Learning in Reading," *Analysis and Metaphysics* 12 (2013): 25–46.

18. In what follows I draw from Chotiga Pattamadilok et al., "On-line Orthographic Influences on Spoken Language in a Semantic Task," *Journal of Cognitive Neuroscience* 21, no. 1 (January 2009): 167–179; Chotiga Pattamadilok et al., "Auditory Word Serial Recall Benefits from Orthographic Dissimilarity," *Language and Speech* 53, no. 3 (2010): 321–341; Chotiga Pattamadilok et al., "Unattentive Speech Processing Is Influenced by Orthographic Knowledge: Evidence from Mismatch Negativity," *Brain and Language* 137 (October 2014): 103–111; and Karla Monzalvo and Ghislaine Dehaene-Lambertz, "How Reading Acquisition Changes Children's Spoken Language Network," *Brain and Language* 127 (December 2013): 356–365.

19. I rely on Sebastian P. Suggate et al., "Incidental Vocabulary Acquisition from Stories: Second and Fourth Graders Learn More from Listening than Reading," *First Language* 33, no. 6 (2013): 551–571, and Erika Christakis, "How the New Preschool Is Crushing Kids," *The Atlantic* 377, no. 1 (January–February 2016).

20. There has been a debate in the pedagogy of reading between the "phonics" method and the "whole language" method, where the former begins with systematic instruction in the alphabet and spelling so that the child can sound out new words, and the latter emphasizes meaningful reading contexts and experiments of pronunciation and spelling, which will gradually build competence. In America, phonics seems to have prevailed, although both methods have advantages, and the decisive variable seems to be a skilled and caring teacher. See "Phonics and Whole Language," *Encyclopedia of the Social and Cultural Foundations of Education*, eds. Eugene F. Provenzo and Asterie Baker Provenzo (Thousand Oaks, CA: Sage Publishing, 2009), 581. Phonics might have an advantage because it honors the actual technology and mechanics of the alphabet as a radical alteration of how language is processed (as a phonic construction *of* meaningful words). Whole word approaches might therefore represent a retrospective error of emphasizing meaning first. There may be an analogy here with learning how to read music. One can certainly perform meaningful music without notation, but it would be odd to say that someone could develop sight reading of music without first mastering the notation as such.

21. See Kevin Robb, *Literacy and Paideia in Ancient Greece* (Oxford University Press, 1994), Chap. 1, and Coulmas, *The Writing Systems of the World*, Chap. 9.

22. Havelock, *The Muse Learns to Write*, chap. 9.

23. Richard Janko, "From Gabii and Gordian to Eretria and Methone: The Rise of the Greek Alphabet," *Bulletin of the Institute of Classical Studies* 58, no. 1 (June 2015): 1–32.

24. See Adam Parry, ed., *The Making of Homeric Verse: The Collected Papers of Milman Parry* (Oxford: Clarendon Press, 1971), Albert Bates Lord, *Epic Singers and Oral Tradition* (Ithaca, NY: Cornell University Press, 1991), and Ong, *Orality and Literacy*, Chaps. 1–2.

25. Barry B. Powell, *Homer and the Origin of the Greek Alphabet* (Cambridge: Cambridge University Press, 1996).

26. See Robb, *Literacy and Paideia in Ancient Greece*, Chap. 9, and Rosalind Thomas, *Literacy and Orality in Ancient Greece* (Cambridge: Cambridge University Press, 1992), Chap. 3.

27. Jonathan L. Ready, "The Textualization of Homeric Epic by Means of Dictation," *Transactions of the American Philological Association* 145, no. 1 (Spring 2015): 1–75.

28. For the educational role of Homeric poetry, see H. I. Marrou, *A History of Education in Antiquity*, trans. George Lamb (Madison, WI: The University of Wisconsin Press, 1956), 3–13.

29. Unless otherwise indicated, some of what follows is drawn from Bruno Gentili, *Poetry and Its Public in Ancient Greece: From Homer to the Fifth Century*, trans. A. Thomas Cole (Baltimore, MD: Johns Hopkins University Press, 1988), Chap. 1. See also Charles Segal, *Singers, Heroes, and Gods in the* Odyssey (Ithaca, NY: Cornell University Press, 1994), Chaps. 6–8.

30. It should be said that even today, the silent, solitary reading of poetry is thought to be impoverished compared to public recitation. The *sound* of poetry is no less important than its "sense."

31. See *Iliad* 2.484–2.487, 9.186–9.289 and *Odyssey* 12.188.

32. See Egbert J. Bakker, "Discourse and Performance: Involvement, Visualization and 'Presence' in Homeric Poetry," *Classical Antiquity* 12, no. 1 (April 1993): 1–29.

33. See Marcel Detienne, *The Masters of Truth in Ancient Greece*, trans. Janet Lloyd (New York: Zone Books, 1996), Chap. 2.

34. The work of Heidegger came to emphasize the world-disclosive character of poetry as a founding mode of unconcealment that precedes (historically and phenomenologically) descriptive and objective capacities of language. See "The Origin of the Work of Art," in *Off the Beaten Track*, trans. Julian Young and Kenneth Haynes (Cambridge: Cambridge University Press, 2002), 1–56; *Poetry, Language, Thought*, trans. Albert Hofstadter (New York: HarperCollins, 1971); and *On the Way to Language*, trans. Peter D. Hertz (New York: HarperCollins, 1982).

35. See Egbert Bakker, "Storytelling in the Future: Truth, Time, and Tense in Homeric Epic," in *Written Voices, Spoken Signs: Tradition, Performance, and the Epic Text*, eds. Egbert Bakker and Ahuvia Kahane (Cambridge, MA: Harvard University Press, 1997), 11–36.

36. See Grace M. Ledbetter, *Poetics before Plato: Interpretation and Authority in Early Greek Theories of Poetry* (Princeton, NJ: Princeton University Press, 2002), Chap. 1; also Segal, *Singers, Heroes, and Gods in the* Odyssey, Chap. 6.

37. See Wolf, *Proust and the Squid*, 67–68.

38. See Ong, *Orality and Literacy*, 31–33, on which I rely for some of what follows.

39. Ibid., 33–36.

40. See Ernst Cassirer, *Language and Myth*, trans. Susan K. Langer (New York: Dover Books, 1953), 45–58.

41. Ong, *Orality and Literacy*, 33.

42. Ibid., 57–67; and Jennifer Wise, *Dionysus Writes: The Invention of Theatre in Ancient Greece* (Ithaca, NY: Cornell University Press, 1998), 25–31.

43. Wise, *Dionysus Writes*, 33.

44. See David R. Olson, *The World on Paper: The Conceptual and Cognitive Implications of Writing and Reading* (Cambridge: Cambridge University Press, 1994), Chap. 5. The hand, of course, is the embodied element in producing non-mechanical writing, literally a manuscript.

45. See Wise, *Dionysus Writes*, 94ff.

46. Ibid., 95–96.

47. See Harvey Yunus, "Writing for Reading: Thucydides, Plato, and the Emergence of the Critical Reader," in *Written Texts and the Rise of Literate Culture in Ancient Greece*, ed. Harvey Yunus (Cambridge: Cambridge University Press, 2003), Chap. 9.

48. I use Yunus' translation in ibid., 193.

49. I draw from Ong's discussion of Alexander Luria's work (*Orality and Literacy*, 46–57).

50. I draw from Olson, *The World on Paper*, 33–44.

51. Ibid., 140–41.

52. See David R. Olson, "Literacy, Rationality, and Logic: The Historical and Developmental Origins of Logical Discourse," *Written Language and Literacy* 15, no. 2 (2012): 153–164.

53. Ong, *Orality and Literacy*, 54.

54. See John F. Ehrich, "Vygotskian Inner Speech and the Reading Process," *Australian Journal of Educational and Developmental Psychology* 6 (2006): 12–25.

55. Part of what follows is taken from Havelock, *The Muse Learns to Write*, 70–78.

56. In the next chapter, I will take up how digital media have brought significant changes to the meaning of a text.

57. See John Marincola, "Herodotus and Poetry of the Past," in *The Cambridge Companion to Herodotus*, eds. Carolyn Dewald and John Marincola (Cambridge: Cambridge University Press, 2006), 13–28.

58. Thucydides, *The War of the Peloponnesians and the Athenians*, ed. Jeremy Mynott (Cambridge: Cambridge University Press, 2013), 14–16. See Andrew Ford, "From Letters to Literature: Reading the 'Song Culture' of Classical Greece," in Yunus, *Written Texts*, 33–34. An *agōnisma*, or competition piece, was typical of public performances. Here Thucydides anticipates Aristotle's distinction in *Rhetoric* 3.12 between a "writerly" style (*graphikē*) and a style meant for public competitions (*agōnistikē*). For a stimulating account of the relationship between philosophy of history and philosophy of language in the Western tradition, see Roy Harris, *The Linguistics of History* (Edinburgh, UK: Edinburgh University Press, 2004).

59. Havelock, *The Muse Learns to Write*, 78.

60. Ezra Pound, *ABC of Reading* (London: Faber and Faber, 1961), 28.

61. See Ong, *Orality and Literacy*, 102–107.

62. Coulmas, *The Writing Systems of the World*, 12–13.

63. What follows is taken from Volume I, 138.

64. See Michael C. Corbalis, *The Recursive Mind: The Origins of Human Language, Thought, and Civilization* (Princeton, NJ: Princeton University Press, 2011).

65. Sometimes students will complain about a critical assessment of their written work: "Well, that's what I was trying to say!" From the standpoint of potentiality, they may be right but not with respect to actuality.

66. See Valerie Hobbs, "Looking Again at Clarity in Philosophy: Writing as a Shaper and Sharpener of Thought," *Philosophy* 90, no. 1 (January 2015); 135–142.

67. See Havelock, *Preface to Plato*, 188–190.

68. *Plato: Complete Works*, ed. John M. Cooper, trans., Stanley Lombardo and Karen Bell (Indianapolis, IN: Hackett, 1997), 760. Subsequent translations of Plato will be taken from this edition. For a discussion of reading education, see Robb, *Literacy and Paideia in Ancient Greece*, Chap. 7. Education in the classical period involved the triad of *mousikē* (music and poetry), *gumnastikē* (physical training), and *grammata* (reading and writing). The growth of literacy was generally due to the documentary operations in democratic politics and imperial functions. See T. J. Morgan, "Literate Education in Classical Athens," *The Classical Quarterly* 49, no. 1 (1999): 46–61. For the role of writing in the development of Greek law, see Michael Gargarin, *Writing Greek Law* (Cambridge: Cambridge University Press, 2008).

69. For a helpful account of Socrates (and the Sophists) in relation to the traditional model of immersive imitation of poetic texts (*mousikē* and *sunousia*), see Robb, *Literacy and Paideia in Ancient Greece*, Chaps. 7–8. See also Ford, "From Letters to Literature."

70. See Brian A. Irwin, "An Enactivist Account of Abstract Words: Lessons from Merleau-Ponty," *Phenomenology and the Cognitive Sciences* 16, no. 1 (2017): 133–153.

71. See Ong, *Orality and Literacy*, 41–42.

72. Coulmas, *The Writing Systems of the World*, 13–14.

73. Ong, *Orality and Literacy*, 105–107.

74. Grammatical analysis of word types began with the Sophists, Plato, and Aristotle. See Plato's *Cratylus* 424b-c and *Sophist* 262a-d; and Aristotle's *Poetics* 20. A fully organized and articulated grammar took shape in the 3rd–1st centuries BCE, particularly in the work of Chrysippius and Apollonius. See Andreas U. Schmidhauser, "The Birth of Grammar in Greece," and James I. Porter, "Language as a System in Ancient Rhetoric and Grammar," both in *A Companion to the Ancient Greek Language*, ed. Egbert J. Bakker (Malden, MA: Wiley-Blackwell, 2010), Chaps. 33–34. For a broader historical treatment, see Vivien Law, *The History of Linguistics in Europe: From Plato to 1600* (Cambridge: Cambridge University Press, 2003).

75. This take on writing is operative in Derrida's work. See especially *Of Grammatology*, trans. Gayatri C. Spivak (Baltimore, MD: Johns Hopkins University Press, 1976).

76. See Wolf, *Proust and the Squid*, 65–66.

77. Ong, *Orality and Literacy*, 33.

78. See David R. Olson and Keith Oatley, "The Quotation Theory of Writing," *Written Communication* 31, no. 1 (2014): 4–26.

79. See Raymond A. Prier, *Thauma Idesthai: The Phenomenology of Sight and Appearance in Archaic Greek* (Gainesville, FL: Florida State University Press, 1989), 169–179.

80. Roy Harris offers an account of writing that challenges "semiotic" theories and their abstract decontextualization of "signs." He stresses the "working sign" that embodies practical realization in specific contexts of use. See his *Rethinking Writing* (New York: Continuum, 2000).

81. Jennifer Anna Gosetti-Ferencei, "The Mimetic Dimension: Literature between Neuroscience and Phenomenology," *British Journal of Aesthetics* 54, no. 4 (October 2014): 425–448.

82. See Benjamin K. Bergen, *Louder Than Words: The New Science of How the Mind Makes Meaning* (New York: Basic Books, 2012).

Chapter 5

Philosophy and Literacy in the Greek World

In an early work, I examined the complex relationship between myth and philosophy, *muthos* and *logos*, in Greek thought from Homer to Aristotle.[1] One goal was to challenge the "progressive" view that philosophical reason displaced and "corrected" the early Greek reliance on myth and poetry. Myth never disappeared in the Greek world, not even in philosophy, and the supposed correction was in many respects rigged according to new assumptions that suppressed the kind of worldview and truth presented in mythopoetic culture. I offered a brief discussion of how the rise of literacy functioned in the advent of philosophy and its implicit shift from the oral base of Greek poetry.[2] Since then I have become convinced that the transition from orality to discourse informed by writing is a crucial guiding thread within the emergence of philosophy.[3] Here I will develop the contours of this historical material, which will supplement, extend, and specify the thrust of chapter 4: the philosophical implications of literacy in concealing what proto-phenomenology aims to highlight.[4]

Philosophy was born as a departure from traditional forms of disclosure in myth and poetry. Although never completely breaking with tradition, philosophical modes of rationality began to contest the stories of gods and heroes that shaped early Greek culture. Myth and poetry, particularly the Homeric epics, expressed in both content and form elements of the lived world that have occupied my investigation. In the next two sections, I sketch some material offered in previous work that can prepare coming discussions of Greek philosophy and literacy.[5] For the sake of economy, I am omitting most of the scholarly references and discussions that were operating in my treatment. This material is important because philosophy emerged not only as a challenge to poetic *form* and its oral character but also its *content*, the way human life was presented in early Greek poetry.

1. MYTH IN ANCIENT GREECE

In this section, I outline the meaning of myth and its manifestations in Greek thought, especially as it bears on a phenomenology of factical life.

1.1. Myth and the Lived World

Since myths have served a core cultural function in all human societies, it does no good to begin with assuming the association of myth with falsehood, as in most modern uses. I define myth as a traditional narrative that discloses a meaningful world infused with something sacred, often concerning the origins of cultural beliefs and formats. The narrative form involves stories that convey living circumstances and deeds performed by exemplary agents—with a temporal-historical shape that reaches back to an immemorial past for the sake of sustaining present and future forms of life. Mythical narratives in their factical expression shape both knowledge and affective attunement in a blended package. Myths depict and enact a lived world because they cannot be separated entirely from rituals, cults, and everyday existence.[6] In their own setting, myths are not proto-theories or even mere stories because they were woven into the lives of a people: establishing communal, educational, and religious values; prescribing daily tasks and ceremonies; inspiring artistic expression; giving meaning to birth, maturation, marriage, social roles, and death. Consequently, myth should be understood as a primal case of culture-formation.

The sacred element is important for understanding the religious aspects of mythical disclosure, at least in a loose sense. The sacred need not refer to something transcendent; in early mythical culture, the sacred is simply counter-posed to the profane, where the latter designates ordinary experience and the former expresses something extraordinary that establishes meaning and that exceeds human power and full comprehension.[7] The sacred is usually rendered as a deity or something divine, in the midst of which human beings are subordinate and recipients of something bestowed or given. The sacred is therefore owed a certain deference and reverence. Mythical culture embodies a lived world that is consonant with key findings in proto-phenomenology: active participation in a meaning-laden environment, which therefore cannot be understood in purely objective terms; yet meaningfulness cannot be cast in merely subjective terms either because it reflects something given *to* humans, exceeding their domain and therefore somehow in the *world* and not just in the mind. In this way, mythical disclosure in many respects displays what I have called *projection*.

1.2. Greek Myth

Myths in the early Greek world were much more than a form of "literature" because they animated a full cultural life, religious significance, and a genuine experience of the sacred.[8] Mythical narratives had a formative effect on cognition, affective attunement, and practical life—in phenomenological terms, they issued a disclosive story-world.[9] As we have seen, oral poetry was the main vehicle for transmitting myths and this public format gave the Greeks a collective identity, as distinct from the esoteric character of cult worship. One reason why Greek myth has usually not been taken as a genuine expression of religious culture is that it does not square well with supposedly model forms of religion originating in the Middle East and Asia. Early Greek myth and religion were thoroughly rooted in earthly existence. Every significant facet of life in the natural world had a sacred association: sun, sea, earth, light, night, love, marriage, war, governance, poetry, song, strife, cunning, craft, among much else. There was even worship of deities who seem to be personified precursors of conceptual thinking: order (*Themis*), persuasion (*Peitho*), retribution (*Nemesis*), health (*Hygieia*), and peace (*Eirene*).[10] Greek polytheism exhibited a pluralism rather than a unified divine sphere; even particular gods were rendered in variable forms. Forces of fate were ever prominent and usually associated with harm, death, or ruin—at times even beyond the control of the gods. Multiple divine forces were often in conflict and so human beings could not rest with a single sacred directive. The gods also behaved in ways considered immoral in later ethical systems. They could not be counted on to always serve human interests. The divine was therefore unpredictable and often unreliable: as Homer put it, a god may or may not bring something to pass, as the god's heart pleases (*Odyssey* 8.570–8.571). We could surmise that the unmanageable character of Greek polytheism aimed to make sense out of the fact that things do not always make sense.[11]

Early Greek religion, at least in its Homeric expression, did not offer immortality to humans, who were called "mortals" as distinct from the deathless gods.[12] Hades was the realm of the dead, which was really an insentient shadow-world that held no attraction for human beings. Departed souls there existed in a ghost-like dimension without the animations of earthly life. We could say that the souls in Hades simply gave a "presence" to the "absence" of death, something more than nothingness but less than life.

All told, the early Greek world exhibited a tragic dimension of necessary limits on human aspirations and power; and yet Greek life was vibrant and life affirming, not despite limits but perhaps because of them.[13] A finite life was not experienced as woeful and debilitating, but as a set of challenges to achieve heroic or noble deeds that will gain "immortal" glory and fame (as commemorated by poets). The gods honored such exploits and even devised scenarios for their execution. The pursuit of excellence gave meaning to life and so Greek culture was replete with settings for a contest (*agōn*) that would test strength, prowess, and achievement by way of conflicting powers—not only in battle, but also in athletics, art, and public debate.

Finally, the pluralism of Greek religion was not simply a multiplicity but also a plasticity, in being fluid, dynamic, malleable, and undogmatic. There was no fixed doctrine, no rigid cult directive, no organized canon, no single story, and no priestly class controlling the populace. There was hermeneutical flexibility and adaptability that was simply a given, without an expectation or inclination that cultural measures should find a fixed form.

2. THE HOMERIC WORLD

Assuming that epic poetry was not simply "literature" but a source of world-disclosive cultural bearings for the early Greeks, we notice elements of the lived world that precede reflective constructions typical in philosophical thinking. In other words, the Homeric world precedes philosophy not only historically but phenomenologically as well. There human existence is presented as (1) thoroughly embedded in earthly, embodied life, (2) informed by capacity and performance, (3) pluralized in different measures of meaning (especially by way of polytheism), (4) disclosed through poetic speech that fuses knowledge and feeling, entrancing its audience with ecstatic force, and (5) fatalistic in being subject to negative forces of fate and divine power, in a manner that cannot be fully comprehended or controlled by mortals.[14]

2.1. The Heroic Ideal

The account of the Trojan war in the *Iliad* was not meant to be an historical record in the modern sense; the poem begins in the midst of the war and ends before the war's completion. The primary focus of the story concerns the existential dilemma of Achilles, who was fated to die young in battle, which however would bring him glory and fame. His choice to fight favored a short heroic life over a long life without distinction. The heroic ideal embraced by Achilles represented a framework of meaning marked by an intrinsic tension: (1) human beings are essentially mortal and subject to fate (*Iliad* 6.488–6.489, 21.99ff.); (2) although the hero's ultimate fate is death, he can achieve the worldly compensation of honor and the immortality of fame (*Iliad* 22.297–22.305); (3) honor, glory, and fame can be achieved by risking one's life and facing death or defeat; and (4) the courage to face death and risk life alienates the hero from normal existence, but it also elevates him above ordinary people (*Iliad* 22.392ff. and 430ff.). When Achilles chooses to fight, he seeks a meaning that dictates his death.

Homer's poetry on occasion explicitly articulates this heroic framework, wherein the value and importance of life is correlated with death.[15] Mortals are often warned against crossing their mortal boundary (*Iliad* 5.440–5.442).

This limit is even affirmed in one case, because when Odysseus is offered immortality by the goddess Calypso (*Odyssey* 5.136), he turns it down so he can return to Penelope and his mortal life in Ithaca. In all, Homeric poetry issues narratives that measure the value of life in relation to death.[16] In this context, we get a different take on Apollo's famous maxim, "Know thyself," which was not a call for self-discovery but a reminder that one is not an immortal god—a pronouncement more akin to "Know your place."[17]

2.2. Non-Centralized Selfhood

The modern sense of selfhood is usually marked by unity, interiority, and autonomy, characteristics that first took shape in Greek philosophy. In Homeric poetry, depictions of human experience generally lack these features in strict terms.[18] Rather than a unified self or even the composite notion of a "body," experience is pluralized according to different psychic functions (*thumos*, *psuchē*, *noos*, *phrenes*) and piecemeal bodily behaviors (e.g., legs running rather than a body or a person running). Such pluralized expressions can be understood phenomenologically as not yet detached from immediate experience in the service of reflective organization or amalgamation.

The characters in Homer also lack the sense of interiority common to modern psychology. The heroes are embedded in fields of performance and social relations (in my terms, an ecstatic social-environing-world). Measures of value stem from this ecological field, not an inward self-estimation. This helps us understand the obsessive concern with honor, which materializes only by way of praise and rewards. Honor requires external confirmation, hence the fixation on tangible prizes and the spoils of victory. Excellence and self-worth can be measured only by public signs of recognition.[19] Language in Homer is typically correlated with overt performance, which has been called a prefiguration of "speech act" theory.[20] We find various collocations of *ergon* and *epos*, deed and word, correlated linguistically and contextually—such as the conjunction "both deed and word" (*ergon te epos te*). Speaking and acting in the world are presumed to go together. That is why the words of Thersites (*Iliad* 2.212) are given low status because he is incapable of effective action: he is a man of "endless talk" (*ametroepēs*), a man of no consequence.

The last element of modern selfhood that seems absent in Homer is autonomy, understood in the strict sense of a causal source of action that entails individual responsibility. The heroes are certainly not automatons because they regularly make choices; but Homeric psychology is caught up in divine intervention, where a deity penetrates a hero's makeup and either initiates or alters his motives, emotions, and capacities. One example: Ares "enters into" Hektor and "fills his limbs with force and fighting strength" (*Iliad* 17.210–17.212).[21]

In all, Homeric selfhood exhibits elements that are comprehensible in proto-phenomenological terms: ecstatic immersion, embedded practice, the social-world, action-fields, pluralism, and projection. The psychological life of heroes is not chaotic; it is gathered in their embodied existence and contextual directives. Selfhood is simply not reduced to a substantive base apart from factical deeds. The description of Odysseus as *polutropos* (*Odyssey* 1.1), meaning many ways or turns of character, can still be organized around his *name* as an "indicative" self, which points to all its instances without the need for a grounding source "behind" its manifestations.

3. THE ADVENT OF PHILOSOPHY

The emergence of philosophy in the Greek world (around the 6th century BCE) was marked by a number of departures from mythopoetic culture. It must be kept in mind, however, that the first philosophers, usually called Pre-Socratics (Thales, Parmenides, Xenophanes, Heraclitus, Anaximander, Empedocles, among others), exhibited much overlap with their traditional heritage.[22] Philosophy did not come out of the blue, and some elements of post-Homeric poetry (in lyric and tragic genres) issued existential, cognitive, and psychological developments that pre-figured philosophical thinking.[23]

In any case, philosophers began to turn away from poetic narratives in favor of abstract concepts that could bring more order to human thought, especially in terms of unified principles. Mythical accounts of the gods were dismissed or downplayed in favor of more naturalized accounts of the world and more intellectualized conceptions of divinity. Most significantly, divine mysteries and inspiration gave way to unaided procedures of human thinking that could appeal to available experience and persuade in the midst of self-directed paths of inquiry.[24] Such developments have commonly been described as the Greek "enlightenment," as the movement from a more primitive mentality to the truth-bearing character of rational thinking (from *muthos* to *logos*). Yet such a progressive script is suspect in many respects, in part because of the phenomenological priority of the lived world advanced in this investigation. If early Greek myth was in fact expressive of the lived world, then the advent of philosophical thinking should be open to interrogation if and when factical experience was unduly suppressed or marginalized.[25]

It should be said that the early philosophical texts we have do not offer much attention to methodological matters concerning *how* rational thinking proceeds. Indeed, the texts are more declarative than inquisitive, even oracular at times. That may be why these thinkers are usually classified as Pre-Socratics, because the figure of Socrates clinched the spirit of philosophy with his interrogative and dialogical posture (as presented in Plato's dialogues). For Socrates, no belief could be taken for granted or shielded from criticism. He wanted his interlocutors to test their beliefs and improve their thinking through logical reasoning, with the aim of grounding beliefs in universal principles that could overcome the ambiguities, confusions, and disparities evident in everyday thinking and received wisdom. As we will see, part of the Socratic-Platonic mission was to challenge traditional myth and poetry on behalf of new rational paradigms.

3.1. *Muthos* and *Logos*

One way to frame the questions at hand emerges from considering the linguistic history of the Greek words *muthos* and *logos*. For us, a myth usually denotes something false or lacking rational grounds. The word *logos* in Greek philosophy did come to mean a reasoned account or reason generally, often in contradistinction to poetic storytelling. But the selective and contingent character of this connotation can be garnered by a genealogical look at *muthos* and *logos*. Both words originally had to do primarily with speech and a range of related meanings: *muthos* could refer to speech, conversation, something said, fact of the matter, purpose, report, tale, and narrative; *logos* could refer to anything said, story, narrative, account, conversation, mere words as opposed to deeds, deceptive talk, agreement, thought, opinion, argument, truth, measure, proportion, law, and reason. Notice that several common meanings appear in both word groups, and that only *logos* carried a sense of deception. Early on, in fact, particularly in Homer, there was a pattern in which *muthos* was associated with authoritative speech from positions of power, and *logos* was associated with speakers in a subordinate position.[26] Indeed, the word *muthos*, understood as a story, was usually not identified with falsehood in Greek thought, even by philosophers. When Plato accused poets of telling "false stories" (*pseudeis muthous*) in *Republic* 377d, *muthos* cannot mean falsehood because then *pseudos* would be redundant; and Aristotle used *muthos* to designate the "plot" of a drama, without any sense of deficiency (*Poetics* 1450a9).[27] In any case, the *muthos-logos* association with speech highlights something distinctive about the ancient Greeks: the degree to which spoken language was at the core of their self-conception.[28]

The meaning of *logos* was not originally or even primarily a matter of reason and logic; but it became so in philosophical expression, generally as a divergence from other modes of speech, including the *muthoi* of poets and storytellers (recall Plato's use of *logos* as "prose" in *Republic* 607d). Philosophers emphasized specific forms of language governed by new criteria of unification, universality, and consistency. The link with non-philosophical uses of *logos* was nevertheless evident because, as noted in chapter 4, the most common and basic meaning of *logos* was "speech that makes sense to an audience."[29] Myths and poetic narratives could surely make sense to an audience, so a delineation of philosophical *logos* apart from mythical language entailed *different* forms of sense. One can even say that rudiments of rational form were implicit in myths.[30] We find there patterns, relationships, structures, comparisons, and causes, but such notions were embedded in the specificity and fluctuations of the lived world. Once the notion of structure, for example, became *explicit* and abstracted from specific uses (by way of writing), there arose a divergence of mythical and rational sense.

Let me sketch an example: Zeus commands a sacrifice. He is a particular god with a particular history and character. A kind of knowledge follows from dealing with him. A form of consistency and purpose is intrinsic to his command. Obedience is due him "because" he is a god; "if" he is disobeyed, "then" humans will be punished. In other words, causes and inferences are implicit, but the form is identical with the content (the command of a particular god). In Greek myth, the command of one deity could be inconsistent with that of another, and yet this was seen to be *in order*, because that was thought to be the way of things (just as the lived world is often unpredictable and conflicted).[31] But with philosophical reason, the notion of consistency was abstracted from factical experience, a development partly influenced by mathematics. Then there could emerge a focus on consistency per se, which prompts the notion of *universal* consistency across the board in discourse—and *now* the mythical field of descriptions can be deemed problematic. Consider Socrates' easy dismissal of Euthyphro's claim that piety is what the gods desire: the different gods are in conflict over what is desirable; so any particular option can be both pious and impious at the same time (*Euthyphro* 7ff.). There is an intrinsic *ambiguity* in Greek myth, namely a co-mingling of opposing forces in a single domain (think of the common motif of family strife), which does not fit the later philosophical logic of non-contradiction, the exclusive separation of opposite conditions. Since language in an oral culture was caught up with action and efficacy, diverging manifestations could be indicated by a common valorizing term or attached to the same agent. As Detienne puts it:

> The divine world is fundamentally ambiguous, and even the most positive gods are tinged with ambiguity. Apollo is the Shining One, but at times he is also the Dark One. While for some he is flanked by the Muses and memory, for others oblivion and silence stand at his side. The gods know the truth but can also deceive: their appearance are traps for men, and their words are always enigmatic, concealing as much as they reveal.[32]

The shift from ambiguity to formal consistency was a central feature in the conflict between philosophy and myth in the Greek world. To sum up thus far, we are engaging the historical tension between an oral/mythical culture (which was embedded in the lived world) and a literate/rational culture (which developed thought constructions abstracted from the lived world).

4. PLATO AND THE POETS

The discord between philosophy and traditional mythopoetic culture reached a climax in the dialogues of Plato. Yet Plato's frequent deployment of myths and the narrative form of his own writings significantly complicate the story at hand—so much so that some interpreters challenge the standard reading of Plato as a staunch opponent of mythopoetic thinking and a proponent of fixed metaphysical doctrines.[33] I think that Plato was serious in his deployment of myth, which provided a vital supplement to rational analysis and even served to delimit the reach and results of philosophical thought. Yet I also believe that Plato was serious when he targeted poetry and myth as obstacles to philosophical wisdom. Am I confused?

The critique of poetry in the *Republic* had little to do with "aesthetics" or a censorship of the arts. Greek poetry was not an "art form" but a world-disclosive source of meaning, and in Plato's day epic and tragic poetry were still primary vehicles for cultural bearings and education. Socrates calls Homer the primary educator of Greece; his poetry has been ordering "our entire lives" (606eff.). Plato's critique had to do with truth, the transmission of cultural values, and pedagogical authority. He was waging a momentous *diaphora* (607b), a contest against established meanings on behalf of new standards of truth and morality. So, Plato's philosophy was not averse to myth and poetry per se—since the dialogues were often informed by such things—but to *traditional* myth and poetry.

Plato's critique of traditional poetry was fundamental because it challenged both the material and formal elements at the heart of epic narratives and tragic drama. The material element can be summed up as the depiction of a tragic world-view; the formal element can be located in the psychological features of poetry's (oral) composition, performance, and reception—each of which involved forces that surpassed conscious control and blocked critical reflection. For Plato, the formal and material core of traditional poetry represented a potent and ingrained cultural barrier that had to be overcome to clear the way for two new ideals: rational inquiry and an overarching justice governing the world and the human soul (602d–604a; 605a–c).

As Socrates tells it in the *Republic*, epic and tragic poetry present a world that is unstable, unpredictable, mysterious, and fatally ruinous of human possibilities; mortality is the baseline limit of life, and death is portrayed as repulsive in its darkness (386–392). Here Plato provides an accurate reading of early mythopoetic culture, in line with what we have seen previously. But Socrates accuses the poets of telling "false stories," where heroes come to grief and surrender to powerful emotions, where the gods act immorally, fight each other, cause evil and ruin, punish the innocent, change form, disguise themselves, and lie (377ff.). One thinks of Oedipus as the paradigm case of tragic life: a noble man faced with a terrible fate, who resists out of moral motives; and yet in this very resistance he actualizes his fate.[34] One might also think of Socrates in this vein, a man who compares himself to a tragic hero (*Phaedo* 115a), and who is destroyed following a divine calling to practice philosophy. The *Republic* displays a wealth of meanings, but I think the text is essentially an anti-tragic *muthos* (a term applied to the account of the *polis* at 376d). The full course of the dialogue can be called a narrative about the possibility and desirability of a just life in a world that resists justice. The virtue of justice is defended by Socrates against Thrasymachus and the cynical implications of the Gyges myth (Books 1–2). The long digression about the *polis* is meant to illuminate on a larger scale the picture of a just soul and its advantages.[35] The political digression unfolds to meet the daunting task posed to Socrates in Book 2: prove not only that the just man is worthy but *happier* than the unjust man, that he will flourish in some way—and this in terms of the toughest case imaginable, pitting the unjust man thought by everyone to be just against the just man thought by everyone to be unjust (361). In Book 10 (612), this task is reiterated as the purpose of the entire dialogue. And the rectification myth of Er (616–618) performs the climax of Socrates' project: immortality serves an essential function in overcoming the limits facing rationality and justice in earthly life.

Homer's depiction of Odysseus was in many ways a stark contrast to Platonic hopes. As we have seen, he is a heterogeneous character, a man of "many ways and turns" (*polutropos*), and his capacity for deceptive cunning (*mētis*) is frequently celebrated (*Odyssey* 13.295ff.). Most notably, Odysseus turns down Calypso's offer of immortality (5.203ff.), preferring his homecoming that includes old age and death. Indeed, the opening of the epic (1.59) points to this episode and tells us that Odysseus "yearns to die" (*thaneein himeretai*)—and Odysseus makes his choice *after* having witnessed the grim reality of Hades described in Book 9. Given this picture of heroic finitude, it is telling that the myth of Er in Plato's text has Odysseus recanting his Homeric persona, choosing for his next embodiment the quiet, unaccomplished life of a private individual (*Republic* 620C).

All told, the fact that the poets and their tragic stories figure prominently at both ends of the dialogue cannot be incidental. Traditional myths were fully expressive of the obstacles blocking the path of Socrates' mission. Plato wants to tell a *better* story than the poets, one that can overcome the possible tragedy of a just life. And one cannot help but recall the fate of Socrates, whose death at the hands of Athens *would* be tragic without the kind of rectification suggested in the *Republic*.

The formal element in Plato's critique concerns the psychological structure of poetic production, performance, and reception. The traditional view was that poets were inspired receptacles for the sacred power of the Muses, a "revelation" more than a "creation." Plato agreed that a poet is "not in his senses but is like a fountain giving free course to the water that keeps flowing on" (*Laws* 719c), that poets are "out of their minds" (*Phaedrus* 245a). This matter of ecstatic immersion in a force exceeding the conscious mind was also implicated in the objections to *mimēsis* in the *Republic*. In Greek, *mimēsis* referred not only to representational likeness but also to psychological identification in poetic performance and audience reception, where actors, reciters, and listeners were "taken over" by the poetic imagery and its emotional power.[36] Here is Gorgias in the *Encomium of Helen*:

> All poetry I judge and define to be speech (*logon*) in verse (*metronēs*); when the audience hears it, terrifying horror, tearful pity, and sorrowful longing enter them, and the soul experiences its own emotion at the actions and feelings of others in their fortunes and misfortunes, produced through speech.[37]

Platonic accounts of *mimēsis* as identification in the context of acting and spoken performance can be found in the *Ion* (533ff.) and the *Sophist* (267). In the *Ion*, the power of poetry is depicted as a chain of magnetic rings, which transmit a compelling force of attraction from the Muses to poets to rhapsodes to audiences. What really mattered to Plato in the *Republic* was not mimetic representation, because the example of painting is described as merely an *analogy* for the genuine matter of concern, mimetic identification with poetic language (603c). And Socrates confesses (605cff.) that even the "best of us" can become enchanted by poetry and swept away by the *pleasure* of empathic union with the sufferings of tragic characters—an effect that ruins the "manly" ideal of silencing and mastering grief (605e). In Books 2 and 3, the censoring of poetry was qualified and seemed restricted to the context of educating children. But later, poetry's power threatens the reflective mental control of adults as well, and for this reason *all* mimetic poetry (epic and tragic) are to be banned from the ideal city (595a). The only forms of poetry permitted are hymns to the gods and songs praising good men (607a–b). The central problem of mimetic identification is that critical reflection is incommensurate with the "captivating" language of poetry; a reflective stance must disable the force of poetic communication. The hymns and songs permitted in the *Republic* are ethically beneficial, and so their mimetic effects are worthy and need not be subjected to critical reflection.[38]

It should be noted that epic poetry itself recognized the enchanting power of poetic speech (*Iliad* 9.186–9.189 and *Odyssey* 11.334); and its danger for mortals was vividly portrayed in the episode of the Sirens (*Odyssey* 12), whose song brings death rather than life by causing men to forget their vital tasks. The Sirens can be seen to embody the sheer power of poetic enchantment *without* its effect of engendering cultural memory. The Sirens, then, are a demonic divergence from the Muses and their role of establishing and sustaining stories for future appropriations of a memorable past (see *Iliad* 6.357–6.358).[39] In line with this divided posture, Plato's critique of myth and poetry was not absolute because his dialogues exhibited their own lived character and artistic force on behalf of culture production. His specific target was traditional mythopoetic disclosure—which was primarily indicative of an *oral* culture. My thesis is that Plato's reproach of poetry on behalf of philosophy is at a certain level a challenge to orality by way of literate skills that figure in philosophical thought. In the next two sections, I develop this thesis in some detail.

5. LITERACY AND PHILOSOPHY

In view of discussions thus far, we can say that reading and writing make possible an array of cognitive abilities that generate philosophical thinking and depart from conditions of orality: the spacialization of language as a discernible object, organization and regulation, decontextualization, disengaged reflection, abstraction, and representation. Historically speaking, a range of intellectual discoveries and cultural achievements in the Greek world—mathematics, law, history, philosophy, science, grammar, theater, among others—cannot be properly understood apart from literacy. Graphic figuration also had formative effects. Mathematics and geometry are figural disciplines, requiring abstract units of numeration and spatial lines that are (1) graphically drawn with formal precision and (2) manipulable in the course of a proof. The manifest rigor of mathematical thinking was a significant influence on philosophical developments. In a wider sense, graphic signs, symbols, and numbers also played a notable role in most forms of cultural documentation.[40]

There is also the interesting case of "elemental" thinking prominent in Greek thought, which aimed to analyze and break down common-sense objects into their basic elements that constitute them or combine to create them. The word for "element" in Greek is *stoicheion*, which originally denoted things in a row and then shifted to the row of alphabetic letters and then to the abstract notion of an element. The expositional analysis of language into sonic letter forms that build words allowed an extension of such a reduction-construction scheme to other areas of inquiry. In *Timaeus* 48b–c, Plato calls earth, air, fire, and water the "letters of the universe" (*stoicheia tou pantos*), and he frequently used lettering as a way to understand philosophical analysis and conceptual order.⁴¹ Aristotle and the Stoics then cemented this derivation of "elemental" thinking for posterity.⁴²

The summary point so far is twofold: (1) Greek philosophy and science could not have taken shape in a preliterate or non-literate culture;⁴³ and (2) "literacy" is not limited to alphabetic script because it includes a host of graphic figures that functioned as affordances for refined rational thought.

5.1. Writing and Conceptualization

The most significant operation in the workings of philosophy is the formation of abstract concepts. How could alphabetic writing have contributed to conceptualization in Greek thinking? Oral speech is thoroughly concrete in its embodied milieu, the specific contexts of speech acts, the sensuous imagery, and the direct immersion in immediate descriptions and expressions. With the conversion of speech into written words, graphic alphabetic lines create a radically different presence. The visual markings that make up t-r-e-e are arbitrary in the sense of being nothing like a tree or the sounded word *tree* in its context of use. Instead of talking about trees in concrete situations, we now *see* this talk separated from contexts, and what we see is not a tree but a visual object utterly unlike a tree or any other sensuous thing in experience. Yet a link with actual speech acts is retained, and once reading and writing become second nature, we develop a new way of accessing the world through the *nonsensuous* visual presence of alphabetic lines. In effect, the power of abstraction can emerge by way of this technological transformation of speech. The written word t-r-e-e itself has no concrete features other than its abstract graphic form in a material medium. And as Bruno Snell has argued, the function of the definite article in Greek language made it possible to recursively create abstract substantives out of concrete nouns, adjectives, and verbs: not "Look at the tree over there," but "the tree," everything that makes up "treeness" in general; and "justice" as "the just," that which is just in general, where the modifier "just" is converted into a subject of modification (*to dikaion*). Seemingly comparable instances in poetry, such as *ta dikai* in Hesiod, were not really substantives but aggregate nouns (the series of just acts).⁴⁴

The Socratic search for definitions was precisely a focus on substantives, and the novelty of his approach is shown in his continual refusal to accept a ready citation of specific examples in response to the question What is X? Socratic definitions aimed for abstract universals that would unify and *govern* the use of particulars, rather than simply collect particulars. Yet definition, as a formal organization of specific uses, seems to be a contingent literate capacity that is not evident in oral cultures, as we saw in chapter 4 when the request to define a tree was rebuffed as unnecessary.⁴⁵ That response indicates not an obstinate refusal of cognitive thought, but a different way in which a tree can be *understood*. The call for a formal definition of a tree is different from its living sense evident in oral culture, where a tree would be comprehended in various situational and practical contexts. Here the definitional question, What *is* a tree?—which suggests an atemporal posit of a fixed form (*Laches* 198dff.)—would not even arise because the sense of trees is woven within a shifting temporal nexus of specific dealings and relations.[46] In this respect, an ostensive pointing to examples would actually suffice for understanding something; but not for Socrates, who looks for an "essence" that cannot be satisfied by any particular instance.

Given the pedagogical milieu of *conversation* presented in Plato's dialogues, the difficulty experienced by many interlocutors in comprehending the conceptual methods at work in the discussions may be easier to understand as a deficit of literate skills, rather than obstinate ignorance. In the *Laches* (192a), Socrates is asking for the general meaning of courage that can unify particular types of courage. When he asks Laches if he understands the point of the *question* (finding a *unity* behind a common word for different instances), Laches replies that he does not. Likewise, in the *Hippias Major*, Hippias is unable to grasp the meaning of Socrates' criticism that examples cannot suffice for capturing the meaning of a general concept. Hippias sees "no difference" between "the fine" and a fine thing (287d–e). The *Theaetetus* shows more success. After attempting to define knowledge with examples, Socrates stresses the different posture of finding a common form. Theaetetus quickly grasps the point by referring to a similar process he learned when seeking a common form in mathematical and geometrical figures (147dff.).[47]

How could such universal forms come to be ascertained as new "objects" of inquiry? Is it the visual graphics of writing that creates a "concrete universal," an accessible presence stripped of all specificity, which nevertheless points back to particular instances now "re-formed" in abstract terms? If true, this would help explain something that otherwise seems puzzling. Plato and Aristotle deployed terms with original meanings of visual perception—*idea, eidos, theōria*—to denote conceptual forms and powers of intelligibility that purportedly exceed or transcend sense perception—as in *Republic* 507b: the true being of each thing is its *idea*, which is thought (*noeisthai*) but not seen (*horasthai*). Yet intellection does seem to involve another kind of "seeing." In the *Euthyphro*, when asking about the nature of piety, Socrates dismisses mere examples of pious behavior; he is looking for the *eidos* or *idea* of piety, that which is "the same with itself (*auto autō*)" in every *praxis* (5dff.), which he can "look at" (*apoblepōn*) and use as a model (*paradeigma*) to measure what is pious in any instance (6e).

In Plato's dialogues, a sensuous *eidos* often provides an analogical gateway to philosophical reflection, as in frequent references to craft, but a true *eidos* can only be ascertained by a qualitatively different kind of intellectual "vision." We might well wonder what Aristotle meant when he said that non-material form is a "look (*eidos*) disclosed in *logos*" (*Physics* 193a3ff.), where *logos* can mean "speech" but also "word" or "sentence." Was it the written word that made possible the abstract "look" of ideas and the revolutionary construction of the "mind's eye," what Aristotle called the "eye of the soul" (*ommati psuchēs*)?[48] Can this be the meaning of the claim in Plato's *Cratylus* (390e) that a name can embody a thing's true *eidos* by positing or setting it down (*tithenai*) in letters and syllables (*grammata kai sullabas*)? Giovanni Manetti tells us that in Greek culture, a sign was a perceptible thing that refers to, or allows knowledge of, something non-manifest (*adēlon, aphanes*); and that in Plato, a linguistic sign is a revelation (*dēlōma*) of a non-manifest, non-perceived reality, either an object or its essence.[49] It is noteworthy that the discussion of "primary names" in *Cratylus* 422e uses the word *stoicheion* to indicate a non-derivable element or essence.

The questions at hand suggest a tempting provocation: that the philosophical deployment of vision words to render abstract concepts was not simply a metaphorical transfer from visual sensation, but rather a new kind of *actual* vision of the abstract lines of meaning-laden written words—recall that skilled readers perceive a word as a higher-order "object," not simply a string of letters.[50] Consequently, the abstract character of written words—*as such* in their visible presence—could well serve philosophical reflection detached from immediate experience.[51] Since literacy provided such radically new openings for thought, Greek philosophers were likely so enthralled by these new possibilities as to be less prone to reflexive awareness of the graphic medium at work in philosophical thinking. Yet there are hints of such awareness, as we have seen and will see again in coming discussions.

5.2. Scriptio Continua

There is a problem with my claim that written words provide new "objects" of attention, which fits well our writing formats because of graphic word separation. Ancient Greek texts, however, did not have routine word separation because of so-called *scriptio continua*, where words were strung together continuously without breaks (continuouslywithoutbreaks). A common and plausible explanation for this practice stems from the fact that written texts were intended primarily for oral recitation and that reading aloud was the norm; word separation was not necessary because the ear would pick up word differentiation more than the eye, since normal speech is generally a seamless flow without perceptible breaks.[52] This complicates my suggestion that written words created new visual objects that aided abstraction and reflection. Nevertheless, *learning* to write—by first learning letters and then writing words down—can serve my analysis because such a practice involves piecemeal attention to the different words. The performance of writing is a more visually focused departure from the oral accent of reading. Acquiring the skill of writing is originally an embodied practice that coordinates hand and eye in relation to speech; and it begins in a fragmented fashion, with the learning of lettering and word formation, which in the context of instruction and assessment would seem to require isolated attention to graphic units.[53]

I would surmise that the very act of writing a philosophical text is a non-oral, reflective redirection of language apart from overt speech. However, the association of *scriptio continua* with oral delivery has been cited to weaken claims that writing was a turn to silent reflection. Yet written texts in the Greek world were not exclusively meant for oral recitation; and the practice of silent reading was not uncommon.[54] The scroll pages carried a narrow span of text, averaging fifteen to twenty-five characters per line, which was an aid to both writing and reading; scanning was easier and the speed and accuracy of reading was enhanced. Silent reading was even more efficient than oral recitation, and it was especially apt for longer scholarly texts. Accordingly, the reading of a philosophical text was more likely to be silent. So there remains a way to speak of silent visual attention to words in Greek reading, which squares with Plato's depiction of a *silent* comprehension of the *logos* associated with writing, as we will see. And in the *Phaedo* 97cff, Socrates tells of having heard a recitation of a book by Anaxagoras, and then eagerly attaining a copy and rapidly reading it himself (presumably in silence). In summation, there is good evidence against the notion that *scriptio continua* rendered silent reading unlikely if not impossible.[55]

What can explain the development of silent reading? Svenbro offers an intriguing theory.[56] *Scriptio continua* is surely not the most amenable format for the reading process, but the invention of word separation had to wait until the Middle Ages, mainly for scholarly purposes.[57] As noted, reading aloud was a common form of engaging a written text and it had certain advantages over silent reading. The word for reading was *anagignōskein*, meaning to recognize, to know words again. For the vocal reader, the ear recognizes what the eye sees (mere letters that do not speak). In silent reading, the eye "sees" the sound, without the mediation of the reader's voice. Only now does there arise the notion of a "pure" representational relation between writing and speech; without the vocal supplement of the reader, written words become more detached from speech. In any case, Greek theater may have provided a pathway to silent reading. Actors speak written lines, while the audience is passive and silent; the actor embodies "vocal writing." The passive audience *sees* this vocal writing (*theatron* stems from *thea*, having to do with seeing). In a fascinating case, there was an explicit rendition of vocal writing in Greek theater, a play by Callias called the "ABC Show" (*Grammatikē Theōria*):

there a chorus of twenty-four women represented all the letters in the alphabet and acted out a series of reading lessons. The point is this: theater presents writing on stage in the voice of actors, viewed by a silent audience; this passive (non-vocalized) relation to a written text can move from silently seeing a play to silently reading the script. Here we notice the possibility of vocal reading transformed into silent reading. In general terms, silent readers could be said to read with their "minds," not their active voices; and the silence provides an "interiorization" of the reading process. Now what is seen can open up "representational" space between writing, speaking, and thinking.

5.3. Qualifying the Literacy Thesis

In exploring the intellectual consequences of writing, I must be careful not to over-state the relationship between literacy and philosophy or the contrast between literacy and orality.[58] First of all, philosophy as we understand it did not arise in some literate cultures. Literacy, I think, is a necessary condition for the development of philosophy but not a sufficient condition. In the Greek case, other elements have to be noted, namely distinctive religious, social, and political factors operating in the culture. Philosophy was in many ways a turn toward the natural world and natural experience, rather than some kind of spiritual transcendence—and it associated with the rise of "natural science" and "humanism."[59] This kind of direction could arise in a religious atmosphere wherein the gods would implore mortals to stay within their earthly realm and not strive to be divine. The flexible and undogmatic character of Greek religion also made philosophical challenges less dangerous—although some thinkers did indeed get into trouble. In addition, legal and political developments generated a tolerance for free speech and inquiry.[60]

The openness of Greek society can also be gathered in its agonistic character. Contests imply no predetermined result but rather an opportunity for achievement pitted against an opponent. Contentious speech was a fixture in classical Greek culture, as displayed in two concurrent formats: tragic drama and democratic politics. Greek tragedy offered composed scenes of interactive speeches in a setting of perspectival tensions arising within social, political, and cultural domains. Democratic politics involved unscripted speech performances in debates vying for citizen approval.[61] Even though philosophers such as Plato and Aristotle had their criticisms of democracy, this very critical spirit was made possible by democratic discourse—which by common consensus was preferable to old aristocratic orders based on wealth and birth.[62] Democratic speech presupposed certain factors that could resonate with philosophical thinking. Discussion began in the midst of professed beliefs offered to a wide audience—not religious revelation and not speech *to* or *from* a ruler or privileged group. The aim to persuade an audience replaced dictation and traditional custom. Argument and persuasion in this respect benefited from broad appeal—yet the philosophical ideal of rational persuasion typically would not want common opinions to be the last word.

Mathematics was also a significant influence on the development of Greek philosophy, but even here an agonistic atmosphere was operative in a manner not exhibited in other cultural traditions.[63] Mathematical science in any form depends on written signs and graphic diagrams. Yet since Greek adversarial customs had writers and speakers contending for audience approval, deductive demonstration in mathematics presumed an *indefeasible* conclusion, where axiomatic implications generated the "force" of compliance with what could not be denied—in Greek, "necessity" (*anankē*) was derived from physical compulsion. The very idea of an "argument" producing a "conclusion" (a decisive result) was born in a particular cultural environment. Chinese mathematical science reflected a more authoritarian outlook, in terms of established knowledge simply handed down from master teachers to student apprentices. The summary point is that (Western) philosophical thinking, understood as an inheritance from the Greek tradition, is not an automatic consequence of literacy because (1) not every literate culture has given birth to its specific features, and (2) other cultural forces in the Greek world besides literacy figured in generating the spirit of philosophy. In other words, literacy was a necessary but not sufficient condition for the emergence of philosophy in ancient Greece.

Another important qualification of my thesis is that full literacy in the Greek world was neither widespread (the percentage of fully literate citizens in classical Athens was 5%–10%) nor separated from oral speech.[64] What matters for our interpretation is not so much literacy *simpliciter*, but the different uses and functions of written texts, many of which were tied to oral performance (as in recitation), but some of which were geared toward rational reflection. Although literacy was indeed implicated in significant intellectual transformations, it never was, and is not even now, a discrete sphere utterly apart from spoken language. In the next section, we will confront a special problem in this regard. In any case, here we take note of Walter Ong's distinction between primary and secondary orality, between an oral culture without writing and oral language within, and much informed by, literacy. We have indicated that there is no such thing as "orality" in primary orality; orality as such is a construction of literate reflection on what is "absent" in a non-literate culture.[65] Although we literates can never access primary orality, my investigation aims to intimate significant differences in oral and written language by reflecting on how these differences can be gleaned from developments in Greek culture. It is evident that despite the oral performative context of early written texts, there did develop in the time of Plato and Aristotle a *selective* culture of engaging written texts simply for reading and studying, rather than performance. And it is this cultural setting that spawned the development of philosophy.[66]

6. PLATO AND WRITING

One thing is clear: Plato was a brilliant philosophical writer. And given the preceding analysis, it seems evident that literacy played a crucial role in the story of philosophy. Yet Plato's dialogues exhibit an ambiguity about writing and its value relative to living speech. For one thing, the dialogue form represents a kind of writing that retains the milieu of conversation as its subject.[67] Also the *Phaedrus* contains a specific critique of writing, which I will get to shortly. I think Plato does give a certain priority to living dialogue, but recalling his concerns about the effects of poetry, the dialogical ideal is not a defense or retrieval of orality per se. I maintain that the kind of philosophical dialogue promoted by Plato requires literate participants. And there are a number of references to writing in the dialogues that lead me to this view.

Yet again, the picture is not entirely clear. In the *Republic*, there is no specific mention of educating citizens in reading and writing, although Socrates does mention the learning of letters (402a); and an earlier dialogue, the *Protagoras*, discusses the learning of letters in education (325cff.). In the *Cratylus* (424b–425a), Socrates describes the building of words from letters and syllables; then nouns and verbs are combined to arrive at "language" (*logon*). There is a consensus that the composition of the *Republic* and the establishment of Plato's Academy were close together in time.[68] The Academy certainly used books for instruction, but we recall that in Plato's day, a common practice was to read books aloud to an audience, which likely was part of philosophical engagement. Nevertheless, silent private reading was practiced at the time. Moreover, mathematical education, so important to Plato, required the careful study and analysis of graphic representations.[69] As far as the dialogues are concerned, it is in the *Laws* that reading and writing are specifically mandated for schooling (810ff.).

One other effect of writing should be noted: the capacity for individualized and internalized reflection made possible by books, which are portable and separable from public speech acts that are socially informed and externally directed. Adding the previous point about the abstract "look" of written words, which permits the reflective alteration of language into new conceptual forms, perhaps certain passages in the dialogues can be clarified by way of the connections between reading, abstraction, and internalization. In the *Philebus* (38eff.), memory and perception are compared to writing (*graphein*) words (*logos*) in the soul. Knowledge is written in the soul in the manner of a book (*biblion*). This account is preceded by the picture of a solitary soul and its self-possession of thought prior to verbalizing aloud to others in spoken conversations—which fits many references in the dialogues to the soul's interior possession of ideas. The *Theaetetus* (189eff.) describes thinking as the soul's *logos* and conversation (*dialegesthai*) with itself, a *logos* not spoken aloud to another person, but "silently to itself" (*sigē pros auton*). And in the *Protagoras* (347cff.), Socrates advocates the self-sufficiency of relying on one's own voice in a conversation. This leads me to think that Plato's dialectical model of philosophy is not *radically* dialogical (in the sense of an irreducible intersubjective practice), and that good results and participation in a conversation involve importing or possessing reflective insight, something made possible by the technology and practice of writing, which would explain the metaphorical use of writing to describe knowledge in the soul. Genuine knowledge of pure Forms is basically an internal intuition, a reflective posture of the soul by itself within itself, as opposed to external sources of knowledge gained by sense perception or hearing the speech of other people (*Theaetetus* 185bff.).

Aristotle also deploys the metaphor of writing in *De Anima* to characterize the development of thought. In the account of *nous* as the potential for thinking forms, Aristotle says that what is thought in the mind is equivalent to "the same way that letters are on a tablet that bears no actual writing; this is just what happens in the mind" (430a1–2). Then after including the soul in processes of making akin to *technē* (artifice) forming matter, Aristotle says that the soul is both a receptive "becoming all things" and an active "making all things" (430a10ff.); and that the soul is like a hand in being an instrument (*organon*) that employs instruments: *nous* is a form (*eidos*) that employs forms (*eidōn*) (432aff.). So, the mind both receives intelligible forms without sensible matter (429a15ff.) and activates intelligible form, and this twofold process is compared with *technē* (430a13). Would it be too much a stretch to detect here a tacit reference to the receptive and active techniques of reading and writing?

6.1. The Critique of Writing in the *Phaedrus*

The *Phaedrus*, of course, complicates my argument because of its overt criticism of writing in favor of living speech. But let's look carefully at the text. Early on, Socrates confesses to preferring life in the city because he "loves learning" (*philomathēs*), which cannot be found in the country. He can be coaxed to leave the city if lured by *logous en bibliois*, "discourse in books" (230d–e). When Socrates tries to compete with Lysias' written speech about love, he does poorly and regrets his performance: he slipped into poetic modes of speech and ecstatic states of mind, in part because of enchantment at the physical presence of the beautiful Phaedrus (234d, 238e). The move to cover his head attests to Socrates' worry about the effects of embodied speech (and anticipates the later picture of the soul needing to control the force of the body). The implication here is that pure orality cannot be the solution to the coming concerns about writing.

In the dialogue, writing is not intrinsically problematic, but it is capable of serving deceptive rhetorical practices (267aff.). Books about speeches do provide guidance for the proper structure and function of speech writing (266d), which should possess the power to "guide the soul" (271c–d). And the story about King Thamus and the god Theuth with respect to writing is prefaced by the task of discerning good from bad writing (274bff.). Then comes the critique of writing (274eff.), which is called a *pharmakon*, with an ambiguous connotation of both a medicine and a poison. A reliance on writing diminishes the skills of memory; and most importantly, writing involves "external" signs belonging to others rather than an internal possession. Writing provides only the appearance of wisdom since it is outside the direct access to knowledge. Once written down, words become dead and mute; they cannot answer questions or defend themselves. Plato's point about question and answer presumably reflects a pedagogical program: "Why do you believe X?" not only prepares the defense of beliefs but the teaching of knowledge by way of personal discovery. Another important element in Plato's criticism of writing has to do with the emerging distinction between what is said and what is meant by what is said. Written texts by themselves "say" the same thing forever; they cannot answer questions about the meaning of the text (275d). Finally, written words can circulate anywhere, indiscriminately to the able and unable alike.

In an interesting passage, the *logos* (speech) that is superior to writing is "written" (*graphetai*) in the soul of the learner and it can both defend itself and distinguish proper from improper recipients (276aff.). Here we also hear of the contrast between the inferior "sowing" of words by pen and ink and a superior form of dialectic, which plants and sows in the soul the words of knowledge that can also be reproduced in others—this seems less like a "dialogue" and more like an "infusion." Then the proper writing of speeches is described as being concerned with truth and deploying the procedures of definition, analysis, division, and collection, which all seem to be literate skills.[70] In the *Philebus* (18b–d), Theuth is cited as the one who distinguishes and organizes the forms of vocal elements into a system of their combinations and differences; such structure must involve a passage from sonic elements to graphic letters, because the knowledge involved is called *technē grammatikē* and its possessor is called a *grammatikos*. In the *Sophist* (253a), the problem of defining things by way of combination and separation calls for a philosopher's expertise, which is likened to a grammarian who can show which letters of the alphabet do and do not fit together linguistically.

Returning to the *Phaedrus*, at 264c, the organic order of a speech is needful of a "bodily" structure that is written out (*gegrammena*) in order to delineate proper relationships.

Something like Plato's dialogues themselves would seem to be emblematic of good writing, and indeed the *Phaedrus* associates philosophy with the best kind of written *logos* (277bff.). A case can be made that Plato's dialogues were not meant to be "published" in our sense of the term (for an open market of readers); rather they were used primarily for the pedagogical purpose of philosophical education in the academy, where the texts were recited, read, studied, and discussed, with the aim of *continuing* intellectual exploration and composition.[71] This might provide telling clues about why the dialogues exhibit an open and "unfinished" character. In any case, Socrates says that any writing for "public" speeches is not worthy of serious attention. What *is* worthy are words "truly written in the soul," marked by a "clear and perfect" *internal* understanding of goodness and justice, which then becomes ready for planting *in* other souls (278a–b). In the *Republic*, the soul's inward possession of knowledge seems essential to counteract the conditioning power of poetry, where the effects of poetic *mimēsis* settle into the very nature of a person, in body, speech, and thought (395). Philosophical knowledge is the antidote (*pharmakon*) against the corrupting effects of poetry (595a), which create falsehood *in* the soul—not simply false "words" (*logoi*) or beliefs but a morally "false life" (382b–c).[72] All told, we can say that Plato's critique of writing is not a preference for oral language per se, but a defense of literate thought (writing "in the soul") against mimetic identification with the oral force of poetry and public oratory.

The ambiguous treatment of writing in the *Phaedrus* can be sorted out by way of a tension between written texts themselves and the intellectual *effects* made possible by literacy (its *powers* and not simply its products). The dialogue raises the problem of the detachability of written words from the milieu of lived conversation. But this does not amount to a defense of "orality," given the persistent criticisms in several dialogues of the power of poetic speech and political rhetoric to overwhelm the mind (and Socrates' own confession of the failure of his own oration in the *Phaedrus*). Rather, the critique of writing amounts to a defense of the *literate* soul against (1) the stand-alone character of a written text set apart from the living reality of knowledge, and (2) the sterility of writing when not originating from, or addressed to, those select souls who are capable of possessing knowledge (*Phaedrus* 275e). So, the *pharmakon* of writing can be associated with both the *remedy* of literacy overcoming mimetic orality and the *poison* threatening philosophy, when writing circulates to the wrong audience.

As we have seen, given (1) the common practice of orally reciting written texts, (2) the pedagogical milieu of conversation in Plato's dialogues, and

(3) the presumption that conversation is the genuine province of philosophical discussion, then the difficulty experienced by some interlocutors in even getting the point of conceptual methods at work in the discussions could be understood as a deficit of literate skills, being "poor in letters" (*ta grammata phaulos*), as Socrates says in the *Phaedrus* (242c). The notion of "literate minds" is suggested in the *Protagoras* (347c–348b): In a discussion of the nature of goodness, poets have been consulted for their insights; Socrates says that in a rational dialogue, he prefers "educated" persons who use their own voice, as opposed to the uneducated who enjoy "extraneous voices" in poetry, music, and dancing. The educated-uneducated distinction here seems to imply the literacy-orality distinction, where the self-activation of a literate mind is superior to the ecstatic dependence of the oral/poetical mind.

Plato's Academy seemed to be in transition from an oral to a literate focus. In the *Laws* (811d–e), after traditional poetry and texts are deemed harmful for education, the kind of discussions being conducted in this dialogue—and "all our other (like) discourses"—are deemed worthy and should be written down for instructional purposes. Aristotle's Lyceum appears to be the first recognizable school dedicated to reading, analyzing, amassing, and composing written texts.[73] Indeed, Aristotle saw much value in books for philosophical thinking. A treatise is useful for mental training, setting out opinions for debate, and enacting rational adjudication (*Topics* 101a25–101b4). Written works (*diagraphas poieisthai*) allow for organization and classification, and they record reputable opinions, which at least avoids having to start every investigation from scratch (*Topics* 105b10–18).[74]

6.2. Writing and Knowledge

The complex question of the written word in relation to genuine knowledge—and of the status of the written dialogues—can perhaps be illuminated by attention to the *Seventh Letter*.[75] The distance between writing and the original experience of living thought can mark the difference between an author's authentic vision of reality and its transmission in a written text, which is judged deficient for two reasons: (1) public dissemination permits access for unworthy readers; and (2) even worthy readers cannot fathom the full vision of reality inevitably concealed by written expression. The *Phaedrus* clearly speaks to the first deficiency: a written book is helpless without its "father" (the author) when it is released to the public and misused or reviled by the wrong kind of readers (275e). The second deficiency is implicitly at issue in the *Phaedrus*, but it is clearly expressed in the *Seventh Letter*. There Plato says that his teachings cannot be captured in *either* written texts *or* spoken language (34ff.). Words as such are insufficient for conveying genuine knowledge that "flashes" in the soul after sustained discussion between teacher and student (341d). In the five steps of discovery (342ff.), the soul's knowledge of true objects is beyond both words and images (a cited example of an image is the visual figure of a circle). No wise person would express his deepest thoughts in words, in either spoken words or especially the "unchangeable" form of written words (343ff.). So language as such cannot do justice to true knowledge. Verbal names (and their extension in definitions) are arbitrary and variable signs that do not convey the eternal nature of true objects. Even the fixed form of written signs does not provide sufficient firmness or certainty (*mēden hikanōs bebaiōs*) because graphic lines are tainted by matter and thus they mislead the soul with a false permanence (343b). This point is clarified in the discussion of the graphic image of a circle, which has physical features that conflict with the true meaning of the *idea* (the image can be "rubbed out" and it "everywhere touches a straight line" in being composed of "points" and thus mixed with an opposite nature). Yet I think we can still say that "knowledge written in the soul" has a *relative* permanence that is implicated in knowledge of the Forms.

The danger of putting thoughts into words and writing is as follows: confining knowledge to the misplaced concreteness of defective images and verbal forms permits endless disputation about different aspects and permutations of the "relative" nature of specified signs, particularly the reciprocal heterogeneity of their dyadic relationships (unity and multiplicity, for instance, where each is understood as not the other). Such disputes are falsely assumed to engage the "soul of the writer" (*hē psuchē tou grapsantos*: 343d). The "false permanence" of graphic signs and images is in fact due to their concrete detachability from reality and their ready availability (as fixed "things") for free deployment and counteraction. Free signification permits the endless possibility of contestable maneuvers. Nevertheless, genuine knowledge can emerge *through* earnest instruction in language and writing, but only with a leap beyond language that flashes suddenly (*exaiphnēs*) in the soul (341d), and only in the chastened milieu of intimate teacher-student exchanges, not the unseemly arena of envy and discord in public discourse. What is most serious and worthy in someone's work cannot be found in books but in the treasured domain of the soul, "stored in the fairest place he possesses" (*ketai de pou en chōra tē kallistē tō toutou*: 344c). Knowledge cannot be fully realized in vocal utterances (*phōnais*) or in physical figures (*sōmatōn schēmasin*) but only in souls (342c).

The *Cratylus* likewise depicts the idea of nominalistic relativism, that names are arbitrary conventions that can admit indiscriminate use (384dff.). Yet Socrates proceeds to critique this notion on behalf of the possibility of proper naming. An ideal name (*estin onoma*) can be fitted to the true nature of an object (389d). A true name can embody a thing's form (*eidos*) by being set down or deposited (*tithenai*) in letters and syllables (*grammata kai sullabas*:

390e). Moreover, the stipulated variability of letters and syllables, even their differentiated forms, are permissible if someone knows the meaning of the proper name. But the uninitiated will not be able to discern this difference, prompted instead to think of different realities, just as a physician's *pharmakon* can appear to be a different substance when simply colored or perfumed. Yet the physician who knows the medical value of the potion will not be confused (393dff.). Once again, we seem to have here a distinction between good and bad writing, which turns on the relative capacity of readers.

6.3. Writing and Philosophy

In summation, let me sort out the complicated relationships between language, writing, and knowledge in Plato's texts by way of the following claims: (1) Traditional poetry and its oral reception are obstacles to genuine knowledge. (2) Knowledge can be gained through philosophical methods made possible by literacy. (3) Philosophical education proceeds through conversations between literate participants. (4) Such conversations can be represented and facilitated by written dialogues. (5) In the process of philosophical education, knowledge can dawn in the soul, an illumination prepared by, but leaping beyond, linguistic/rational discourse. (6) The living process of discovery and the intrinsic limits of language are appropriately presented in dialogues that are "open" in both form and content, and that partly deploy mythopoetic supplements to, and constraints on, rational discourse. (7) Philosophical dialogues are primarily geared toward selective pedagogy, suitable only for the right kind of audience, one that is capable of philosophical learning and attuned with humility and reverence for the transcendent aims of philosophy. (8) Written texts must be protected from the misuses and abuses that follow indiscriminate publication, and thus must be restricted to the proper milieu of instruction. (9) Genuine knowledge is made possible by literate dialogue but is consummated in the leap of the soul's "inward vision" that cannot be directly communicated or produced by rational inference. (10) Philosophical writing embodies a complex set of forces that both displaces and transforms traditional poetic language, in the direction of rational discourse that breaks out into an "inspired," receptive vision; the difference between poetry and philosophy is that poetry begins with inspiration and philosophy ends with it.

In the *Cratylus* (396d), Socrates concludes an extensive discussion concerning the correct use of names by mentioning in this regard a wisdom that came to him suddenly (*exaiphnēs*), the source of which is unknown to him. Hermogenes says that Socrates does seem to be *atechnōs*, an inspired prophet spontaneously uttering oracles (*enthousiōntes exaiphnēs chrēsmōdein*). And the *Phaedrus* gives us Socrates' second speech on love (243eff.), which praises four kinds of sacred madness (*mania*), which are extraordinary states of inspiration (*enthousiaseōn*) that "possess" the soul with nondiscursive revelations. The first three forms are prophecy, ritual healing, and poetry. The fourth and highest kind of *mania* is the force of love that culminates in the philosophical search and discovery of "true realities" (*ta onta*). The many references in the dialogues to inspired states (e.g., the *Ion* and *Meno*) need not be read as polemics, irony, or condescension. I believe that the *Phaedrus* and the *Seventh Letter* show that Plato was interested in these traditional phenomena as analogies for the deepest level of philosophical discovery. Philosophical inspiration is different from the other types because it follows from the initial execution of rational methods, which rely on literate skills that depart extensively from traditional oral and religious experience. We could say that Plato's deployment of mythic and traditional modes of expression is not a facilitating gesture to lesser minds but a self-conscious acknowledgment of the limits of language and rational discourse in the conveyance of philosophical truths.[76]

In this rich array of forces in Plato's thought, writing exhibits an essential ambiguity in being both (1) an empowerment of philosophy over the impediment of orality, and (2) an impediment to the ultimate aims of philosophy. Such ambiguity may help us understand the way in which writing is both critiqued and sustained in the *Phaedrus*: the movement from knowledge written on the page and performed on the stage of public debate to the "invisible vision" of knowledge written in the soul. I read this metaphorical transformation of writing as *sustaining* the power of literacy while warning against the limitations and drawbacks of written texts as such. Rather than a division between writing and something altogether different, we may have here a distinction between written texts and literate knowledge, which I think is shown in *Phaedrus* 276a: The written word is an image (*eidōlon*) of the true word (*logos*), the "living and breathing word" characterized as "knowledge written in the soul of the learner" (*epistēmēs graphetai en tē tou manthanontas psuchē*). The true word is described as (1) the "legitimate brother" of the "bastard" written word (the word apart from its father/author) and (2) an intelligible reality possessing a "more powerful nature" (*dunatōteros toutou phuetai*). The distinction here between (written) image and genuine (written) reality—where *both* denote a form of writing—suggests that "writing in the soul" is not *merely* a metaphor, but, as I would put it, an irreducible metaphor that embodies the distinction between written words as such and the *power* of literacy in its intellectual effects and capacities for new discoveries, a power animated by the *visual* presence of a graphic *eidōlon*.

Within this story of philosophical writing, there lurks the specter of philosophy's Other, the phono-ecstatics of original orality, which literacy conceals in its transformative effects. Such an oral speech-world identified in proto-phenomenology does not fit Derrida's attribution of speech being "phono-centric" (as a governing authority in Plato's account) because no "center" is given in primary orality, which is no more than world-disclosive transactional speech acts passing in time and preserved only through the fragile power of memory. Yet even in a literate culture, a secondary orality persists as the disclosive atmosphere of dwelling in speech, which precedes and haunts reflection as an immanent background that cannot be reduced to any expositional ground.

6.4. Writing and Deconstruction

These last remarks harbor an interrogation of both Plato and Derrida's deconstructive critique of Plato's account of writing.[77] The problem I want to raise is as follows. Derrida's reading of Plato on the matter at hand is impressive in destabilizing the purported privilege of an "authorial voice" that is threatened by writing and the openness of textual circulation. Yet I hope that my investigation has established something missing or submerged in Derrida's analysis, namely the phenomenon of orality and its importance for addressing the question of writing in Plato and broader issues in the philosophy of language.

I agree with Derrida that Plato's critique of writing entails a certain metaphysical bulwark against the differential structure of writing and its disseminating force. But with my focus on the background elements of literacy and orality, I do not take those moments where the "trace" of writing shows up in its alleged Other ("writing in the soul") to be a deconstructive disturbance in Plato's account. Rather, I read them as coherent within the overall picture I have tried to sketch. The phono-centrism diagnosed in Derrida's reading is from my perspective a phono-graphic center—which is to say, a *literate* voice, whose ultimate Other is not writing per se, but the illegible voice of orality and its persisting effects in Greek culture, especially in poetry and rhetoric.

The voice of the Platonic soul departs significantly from the structure of selfhood in an oral culture and poetic texts. As we have seen, selfhood in Homer is (1) "externalized" in action, factical circumstances, and social relations; (2) "decentered" in a plurality of capacities; and (3) "vulnerable" in being subjected to fate and divine management. Even when selfhood is more sharply focused in Greek tragedy, as in the case of Oedipus, a fatal excess remains at the heart of human existence. Plato advances a strict diversion from such depictions of selfhood by rendering the soul as a triadic constellation of internality, unity, and self-mastery (*Republic* 433cff.). Moreover, the psychology of poetic creation, performance, and reception shows an ecstatic immersion in a nexus of forces that "overcome" the normal self and mutes the possibility of critical reflection. The phono-ecstatic character of this nexus is precisely the force of *mimēsis* targeted by Plato. Derrida seems to miss this element in the dialogues by reading *mimēsis* as representational likeness.[78] Finally, Derrida's alternative to the Platonic authorial voice need not rely exclusively on the dissemination of writing. As we have seen, oral poetry renders "authorship" ambiguous and lacking signature.

Derrida's critique is apt in disturbing Plato's concerns about writing as an uncontrollable dissemination of texts that undermines philosophical authority and foundational aims. I want to stress that Plato's main worry about dissemination was the intrinsically agonistic character of Greek cultural life, where philosophy would be subjected to an ungoverned and incessant contestability. Plato's polemic was in part political and reflected his persistent critique of democracy as an unhinged contest of speeches aiming for nothing more than public persuasion.[79] In this respect, the philosophical dialogues are not radically open because they are governed by rational guidelines and elitist assumptions about the capacity and virtue of participants.

With regard to writing, the issue of contestability indicates that Plato and Derrida appear to be on the same page in some respects. If we recall the *Seventh Letter*, when thought is put into written or spoken words, a misplaced concreteness allows endless debate about these semantic "objects" and their heterogeneous relativity. Plato seems to be saying, *with* Derrida, that language as such is radically differential and productive of an infinite play of signifiers—the difference being that Plato proposes an extra-linguistic metaphysical resolution of the differential force of language. In any case, the beauty of Derrida's account is that he is able to turn Plato's critique around and celebrate the "false permanence" of writing and its emancipation from authorial governance. Writing, on the one hand, instantiates fixed texts that can preserve, sustain, and transmit a culture over time, while on the other hand, it releases a portable distribution and circulation of texts beyond their origin, both synchronically and diachronically—which opens texts to continual interpretation, disputation, and application, thereby extending exponentially the creative potential of cultural production. A written text by itself is not really a text because it has not yet been "actualized" until it is read; and reading is the particular occasion of an individual reader in a certain context, which issues a reception that is never simply a reiteration of the written text. The "permanence" of a text only applies to its physical inscription. An actualized text is an engine of interpretation that never ceases as long as it generates a readership. In this respect, writing sustains in its own way the open, addressive, and dialogical character of oral language.[80]

In the context of my overall analysis, there are a number of ways in which I find Derrida's notion of arche-writing congenial. The "priority" of arche-writing, of course, is not a historical thesis, since orality preceded literacy; rather it is a philosophical trope that illuminates the differential structure of language. I think it is right to say that the technology and form of writing permit not only the possibility of abstract reason, but also the distancing effects and recursive juxtapositions that draw out the open, ungrounded character of language as such, which is implicit or concealed in orality. This helps us understand why Plato's project wound up extending the critique of writing all the way to withdrawing *any* form of language from the ultimate aims of philosophy.

Another sense in which arche-writing accords with my treatment is the pervasive manner in which literacy alters human existence once it is in place. A literate culture cannot help but engage the world through the lens of literate skills and the inheritance of a literate past. As we have noted, for us, there is no access to primary orality, which itself is a construction of literacy. Even when we might make contact with an illiterate culture, the way in which we engage it or come to understand it is informed by our literate background. Nevertheless, as I have suggested, this does not mean that the distinction between orality and literacy cannot bear fruit in working to understand the nature of language and human thought. In my view, this is where Derrida's analysis of writing falls short.

A literate culture can only manifest secondary orality, but even this form of language shares with primary orality an immediacy of inhabited speech in pre-reflective social relations that are not as such divisible into "word" and "referent" or separate selves launching thoughts out to each other by means of words. In proto-phenomenological terms, the self is originally immersed in factical practices, ecstatically "there" in its world of concernful dealings. This nexus can become exposited into "self" and "world" when disruptions bring a pause that allows reflection on the environment. Natural language has the same ecstatic structure as communicative practice, where we spontaneously speak with each other about circumstances of concern. Here speech is immediately disclosive of the world, and we *dwell* in language in such a way that it is not even identified as "language," as a transaction of "words" between "speakers" about "things." Language in this exposited sense is effaced in favor of the specific occasions of disclosure.

The ecstatic social structure of lived speech is precisely what was implicated in the form of *mimēsis* critiqued by Plato, where an audience is immersed in the power of poetic and political performances. The province and effects of poetry and oratory were Plato's particular concerns about *mimēsis*, but we can say that ecstatic immersion is evident in any form of language when practiced without reflective distance. Consequently, the nexus of dwelling intrinsic to the speech-world of orality, which was modified by literacy and its philosophical powers, has an indefinite range, since we have seen that even reading and writing can exhibit an ecstatic structure. Although literacy is a significant alteration of "natural" language, once reading and writing become second nature, they too can operate in a non-reflective, spontaneous manner; and they too can be immediately disclosive in their operational contexts. Yet oral language—speech that is spoken, heard, and visually engaged in face-to-face, body-to-body communicative energy—is our "first nature," and its priority shows the enduring significance of the orality-literacy question we are exploring.

Given a phenomenological perspective on orality broadly understood, I wonder if Derrida and Plato share a certain complicity in their approaches. I have suggested that both thinkers in their own way deploy writing for their philosophical purposes: for Plato, writing prepares and allows access to an ultimate permanence; for Derrida, writing shows the ultimate impermanence of language in the play of signifiers. Yet Plato appears to approximate Derrida's account of writing as an interminable circulation of signs, so the difference turns on the status of metaphysical permanence. If we focus on the phenomenology of oral language, however, both the Platonic and Derridean deployment of writing seem to share a discomfort with orality, but in markedly different ways. Lived speech exhibits a temporal-contextual-practical plurality, a differential element that eludes formal governance; but speech also issues bearings of fitness in an unstable world, as modes of dwelling. In light of this orientation, we might say that for Plato lived speech blocks access to metaphysical permanence, while for Derrida dwelling in speech conceals the radical *impermanence* of linguistic differentiation. I take proto-phenomenology to be offering an effective middle position by advancing the nature of language as differential fitness, which is neither permanent nor impermanent in a strict sense. One way to put my suggestion about the possible complicity of Plato and Derrida in their deployment of writing is as follows: writing, by its nature, requires a distancing from lived speech, a distance that opens space for reflection *on* language. Although Platonic philosophy and Derridean arche-writing go in very different directions, can they *both* be said to privilege literate reflection over lived speech? Are they both writing off speech?[81]

My approach has the advantage of *beginning* with language as communicative practice, construed as a positive, world-disclosive phenomenon that yet shows itself to be differentiated and finite. Phenomenology, of course, is a literate enterprise, and its concepts are literate constructions. But an indicative model of concepts provides a "bridge" between literacy and orality with a medial sensitivity to both forms of language on their own terms. Oral speech is the factical setting of language. Yet since the very articulation of "orality" is a literate product, literacy allows us to see more explicitly what is only implicit in primary orality. But an indicative deployment of literate analysis can keep us alert to the differences between orality and literacy, and how these differences can modify hyper-literate biases in philosophy that miss or even disparage the lived nexus of oral language. A phenomenological approach to philosophy and language allows us to be more careful and circumspect in this regard. Rather than write off speech, we can write "on" speech, both topically and metaphorically—analogous to the way in which we write "on" a material medium that receives letters, without which the words would have no place or direction. Writing is "on" speech as an original mode of inhabitance.

7. SOME EFFECTS OF LITERACY IN GREEK PHILOSOPHY

I close this chapter with a discussion of three philosophical discoveries in Greek thought that were animated by the technology of writing: propositional truth, substantial being, and logic. With truth and logic in place, I then consider the philosophical revision of orality as "rhetoric."

7.1. Propositional Truth

We have seen in chapter 4 that mythopoetic language can have "truth" in a broad sense, in line with the Greek word *alētheia*, or unconcealment. Poetic truth is a mode of revelation from sacred sources, where cultural meanings are simply brought forth *to* humans out of inspired poetic performances. Oral poetry in a non-literate world was also the only way in which cultural traditions could be preserved against the concealment of forgetfulness. The opposite of truth in this sense is not falsehood, but oblivion.

The relationship between truth/*alētheia* and falsehood/*pseudos* in early Greek culture did not operate in the manner of later philosophical conceptions, although some overlap can be seen. There was indeed a notion of falsehood in the sense of a mistake or error, not in a setting of "propositions" but rather living contexts of speech issuing infelicitous effects. The most common meaning of *pseudos* in Homer had to do with concealment in the manner of deception or hiding. Accordingly, truth had less to do with accuracy and more to do with honesty, sincerity, and reliability. We have also seen that *muthos* did not carry a meaning of falsehood; in fact, it often reflected authoritative speech. In the *Odyssey* (17.15), Telemachus proclaims, "I love to speak the truth." The Greek is *phil' alētheia muthēsasthai*, which more literally means "telling true stories." The verb form *mutheomai*, "I speak," was used to connote telling the truth. In Homer, there occur other positive uses of *muthos* coupled with *orthos*, which later came to mean "correct," but which in epic poetry referred to standing up from a fallen or reclined position (derived from the verb *orthoō*). Given the nobility and active lives of heroes, we can see a relation to other meanings of the word *orthos* in Greek usage: real, genuine, steadfast, straightforward (something like a "standup guy"). In Book 23 of the *Iliad*, there are seven instances of the phrase *orthos kai muthon*, meaning "stand up and speak," which in contextual terms reflects the heroic virtue of what can be called "upright readiness for action."

The *alētheia-pseudos* relation in early Greek culture also exhibited a complex meaning in poetic expression. The Greek language had one word, *pseudos*, covering both error and deception, and it frequently was associated with poets telling "lies." In retrospect, this might be taken as self-conscious recognition of mythopoetic falsehood, but that is not the case. The Greeks were well aware, from the earliest times, that poetic performances were different from "actual" events; and the performances themselves offered a "pause" from normal life pursuits. The word commonly used to denote this different sphere was *pseudos*, which in its cultural setting could not mean "falsehood" or "lie" in strict terms. The word *pseudos* had remarkable flexibility and extension depending on the context.[82] Given the competitive nature of Greek poetry, an attribution of "falsehood" could simply mean "inferior" or "ineffective." Assuming the recognition of poetry's departure from normal events and speech, *pseudos* could refer to what we would call "fiction" as opposed to "fact," but that distinction does not capture the cultural authority and impact of Greek poetry. We might call it "fictive truth," but that would have to include the revelatory power of poetic inspiration and mimetic identification. Finally, there are cases where *alētheia* and *pseudos* are co-mingled in such a way as to blur their lines.[83]

With the advent of philosophy, mythopoetic senses of truth gave way to models we are familiar with. *Logos* understood as rational discourse (and prose) ascended over *muthos* (especially given the latter's heterogeneous and fatalistic worldview). More naturalized and empirical explanations were counter-posed to poetic imagination and mythical mysteries. Especially pertinent here is the medical tradition, which specifically set itself against magical thinking and "sacred" explanations for human maladies in favor of natural causes and remedies.[84] Plato's philosophy began to draw lines of distinction between *muthos* and *logos*, although primarily in the face of traditional storytelling: "Give an ear, then, as they say, to a very beautiful *logos*, which you will regard as a *muthos*, I believe, but I take as a *logos*, for what I am about to say I will tell you as true" (*Gorgias* 523a). The irony is that the *logos* Socrates will relate is a story told about moral consequences in the afterlife.

It is Aristotle who formalized a sense of propositional truth and prepared the representational theory of correspondence. In the *Metaphysics* (1011b25), truth is defined as saying of what is that it is, and of what is not that it is not. Here truth has been relegated to the sphere of descriptive language (although he includes a robust sense of "being" that exceeds a mere copula function). Aristotle's *On Interpretation* comes closest to a correspondence theory.[85] We have seen how Aristotle in this text sets out a signification chain running from things to their mental affections, then to their spoken signs, then to their written signs. Even though written signs are the last stop, it seems clear that graphic presentation underwrites a signification scheme in the first place. With the purported links between actuality, mentality, speech, and writing, Aristotle in his account of truth is able to locate linguistic "objects" that are not exhibited in orality: a "proposition" (*apophansis*) and a "sentence" (*logos*). A truth-bearing proposition is a sentence that properly affirms or denies the presence or absence of something in the subject of inquiry. Writing not only provides the linguistic "objects" at work here, it also allows the most reliable *record* of language that can then be subjected to a veridical test. Writing affords the reification of language, which at least establishes a secure presence to counter the fluid domain of speech. What is momentous in Aristotle's formulation is that the grammatical construction of a "proposition" allows for an accessible *model* of truth in general terms, which can exceed the question "Is that true?" by addressing the question "What is truth?"—the disclosive relation between sentences and things in the world. Now the mind is given extendable guidance on how to focus and judge assertions about reality.

We should hesitate to identify Aristotle's position with representational correspondence in modern parlance because he does not begin with a subject-object binary that requires an explanation of how the two domains can connect. For Aristotle, mind and world co-actualize each other when truth obtains.[86] In addition, the early association of *alētheia* with unconcealment and honesty can be found in Aristotle's discussion of magnanimity in the *Nicomachean Ethics* (1124b26ff.). Magnanimous persons should be forthcoming in their loves and hates because concealing them (*lanthanein*) stems from fear about how people will react; one should care about truth (*alētheia*) more than the opinions of others.

7.2. Substantial Being

Plato began the precise philosophical examination of how the mind comes to know things. A simple statement like "this is a horse" is in fact complex because there are two dimensions at work, the perceived "this" and the concept "horse" that explains what the perceptible entity is. The universal concept as such grounds all the particulars and thereby exceeds their aspects (color, size, activities, etc.). The concept "horse" itself is not brown, it does not run, and it remains what it is despite the passing of individual horses. To accommodate and accentuate the particular-universal distinction, Plato set up two domains, the sensible world and the world of Forms, those concepts and principles that remain the same and do not exhibit the changeable variations of sense experience. The Forms that most interested Plato were concepts such as justice, love, courage, goodness, and so on, pertaining to deep cultural issues, but understood *in themselves* apart from particular instances. If the soul could ascend to the domain of Forms, it could ground its knowledge with stable universals that never change or pass away. As I have suggested, it may be the permanence and decontextualized system of written words that can focus this kind of intellectual work, especially by way of the detached mentality of a "reader." And recall that the Greek definite article could do something not generally exhibited in factical speech; it could turn adjectives into nouns: the good, the true, the beautiful. Such recursive grammatical constructions did not by themselves *cause* the new philosophical thinking, but they served the impulses of Greek thinkers to discover something unified, universal, and lasting above or within temporal experience and ordinary speech. Writing increases the recursive power of language exponentially, which philosophers like Plato could exploit.[87] Now abstractions like "the good" and "the mind" could bank on the grammar of natural language and take on a life of their own in philosophical sentences: the good is the source of all striving; the mind governs the body; concepts organize sense experience, and so on.

Aristotle did not abide Plato's ontological divide between Forms and sensible things, but he shared the philosophical drive to organize human thinking and ground it in universal concepts. For Aristotle, such concepts are not beyond the perceptible world because they are discovered in that world through empirical processes of collection and division, after which the universal "settles" into the soul (*Posterior Analytics* 100a4–100b1). If we look at Aristotle's nomenclature, we can see how the recursive capacity of literacy can turn language in new directions. Aristotle wanted to discover "essences," namely the fundamental nature of things that exceeds and grounds the mere perceptible presence of things—the *what* that explains the *that*. The common translation term *essence* in Aristotle's texts is in Greek actually a phrase: *to ti ēn einai*, literally "the what it is to be" something. What Aristotle has done is transform an interrogative into a declarative: from "what (*ti*) is that?" to "what (*ti*) it is." In normal speech, this would not fare well: "What are you doing?" "What I am doing." But Aristotle is able to graphically manipulate the transformation that will simply stand as a focal point for the investigative work that will specifically answer the question concerning what something is. Even Aristotle's four causes are said by him to follow from four kinds of questions (*Posterior Analytics* 89b23–24): *as* what (formal), *out of* what (material), *from* what (efficient), and *for* what (final). The graphic objectification of questions apart from familiar answers served the spirit of philosophy, namely a deliberate departure from received wisdom for the sake of rational inquiry.

The recursive power launched by writing is most evident in a classic question that occupied Greek philosophy: the nature of *being*. "What" something "is" will deliver a substantive "essence," but the Greeks were also fascinated by the "is" itself, especially when it could highlight a fundamental issue facing finite existence: the constant possibility of non-being in the midst of being, of things passing away or losing their aspects in a changing world—and most pressing for human beings, issues concerning success and failure, having and losing, aging and dying. Parmenides began the cognitive venture by emphasizing the radical opposition of being and non-being, to the point where we cannot even talk about or think non-being, which calls into question the reality of change. The problems created by this dramatic set up was explored in various contexts pertaining to questions in epistemology, psychology, ethics, politics, and metaphysics. The basic question at work throughout was: Can there be any sense of lasting being in a temporal world of becoming?

Despite the many important philosophical findings that emerged from investigating the nature of being, the very question itself amounts to a grammatical trick, turning a verb (to be) into a noun (being and beings). The literate discipline of grammar itself set the stage for such maneuvers by naming forms of speech (verbs, nouns, adjectives, etc.) and organizing all the possible instances of word usage (e.g., verb tenses and case declensions). With respect to being, the first-person singular form *eimi* headed all the possible permutations of the verb form in graphic organization. The format of grammar took word usage out of factical contexts and simply listed them as abstract tokens without concrete associations (from "I am hungry" to "I am"). A grammatical chart posted word forms as discrete objects that were ready for recursive use and transformation. For example, with *eimi*, the participle *ōn* could be paired with a definite article to produce *to on* and *ta onta*, which covered broad meanings such as *what is the case* and *what exists*. Inflections of the verb also issued words like presence (*parousia*) and absence (*apousia*), and the word *ousia* came to have general ontological significance, especially in Aristotle as the keyword for "being."[88] The infinitive form *einai*, with its lack of specificity, could be nominalized as *to einai*, and because of its generality, it could serve a philosophical interest in universals.[89]

Familiar philosophical theories about "being" have run from grammatical functions (copula and predication) to metaphysical proposals of universal foundations and permanence. In recent philosophy, there have been complaints about illicit transmutations of being in metaphysical language: as in logical positivism and ordinary language philosophy, where the search for "being" is driven by a misplaced grammatical operator. From a proto-phenomenological perspective, I share suspicions about metaphysical deployments of "being." The very transformation of being from a verb to a noun can be challenged, especially if it suggests something exceeding the finite world of factical existence. At the same time, the word "being" can serve as a focal concept that simply points indicatively to the wide range of usage in natural language. Attention to the varieties of use in ancient Greek can effectively show the rich and complex contours of the word "being" without any metaphysical pretense. Although literacy and grammar provided a useful focus for certain suspect philosophical projects, the written record of a dictionary happily can display all the possible and varied uses that could be gathered around the word "being" in an indicative manner.[90] The abstract concept of being, as a verbal substantive, conceals the many ways in which "is" functions in factical language—where the "is" is not simply a copula linking subjects and predicates but meaningful disclosure in actual circumstances of use: the war is over; your father is dead; she is in trouble; he is coming home. Being as a verb did not originally possess an indefinite or abstract character. Sanskrit and Indo-European roots show more concrete senses of living, emerging, and abiding. And the Greek verb forms *eimi* and *einai* exhibited in their variations a surprising range of contextual and situational meanings: to be, to live, the living, to be in hand, property, to happen, true, truth, real, to exist, to be possible, to express, to signify, to predicate, to have to do with, goings-on, and motions. In proto-phenomenological terms, the question concerning the meaning of being that arose in the Greek world could be gathered in a focal word "being" that simply tracks all those uses without the need for a unified essence that illuminates and governs all the different meanings. In this respect, a dictionary entry would be more apt than a taxonomic treatise.

An indicative focalization of the word "being" precludes nominalizing it into a metaphysical substantive that is given pride of place in philosophical thinking. A significant advantage of this constraint is that we find a way around common claims about philosophical limits in non-Western languages. It may be that some languages do not have the same kind of abstract resources inherited from Greek philosophy, such as the universal concept of "being." But since those languages surely do exhibit many of the factical meanings noted in the usage of *eimi* and *einai* in Greek, the supposed philosophical gap can be narrowed significantly, if not closed altogether.[91]

7.3. Logic

As we have seen, mythopoetic disclosure made sense in certain contexts, yet it was tied to the particularity and variability of facticity, in such a way that global order was not exhibited and people were prone to accept uncertainty and ambiguity in cultural life. Philosophical writing was able to shape abstract concepts that brought more order and stability to human thinking. Platonic Forms, for example, could gather all instances of a phenomenon under a governing principle, which can provide certainty and efficiency when engaging the world. If you know that all acts of courage require risk for the sake of some good, then a non-risky situation or a brave act for a bad end can be ruled out with confidence, without having to start from scratch. Platonic dialogues are filled with investigations into conceivable principles that are scrutinized for consistency and extendibility—namely a stable conception broad enough to cover all relevant cases and narrow enough to exclude extraneous cases. Here we find logical analysis and argumentation at work when interlocutors would test proffered answers to philosophical questions.

Aristotle was the first to explicitly distinguish the logical form of an argument from its material content. His discovery of formal logic was animated by graphic inscription because he took letters of the alphabet as placeholders for any particular content (see, for instance, *Prior Analytics* 25a15ff.). Letters by themselves have no semantic or experiential meaning, but this vacuity was able to signify the position of any content in an argument, along with the set of logical relations and entailments between propositions supporting a conclusion. The inscribed form is such that the structure of logical demonstration can be *put into view* and regarded *as* a rational blueprint. The power of abstracted logical form was an enormous discovery that continued to drive Western thinking. Aristotle tells us that he and his circle were the first to recognize and work out this schematic arrangement (*On Sophistical Refutations* 183b35–184b4). Demonstrative syllogisms may have been implicit in Platonic dialogues, but their formal inscription was not articulated. Figurations such as "every B," "no A," and "some C," could be arranged as subject-predicate relations without existential import to sort out valid formats of deductive reasoning. If I know that X is C (included in the class C) and every member of that class C possesses a property P, then X must possess P. The structure (X is C/all C is P/therefore X is P) is such that *any* content plugged into that formal arrangement will have a valid logical form; if the premises are true, then the form issues a demonstrated conclusion, which follows necessarily from affirming the premises. "Socrates is a human/all humans are horses/ therefore Socrates is a horse" is logically valid but not sound, because one premise is false. "Socrates is human/all humans are mortal/therefore Socrates is mortal," is both valid and sound. Aristotle's discovery of logic was facilitated by the technology of graphic figuration and its impact was enormous. One can now understand the difference between *what* is said and *how* sentences are arranged structurally (in Greek, *sul-logismos*). If I have mastered the syllogism models and their valid/invalid forms, I am armed with a method that can identify good and bad reasoning *in any given content*. The power of logic is such that if I believe that Socrates is human and that all humans are mortal, I *must* conclude that Socrates is mortal. Otherwise I contradict the implications of my own beliefs. If I contradict my own beliefs, no one will want to talk to me anymore. Of course, the truth of premises in a philosophical argument can be a matter of significant dispute, but not their logical consequences if true and properly structured. Written graphics assisted these developments by way of abstract symbols fixed in place so that consistency and propositional implication could be *recognized* as an objective phenomenon.[92] The abstract format of logical structures also converted natural language utterances into "propositions," the content of which was decontextualized and isolated from factical situations of usage, for the purpose of pruning away as much ambiguity and contingency as possible—so that the movements of logical relations could have a clean and clear path.

The most basic logical principle was explicitly formulated by Aristotle: the principle of non-contradiction (PNC), whereby something cannot both be and not be at the same time.[93] We will see that this principle is not as severe as Parmenidean reasoning. In normal experience and natural language, we talk about countless instances of being and non-being in concrete terms: life and death, change, contraventions, and presence and absence. Parmenides seems to abstract from natural life and simply consider the *concept* of being *by itself*, which I maintain is constructed and identified by the reifying effects of writing, at least as a necessary condition for "positioning" concepts apart from each other. In deductive fashion, Parmenides shows that non-being is an impossible thought: How can anything that "is not" *be*? Consequently, being can never be contravened, and being can never change because that would mean the negation of one condition into another condition that previously was not. Here we have a classic example of how philosophical reflection can become alienated from the lived world.[94]

Aristotle's PNC serves a stable sense of "being" and critiques anyone who might entertain the co-existence of opposite conditions, especially being and non-being. The insulation of being from non-being supports Aristotle's ontology (discrete beings) and epistemology (stable explanations and demonstrative starting points). Aristotle's principle has taken three compatible forms: identity (A equals A), non-contradiction (A cannot equal −A), and excluded middle (either A or −A). Here I believe Aristotle is elaborating on a basic effect of literacy—the objectification of speech in perceptible graphic form—for significant philosophical purposes. Aristotle provides his signature defense of the PNC in the *Metaphysics* (beginning at 1005b8–34): it is impossible for the same thing to belong and not belong to the same thing at the same time and in the same respect; or for the same thing to both be and not be (*einai kai mē einai*) at the same time (*hama*). Aristotle tells us that this principle or starting point (*archē*) is the most certain of all thoughts, about which one cannot be mistaken. We must already possess it to know anything about beings; it is therefore an "ultimate belief" (*eschatēn doxan*) that grounds all other axioms.

Aristotle goes on (1005b35–1006a26): some who believe in the coincidence of opposites might ask for a demonstration of the PNC, but like all first principles, it cannot be derived from something else. But it can be defended "by refutation" as long as the opponent advances some statement (*logon*). The "argument" for the PNC is that the opponent is caught in a performative contradiction when attempting any communicative act.[95] It might seem odd that Aristotle proceeds for over twenty pages defending an indubitable principle, but it is interesting as a pragmatic argument in line with what I have called the factical speech-world. If anything can both be and not be what it is, no focal point can hold for conversations to proceed effectively. If speech about things cannot hold (or fit), if an utterance is both true and false, then nothing significant can be said of anything because one is both asserting and denying something simultaneously—literally a contra-diction. Language as such implodes and then we are no different from plants (1008b). Even practical life is ruined (1008b14–25) because any focus of action would both be and not be what it is. How can I concurrently walk toward and away from a door that is not a door?[96]

In the setting of metaphysical and logical musings, Aristotle is actually enlisting a proto-phenomenological defense of communicative speech and common-sense ontology against a useless philosophical posture, not only a denial of the PNC but also a Parmenidean dismissal of familiar forms of negation. Change, for instance, is real and is manifest in "beings" that undergo change (1010d15–20), negating one condition for another. Moreover, the qualifications in the PNC (at the same time, in the same respect) allow for many correlations of opposite conditions. One can walk an uphill road that is also a downhill road, but it is downhill when you walk back; you cannot walk uphill and downhill at the same time (see *Physics* 202a20). Finally, Aristotle's use of normal speech in his defense of the PNC is not actually segregated from philosophical thinking in his estimation. A mark of Aristotle's work is taking seriously what is commonly said of something. He will often take up what "is said" or what "we say" in his investigations. Language, for Aristotle, has a default fitness that cannot be ignored or put aside. Philosophical understanding works with and through what is disclosed in natural language. The elements of being cannot be understood apart from what is said of them (*Metaphysics* 992b19–22).[97]

7.4. Orality and Rhetoric

A significant aim in Plato's philosophy was the promotion of rational thinking as a challenge to the Sophists, who professed to educate people in the art of public speaking and political persuasion. Given the setting of democratic assemblies as a forum for debate about civic concerns, an ability to garner favor with an audience was a valuable asset. Plato's interest in reason was not simply academic because he recognized the possibility of sacrificing truth for political expediency. Ever since, philosophy has distinguished between *logic* as the rational force of an argument based on evidence, consistency, and entailment, and *rhetoric* as the psychological force of an argument appealing to an audience's emotions or vested interests.

It is clear that political rhetoric in this sense can be consistent with basic features of oral poetry discussed in this chapter—and Plato saw poets, Sophists, and orators as common threats to disciplined reason.[98] Political oratory can be effective when appealing to emotions, existential needs, and factical specificity; also when deploying narrative storytelling and attractive sonic powers of speech (tone, rhythm, emphasis, etc.). Ecstatic enchantment is a significant capacity of oral language, and public oratory can trigger it to great effect. Philosophical complaints about rhetorical speech are not unfounded, but our analysis calls for a measured critique because natural language *is* an embodied, social, practical, addressive, and captivating phenomenon, and political speech *does* require "moving" an audience—so that a political ideal of strictly "logical" adjudication and governance would be unrealistic and naïve.

Aristotle's *Rhetoric* recognized the positive role that oral communication can play in politics—as opposed to the modern use of this text as a classic guidebook for effective *writing*.[99] Within certain bounds, Aristotle understood that public speech calls for noncognitive motivation and passional attraction, as well as the personal appeal of the speaker. If politics were nothing but rhetoric and charisma, that would be dangerous; but politics without capacious speech would be lifeless and debilitated. Oratorical style can run deep into the natural energies of human speech and tap into less mediated intimations—which can be dark, but also noble. For every Adolph Hitler, there is a Martin Luther King. The "content" of a King speech cannot be separated from his character and oratorical gifts. The same speech in a different voice would not be the same speech. Language in this respect is far richer than any expositional or analytical account typically advanced in philosophy and linguistics.[100]

7.5. Philosophy as Hyper-Literacy

In closing this chapter, I offer some further remarks about philosophy and literacy. I have argued that writing was a necessary condition for the development of philosophy in the Greek world. I have also noted that Havelock's thesis in this regard has been criticized for over-stating the philosophy-literacy connection and the divide between oral and written language. A key reason for this critique is that Greek written texts in most cases retained an association with oral performance, even in philosophical circles. Accordingly, the role of literacy in the beginnings of philosophy should be qualified and not segregated from orality. This is a fair criticism, but I think that Havelock is on firmer ground when it comes to certain specific philosophical discoveries and methods, such as those discussed in this chapter, which involve significant disengagement from oral language. This is especially true with the capacity to "objectify" language in graphic form, which opens up different spaces for cognition and ideation that are not available in factical speech.[101] Nevertheless, it is true that philosophical literacy in the ancient world was much more intertwined with oral practices than is the case today. Indeed, it took many centuries and a variety of cultural forces for the full effects of reading and writing to saturate the discipline of philosophy in its modern form. That historical course of development will be given specific attention in the next chapter.

In any case, when it comes to the role that writing played in Greek philosophy, if we want to both recognize and limit the literacy factor, it would be preferable not to associate philosophy with literacy *simpliciter*, but rather *hyper-literacy*, which involves (1) a refined concentration on rational investigation and methods that are afforded by reading and writing skills (even if connected to oral practices), and (2) a specialized domain that most literate persons are not inclined to explore or find compelling. Hyper-literacy is thereby in line with the notion of theoretical literacy identified in chapter 4. Accordingly, when discussing literacy in philosophy (or any advanced academic discipline), I mean more precisely a hyper-literate orientation—which normal reading and writing skills by themselves might be hard-pressed to fathom. Here, I refrain from either elitist or populist responses to this selective picture. In the spirit of my investigation, however, I do maintain that hyper-literacy in its historical manifestations has concealed or suppressed the dimension of factical dwelling that calls for phenomenological retrieval.

It should be said that all developed cultures—Western and non-Western, including those with a non-alphabetic script—exhibit degrees of hyper-literacy in the following manner: the province of those who engage a literate domain and its disclosive powers, who speak for or to a wider audience of less-educated, ordinary members of society. Such specialists can be rulers, priests, sages, teachers, experts, and so on. Hyper-literacy in any culture has always been "elitist" in one way or another.[102] One can accept the fact that any culture will display gradations of expertise and authority. Proto-phenomenology, however, stipulates that "ordinary" spheres of life are a common reservoir of factical meanings, in the midst of which everyone gets their start. Accordingly, any "elite" standpoint is not a sheer departure from that first world and so cannot presume a "superior" cognitive standpoint in every respect or circumstance.

NOTES

1. Lawrence J. Hatab, *Myth and Philosophy: A Contest of Truths* (Chicago, IL: Open Court, 1990).
2. Ibid., 88–90.
3. The classic founding work in this regard is Havelock, *Preface to Plato*. Ong is among those who believe that philosophy as we understand it is not possible apart from literacy (*Orality and Literacy*, 169–170).
4. In addition to sources I have cited and will reference in this chapter, an important precedent for my analysis can be found in two works by P. Christopher Smith: "Orality and Writing: Plato's *Phaedrus* and the *Pharmakon* Revisited," in *Between Philosophy and Poetry: Writing Rhythm History*, eds. Massimo Verdiccio and Robert Burch (New York: Continuum, 2002), 73–89; and *The Hermeneutics of Original Argument: Demonstration, Dialectic, Rhetoric* (Evanston, IL: Northwestern University Press, 1998), Chap. 4.
5. The sections are drawn from Hatab, *Myth and Philosophy*, Chaps. 1–3.
6. For the myth-ritual association in the Greek context, see Walter Burkert, *Savage Energies: Lessons of Myth and Ritual in Ancient Greece*, trans. Peter Bing (Chicago, IL: The University of Chicago Press, 2001).
7. See Ernst Cassirer, *The Philosophy of Symbolic Forms*, Volume 2: *Mythical Thought*, trans. Ralph Manheim (New Haven, CT: Yale University Press, 1955), 77–79 and throughout.
8. See Walter Burkert, *Greek Religion*, trans. John Raffan (Cambridge, MA: Harvard University Press, 1985) and two works by Jean-Pierre Vernant: *Myth and Thought among the Greeks*, trans. Janet Lloyd (New York: Zone Books, 2006) and *Myth and Society in Ancient Greece*, trans. Janet Lloyd (New York: Zone Books, 1990).
9. See two articles by Sarah Iles Johnston: "Narrating Myths: Story and Belief in Ancient Greece," *Arethusa* 48, no. 2 (Spring 2015): 173–218, and "The Greek Mythic Story World," *Arethusa* 48, no. 3 (Fall 2015): 283–311.
10. See Emma Stafford, *Worshipping Virtues: Personification and the Divine in Ancient Greece* (Swansea, UK: Duckworth, 2001).
11. See John Gould, "On Making Sense of Greek Religion," in *Greek Religion and Society*, eds. P. E. Easterling and J. V. Muir (Cambridge: Cambridge University Press, 1985), 1–33.
12. Segal, *Singers, Heroes, and Gods in the* Odyssey, Chaps. 2–3.
13. See my "Tragic Values in Homer and Sophocles," in *Logoi and Muthoi: Further Philosophical Essays in Greek Literature*, ed. William Wians (Albany, NY: SUNY Press, 2019), Chap. 6.
14. For a vivid depiction of the Homeric world, see the description of the great shield of Achilles, on which the full range of scenes from earthly life have been crafted (*Iliad* 18.504–661).
15. See *Iliad* 12.310–12.328; 3.428ff.; 22.355–22.356; *Odyssey* 11.485ff.
16. For an illuminating study, see Jasper Griffin, *Homer on Life and Death* (Oxford University Press, 1980).

17. Burkert, *Greek Religion*, 148.
18. For a detailed discussion with references, see Hatab, *Myth and Philosophy*, 75–83.
19. The wrath and withdrawal of Achilles may be extreme, but he was motivated by Agamemnon's seizure of his captured concubine, which was indeed an offense to heroic honor.
20. I draw from David Roochnik, "Homeric Speech Acts: Word and Deed in the Epics," *The Classical Journal* 85, no. 4 (April–May 1990): 289–299.
21. Other examples can be found in *Iliad* 5.185, 13.59–60, and 19.86ff. For a comprehensive study of extra-conscious forces in Greek culture, see Ruth Padel, *In and Out of the Mind: Greek Images of the Tragic Self* (Princeton, NJ: Princeton University Press, 1992).
22. See Hatab, *Myth and Philosophy*, Chap. 6.
23. Ibid., Chaps. 4–5. See also Edward T. Jeremiah, *The Emergence of Reflexivity in Greek Language and Thought: From Homer to Plato and Beyond* (Boston, MA: Brill, 2012).
24. In the *Metaphysics* (I.2), Aristotle says that myth is in a way philosophical because it is composed of "wonders," and philosophy begins with wonder. Yet the aim of philosophy is to achieve the "opposite" condition of wonder, namely knowledge.
25. Volume I discussed pre-reflective senses of temporality and place that are intelligible preconditions for objective conceptions of time and space (53–58, 62–63). In mythical thinking, comparable pre-reflective intimations of time and space are displayed in practical, cultural, and linguistic formats. See Hatab, *Myth and Philosophy*, 37–39.
26. See Richard P. Martin, *The Language of Heroes* (Ithaca, NY: Cornell University Press, 1989), Chap. 1; also Bruce Lincoln, *Theorizing Myth* (University of Chicago Press, 1999), Chaps. 1–2.
27. Thucydides and Pindar did seem to associate *muthos* with an unverifiable fiction. See Richard Martin, "The 'Myth before the Myth Began,'" in *Writing Down the Myths*, ed. Joseph F. Nagy (Turnhout, Belgium: Brepols, 2013), 45–46.
28. See John Heath, *The Talking Greeks: Speech, Animals, and the Other in Homer, Aeschylus, and Plato* (Cambridge: Cambridge University Press, 2005).
29. G. R. F. Ferrari, "Logos," in *Classical Papers* (Department of Classics, University of California at Berkeley, 1997). Even in Aristotle's work, *logos* was used in different senses, so that we get varying translations such as reason, argument, proposition, sentence, language, speech, and utterance. Sometimes the "rationality" of *logos* was not in line with modern expectations. See my *Phainomenon* and *Logos* in Aristotle's Ethics," in *Phenomenology and Virtue Ethics*, eds. Kevin Hermberg and Paul Gyllenhammer (London: Bloomsbury, 2013), 9–28.
30. See Bruno Snell, *The Discovery of the Mind*, trans. T. G. Rosenmeyer (New York: Harper and Row, 1960), Chap. 9; and G. E. R. Lloyd, *Magic, Reason, and Experience* (Cambridge: Cambridge University Press, 1979).
31. See H. S. Versnel, *Coping with the Gods: Wayward Readings in Greek Theology* (Leiden: Brill, 2011).

32. Detienne, *The Masters of Truth in Ancient Greece*, 84–85.

33. Among several important studies in this vein, see two works by John Sallis: *Being and Logos: Reading the Platonic Dialogues*, 3rd Edition (Bloomington, IN: Indiana University Press, 1996) and *Chorology: On Beginning in Plato's Timaeus* (Bloomington, IN: Indiana University Press, 1999). See also Drew Hyland, *Finitude and Transcendence in the Platonic Dialogues* (Albany, NY: SUNY Press, 1995).

34. See my discussion of tragic poetry in *Myth and Philosophy*, Chap. 5; also my article, "Tragic Values in Homer and Sophocles."

35. It is noteworthy that the scale function of the *polis* is compared to enlarged letters that will assist when trying to read something far away and too small to discern (368d–e).

36. See Stephen Halliwell, *The Aesthetics of Mimesis* (Princeton, NJ: Princeton University Press, 2002), 1–33, and Raymond A. Prier, *Thauma Idesthai* (Gainesville, FL: Florida State University Press, 1989), 169–179.

37. *The Texts of Early Greek Philosophy*, Part II, trans. Daniel W. Graham (Cambridge: Cambridge University Press, 2010), 759.

38. Plato and Aristotle in their epistemology and psychology did take up a representational sense of *mimēsis* in poetic production and reception. See Ekaterina V. Haskins, "'Mimesis' between Poetics and Rhetoric: Performance Culture and Civic Education in Plato, Isocrates, and Aristotle," *Rhetoric Society Quarterly* 30, no. 3 (Summer 2000): 7–33.

39. See Segal, *Singers, Heroes, and Gods in the* Odyssey, 100ff.

40. See Greg Woolf, "Ancient Literacy?" *Bulletin of the Institute of Classical Studies* 58, no. 2 (December 2015): 31–42. For a study of Greek mathematics and graphics, see Reviel Netz, *The Shaping of Deduction in Greek Mathematics* (Cambridge: Cambridge University Press, 1999).

41. *Philebus* 17a–18d, *Theaetetus* 201e–210, and *Republic* 402a–c.

42. See Andrea Falcon, *Aristotle and the Science of Nature: Unity without Uniformity* (Cambridge: Cambridge University Press, 2005), 48–51.

43. Charles H. Kahn, "Writing Philosophy," in Yunus, *Written Texts*, 139–161.

44. Snell, *The Discovery of the Mind*, Chap. 10.

45. See Ong, *Orality and Literacy*, 49–57.

46. Ong, "Writing Is a Technology That Restructures Thought," 43–45. As suggested in chapter 4, the word *tree* simply spans these different meanings with an indicative focal function in the course of enactive interpretation.

47. Even in conversation, literacy can promote different ways of hearing and comprehension, as well as varying capacities to engage the recitation of written texts (consider hearing a conference presentation without the text at hand). One could say that the varying degrees of comprehension in such milieus would be proportional to the degree to which literate knowledge and skills have been mastered and internalized.

48. *Nicomachean* Ethics 1144a30. See Havelock, *The Muse Learns to Write*, 111. When I pose typical philosophical questions in class—say, What is courage?—if students have any initial mental image, is it likely to be the graphic word "courage," even if I don't write it on the board?

49. Giovanni Manetti, *Theories of the Sign in Classical Antiquity*, trans. Christine Richardson (Indianapolis, IN: Indiana University Press, 1993), 56.

50. Grainger and Hannagan, "What Is Special about Orthographic Processing?"

51. See Carlo Sini, "Gesture and Word: The Practice of Philosophy and the Practice of Poetry," in Verdiccio and Burch, *Between Philosophy and Poetry*, 15–25.

52. See Jesper Svenbro, "The Interior Voice: On the Invention of Silent Reading," in *Nothing to Do with Dionysos? Athenian Drama in Its Social Context*, eds. John J. Winkler and Froma I. Zeitlin (Princeton, NJ: Princeton University Press, 1990), 366–384.

53. See Nancy A. Mavrogenes, "Reading in Ancient Greece," *Journal of Reading* 23, no. 8 (May 1980): 691–697.

54. See Jesper Svenbro, *Phrasikleia: An Anthropology of Reading in Ancient Greece*, trans. Janet Lloyd (Ithaca, NY: Cornell University Press, 1993), Chap. 9; also Luigi Battezzato, "Techniques of Reading and Textual Layout in Ancient Greek Texts," *The Cambridge Classical Journal* 55 (January 2009): 1–23, on which I rely for the rest of the paragraph. For a broader perspective on silent reading in the ancient world, see R. W. McCutcheon, "Silent Reading and Antiquity and the Future History of the Book," *Book History* 18 (2015): 1–32.

55. Alessandro Vatri, "The Physiology of Ancient Greek Reading," *The Classical Quarterly* 62, no. 2 (December 2012): 633–647.

56. The rest of this discussion is drawn from Svenbro, *Phasikleia*, Chap. 9.

57. Word separation began around the 7th century and became common in the 9th century: Christian Vandendorpe, *From Papyrus to Hypertext*, trans. Phyllis Aronoff and Howard Scott (Urbana, IL: University of Illinois Press, 2009), 7.

58. Havelock seems to be guilty of such polarizing tendencies, which have been duly criticized. See the work by Rosalind Thomas, *Literacy and Orality in Ancient Greece*, and Kahn, "Writing Philosophy."

59. Greek culture did exhibit certain world-transcending tendencies in Orphic and Pythagorean circles, which had an influence on Plato and his supposed two-worlds doctrine. In any case, such tendencies were not in the mainstream.

60. Detienne, *The Masters of Truth in Ancient Greece*, 104.

61. For connections between Greek democracy and contests, see Vernant, *Myth and Society in Ancient Greece*, 19–44.

62. See Josiah Ober, *Political Dissent in Classical Athens* (Princeton, NJ: Princeton University Press, 1998), Chap. 1.

63. See Geoffrey Lloyd, "Literacy in Greek and Chinese Science," in Yunus, *Written Texts*, 122–138, on which I rely in this discussion.

64. William V. Harris, *Ancient Literacy* (Cambridge, MA: Harvard University Press, 1991), 114–115, and Thomas, *Literacy and Orality in Ancient Greece*, Chaps. 4–6.

65. See "Writing Is a Technology That Restructures Thought," in *The Written Word: Literacy in Transition*, ed. Gerd Baumann (Oxford University Press, 1986), 23–50.

66. See Andrew Ford, "From Letters to Literature: Reading the 'Song Culture' of Classical Greece," in Yunis, *Written Texts*, 15–37.

67. The setting at the start of the *Theaetetus* is rich with a remarkable ambiguity: Euclides wrote down the *logos* of a conversation, which is then read aloud to the group—so here we have a written dialogue portraying a conversation that turns to the reading/reciting of a written text that recorded a conversation.

68. Robb, *Literacy and Paideia in Ancient Greece*, 232.

69. In the *Meno*, just before the instruction of the slave boy, Socrates discusses the graphic example of a geometrical figure (*schēma*), defined as the limit (*peras*) of a solid (76a). Before he talks with the boy, Socrates asks if he speaks Greek, and he then draws a square figure in the sand (82b). The boy's difficulty with the problem of doubling the figure's area is that he merely supposes (*oietai*) the answer by doubling the sides (82e). Socrates tells him to visually point out the line rather than "reckon" (*arithmein*) the answer. Socrates then draws the diagonal line (*grammē*) that will show the boy the answer.

70. For discussions of the shifts from oral to written practices pertaining to cultural education, see Svenbro, *Phrasikleia*, Chap. 9, and Wise, *Dionysus Writes*, Chap. 1.

71. See Robb, *Literacy and Paideia in Ancient Greece*, 235ff. As we have noted, recitation was a common use of written texts, but Plato objected to traditional methods of recitation that involved vivid gesturing and dramatization (Mavrogenes, "Reading in Ancient Greece," 694).

72. See Christopher Gill, "Plato on Falsehood—Not Fiction," in *Lies and Fictions in the Ancient World*, eds. Christopher Gill and T. P. Wiseman (Austin, TX: University of Texas Press, 1993), 38–87.

73. Robb, *Literacy and Paideia in Ancient Greece*, 235ff.

74. It should be said that Plato's critique of writing was not unique in the Greek world. See Mathilde Cambron-Goulet, "The Criticism—and the Practice—of Literacy in the Ancient Philosophical Tradition," *Mnemosyne: Supplements* 335 (Leiden, The Netherlands: Brill, 2012), 201–226. Books were valuable commodities and could be collected simply for prestige. Manuscripts were also hard to read accurately, and they were detached from face-to-face apprenticeship and friendship relations that were highly esteemed.

75. There is dispute over the authenticity of the *Seventh Letter*, but it is noteworthy how this text can resolve some of the issues at hand.

76. See Kathryn A. Morgen, *Myth and Philosophy from the Pre-Socratics to Plato* (Cambridge: Cambridge University Press, 2000).

77. For Derrida's seminal account, see "Plato's Pharmacy," in Jacques Derrida, *Dissemination*, trans. Barbara Johnson (Chicago, IL: The University of Chicago Press, 1981), 63–171.

78. Derrida, *Dissemination*, 138–139.

79. Indeed, oral performance as such seems to have been understood competitively. When Aristotle distinguishes between written style *(lexis graphikē)* and style in public speeches, he calls the latter *lexis agōnistikē* (*Rhetoric* 3.12). Derrida does recognize that the critique of writing mirrors the critique of democracy in the *Republic* (*Dissemination*, 142–147).

80. See Walter J. Ong, "Before Textuality: Orality and Interpretation," *Oral Tradition* 3, no. 3 (1988): 259–269.

81. Ong believes that Derridean deconstruction itself is caught up in literate textuality and lacks sufficient historical depth that can explore primary orality and how it was altered by literacy (*Orality and Literacy*, 162–166). Prier cautions that Derrida's thinking remains within representational linguistics, albeit in a dynamic manner

(*Thauma Idesthai*, 216–226). I should note that in one text, Derrida talks about his native tongue as a habitat, as a "dwelling" in which he draws his very breath: *Monolingualism of the Other: or the Prosthesis of Origin*, trans. Patrick Mensah (Stanford, CA: Stanford University Press, 1998), 1. I owe this reference to Carolyn Culbertson, "My Language Which Is Not My Own: Heidegger and Derrida on the Ambiguity of Linguistic Life," *Southwest Philosophy Review* 32, no. 2 (July 2016): 115–136.

82. See Louise H. Pratt, *Lying and Poetry from Homer to Pindar* (Ann Arbor, MI: University of Michigan Press, 1993), Chap. 1.

83. See especially Hesiod's *Theogony* 23–28 and the character of Odysseus, who regularly shifts back and forth between truth-telling and deception.

84. See my discussion in *Myth and Philosophy*, 262–266. For a definitive treatment, see Lloyd, *Magic, Reason, and Experience*.

85. 17a3–5, 23–24.

86. See my discussion in "*Phainomenon* and *Logos* in Aristotle's Ethics," 11–12.

87. See Havelock, *Preface to Plato*, Chap. 14, and *The Muse Learns to Write*, Chap. 9.

88. The word *ousia* in ordinary usage referred to property, particularly land, the sustainability of which throughout changing fortunes resonated with the search for a stable ontological concept.

89. For the definitive study of Greek ontology and its grammatical roots, see Charles H. Kahn, *The Verb "Be" in Ancient Greek* (Indianapolis, IN: Hackett, 2003).

90. See the Liddell-Scott *Greek-English Lexicon*; also my article, "The Point of Language in Heidegger's Thinking: A Call for the Retrieval of Formal Indication," *Gatherings: The Heidegger Circle Annual* 6 (2016): 1–22. Some of what follows is drawn from both sources.

91. See Jiyuan Yu, "The Language of Being: Between Aristotle and Chinese Philosophy," *International Philosophical Quarterly* 39, no. 4 (December 1999): 439–454. Yu shows how Western notions of "being"—such as a copula, predication, or existential function, and a nominalized conversion from verb usage—cannot find ready counterparts in the Chinese language. Chinese readers have a hard time with abstract entities nominalized and held apart from sensible things. And some words in Chinese that have been suggested as translations of "being"—*you* and *cunzai*, for instance—have meanings such as "to have," "to survive," and "this," which do not really compare with Western philosophical usage. The author calls for a revision of Chinese grammar that can approximate Western ontology. My analysis, however, finds such reform questionable and even calls for revising Western ontology in the direction of factical meanings that any developed language can exhibit.

92. In *On Memory and Recollection*, Aristotle seems to offer an indirect or implicit recognition of the "graphic" component of thought (449b24–450b30). In the context of considering how the mind can think things that are not present, Aristotle says that thought requires imagination (*phantasia*), which is compared to drawing a diagram (*diagraphein*), something that can be put before one's eyes. Memory is like a picture (*zōgraphēma*), which "traces" (*ensēmainetai*) an "outline" (*tupon*) of an experience. In this way, the trace of a picture (*graphē*) enables access to things not immediately present. In Greek, *gramma* and *graphē* both referred to letters/letter-making as well as drawings/figure-making.

93. In Book 4 of the *Republic,* Plato presents an account of the PNC in quasi-formal terms, albeit through examples.

94. The deductive reading of Parmenides is standard. I have tried to loosen the grip of this approach by pointing out mythopoetic elements in his writings: the text is written in hexameter verse and the prologue is infused with mythical imagery depicting revelation by a goddess. Moreover, if "being" is understood as *disclosure*, then its ubiquity can make more sense. Even non-being must be disclosed as such in language and thought. See *Myth and Philosophy*, 183–191.

95. See Scott Roniger, "Speech and Being in Aristotle's *Metaphysics*," *International Philosophical Quarterly* 57, no. 1 (March 2017): 31–41.

96. Binary logic has been a staple in Western thinking. It seems that the graphic space of writing facilitated the isolation of a unit of thought from other thoughts and from negative instances. But there are other possibilities of an "expanded" logic that discerns a constitutive relation between positive and negative meanings—a dialectical logic—which was recognized by Heraclitus (and later thinkers such as Hegel, Nietzsche, and Heidegger). The proto-phenomenological account of the relation between contravention and meaning works in this domain as well.

97. See Christopher P. Long, *Aristotle on the Nature of Truth* (Cambridge: Cambridge University Press, 2011), 49–56.

98. See Ong, *Orality and Literacy*, 107–110.

99. Ibid., 114.

100. For insightful discussions of "non-logical" elements of human language and persuasive discourse, see two works by Douglas Walton: *The Place of Emotion in Argument* (University Park, PA: Penn State University Press, 1992) and *The New Dialectic: Conversational Contexts of Argument* (Toronto, Canada: University of Toronto Press, 1998). The latter work is consistent with what I have called enactive interpretation because it details different types of dialogue with different goals, expectations, and measures: persuasion, inquiry, negotiation, debate, information-seeking, and deliberation, among others.

101. Olson, *The World on Paper*, 241.

102. For a cogent treatment of cross-cultural cognition, see G. E. R. Lloyd, *The Ambivalences of Rationality: Ancient and Modern Cross-Cultural Explorations* (Cambridge: Cambridge University Press, 2018).

Chapter 6

The Transcribed World

The American philosopher Theodore Sider recently published a work with the title *Writing the Book of the World*.[1] The text advances a realist metaphysics wherein conceptual language can correspond to fundamental structures of reality—a representational relation that offers an objectively correct way to "write the book of the world."[2] This metaphor is simply stated a few times with no explicit attention to its meaning; and there are no index entries for "language," "writing," or "book." The title could be taken as an unconscious or inadvertent expression of my thesis that philosophy looks at the world through a literate lens. Is literacy so ingrained that the author takes the metaphor to be effective and illuminating without having to explain its use?

My investigation could be called an extensive inquiry into the meaning of this metaphor—but as something more than metaphorical. Someone skeptical of this approach might say that Sider's image of writing is innocuous, that philosophy is obviously a literate endeavor and leave it at that. But my work has explored a phenomenology of language and literacy, wherein the notion of writing is far from innocuous and obvious because it has significant philosophical implications. Literacy is a derivative mode of language that alters the way in which the world is disclosed. Reading and writing emerge out of oral language inhabiting a lived world—understood as dwelling in speech. Again, one might concede this but in a progressive spirit, whereby literacy advances human understanding beyond naïve common sense in the direction of rational knowledge and analysis. Proto-phenomenology, however, with its presumption of immanence, assumes that the "first world" of dwelling in speech has its own disclosive integrity that cannot be dismissed or ignored. Philosophy is always already *in medias res*, in the midst of a lived world that makes philosophy possible and that must be given indicative attention if philosophy is to be truly comprehensive.

Philosophy's reflective disengagement from the factical speech-world is animated and facilitated by the acquisition of literate skills. The case for this claim rests on two historical pillars: (1) the cultural history of ancient Greece, where the advent of literacy was a necessary condition for the development of philosophy; and (2) the personal history of anyone learning how to read and write as a preparation for taking up philosophy. In this respect, philosophy (and other modern disciplines) could be said to access the world *in mediam scripturam*, in the midst of rational literacy, which does not literally write the book of the world but rather renders the world *transcribed* and *legible*—which means decipherable by literate minds working with an archival store of documented findings and methods. Such historical attention provides a concrete scenario for understanding philosophy as derived from its pre-philosophical environment, not in the manner of progressive deliverance but a disclosive transformation that should not lose sight of its factical background.

Chapters 4 and 5 of this volume argue that philosophical concepts, logical methods, and representational models of truth are constructed from an orthographic base. We can say more about this by retrieving the notion of reification mentioned in chapter 1. Reification is a consequence of expositional specification, namely a framing of discrete "entities" marked off from other entities, relations, and movements. Reification here does not pertain to physical objects in the familiar sense; it involves an "objectification" of non-tangible or fluid phenomena, where a concentrated focus of demarcation issues "concepts" as distinct from "percepts," a "mind" apart from the body, or the conversion of active engagements into stable references, such as "knowledge" and "experience." Reification generates important expositional comprehension, but the priority of immersion in an ecological field of dynamic involvement limits its explanatory scope. In any case, the primary productive source of reification is the material transformation of speech into written "objects," which generates not only the stable "presence" of abstractions and processes in script, but also the recursive power of inter-lexical composition and reconstruction, where verbal notions are iterable and overtly manipulable—so that they can be deployed to mimic the grammar of natural language and have a life of their own in philosophical sentences: knowledge is the organization of sense data; truth is the correspondence of mental representations and states of affairs; the good is the happiness of the greatest number; exposition is derived from immersion. Philosophers become so habituated to such sentences that they seem normal and straightforward, which of course they are not (ask most first-year students in general education courses). Such facility with philosophical sentences conceals the complex history of their development, in both cultural and personal terms—which my investigation tries to bring into view.

This last chapter will explore a number of historical and conceptual developments that succeeded the ancient Greek period, with the aim of expanding the story of literacy and philosophy as it evolved toward our own time. This is an enormously complex story that could not possibly be done justice in a single chapter. My discussion will be selective and provisional. I have chosen a few topics that can highlight and extend the themes of this investigation, but in the manner of broad sketches that require further research and articulation.

Before pursuing these topics, I offer some remarks about philosophy in the ancient world. Pierre Hadot has forcefully shown how Greek and Roman philosophy was not simply a theoretical/reflective endeavor but also caught up with concrete existence—as *a way of life*.³ Despite the manner in which philosophical literacy disengaged from normal existence, that disengagement itself was taken to be a recipe for achieving fulfillment in life and guiding civic affairs. In the context of the last two chapters, the existential significance of ancient philosophy can be indicated in the degree to which literacy remained intertwined with oral practices, which were embedded in the personal-social-environing-world. Hadot's focus does not suggest that philosophy after the ancient period had nothing to do with life; his target is the academic professionalization of philosophy that has gradually segregated itself from the wider world and muted the life-enhancing possibilities of philosophy. The hyper-literate "discipline" of philosophy has compressed its scope and reach to the point where its "legibility" is largely limited to academic specialization and inter-textual communication.

Hadot maintains that the ancient conception of philosophy as a way of life began to diminish with the rise of Christianity, especially because of the latter's early disdain for pagan philosophy as a fallen worldly distraction. In the Medieval period, ancient philosophy did come to be rigorously studied and sophisticated philosophical texts were written, but usually in the service of Christian theology and its specific intellectual questions. Medieval monasticism and its development into the first universities sustained a reserved domain for philosophical thinking. The Renaissance and early Modern period began to move away from Medieval scholasticism toward more worldly perspectives. Modern philosophy and its association with the scientific revolution, however, reflected its own kind of "other-worldliness" in adopting the scientific disengagement from the world of common sense and factical experience. In the first four sections of this chapter, I sketch the movement from ancient to modern philosophy, beginning with a linguistic perspective covering the translation of Greek philosophy into Latin and then the role that "learned Latin" played in the technical vocabulary of European philosophy and science up through the early Modern period.

1. FROM GREEK TO LATIN

The Western inheritance of Greek philosophy was in the main transmitted through the Latin language. That transmission up through the 18th century involved two elements I want to emphasize: (1) how the translation into Latin altered some aspects of Greek philosophical language; and (2) how later developments of Latin usage magnified and sharpened the effects of literacy in philosophical thinking.

1.1. The Translation of Greek Philosophy

The Roman reception of Greek philosophy launched the Western scholarly tradition.[4] Most Latin philosophical terms originated in the Greek language: some were simply transliterations of the Greek, others were translations or coinages if Latin equivalents were lacking. The ancient process of transmission was less a "translation" measured by modern standards of faithful rendition and more a "transformation" of Greek words for usage in a new tongue. Most early Roman philosophers such as Cicero were bilingual. Seneca and other Roman authors perceived Latin deficiencies in rendering Greek philosophical terms; often the Greek word was simply included alongside the Latin translation. Up until the 13th century, it was common to rate Greek higher than Latin in philosophical value. After that, however, confidence in Latin expression grew and became more secured.

Since most Greek philosophical words were originally drawn from natural usage in a mother tongue, their special deployment for intellectual purposes could still resonate with wider meanings, at least for native speakers. Translation into Latin, especially for narrow deployment in philosophical work, could mute the richer resonance of Greek words, at least for those who were not fluent in Greek. Here are some Greek terms coupled with their common English translation, followed in parenthesis by some of their meanings in natural Greek usage: *aition*/cause (responsibility); *anankē*/necessity (force, violence, chance); *archē*/principle (starting-point, governance); *eidos*/species (visual form); *ousia*/substance (property, holdings); *psuchē*/soul (breath, life); *theōria*/contemplation (report after visiting a foreign land). We have already discussed various vernacular meanings of *einai* (being), *logos* (reason), and *phusis* (nature). In addition, Greek words designating "knowledge" in philosophical usage (*epistēmē, phronēsis, sophia, gnosis*) had pre-philosophical senses having to do with knowing-how rather than knowing-that. And two central Aristotelian terms—*dunamis*/potentiality and *energeia*/actuality—had respective meanings of "capacity" and "at work."[5] It is worthwhile to consider what might have been lost or muted when the Greek language gave birth to philosophical nomenclature.

Greek philosophical words were generally used in a more technical manner compared to normal usage; but again, echoes of natural language were likely to be intimated by native speakers. Translation into Latin philosophical terms emphasized technical meanings more pointedly, which consequently diminished any echoes of factical sense. The subsequent history of Latin in scholarly work thereby cemented the nature and function of so-called technical language, which (1) pertained to objective, factual, and descriptive content (as distinct from personal expression, affective force, or the literary arts) and (2) aimed for precision and standardization. The evolution of philosophical and scholarly Latin, therefore, was a literate transformation of language that emphasized abstract cognitive functions and generated a semantic shift away from natural speech. In other words, the intellectual impulses of philosophy and other disciplines were enhanced and furthered by Latin literacy—especially in post-Roman periods when Latin gradually became confined to academic work after the emergence of vernacular Romance languages and the eclipse of Latin as a mother tongue.

In the history of the West, Greek intellectual developments were unique in emerging from the "natural" background of a native tongue.[6] Latin borrowed its cognitive bearings and grammatical formats from a foreign language (Greek). Moreover, the imperial mandate of Latin as the official language of the realm required formal instruction for foreigners. Latin thinking on language and knowledge therefore operated with a decidedly reflective and expositional mind-set (drawn *from* the Greek tongue and prepared *for* imperial transmission)—whereas Greek reflective thought was embedded in a background of native speech. With its Latin sources, then, subsequent Western thinking was from the start inflected by a reflective/expositional orientation set apart from an indigenous atmosphere of natural language.

Latin's post-Roman philosophical career in the early Medieval period (4th–6th centuries) can be gathered in Augustine's appropriation of Neoplatonism and Boethius's work on Aristotelian texts (which became the basis for Western scholasticism). The later Medieval period (10th–12th centuries) saw the heyday of philosophical production in Latin, which in its very impetus was a technical discipline emphasizing abstract analysis, linguistic theory, grammatical structure, and logical argument (following the transmission of Greek philosophy largely from Arabic sources). In all, the story of Latin highlights historical and linguistic factors that shaped the reflective posture of Western philosophy in its refined disengagement from factical life.

1.2. Neo-Latin

In the Roman period, Latin was the native tongue of philosophers and scholars. In the course of time, offshoots of Latin developed into budding Romance languages and other vernacular domains of speech. For intellectual work, however, *written* Latin survived and was sustained by educated elites. Eventually, Latin died out as a native tongue learned in childhood, but it stayed alive in the academic world as what is now called "Neo-Latin" or "learned Latin."[7] In the face of so many different spoken languages and dialects, written Latin and its advanced vocabulary served the crucial function of an international standardized language, which was useful for the global reach of the Catholic Church, for international diplomacy, and especially for the sciences and scholarly disciplines that saw their paramount purpose to be the search for rational knowledge, which exceeds and surpasses the ordinary realm of practical affairs and common beliefs. In philosophy, Latin provided a language whose very character, form, and vocabulary were segregated from natural speech and predisposed to articulating objective analysis, abstract concepts, and universal principles. For centuries after the Roman period, Latin was the only written language in Europe, and it was specifically geared toward the methods and types of cognition pursued by philosophy. Accordingly, written Latin maximized and sustained philosophy's literate revision of oral language—without immediate competition from factical speech. Ong summarizes the point well:

> Devoid of baby-talk, insulated from the earliest life of childhood where language has its deepest psychic roots, a first language to none of its users, pronounced across Europe in often mutually unintelligible ways but always written the same way, learned Latin was a striking exemplification of the power of writing for isolating discourse and of the unparalleled productivity of such isolation. Writing . . . serves to separate and distance the knower and the known and thus to establish objectivity. . . . Learned Latin affects even greater objectivity by establishing knowledge in a medium insulated from the emotion-charged depths of one's mother tongue, thus reducing interference from the human life-world and making possible the exquisitely abstract world of medieval scholasticism and of the new mathematical modern science which followed on the scholastic experience. Without learned Latin, it appears that modern science would have got under way with greater difficulty, if it had got under way at all. Modern science grew in Latin soil, for philosophers and scientists through the time of Sir Isaac Newton commonly both wrote and did their abstract thinking in Latin.[8]

Neo-Latin was a language thoroughly governed by the structures of writing and thus not susceptible to the dispersal and fluidity of speech practices. Therefore, it was able to sustain a relatively stable structure, syntax, grammatical format, and vocabulary. Dante celebrated the virtues of Latin as a model for shaping vernacular languages into formats amenable to scholarly work.[9] Vernacular language, he wrote, is given by nature, without rules, learned at a mother's knee, and continually subject to random fluctuation. Latin is shaped by art, governed by rules, learned through formal study, and unchanging through time and across geographical locations. For a thousand years (800–1800), Latin was the indispensable language of cultural production (and as late as the 20th century, it was considered part of a good education).

The paradigmatic character of Latin was such that when European vernacular languages were transposed into written form, the rules and contours of Latin were the guiding measure for these new literacies. Moreover, the technical vocabulary of Latin was sustained in European writing, and even today new scientific terminology will often be rendered by classical nomenclature, which is an effective way of highlighting and reinforcing technical language in its departure from natural speech.

2. THE EVOLUTION OF LITERACY

The constitutive role of literacy in philosophy is a good deal more pronounced in the modern world than it was in ancient Greek and Roman culture. In those times, written works were still caught up in oral practices (recitation, political speech, philosophical discussion, group readings, reading aloud). The same can be said for Medieval culture, where scholarly training was measured by oral examination, not written work. To whatever extent oral language was involved, the function of non-lexical elements of speech (gesture, facial expression, intonation, tempo, emphasis) needed less explication or indication in written texts. Between the Medieval and early Modern period, oral associations with literacy diminished to the degree that writing gradually disengaged from speech and gravitated toward its own domain. Consequently, the force of literacy in intellectual work was sharpened and enhanced. In time, this course of development (1) altered how reading and writing were perceived and practiced, and (2) opened up new ways in which the mind and the world would be understood. In this section, I will draw from the work of David Olson, which examines the evolution of literacy from the Medieval to the early Modern era, with an emphasis on scholarly writing that can serve my focus on philosophy.[10] First, some orientation. Olson's analysis emphasizes what I would call a literate-world, in the sense that writing per se cannot be separated from reading and wider contexts in which writing and reading are shaped and construed. Literacy in this sense inhabits different hermeneutical orientations, different types of writing and reading, each with their social-world of shared assumptions and expectations concerning the production, assessment, and distribution of written texts, particularly with guidance in how texts are to be read.

Olson emphasizes the world of scholarship and details the ways in which that kind of writing developed a gradual dissociation from oral language and accordingly had to pay more attention to authorial intent. Such a task went hand-in-hand with a growing emphasis on literal language and objective description.[11] Between medieval and modern times, written texts began to be emphasized as such, understood as writers communicating their intended meaning to readers, in a manner distinct from spoken conversation. With the influence of Renaissance humanism and the Reformation, textual meaning came to be seen as transparently evident in the text as *written by authors*—as opposed to (1) "spiritual" sources of revelation, (2) allegorical indirection or poetic expression, and (3) dogmatic governance of interpretation by institutional authorities. Here was evolving a new conception of writing and reading as the communication of a writer's "thought" that is expressed in the text. The notion of authorial intent took shape in a writer-text-reader domain set apart from oral communication, cultural authorities, artistic effects, and hidden mysteries. A preference for "literal" language animated this sphere of transparency with less emphasis on imprecise aspects of language (which can hinder a reader's discernment) and the promotion of more direct, descriptive prose. Such tendencies were consonant with the early Modern interest in scientific objectivity. In rough terms, then, there emerged an association of "as written" with "as is." A guiding thread in these developments was the need faced by written language to compensate for what is lost when disengaged from face-to-face speech.

2.1. Writing and Illocution

Olson spotlights the error in understanding literacy as simply the written transcription of spoken language.[12] Writing can indeed faithfully record what is said, but there remains the matter of how what is said *is to be taken*, which can be gathered in Austin's idea of the illocutionary force of language, the intended meaning of an utterance.[13] There are differences between declarations, commands, requests, and inquiries; between praise, sarcasm, irony, warning, and threat. With face-to-face speech, illocutionary force can be sensed in non-lexical elements of tone, tempo, gesture, and other modes of embodied communication. Written language by its very nature omits non-lexical features of spoken exchanges. When writing is necessarily coupled with reading (rather than, say, recitation), there comes the task of attending to *how* texts are written to be read.[14] The more that texts are isolated from speech, the more pronounced is the burden of *explicating* the illocutionary force of language.

Since writing amounts to an externalized objectification of language, it can serve the conscious explication of illocutionary meanings that are not lexically expressed in speech (from hearing a sarcastic tone to "She said sarcastically. . . "). The nominalization of modes of expression and reception allows more focused attention on linguistic capacities that are implicit in modes of oral communication. With the objectification of speech allowed by writing, there can arise a conscious articulation of "language," its aspects, structures, and types of disclosure. An overt awareness of grammar, sentences, words, phonemes, and so forth is the *product* of writing, not something "expressed" by writing.[15] Literacy is much more than a record of speech; it provides a model for *understanding* speech.[16]

The explication of "language" was at work in the evolution of literacy up through the early Modern period—not just regarding linguistic formats but also the different kinds of disclosure afforded by language. With the turn toward transparency and objectivity, specific forms of discourse were identified and sorted out: describing, inquiring, evaluating, hypothesizing, inferring, deducing, and so on. For the sake of precision and demonstration, there developed a predilection for definition, analysis, and the accumulation of evidence, which could be gathered in either lexical, syntactical, logical, or empirical terms. All told, by way of writing, the phonic, grammatical, and disclosive aspects of language became articulable and then *directable* toward the world in an organized and more precise manner. Literacy, then, was far more than an "expression" of thought; it generated a literate mentality.

2.2. The Literate Mind

The illocutionary force of language is hard to convey simply by the written record of spoken words, since it lacks the non-lexical elements of communication that can be intimated in face-to-face conversation. Specifying illocutionary force is a key task of writing, and recovering it is the initial assignment of reading.[17] The recursive plasticity of language is enhanced by writing and its ability to devise expressions for conveying intended meanings, such as how something is said: angrily, sarcastically, eagerly, coldly. Likewise with verbs describing a speech act: declared, asked, insisted, denied, agreed. When we speak, we do not usually add: "I am saying angrily. . . ." or "I am declaring. . . ." Also emergent are new concepts drawn from illocutionary descriptions: from "stated" to statement, from "implied" to implication. Consider a partial list of speech act and mental state verbs in English that first appeared in the 15th and 16th centuries: assert, conclude, confirm, contradict, criticize, define, discover, doubt, interpret, and prove. What now seems natural in such terms was originally a construction of literacy for the purpose of articulating illocutionary meaning. In effect, writing is able to convert non-lexical elements of (oral) language into lexical form. Such words now become objects of consideration, whereby new or implicit dimensions of "mentality" are brought into view for self-reflection and deployment. These recursive processes of construction, conversion, and reflexivity are characteristic of *literate* discourse and thought.

Proto-phenomenology advances a hermeneutical posture in claiming that interpretation goes all the way down in world-disclosure. Language is the obvious vehicle for interpretation, and it calls for self-interpretation when what is said can be modified by how it is said or the context in which it is said (insisting, exaggerating, imploring, requesting, ridiculing, commanding, advising, asserting, teaching, exclaiming). Immediate embodied occasions of speech can provide interpretive cues, often by direct means or impact without the need for considered attention. Written texts intensify the task of interpretation because the writer is usually absent to the reader and more explicit articulation of meaning is called for. Reflective attention to "the meaning of words" and their various uses is the core function of literacy-based schooling, as is the identification and execution of different types of writing: exposition, narrative, fiction, poetry, and various disciplinary texts. So, the central task in a literate education is learning the difference between what is said and what is meant, along with the studied application of different discourses. Such tasks exceed natural linguistic capacity and so it takes time and significant effort to learn their refined practice.[18] The "distance" traveled from natural language use in literate education is consummated by the hyper-literacy of academic disciplines.

2.3. Hyper-Literacy

Refined literate knowledge in schooling develops relatively late in a student's career, if at all. Since teachers have been habituated to their disciplines, the complex transformational effects of literacy can seem more natural than it is for students first coming to learn *how* subjects are treated in school, especially in higher education.[19] The literacy in question is much more than simply reading and writing skills; it follows from specific developments in Western intellectual history concerning how texts are to be written, read, and deployed for understanding the world. Consequently, "illiteracy" in this context is not a lack of intelligence or the sign of a "backward" mentality; it just means non-exposure to specific conceptual horizons opened up in Western disciplines of science, law, history, and philosophy, among others.

The question, therefore, is not simply a matter of literacy and orality, but how hyper-literacy has generated particular modes of thinking that demand a refined education in particular kinds of reading and writing.[20] The interrogation of hyper-literacy in this investigation does not dispute or derogate the disclosive power of academic knowledge, which can be apt in contextual terms, as responses to certain types of questions, analytical tasks, and explanatory aims. Hyper-literacy involves particular types of disclosure governed by disciplinary methods and institutional provisions, which promote regimes of writing and reading geared toward rational, reflective, and objective thinking. The problem at hand is not the nature and execution of these disciplines, but rather the pretense of exclusivity and fundamentality in hyper-literacy, which not only can conceal and distort the lived world, but also do harm when its effects amount to an undue colonization of that world. This opens up an extensive critical enterprise concerning the consequences of rationalized knowledge schemes in objectifying, regulating, and controlling nature and human life—in technological, social, and political domains, among others. My investigation has not focused on that critical project, but the delimitation of disciplinary knowledge at least sets the stage for how and why critique can be a legitimate response to over-reach and exclusionary effects.

3. PRINT

Approaching the year 2000, scholars were asked to nominate the most important discovery or invention in the previous thousand years. The consensus was the printing press (1450). There are many reasons supporting that choice, and I would like to frame the discussion in terms of how print (1) transformed literacy by concentrating and extending the effects of writing far beyond earlier periods, and (2) clinched the constitutive role of written language in Western thought.[21]

3.1. Spatialization and Objectification

The written visualization and spatialization of speech sounds was reinforced and intensified with the invention of the letter press and movable type in 15th-century Europe. Manual written letters do not exist apart from their texts. With printed type, the letters are actual material units unto themselves. The elemental objectification of language was thereby perfected by the store of piecemeal letters assembled into printed words. The precise and mechanical printing process—requiring some twelve to sixteen steps of production between a manuscript and the final page sheets—helped engender an objective, systematic, and technological model of language.[22]

3.2. Standardization

Written standards of usage and grammar in Europe, accomplished in scholarly writing by Neo-Latin measures, became more extensive and pervasive with printed texts—from both a production standpoint and the commercial spread of publications to more audiences and wider territories. A common method of printing for an expansive trans-geographical readership benefited from more generic and standard patterns of language.

The emergence of dictionaries promoted the further codification of usage, spelling, pronunciation, and meaning. A dictionary as a "lexicon" concentrates a lexical focus on language by way of written words. An alphabetized catalog has practical value as a reference, but it represents an utterly artificial manner of displaying words as individual units isolated from their intrinsic correlations with other words in natural language. The aim is to collect in comprehensive form an empirical record of actual usage, but the selection process cannot help but be colored by assumptions governing the discernment of compilers.[23] Much in natural speech can be screened out by scholarly and literate measures. Dictionaries not only reflect cultural usage, they shape future usage. Much more than a catalog of words, dictionaries are "empires of words."[24]

The governing effects and verbal isolations issued by dictionaries have become so commonplace in literate cultures that language and meaning have been conceptually colonized by this very particular expositional format. The human store of words has even been called a "mental lexicon," in a manner that reiterates the regulation and piecemeal precision of a dictionary framework.[25] In this way, an understanding of language is restricted to textual codifications that cannot fully accord with a factical speech-world. The selective and supervisory character of a lexical record is unable to fit or reflect wide variations in pronunciation, syntax, context, correlational scope, embodied communication, affective attunement, and especially the creative spontaneity of everyday usage. In general terms, dictionaries, grammar books, and most expositional accounts in linguistics overlook (and suppress) the messier functions of human speech that nevertheless *work* in practical terms.

Philosophical and linguistic theories have preferred or stipulated "essential" meanings for words, along with execution governed by clarity, precision, and disambiguation. Yet we have seen that contextual interpretation and the differential dynamic of language will ever frustrate such preferences. In factical speech, word usage has vague boundaries, fuzzy edges, and slippery meanings. Speakers do tend to rely on certain prototypical meanings of words, but they are also comfortable with rough approximations, metaphorical extensions, and contextual shifts—where coherence is sustained by context and degrees of overlapping resonance. Some words exhibit so many variations as to defy even loose constellations: consider the remarkable flexibility in the word "over."[26] In any case, the isolation of individual words in dictionaries—along with the visual demarcation of printed words—encourages an impulse for lexical stability, precision, and specificity that will not always fit well with natural speech practices—which exhibit, in Lloyd's nice phrase, "semantic stretch."[27] The polysemic energy of language is continually shifting meaning and usage. With contextual variation, words will expand or contract meaning, associate or dissociate with other words, gather layers of indicative use, adopt compound meanings, undergo grammatical conversion (nouns, verbs, and adjectives exchanging form), and take on morpheme affixation (-ness, -ity, -ly), sometimes with dizzying redundancy—as in the awful managerial word "operationalize," which travels from verb to noun to adjective and back to verb.

The fitness of language and its communicative function do require degrees of regularity, but the "sense" of language is a fluid, multi-faceted, and episodic sojourn that gathers comprehension in different contexts and shifts of enactive interpretation. Ironically, despite the regulating effects of "lexiconic" documents, a good dictionary provides a rich indication of the complexity and plasticity of language, if one reads comprehensively. A single word entry can display a wide array of meanings, while etymologies and examples of past usage highlight the historical dynamism of language (The *Oxford English Dictionary* is a stellar example of documenting the intricacy and fluidity of a language). Finally, the periodic selection of new entries to reflect changes or innovation enacts the flexible measure of language over time, which is neither rigidly exclusive nor wide open to any anomaly. Linguistic novelty should register some settlement in a community of users before it becomes part of the lexicon.

3.3. Typographic Accuracy and Science

Unlike a manuscript culture, where even copying a text would involve alterations, deliberate or otherwise, print allows the precise duplication of a text in its production. Oral poetry, as we have seen, involved modification with each performance. While manuscript culture provided more decisive means of comparing texts for the sake of identity and difference, there was no expectation that a written text would represent an authoritative "original" or could take a final "complete" form. The printing press fed the notion of a fixed text, with different copies taking an identical form and the text itself taking on a finished form. That sense of objective accuracy and finality went hand-in-hand with the scientific spirit of precision and accuracy in "reading" the natural world—in other words, the conjunction of exact observation and exact description in language, along with a presumption of discursive completion.[28] The standardization and dissemination made possible by print served science well by spreading identical texts to a wider audience than was possible in manuscript form. Extensive exposure was effective because the more minds brought into the scientific domain, the stronger the force of corroboration—and also the greater chance of productive critique or dissent that could prompt new directions.

3.4. The Individual Reader

The manuscript culture in Europe retained an oral element, with vocalized reading and especially the recitation of books in group gatherings. The print revolution afforded a more individualized relationship with books in a number of ways.[29] Manuscripts were not easy to read. Print facilitated reading with a uniform format and a clearer delineation of word units and spatial relations. Accordingly, the visual element of writing was accentuated and enhanced. Greater legibility made for faster processing—and consequently a preference for silent reading. Printed books were cheaper to purchase and smaller in size than manuscripts, which meant that written texts were more likely to become personal property and their easy portability could follow a reader's mobility. In all, print promoted a silent-visual-individual element of literacy that shifted from an earlier oral-aural-social framework. That tendency also nurtured an individualized posture of thinking, notably illustrated by Descartes isolating himself from the social-world and taking the pathway of individual reflection, a movement from dialectical processes to internal "meditation."[30]

3.5. The Literate Lens

In the early Modern period, print and its effects on literacy were such that language and thinking came to be understood more and more through the lens of writing. This went further than the regulation of language by grammar books, dictionaries, methodological treatises, and Neo-Latin guidelines. By the 18th century, a common view was that writing was subsequent to speech in the order of time (historically and pedagogically), but not in the order of nature. The visual spacialization of language took hold to such an extent that writing was overtly taken to represent the very nature of language—even in a generative sense, wherein writing was thought to be the cause of reading and reading the cause of oral speech.[31]

Philosophy in the early Modern period also displayed the effects of a literate lens. The next section will explore this notion by focusing on the parallel association of philosophy and science in the Modern period. But here I point to Locke's account of empirical knowledge as analogous to grammatical construction: simple ideas (of color and shape, for instance) stem from the primary data of experience, which then are combined into complex ideas (a red ball). Locke employed the "elemental" sense of lettering when he compared the wide variety of complex ideas assembled from simple ideas to the extensive number of words assembled from letters of the alphabet.[32] The concrete visual perspective of written words and their letter parts continued to be deployed for elemental, analytical, and synthetic thinking. And the displacement of oral sound by the perspective of vision played a role in the emphasis on sight in epistemology, where the conceptual organization of "sense experience" was usually cast in visual terms, where hearing and touching, for instance, were rarely referenced. Here was a Western perspective that was less pronounced in Asian and African cultures, where "hearing" played a significant role in the acquisition of knowledge.[33]

4. SCIENCE AND THE BOOK OF NATURE

The early Modern period saw the rise of the New Science, and philosophers found themselves articulating its epistemological implications. Literacy was essential to this new thinking—combining both linguistic and mathematical literacy. We have seen how literate techniques played a preparatory role in the development of scientific thinking. The need to represent authorial intent led to delineations of cognition, reflection on the language of thought processes, and a preference for literal language and transparency of meaning. The emphasis was on (1) "ideas" divorced from poetic, rhetorical, and ambiguous aspects of natural language, and (2) the representational relation between ideas and the natural world. It is telling that science was at times rendered as reading the "book of nature."[34] Francis Bacon, in *The New Organon*, maintained that mere (spoken) words could get in the way of refined ideas in science. He called proper thinking "literate experience," where writing could overcome the contingencies of natural language and where careful observation and analysis would provide the "alphabet of the world."[35] Descartes, Locke, Hume, and Hobbes likewise stressed scientific ideas over mere linguistic signs, but it was new modes of reading and writing that supported this turn to scientific objectivity.[36] Reading the book of nature "as it is" was the goal, which required a departure from the vagaries of natural speech, religious revelation, imagination, guesswork, and interpretation.[37]

Mathematical literacy was essential to the development of modern science, combining numerical and geometrical figuration. Galileo said that natural philosophy (physics) "is written in the grand book—I mean the universe—which . . . is written in the language of mathematics, without which it is impossible to understand a single word of it." Without mathematics, one wanders around in a "dark labyrinth."[38] Galileo's geometrical mathematics was supplanted in the 16th century by the symbolic mathematics of algebraic calculus, yet both forms of scientific thinking would be impossible without script, which operates by way of visual and spatial perception.[39] Algebraic calculus was superior to geometrical illustration in devising an operational analysis that could offer an explication of mechanical motion, which could be manipulated for experimental work. This was not simply a mechanical science but a new picture of a mechanical world.[40] The transformation of mathematics by way of letter signs and formulas allowed an objectification of mathematics as its own domain of thinking, as opposed to the Greek notion of number as simply counting things in the world.[41]

Mathematical models and structures fostered the nomological-causal thinking that is essential to modern science.[42]

4.1. The New Nature

The mathematical character of modern physics created a new sense of "nature," which was transformed into a set of material objects properly ascertained only through empirical observation and quantitative measurement. The reach of this model has been such that in some circles philosophy itself is conceived as a form of "naturalism"—shorthand for scientific naturalism—wherein philosophical topics are best explained by, or at least must be consistent with, findings in natural science. Analytic philosophers often complain that continental philosophy is bereft of precision and commitment to scientific reason. Continental philosophers complain that analytic philosophy takes for granted terms or criteria that are not timeless but historically emergent and contingent, and therefore worthy of interrogation. Nature is a good example. One might think that our sense of physical nature is nicely collected in the Greek word *phusis*, usually translated as "nature," but this word had a much more complex meaning for the Greeks. *Phusis* is derived from the verb *phuō*, meaning to grow, to bring forth, to give birth.[43] With Aristotle we get a philosophical articulation of *phusis* as nature, but here too we have to be careful. Aristotle does not equate *phusis* with physical matter because it is manifest more in form than in matter (*Physics* 193b5ff.). And a prime instance of *phusis*, for Aristotle, is *psuchē*, exemplified by the human soul (*On the Soul* 412a20ff.). *Phusis* is not contrasted with the "supernatural," it is simply identified with movement and change (*Physics* 200b12) and is specified as self-manifesting movement, as distinct from *technē* (artifice) or movement caused by an external agent in human production (*Physics* 192b10ff.). Aristotle even gives *phusis* a comprehensive ontological significance, going so far as to connect it with being itself (*Metaphysics* 1003a26–32). To repeat, Aristotelian *phusis* is not strictly material because it includes a teleological principle of form, where all natural beings are essentially purposeful in the process of actualizing potentialities that are intrinsic to their being.

In general, the modern concept of nature developed out of two guiding criteria in modern science that, despite their apparent divergence into empirical and conceptual standards, were reciprocally related in scientific work: experimental verification and mathematical formalization. Both Descartes and Kant, among others, insisted that a science of nature was grounded in mathematics.[44] Modern science was a self-conscious repudiation of Aristotelian "physics," in part because central Aristotelian concepts of purpose and potentiality elude precise formalization and verification. As Newton put it, "The moderns, rejecting substantial forms and occult qualities, have endeavored to subject the phenomena of nature to the laws of mathematics."[45] And Descartes described his *Meditations* as the foundation of his physics, which dealt a mortal blow to Aristotelian physics.[46] Consequently "nature" in modern science was no longer understood in an Aristotelian manner as the field of self-manifesting phenomena that guide inquiry according to their evident formations, but as re-formed phenomena according to a priori constructs and principles that are *not* evident in immediate experience. In *Meditations* V, Descartes claimed that corporeal things in nature exist, but their true existence cannot be ascertained as a match with our sensory grasp (as in Aristotle), because sense experience can be confused. Things in nature exist only in the manner of clear and distinct ideas, which are ultimately grounded in pure mathematics, which is the ground of mechanical physics, and which, for Descartes, is ultimately guaranteed by knowledge of God.[47]

It can be argued that God, for Descartes, was not only a warrant for physics but also the source of the non-teleological conception of mechanics. Descartes held that God's perfection includes radical freedom, especially with respect to creation as a result of sheer divine will, as not bound by any prior conception, even goodness and purpose.[48] Divine "indifference" with respect to the quality of nature underwrites the legitimacy of the "purposeless" axioms of mechanical physics.[49] Moreover, since nature has no intrinsic ends of its own, the door is open to the modern technological spirit of subjecting natural processes to human ends. Descartes himself claimed that the chief benefit of the new mechanical model of nature is the power of control it grants to those who understand the secrets of nature's workings. Human beings can then become "the lords and masters of nature."[50]

I have noted that one of the meanings of "natural" is that which is "native" to experience, what we are born into, which is indicated in the sphere of common sense that Descartes had to withdraw from and even fight off in his method of radical doubt. Modern science exhibits a similar kind of contested disposition toward natural experience and understanding (which are sometimes called "folk knowledge"). Indeed, the posture of experimental science toward nature is far from a cooperative relationship (which marked Aristotle's account of scientific knowledge). Francis Bacon is disarmingly honest on this matter. The experimental method investigates "nature under constraint and vexed; that is to say, when by art and the hand of man she is forced out of her natural state, and squeezed and molded."[51] The point is that modern scientific naturalism emerged as a *struggle* with erstwhile conceptions of nature and lived experience. Kant as well claimed that scientific reason "has insight only into what it itself produces according to its own plan," and that, armed with necessary laws, it must "compel nature to answer reason's own questions."[52] We can conclude that the construal of nature as a scientific and technological "object" is itself far from an objective discovery.

For such a scheme to emerge, the rational "subject" has to withdraw from natural experience to reconstitute the *being* of nature by way of mathematics and experimental intervention. The transformative character of this modern scheme is shown in its reversal of Aristotle's analysis of mathematics. In *Metaphysics* 13, Aristotle claimed that mathematical form is indeed disclosive of being, but only in the manner of secondary *ousia*, not the primary *ousia* of particular phenomena in nature. Mathematical form is *derived* from primary *ousia* through the operation of *aphaeresis*, or *abstraction*, which means to pull away or take away from (*Metaphysics* 1061a30ff.)—a term that Aristotle used exclusively for mathematics, and that exemplified his critique of Platonic Forms, which were falsely assumed to be conditions of primary *ousia*. Analogously, modern physics would count as a comparable distortion of nature by giving primacy to mathematical form.

The mathematization of nature in early modern science was a complex story, with different applications and emphases.[53] Physics and astronomy deployed mathematics to the greatest extent, compared to chemistry and biology. There were debates between realist and instrumentalist conceptions of mathematics, but practical applications were often decisive for the status of science, largely because of the influence of mechanical engineering. The quantification of nature allowed for technological control and significant predictive power. The subsequent regulation of life and knowledge extended to many domains: navigation, ballistics, surveying, commerce, economics, music, statistics, and even techniques of perspective in painting.

4.2. Philosophers on Literacy

A common reflection on literate knowledge concerned figuration, which in scientific and epistemological pursuits played a significant role in techniques of objectification and calculative thinking. In Greek, *gramma* and *graphē* could refer, respectively, to letters/letter-making and drawings/figure-making. Both Descartes and Kant specifically referred to figuration as central to the power of imagination in the construction of knowledge.[54] Kant maintained that the mind cannot conceive of three-dimensional space without "drawing" lines in thought and configuring them; even understanding the course of time requires linear figuration.

Leibniz is noteworthy in devising his *characteristica universalis*, which offered an "alphabet" of human thought that would display the conceptual elements of a universal language—pictographic symbols that were manipulable by algebraic means in a *calculus ratiocinator*. Such a technical language system was thought to be superior to the messy ambiguity of natural language.[55] Leibniz's device and the use of figuration are both examples of literate constructions that embody abstract thinking. In a functional sense, the objective/external space of figuration and its role in cognition illustrate the notion of an extended mind, where certain areas of knowledge depend on graphic objectifications that spawn or enable reflective thought.

I should mention one thinker, shortly after the Modern period, who recognized the abstract power of alphabetic script along the lines of my account, namely Hegel. In Part Three of his *Encyclopaedia*, the treatment of psychology came to detail the power of imagination in human cognition.[56] In a discussion of language, signs, and symbols, Hegel offered some passing thoughts on written language. Alphabetic writing, he said, allows for a progressive development of language beyond its oral form, because now language can become an "object of reflection" and the sensible element in speech can be raised to "the form of universality."[57] The very form of alphabetic writing, compared to sense experience, aids the "capacity of abstraction." In accord with my analysis of writing and reading generating abstract verbal objects, mental habits, and internalization, Hegel remarked:

> What has been said shows the inestimable and not sufficiently appreciated educational value of learning to read and write an alphabetic character. It leads the mind from the sensibly concrete image to attend to the more formal structure of the vocal word and its abstract elements, and contributes much to give stability and independence to the inward realm of mental life. Acquired habit subsequently effaces the peculiarity by which alphabetic writing appears, in the interest of vision, as a roundabout way to ideas by means of audibility; it makes them a sort of hieroglyphic to us, so that in using them we need not consciously realize them by means of tones, whereas people unpracticed in reading utter aloud what they read in order to catch its meaning in the sound.[58]

5. REPRESENTATION AND SUBJECTIVITY

The personal-social-environing-world advanced in this investigation is meant to challenge (1) the subject-object divide constructed by modern philosophy in its association with scientific thought, and (2) the near ubiquity of representational models of cognition, which presume to correlate mind and world with some kind of referential mental state—even if physicalized into brain states.[59] In this section, I sketch (1) the way in which literacy helped spawn representational thinking, and (2) how the modern "subject" emerged as the site of both referential cognition and the construction of scientific "objectivity."

5.1. Literacy and Representation

The notion of a mind processing or deploying representations is derived from the actual practices of literate work: reading, writing, using dictionaries, and learning from grammar books.⁶⁰ In more schematic terms, the formal properties of language become evident in writing's capacity to construct abstract referential patterns, which then allows thinking to be understood as a representational system, as a rule-governed manipulation of concepts and symbols.⁶¹ The visual permanence of written words suggests cognitive stability and fosters a monological perspective—as opposed to the temporal impermanence and distributed features of face-to-face conversation. The very notion of a representation underwrites such stabilizing and monologizing effects.⁶² Now denotative and descriptive functions of language come more to the fore and take precedence over expressive, emotive, and conative functions that figure strongly in interpersonal communicative practices.⁶³

Revisiting Olson's account of literacy, between the Medieval and early Modern period, written texts evolved from a mnemonic to a representational function, from a record and reminder of what has been said to designating the beliefs and intentions of an author.⁶⁴ Writing came to be understood more as a lexical and compositional technique to communicate the cognitive meaning of a text that accurately represents the mind of the writer. In an oral society, hearing the "same story" is not equivalent to the "same words." Lexical or sonic "identity" is not what is "heard" or expected.⁶⁵ With literate expectations of a cognitive transfer from writer to reader, a more precise relation between what is written and what is meant came to be expected. A preference for literal language, descriptive accuracy, decisive results, and the specification of meaning came to govern how a text should be composed and comprehended. Legal "writs" in English law became influential examples of specification, disambiguation, and transparent representation of cognition (Robert Hooke considered legal writs to be a model for scientific writing). In 17th-century Europe, representational thinking took shape in a variety of graphic forms: maps, diagrams, imaginative fiction, Dutch painting, mathematical figuration, and musical notation. In Olson's terms, there was a general movement from knowledge embedded in the world to reflective, representational knowledge of the "world on paper."

Concurrent with such developments was the construction of a representational mind, the modern "subject" as the site of cognition. Yet that sense of subjectivity was made possible by the material presence of written words as an "objectification" of thinking. Modern writing and reading involved implicit or explicit attention to the "mind" of a writer or reader. With written works, dictionaries, grammar books, methodological treatises, and intertextual critical analysis, literacy presented on objectified extension of language and its meaning. Such occasions afforded self-conscious attention to language and its cognitive functions, which launched the refined articulation of thinking that has characterized modern intellectual life. In some respects, we have literally come to "reading minds."

5.2. Subjectivity and Objectivity

Modern subjectivity is the site of representational thinking, but also an expression of independent thought liberated from the force of tradition and common sense. Central figures such as Descartes, Locke, and Kant held that self-conscious reflective attention to mental representations is essential for thinking because otherwise there is no format for intelligibility linking mental states and the world. It was Kant who clinched this account with his notion of representation (*Vorstellung*) constituting objects of experience and shaping them into knowledge. My investigation has challenged the primacy of representational subjectivity and objectivity. Aside from a phenomenological alternative for understanding selfhood and knowledge, another avenue for critique follows from the contingency of the subject-object relation, owing to its historical emergence in the Modern period, which undermines the presumption of its universality—a critical task that I explore in this section.[66]

The subject as the "I think" (*cogito*) in modern philosophy is a transubstantiation of the Medieval *subjectum*, which was the Latin descendent of the Greek *hupokeimenon*, which was understood as the substantive bearer or base of properties and attributions. In a 1935–1936 lecture course, Heidegger discusses the origins of the modern subject-object distinction in terms of Descartes' task of positing a self-grounding fundament for the mathematical character of modern science, wherein the radical divorce of mathematical physics from ancient, medieval, and customary beliefs demanded a grounding in a disengaged thinking sphere.[67] Descartes's reflective journey in the *Meditations* was aiming for a sphere of certainty that could resolve the vexing debates of his time. His extreme method of doubt allowed that genuine certainty could only be found in reflective thought as such—because he could doubt everything except his mental state of doubting. His "existence" could only be guaranteed as a mode of "thought" ("I think, therefore I am") rather than any kind of material or sensuous condition.

Because of this powerful *warrant* found in the thinking sphere, the a priori methodology and abstract mechanical principles of the New Science could be secured and liberated from all external dependencies and contingencies. Heidegger mentions Galileo's work as an example of such a methodological a priori.[68] In the *Discourses*, Galileo recounted how the discovery of universal principles of motion required that he conceive of a body on a horizontal plane free of any obstacles, a conception that no experience will give him ("I conceive in my mind. . . . ").[69] Heidegger claims that with such developments, the erstwhile meanings of *subjectum* and *objectum* became transformed in a remarkable way. The *cogito* became identified as a special, privileged *subjectum*, construed as the underlying *hupokeimenon* or substantial basis of mathematical thinking. Originally a "subject" indicated any referential base, more in line with Aristotelian *ousia*, which was Latinized as "substance," as that which stands under, behind, or within particular features of an entity.[70] Before Descartes, according to Heidegger, *subjectum* showed no exclusive identification with the thinking mind. But now the *cogito* as *subjectum* became something unique in line with the modern mathematical project: a *self*-grounding *subjectum* that freely grounds the thinking of nature as a set of "objects," namely the "disenchanted" entities of modern science denuded of relations to human interests and values on behalf of a mechanistic/causal world view.[71] In the light of physics, "nature" was transformed into a set of material objects properly ascertained exclusively through empirical observation and quantitative measurement.

The mathematized being of nature sets up and guarantees the modern sense of "objectivity," in the manner of *independence* from interests, values, and purposes. Yet the *selectivity* evident in this transformation of nature is another angle on the history of subjectivity and objectivity. Such selectivity can be seen in the shift that occurred in the meaning of *objectum*. In *What Is a Thing?* Heidegger notes that *objectum* originally referred to something present in the mind rather than something existing in reality (an imagination would be an example). *Objectum* was the Scholastic translation of the Greek *antikeimenon*, meaning "set over against," which Aristotle used not to designate an "object" but opposition. In Medieval and early Modern philosophy, *objectum* usually referred to an intentional object or representation, something thrown before or presented to the mind, as distinct from the independent reality of a thing. When the idealist Berkeley claimed that "to be is to be perceived," he was equating *esse* and *objectum*. As he said with respect to natural phenomena, "their real and objective natures are therefore the same."[72]

What is unusual in all of this, Heidegger remarks, is that the modern senses of subjectivity and objectivity represent a reversal of the original meanings of *subjectum* and *objectum*. *Subjectum* in the old sense indicated something we would call "objective," and *objectum* something we would call "subjective." The *Oxford English Dictionary* bears this out in recognizing "an exchange of sense" between subjectivity and objectivity in the course of time.[73] Objectivity originally meant something only in the mind while subjectivity meant real existence outside the mind. A 1647 passage cited in the *OED* calls personal confession the objective foundation of Christian faith, while Christ is called the subjective foundation.[74]

The implication of Heidegger's analysis of this meaning reversal is, I think, as follows: When the *cogito* became the self-grounding *subjectum*, its substantive reconstruction of nature as a mathematical system out of its own thinking sphere privileged the mind's self-positing capacity (more in line with the original meaning of *objectum*); and from this privileging of the new *subjectum's* positing power, there eventually arose the modern sense of "objectivity," namely real things existing independent of the mind as discerned by scientific reason. In other words, after Descartes, the *cogito* as the primal "subject" now can deploy its own mental "objects" (ideas and laws) to refashion nature by way of a new sense of being that is stripped of non-measurable qualities such as values and purposes—what we now call "objective being."[75] Regarding the existence of material things, Descartes says: "I now know that they are capable of existing in so far as they are the subject-matter (*objectum*) of pure mathematics, since I perceive them purely and distinctly."[76] Heidegger's account is in no way a dismissal of the modern project but an attempt to clarify its deepest conditions of thought. It could even be said that the terminological shifts were necessary for the radical reshaping of nature in modern science. Heidegger's critique would target the subsequent exclusive role played by such thinking in epistemology and ontology. In other words, the positive disclosive power of modern science prompted an inappropriate extension to all manner of philosophical topics.

With respect to the historical developments in question, Heidegger's analysis of Descartes and modern thought is in a technical sense a premature compression of a transitional process that took a long time to unfold. To my knowledge, Descartes did not use the term *subjectum* in reference to the *cogito*. There is, however, an interesting moment in one of Hobbes' objections to the *Meditations*.[77] He suggests that Descartes is applying the substantive sense of the subject (*subjectum*) to the thinking mind—hence a thinking thing (*res cogitans*) becomes "the subject of the mind, reason, or understanding." But for Hobbes, a substantive subject is corporeal (following one of the common meanings of "subject"), so he asks how a mind can be a subject. In effect, Hobbes is accusing Descartes of arbitrarily connecting a subject with a nonmaterial entity. Descartes replies that indeed a subject is a substance, but not on that account necessarily material (citing non-corporeal senses of "subject"). This is a hint of things to come, but not yet a technical employment of modern subjectivity. The same is true for objectivity, given Descartes' distinction between formal reality (more in line with the original substantive sense of *subjectum*) and objective reality (more like the modern sense of subjectivity). In *Meditations* III, formal reality refers to a thing's actual existence as distinct from the objective reality of the mind's representation.[78]

Spinoza also does not use "subject" in the modern sense, and like Descartes, he distinguishes between formal and objective essence. Locke does describe external "objects" as the source of the mind's ideas, as does Hume, but neither Locke, Berkeley, nor Hume uses the term *subject* in reference to the mind, but rather to the old sense of *hupokeimenon*. For Hume, "subject" even refers to "external objects."[79] It is in Kant that the modern configuration of subject and object is clinched and indeed perfected with respect to Heidegger's analysis. Inheriting the Cartesian *cogito*, Kant proclaims in

Critique of Pure Reason: "The *I think* must be *capable* of accompanying all my representations," and it is the ground of any knowledge of "objects."[80] For Kant, to be an object is to be constituted by the a priori structures of the "thinking subject," and therefore objects do not exist "in themselves"—the *noumenon* is not an "object" (A 191/B 236). An "object of experience" must be governed by necessary rules, otherwise we are left with *merely* subjective apprehension, merely a play of representations and thus not an "object" of knowledge (A 194–95/B 239–240). For Kant, the modern sense of objectivity is secured because of the inter-subjective validity and necessity of the mind's categories: subjective knowledge is *transcendentally* more certain than objective knowledge (since a priori categories guarantee scientific knowledge); but *empirically*, subjective knowledge (in individual minds) is less certain than objective knowledge. Thus, Kant denotes a distinction that posed an enduring problem in modern philosophy: the difference between transcendental subjectivity as the ground of knowledge and individual subjectivity as a possible site of cognitive deficiency (non-objective belief based solely in an individual mind).[81]

In many respects the individual, psychological sense of subjectivity has come to eclipse the more foundational, cognitive character of the subject that we find in Kant and Hegel. With Kierkegaard, we come to the valorization of non-objective, personal subjectivity in its proper existential domain (the aesthetic, the ethical, and the religious)—which accordingly rejects Kant's attempt to ground the value realm in intersubjective universals. All told in this historical discussion, we encounter a complex and convoluted movement from *subjectum* as substance, to the subject as ground of knowledge, to subjectivity as individual, personal selfhood; and all of this intertwined with a concurrent movement from *objectum* as mind-dependent, to objects as constituted by the subject, to objectivity as a reality independent of minds and selves. Now we have the familiar distinction between subjective belief (as mind-dependent) and objective truth (as mind-independent).

The terms *subject* and *object*, subjective and objective, have come to be used in different ways that cannot be reduced to any common genus—largely because of the variegated history of these words. With "subject" we note the following meanings: (1) the subject as the ground of cognition, the rational mind, which can be taken as universal and identical across individual minds (as in Kant); (2) the subject as the individual self or person; (3) the subjective as non-objective, as the immediate content of individual consciousness, and then as (4) the *merely* subjective, as corrigible content contrasted with objective truth; (5) the grammatical subject of a sentence; (6) a disciplinary subject of study; (7) a subject of investigation; (8) political subjects (as in a monarch's subjects); and (9) passive subjection in a general sense, as in being subject to ridicule. With "object" we have: (1) an object counter-posed to a knowing subject; (2) an object as a material thing in the world; (3) an object of thought, which can therefore be immaterial; (4) an object of investigation (thus identical to # 7 above); (5) an objective as a goal; and (6) objective truth that is independent of subjective beliefs, desires, or interests.

The confusing historical and semantic thicket just described demonstrates the contingency of some familiar philosophical concepts. With so many different meanings attaching to the subject and subjectivity, the attempt to think beyond them in proto-phenomenology is given more credence. One might argue for the use of subjectivity as a defensible term for the phenomenology of selfhood explored in this investigation, especially since subjectivity and personal selfhood have come to be joined so much in common usage, often in rich ways. I concede that subjectivity in the "existentialist" sense (especially in Kierkegaard) might work for the kind of existential selfhood that I am advancing, but I have three reasons for resisting this philosophically: (1) subjectivity came to mean personal selfhood *only* out of the modern transubstantiation of subject and object, and the subsequent differentiation between scientific objectivity and (merely) subjective psychological states—thus subjectivity never harbored an authentic phenomenological significance prior to this "impersonal" philosophical framework; (2) in some quarters, personal subjectivity has itself come to represent a kind of individual *subjectum*—as a *ground* of beliefs and values—which continues to vex the philosophical prospects of objectivity, especially in epistemology, ethics, and political philosophy; (3) for these and other reasons, subjectivity blocks the "extended" sense of selfhood that I have advanced in the triadic unity of the personal-social-environing-world.

The perennial problem of subjectivism—where truth is reduced to individual beliefs, with no warrant beyond the subject's self-assertion—is a vestige of the grounding character of the subject in the history of modern philosophy. Even modern "objectivity" has "subjective" roots (understood transcendentally). As a consequence of the subject-object binary, the fact-value divide has reduced important cultural beliefs to a "merely" subjective status (understood empirically). Proto-phenomenology is different because elements of "value" can be world-disclosive. In ethical and political domains, any baseline subjectivism or individualism will haunt the "claim" of social projects. Moreover, if individualism is assumed and manifested in ways of life, there can result the reactive formation of oppressive or consuming regimes that overwhelm individual selves. Overall, I have tried to outline a number of reasons why the subject is problematic in philosophy, mainly because of its grounding-character, whether in the rational or personal subject: the rational subject is insulated from the instability and finitude of factical life, while the individual subject is too much wedded to an interior consciousness that misses the ecological character of the personal-*world*. A significant opening for the critique of such long-standing assumptions is the contingency and selectivity of supposedly timeless concepts governing the matters at hand. As we have seen, in the background of scientific, epistemological, and psychological measures of subjectivity in modern thought stand the contours of mentality that took shape primarily in the practices and effects of literacy, which is far from a context-free, objective standard of analysis. The door is open for other pathways of philosophical thought.

6. LITERAL AND METAPHORICAL LANGUAGE

A perennial topic in linguistics and philosophy is the distinction between metaphorical and literal language. A metaphor is a comparison of one thing or condition with another for the sake of comprehension, often a comparison of something abstract with something concrete and perceptible. A literal description is a non-comparative, straightforward account of something just as it is, with no embellishment, transference, or analogy. Olson's work tracks the development of modern literacy, wherein the task of communicating and discerning authorial meaning came to prize specificity, directness, and transparency. This together with the ascendancy of natural science and legal writings generated an emphasis on literal description over indirect and ornamental language.[82] A distinction between the "spirit" and the "letter" of a text diminished; now the spirit could be discerned by a careful reading of the letter.[83] Such a shift crystallized a distrust of metaphor that was common among philosophers.[84] Aristotle's classic account in the *Poetics* and *Rhetoric* extolled the effectiveness of metaphor for the arts and oratory in bringing vivid concreteness to ideas, but he maintained that logic and natural philosophy require a separation from metaphorical expression.[85] In the Modern period, the British empiricists Bacon, Hobbes, and Locke specifically argued against the use of metaphor in philosophical and scientific prose—yet their writings often deployed metaphorical expressions (especially in the very title of Hobbes's major work, *Leviathan*).[86]

As noted in chapter 1, we have come to realize that human thinking cannot bypass metaphor, especially when we look beyond comparison tropes and notice how much cognition and description rely on resonances of embodied perception that have settled into routine expressions: I see what you mean; his ideas are not clear; let's get to the bottom of things, and so on. When child development and language acquisition are brought to bear on the question, we see how important embodied practices in an environment are to the emergence of language. Human understanding and expression are grounded in a body-world nexus that depends on somatic abilities and sensorimotor circuits.[87] Accordingly, "holding" a belief or "constructing" a theory are not *mere* metaphors because the genesis of human intelligence cannot be separated from engagements with the physical world.[88] Embedded metaphors become so tacit and customary that they escape notice as such, to the point where we wrongly assume literal meanings to be more prevalent than they are. Indeed, written language generates the habit of thinking that the "meaning" we read is just *there* in the wording of a text—due in part to the acquired skill of immersed reading—which can conceal the hermeneutical openness and flexibility of language.[89] In any case, the differential character of metaphors can display functional fitness and be directly disclosive, which is more evident when we consider their early acquisition becoming second-nature habituation.

6.1. Metaphor and Understanding the World

Metaphorical disclosure is drawn from embodied immersion in tangible environments, and it is arguably ineliminable for human understanding—which calls for an expanded sense of what "cognition" means.[90] A common view in philosophy has been that concepts have a literal meaning that can be rationally comprehended apart from embodied experience or resonances of perception—and so metaphors are either translatable into literal conceptual meanings or negligible for cognition. Yet metaphor is evidently pervasive in conceptual understanding and linguistic expression, usually in an implicit and non-conscious manner. Abstract thought operates with a wide range of metaphorical meanings and is accordingly grounded in everyday experience.[91] In my terms, metaphor is world-disclosive and anchored in factical life.

The kinds of metaphorical usage are vast and multifarious.[92] Philosophical "arguments" are often pitched in martial terms: winning and losing an argument, attacking and defending a position. Time is frequently rendered as a resource: saving, wasting, or spending time; investing, costing, or running out of time; using or losing time; having time to give. Ideas can be objects and containers, communicated by transport: you gave me a good idea; the speech had little weight; her statement has no meaning; that idea came across well. There are orientation metaphors having to do with spatial relations: being on or off point, feeling up or down; deep or shallow thought; and various renditions of in and out, center and periphery, under and over. Such metaphors have salience because they are rooted in natural experience and socio-cultural settings. There are ontological metaphors, where ideas or emotions are reified and take on agency: fear having properties, causes, and effects; having or losing patience; hatred spreading; anger causing violence; marriage as a journey; being in trouble; seeking fame; a fragile ego. Concepts can be personified: theories explain; religion teaches; inflation hurts the economy. Ideas can be structured like buildings or function as nourishment or products; emotions can be shown in the eyes or have a physical impact; and knowledge usually is expressed in visual terms: having a point of view; thinking clearly; a murky argument. In general terms, context is essential for the creation, production, use, and comprehension of metaphor—in a wide range of circumstances, practices, social relationships, and cultural domains.[93] Moreover, literacy expands the production of metaphors and enhances the comprehension of how thought operates in metaphorical ways.[94] At the same time, as we have seen, writing contributes to the evolution of, and tendencies toward, a "literal" conception of language.

6.2. Writing and the Literal-Metaphorical Distinction

Philosophical concerns about metaphor and the preference for literal language should diminish because of the degree to which metaphor operates at every level of thought and expression. Epistemological worries stem from descriptive and referential assumptions that are even reflected in common usage: "literally true" can be equivalent to "factually accurate." Unembellished literal accounts have become the mark of proper cognition. Yet we have noted the limits of such a presupposition.

The valorization of literal description as superior to metaphorical expression faces another hurdle when we consider the very nature and history of the literal-metaphorical distinction, particularly in relation to writing. The distinction itself in the end may not hold up.[95] A look at the *Oxford English Dictionary* reveals a complex history of usage that opens up many questions about literal language. The original meaning of "literal" pertained simply to alphabetic letters, and thus not to a differentiation from metaphor (since metaphors have letters). In this sense, a "literal mistake" would refer not to a descriptive error but a misprint. Other meanings then grew out of and modified this primary sense: word-for-word transcription (quotation versus paraphrase); taking words in their natural or customary meaning; the core sense of a word or the direct wording of a passage, as distinguished from indirect or suggestive meaning; a matter-of-fact, unimaginative disposition; accurate meaning or reference, free of distortion, exaggeration, or error. We notice here a shift from "literal" in an *orthographic* sense, pertaining to written words as such, to a *descriptive* sense pertaining to how a text (or the world) is to be understood, commonly in terms of unadulterated facts.

The tendency to conflate literal descriptions and factual accounts opens up another complex history of usage. The Latin *factum* originally referred to actions and deeds as opposed to words (the Greek *ergon* had the same sense). Then fact came to mean an actual event known through direct observation or reliable testimony, as opposed to conjecture, fiction, or mis-recollection. In modern thought, a fact mainly denotes the findings of scientific inquiry and its rigorous, controlled methods of testing observations governed by theoretical postulates and mathematical formulas.[96] A historical look at language usage thus shows that current familiar senses of the literal and the factual have arisen out of linguistic shifts and relations that exhibit anything but clear, direct references, and thus anything but "literal" or "factual" sources. The same holds true for the literal-metaphorical distinction. As Derrida has shown, the distinction between the metaphorical and the literal cannot be drawn in a nonmetaphorical manner.[97] The distinction itself has a philosophical history within Greek thought, when new frameworks emerged for understanding natural speech and mythopoetic language, frameworks that generally presumed deficiencies in these pre-philosophical forms of discourse.[98] The problem is that "metaphor" itself is metaphorical: *metaphero* in Greek means "to carry over," and so the familiar notion of metaphor—as "combining" one sense with another owing to a similar, though nonequivalent likeness—is itself a metaphorical trope. As we have seen, the connotations of "literal"—as univocal (non-combined) meaning and descriptive accuracy—are themselves "carried over" from a reference to written letters. One can say then that such extended connotations are no longer "literally" literal (in the original orthographic sense). A similar metaphorical process is located in the meaning of "factual" as carried-over from doing-versus-speaking. So, the purported meaning of the literal-factual dyad, which presumes a secured, unambiguous actuality (as-is), is itself an ambiguous extension of even more direct meanings (as-written, as-done). Consequently, it is hard to avoid the conclusion that indirect, nonliteral forces such as metaphor go all the way down in human language, thus undermining the privilege bestowed on the literal-factual nexus. Indeed, in cases where metaphorical uses might be irreducible and thus indispensable in expressing a meaning (e.g., the concept of "force" in physics), we could say that a metaphor can be "literally" true because of its descriptive necessity.[99]

 The story of the literal-factual nexus cannot be told apart from the complex history of orality and literacy in the Greek world. We have seen how oral culture was shaped according to structures of poetic production and audience reception that in retrospect exhibit a nonreflective immediacy: poets were "inspired" vehicles for sacred transmissions, and audiences were "enchanted" recipients of enthralling poetic performances. The graphics of writing allowed an isolation of texts from such performance milieus, and the fixity of written words permitted a host of reflective operations that greatly altered *how* the linguistic resources of Greek culture would be understood. I retrieve this point to highlight the "literal" effect of graphic letters in crafting a reflective departure from an *oral* sense of "literalness" that has nothing to do with familiar senses of factuality, but rather the *immediate disclosive force* of poetic language in performance. As we have seen, Plato critiqued poets and rhetors because they were "out of their minds" when performing their creative and oral functions. Their inspired condition overtook self-control and was incapable of reflective analysis of what they were saying and why they were saying it. Plato was concerned about the psychological effects of mimetic identification, wherein performers and audiences would be captured by, and immersed in, oral presentations, thus losing reflective self-control and being enraptured by the "reality" of poetic speech and disclosure.

What is important for my analysis here is the notion of mimetic literality, that is to say, the immersive, ecstatic, immediate disclosive effects of language, whether oral or written, whether literal or metaphorical, whether factual or fictional. When we designate epic poetry, for instance, simply as "literature," as fiction or allegory counterposed to actual reality, we miss the disclosive import and impact of poetry in opening up and sustaining the Greeks' sense of their world. On a less grand level, mimetic literality can show how a metaphorical expression can be taken "literally," in the sense of being irreducible or immediately expressive without further analysis. Consider being told (or reading): "Your mother passed away," or "Your book proposal has gone through with flying colors." Even technical slips that are fun to expose ("He literally exploded with anger") may in fact harbor a certain truth (the *word* "exploded" can simply *work* with direct force).

Historically, mimetic literality in the context of Greek poetry was *working*, which is why Plato was preoccupied with challenging its cultural status (as opposed to simply venturing a proper theory of "aesthetics"). Mimetic literality can be called "make believe" in a positive sense, as making-belief in the milieu of poetic performance and reception (*poiēsis* in Greek generally meant to make or create). Poetic speech makes or produces a belief-world through the immediate power of words. Mimetic literality can also be understood to operate in the familiar aesthetic phenomenon of "suspension of disbelief." The reception of "fictive truth" requires that we "forget" the fiction, that we conceal the artificial contrivance of, say, a theatrical production so that we can respond to it *as if* it were real; and we *do* so respond when we react emotionally to scenes that are not "really" happening. Here we are no different from a "primitive" mentality, wherein beliefs that might seem "metaphorical" to us were *taken* "literally" as directly disclosive of a meaningful world.[100]

There is, however, a certain loaded connotation in suspension of disbelief, wherein "real belief" is the guiding standard. Surely Greek dramatic performances were understood in a fictive manner: *as* dramatic performances, the plays were not identical with their traditional sources (e.g., the story of Oedipus). But we should not think that mimetic "identification" in dramatic performances was nothing more than an aesthetic zone of experience. The civic and religious functions of tragedy must be kept in mind to comprehend its *world*-disclosive effects and central role in Greek self-understanding.[101] In the case of epic poetry, particularly its oral mode, suspension of disbelief is even more tenuous. The immersion of the poet and audience was more a departure from *everyday* belief in the direction of extraordinary, sacred disclosures that opened up the meaning of the Greek world. So, there is an element of mimetic identification that *produces* belief in a manner different from ordinary experience, reflective analysis, or the discovery of "facts." Art, then, would involve not simply making-belief, but making-*special*.[102] The Greek art-world was disclosive of special existential meanings at the heart of their culture.

7. A POST-LITERATE WORLD?

This section will consider the status of literacy from two perspectives: (1) the proto-phenomenological critique of a literate bias in philosophy, and (2) developments in digital technology that are both extending and surpassing traditional manifestations of literacy. Both perspectives suggest the possibility of a post-literate orientation, which should not, however, be understood as an anti-literate posture. The virtues of literacy are an indelible enhancement of human life, including the hyper-literacy of philosophy, science, and other academic disciplines. Digital technology is a notable product of hyper-literacy and yet new systems of communication have exhibited some resonance with orality in their cultural operation. Such effects, however, are ambiguous in their repercussions. In particular, a liberation from traditional writing formats and editorial controls carries with it a significant threat to the virtue of truthfulness, by which I mean the following: the disposition of caring about truth and the capacity to produce discourse that is aptly disclosive in any given area of inquiry or expression. In general terms, traditional standards of literate discourse are being altered in unprecedented ways, with decidedly mixed results.

7.1. The Value of Literacy

When "primitive" people were first exposed to writing in Lévy-Bruhl's researches, they took it to be "magical," as a force possessing *powers* in its operation—something quite different from a mere representational function.[103] There is something profound in this reaction, which a phenomenological approach can help illuminate. When written communication becomes second nature and is engaged in the mode of ecstatic immersion, we can miss the marvel of its disclosive power. As noted early in this investigation, reading a message that one's manuscript has been accepted for publication is an immediate presentation of meaningful world-disclosive import—but delivered by marks on a page that in themselves are nothing like the circumstance so disclosed. It does seem almost magical, and yet our investigation has hopefully gone some way toward showing how the magic works. In any case, the disclosive capacity and effects of written language are certainly a wonder, which even sophisticated literates can recognize if they step back a bit from normal familiarity. Consider these remarks by Galileo:

> But surpassing all stupendous inventions, what sublimity of mind was his who dreamed of finding means to communicate his deepest thoughts to any other person, though distant by mighty intervals of space and time! Of talking with those who are in India; of speaking to those who are not yet born and will not be born for a thousand or ten thousand years; and with what faculty, by the different arrangements of 20 characters upon a page![104]

The expositional and revelatory power of literacy is an enormous benefit to human culture. Given the degree to which literate knowledge and its consequences saturate our existence—at the very least in education systems and the techno-scientific transformation of the earth—it is daunting to fathom what a world devoid of written language would be like (even the critical interrogation of writing measured against original orality is a consequence of literate thinking). The technology of writing expands the disclosive power of language beyond its normal mode of differential fitness in face-to-face speech by launching a liberation from immediate audiences that can reach any audience in any place at any time. For readers, their own experience and understanding can expand exponentially by way of written texts, which offer historical, scientific, intellectual, practical, and other forms of disclosure that far exceed what individuals or groups on their own could ever amass. Literature in particular presents novel and enriched vistas of life—in the full existential sense of a lived world—that enlarge the perspectives and sensibilities of readers.

We have explored how language is constitutive of human nature in a developmental and disclosive sense. Written language is not a natural phenomenon, but its "artificial" character can nonetheless be understood as transformative of human nature, especially when reading and writing become second nature and transmissive of wider horizons, both internal and external. A literate person is simply *more* human than is otherwise possible.[105] This does not entail being a "superior" human, but simply an amplification of human possibilities. In any case, regarding the natural-artificial distinction, the *capacity* for artifice is itself something natural to the human condition, as Aristotle recognized.[106] Moreover, when he said (*Physics* 199a17) that art (*technē*) imitates nature (*phusis*), he did not mean representational likeness but rather an *extension* and *expansion* of purposeful activity exhibited in nature. Indeed, *technē* can improve or complete natural conditions beyond their actual manifestations.[107] Such is the case with medicine and housebuilding, for example, compared to natural healing and shelter. We can say, then, that the technology of writing is a material affordance allowing the extension and expansion of the disclosive possibilities of language—and thereby an evolution of human nature, the emergence of new actualities.[108] Whatever debates there may be within literate disciplines about the way the world is, the domain of literacy itself is of unquestionable importance in human history.

7.2. Literacy and Progress

The manner in which writing alters oral language, together with the many consequential results of literate thinking, has readily prompted a "progressive" narrative wherein literacy is an advance beyond a more "primitive" mentality. Accordingly, the features of orality discussed in this investigation are then construed as an unruly confusion or constraint blocking the rational governance of thought and cultural life. Historically, this progressive script animated European colonialism, by not only sanctifying the domination and exploitation of "backward" peoples, but also engendering the paternalistic belief that colonial rule was a benefit for such peoples, an opportunity to improve their existence.

Proto-phenomenology at a basic level is an interrogation of the literate inflection of philosophy, a reclamation of the worthy intelligence and world-disclosive character of oral language—calling for a more comprehensive philosophy of language that can include pre-reflective, pre-literate elements of language, of dwelling in speech. This philosophical project, then, will not countenance an indiscriminate progressive story of literacy advancing beyond primitive illiteracy—and it thereby poses a critical challenge to historical cases of cultural hegemony presumed to be justified by comparable progressive assumptions. It does not follow from this challenge that literate rationality is a regressive decline from more noble origins. What is needed is a contextual approach that can (1) identify the benefits of literacy in terms of specific disclosive possibilities pertaining to specific kinds of questions and purposes, (2) address the features of orality that have their own cogency, and (3) attend to intersecting elements of writing and speech that broaden and enrich a philosophical account of language.

My study has combined proto-phenomenology with the developmental domain of language learning to show how so-called primitive features of orality are preparatory for, and remain operative in, a literate world—such that these features are not "backward" but rather *primal* conditions of proto-language, the *first* world of factical speech that makes written language possible and that cannot be fully absorbed by literate constructs and methods. The philosophical target has been the hyper-literacy of academic disciplines, which are a specific kind of writing and reading, which have their own legitimate disclosive roles, but which have presumed to deliver sufficient accounts of nature, selfhood, social relations, knowledge, action, time, space, and language. The many ways in which natural sciences, social sciences, and the humanities contribute objective, analytical, and rational modes of understanding should be supplemented by (1) indicative reflection on factical life and (2) the posture of hermeneutical pluralism.[109]

To focus on hermeneutical pluralism, let me explore an example that (1) broadens the discussion beyond language, (2) displays the complex correlational scope of cultural phenomena, and (3) embodies the multi-faceted movements of interpretation. Consider the performance of a symphony, which can be understood and articulated from many different perspectives: its composition and history; its notation, structure, and style; the performance as an interpretation of the score; aesthetic judgments of the score and performance; the symphony hall and its construction for the sake of performances; the physics of sound that figures in the discernment of acoustical properties; the musical instruments with their material makeup and sonic capacities; the persons dealing with management, finance, and promotion; audience interest and reception; the musicians and their own histories, their development from raw beginners to expert players with know-how and habituated skills; rehearsals involving immersed performance, contravention, and exposition shaping the interpretation of the piece; the blended personal-social-environing-world, especially in musical performance and the dynamic of joint engagement that allows the reciprocal interplay of the conductor and orchestra; the figure-eight structure of temporality that constitutes the capacity to perform, hear, and comprehend the sonic movement of music; the remarkable integration of mathematical structure—the figural notation of the written score—and the decidedly non-quantifiable nature of interpreting, performing, and experiencing music; and finally the immersed enjoyment of the performance issuing whatever cognitive, affective, or existential effects an audience might receive from the music. All told, the nature of a symphony—what a symphony *is*—reaches far and wide with a range of different conditions, perspectives, and histories coming to bear on a performance, a mix of factical, practical, individual, social, environmental, temporal, historical, objective, factual, evaluative, and experiential elements that proto-phenomenology has deemed to incorporate in philosophical inquiry. The complexity of "being" shown in this example is not an amorphous confusion or imprecise dissipation but a meaningful reality, with interpretive dimensions that cohere not by way of some substantive essence or systematic order, but rather hermeneutical shifts of perspective directly intimated by participants as contextually relevant in the foreground and background of a musical performance. The "world" of a symphony is an animated horizon of meaning, the complex coherence of which is exhibited in different ways by any number of human endeavors.

As this example aims to suggest, a post-literate orientation does not move beyond literacy; it simply attends to the hermeneutical complexity of cultural phenomena, which includes non-literate and non-reflective elements that remain operative in even the most refined cognitive pursuits, including the world of science when it is understood as an existential project enacted by human beings—arising from, and presumed to serve, the interests of factical life. What is superseded in a post-literate orientation is simply the narrowed horizon that presumes literate thinking to be exclusively fundamental for world-disclosive truth.

7.3. Literacy and Digital Media

Digital computer technology is among the most advanced and consequential products of scientific literacy. Its evolution has given us the Internet, personalized computer access, multimedia formats, and various venues of interactive social media. Such technologies far exceed the effects of the printing press and traditional forms of literacy, while also incorporating elements of pre-literate or non-literate modes of disclosure and communication. In my brief discussion, I cannot possibly do justice to the complexity and extent of these momentous developments. I will select a few broad-based and focused topics that at least can fit the tenor of my overall investigation.

The abstract visual space of alphabetic script was a departure from the acoustic space of orality, which included an embodied ecological holism. Modern communication technologies before the Internet retrieved an oral nexus in many respects.[110] Radio and television provided mass communication with acoustical and embodied/visual dimensions. Digital technologies have expanded and exceeded such non-orthographic elements by creating virtual worlds far beyond the bounds of any previous oral or literate culture.[111] Such innovations include: multimedia productions that integrate speech, sound, vision, embodiment, imagery, movement, narrative, and fictional effects; hyper-text linkage to other texts and media, which outstrips the traditional notion of a written text as a self-contained and completed document restricted to a lexical format; interactive features that bring the audience into play, no longer as passive spectators or recipients; virtual realities and mixed media that can mimic, bend, or surpass normal empirical accuracy; and production no longer based in the select domains of publishers, studios, or networks—a democratized and unregulated market of presentation open to anyone with access to the new media.

There are four primary benefits provided by digital computer technology. First is an enriched disclosive milieu that goes beyond traditional print with multimedia effects, which can incorporate more vivid dimensions that accord with the phenomenology of lived experience (affective attunement, factical imagery, embodied enactment, engaged participation). Second is the extent of access to information, media formats, documents, and academic research. In a sense, an entire cultural world is available to any user of the Internet, including portable access at any time and in any place thanks to smartphones, tablets, and laptops. Third is the accelerated pace of access, with almost instant availability. In the past, doing research on foot by way of card catalogs and book stacks in the library was a significant constraint on how much and how quickly research could be gathered. Now one can search, access, and receive documents from venues all over the world—quickly and without ever leaving an office chair. Fourth is the enormous contribution of word processing technology to the production of texts, which someone like myself can particularly appreciate—having composed my first book on a manual typewriter.

There are significant downsides to such benefits, and I will focus on three concerns having to do with virtuality, pace, and truth. First, the multidimensionality of digital technology allows enriched disclosive possibilities compared with written texts. The magnified access, exposure, and interactive participation offer more to users than any previous communication system. Yet compared with the first world of factical embodied existence, digital disclosure is still a virtual world, which disengages from natural experience. The growing saturation of digital communication and the degree to which people have become absorbed in their devices—more and more heads lowered to their phones apart from the immediate world around them—creates a dramatic dimensional rival to factical life.[112] The new virtuality is more like life than previous technologies could provide, but its artificial relation to actual embodiment and direct experience of a lived world will be a consuming question long into the future.

Second, modern communication and transportation systems have been recognized for compressing distances and increasing the pace of life. Digital technologies have magnified such spatial and temporal effects to a remarkable degree. Instant access to world events and communication outlets has quickened visibility, exposure, media reporting, and social responses. Whatever advantages might attach to such developments—especially the ready exposure of grievous activity—the rapid acceleration of cultural communication crowds out the role of careful, extensive analysis, of penetrating reflection on the meaning and possible consequences of world events. When human dwelling speeds up, the benefits of dwelling *on* things with more judicious circumspection get sidelined. In general terms, the accelerated pace of digital disclosure and a kind of quick-cut style of presentation have created an aversion to delay. (In the past it could take some time to find and access an article in the library; now I get a little frustrated if a file takes more than ten seconds to download.) Sustained time for reflection is being eclipsed by more instantaneous delivery and rapid exposure to the "next new thing." The traditional literate ideal of close reading and dissection of complex, intricate texts is getting harder to promote and execute.

Finally, a concern about truth. In the *Phaedrus*, Plato was suspicious of writing because the portability of a text meant that anyone could have access to it, the worthy and unworthy alike, separated from the "authority" of (literate) speech in philosophical conversation. Derrida responded that writing does indeed exceed the "author," but this serves the worthy differential character of language and the circulation of texts amid counter-texts and the interpretive openness of a continuing readership. The hyper-textual and multidimensional character of digital media only magnifies Derrida's point about differential openness, but Plato's complaint about indiscriminate exposure has some resonance today.

Plato seemed to espouse an anti-democratic elitism, at least with respect to intellectual work. Derrida was right to counter regulatory principles with the circulatory character of writing that keeps language and thought ever productive of new vistas. Yet traditional venues for written work have indeed been elitist in the following sense: the production and economics of publishing—the creation of texts by writers, the costs of printing, binding, and distributing physical volumes—placed constraints on the extent to which writing would or could be exposed to a reading public. In various ways, publishing performed a gatekeeping function regarding what *should* be published, what was *worth* reading by a public interested in good writing. Publishing, therefore, was elitist in a meritocratic sense, as measured by editorial judgment and the estimation of readers. Academic publishing and journalism, for example, in the main have been guided by intellectual work and reporting that can blend quality writing with truthfulness, in the sense that whatever is offered to readers should be aptly disclosive of the matters at hand, that false, mistaken, or weakly argued material should not see the light of day. Such measures, of course, have been open to interpretation in any given case; and they have been violated by some venues now and again. But the publication of written work has usually/ideally been guided by a gatekeeping standard, which readers could rely on to one degree or another.

In the early days of the Internet and digital communication, proponents touted the democratic character of the new technology, a kind of utopian vision of open human expression released from institutional controls, where wide-open venues would allow all voices to be heard, especially those who might be unduly silenced by editorial or governmental restrictions. Yet, whatever gatekeeping exclusions or mistakes may have occurred in the history of publishing (for reasons heinous, inept, or short-sighted), the remedy surely should not be indiscriminate publication. Plato may have been wrong about the open availability of writing, but the Internet has given his point a new spin. Anyone can be their own publisher, and the results have been something of a nightmare.

Early utopian hopes were naïve for the following reasons: not everyone has something worthy to say; not everyone is able to fashion worthy discourse that is truthful (aptly disclosive) in a given area of interest; and some people are motivated to purvey falsehood and misdirection. We have recently witnessed the political manifestations of indiscriminate publication, with demoralizing effects. Deliberate deception is nothing new in politics; and the history of publication has had its share of manipulation, prevarication, and "fake news." People have always been susceptible to such things and lacking in critical judgment. But in the past, access to audiences was limited. Now inept or deceptive publication can easily find an audience, indeed many millions of people. Traditional publishing has generally relied on the discernment of editors. Digital "publishing" is indiscriminate and relies on the discernment of the audience. The results in many respects are disturbing and dangerous.[113] Here a post-literate world is deleterious in diminishing publication standards that have been operative or aspirational in a literate culture. In past work, I have defended democratic politics while challenging hyper-egalitarian assumptions. Democracy can and should rely on "elitist" aspects of culture and intelligence, which citizens can and should rely on in political discourse and institutional practices (not indiscriminately, of course). Russian interference in the recent American election is heinous, but I can imagine the Russian retort: yes, we tried to influence your politics with false and manipulative stories, but millions of American citizens believed them.

8. CONCLUDING REMARKS

As indicated in Volume I (7–8), my investigation amounts to a special sort of meta-philosophical analysis, which takes up basic differences between traditional philosophical constructs and pre-philosophical existence—with the aim of *situating* philosophy in its erstwhile environment and therefore revising remedial scripts that have taken that environment to be a barrier to, or deficit of, rational analysis and governance. Both volumes have offered a proto-phenomenological account of the *first* world preceding philosophical reflection, and my approach has delineated that world into three fundamental areas: the lived world, child development, and orality—with oral poetry identified as a cultural precedent in ancient Greece before the advent of philosophy. I call these areas "borderlands" of philosophy, which all human beings inhabit before philosophy becomes a possibility (with myth and poetry in the Greek world being their pre-philosophical abode). To repeat from Volume I: none of us is a native to philosophy-land; we are immigrants from the borderlands. Proto-phenomenology is an alert about over-assimilation in philosophy-land, which dims the memory of native habitats. It is also a call for open borders, whereby the borderland can benefit from philosophical thinking and philosophy can be more attentive to the borderland on its own terms, which can help resolve many philosophical problems that stem from amnesia and conceptual gentrification.

The original environment of the lived world (1) allows philosophy and science to take shape and (2) continues to operate in the background of philosophical and scientific work. Factical life is not grounded in objective analysis and reflective categories, but rather the meaning-laden inhabitance of immersed practices—where something like reason-giving or reflective analysis first emerges when contraventions disturb ecstatic immersion. Traditional philosophy has turned the sequence around and given primacy to reason-giving and analysis. That reversal tends to find the first world problematic and deficient, largely because of its unruly, affective, practical, and finite character. But the presumption of immanence implicit in this investigation finds such a remedial reversal strange and unwarranted. Philosophical reflection is drawn *from* an already-functioning meaningful world, and proto-phenomenology aims to see that world not as a foil but the soil of philosophical thought.

The primary focus of this revision of philosophy has been the question of language. The phenomenological priority of language advanced in Volume I has been fortified by a consideration of language acquisition and literacy. The effects of language begin to shape an infant's experience from the earliest days of life. The face-to-face speech-world in a child's environment reinforces the primacy of pre-reflective phenomenological concepts. Oral language then makes possible the transition to literacy when children learn to read and write. Literacy transforms language into new visual dimensions, which help build the refined concepts and rational-thinking skills that operate in philosophy and other academic disciplines. So, the *continuity* of movement from the lived world of childhood and the inhabitance of speech to a literate mentality offers developmental evidence for the derivative character of advanced rational thought—and the cogency of incorporating this generative background of rationality in the agenda of philosophy. How one *comes to be* a philosopher is just as important as any specific philosophical concern.

At the beginning and end of the first volume, I addressed vexing problems facing my kind of investigation, which bears repeating here at the end of Volume II. How can a philosophical work such as mine genuinely incorporate pre-reflective experience, since the work itself is a reflective endeavor? The proposed answer was the deployment of indicative concepts, which simply *point* to pre-reflective factical life, whereby readers can attend to their own first-person experience to see if the concepts can bear fruit. Rather than address baseline philosophical questions *at the start* with abstract philosophical concepts and logistics at the ready, proto-phenomenology aims to bring philosophical reflection to the pre-philosophical lived world on its own terms, thus acting as a kind of "double agent."

The same kind of problem attaches to examining orality as a more original sphere of language than that afforded by the technology of writing. The critical interrogation of the literate lens of philosophy is itself a literate project—and "orality" is itself a literate construction. The effects of literacy are so pervasive and transformative that a direct or eliminative critique is impossible. Nevertheless, the hope has been that a proto-phenomenological perspective and attention to relevant research in orality studies can provide an effective lens for engaging this difficult methodological question.

Such a conundrum and its possible resolution harbors something noteworthy. Orality is part of a proto-phenomenological project. But a purely oral world would allow little of the expositional articulation and reflection made possible by literacy. If the philosophical pathway of phenomenology succeeds to any significant degree, the result can be an account of language inhabiting the best of both worlds: (1) a sensitivity to the factical base of dwelling in oral speech, which a hyper-literate framework would miss or suppress, and (2) a comprehensive picture of language that includes and requires literate exposition, which would remain concealed in a purely oral domain. Literate philosophical analysis can (1) attend indicatively to dwelling in speech and (2) open up a reflective dwelling *on* language in a richer and more thoroughgoing manner, which is illuminating and fulfilling in its own right if philosophy is one's calling.

NOTES

1. Theodore Sider, *Writing the Book of the World* (Oxford University Press, 2011).
2. Ibid., vii.
3. Pierre Hadot, *What Is Ancient Philosophy?* trans. Michael Chase (Cambridge, MA: Belknap Press, 2002).
4. In this section, I rely on Sten Ebbesen, *Greek-Latin Philosophical Interaction* (New York: Routledge, 2016) and Thorsten Fögen, "Latin as a Technical and Scientific Language," in *A Companion to the Latin Language*, ed. James Clackson (Malden, MA: Wiley-Blackwell, 2011), Chap. 25.
5. The word *energeia* was coined by Aristotle, drawing from *ergon*, meaning "work" or "deeds."
6. See Law, *The History of Linguistics in Europe*, 58–60.
7. See Jürgen Leonhardt, *Latin: Story of a World Language*, trans. Kenneth Kronenberg (Cambridge, MA: Belknap Press, 2013), David Butterfield, "Neo-Latin," in *A Companion to the Latin Language*, Chap. 18, J. I. Jsewijen and D. Sacré, "The Ultimate Effort to Save Latin as a Means of International Communication," *History of*

European Ideas 16, no. 1–3 (1993): 51–66, and Ong, *Orality and Literacy*, 110–113. I draw from these sources in what follows.

8. Ong, *Orality and Literacy*, 112.

9. Dante's text, *De Vulgari Eloquentia*, was written in 1304 but was widely read only after its printing in 1529. I draw this reference from Law, *The History of Linguistics in Europe*, 230–232.

10. Olson's book, *The World on Paper*, is a source for much of what follows.

11. Ibid., Chap 7.

12. Ibid., Chap 1.

13. Ibid., 19, 92.

14. Ibid., 18–19.

15. Ibid., 68.

16. Ibid., 85.

17. Ibid., Chap. 5, on which I rely in this section.

18. Ibid., 124–135.

19. Ibid., 282.

20. Ibid., 18–44.

21. In this discussion, I draw from two works of Walter Ong: *Orality and Literacy*, Chap. 5, and *The Presence of the Word*, Chap. 2.

22. With Searle's Chinese Room in mind, print production is analogous to computerized manipulation of signs in that one could in principle produce a book without understanding the language, by simply following all the lettering in the manuscript.

23. See Marco Annoni, "What Lexicography Reveals about Cultural Objects," *Semiotica* 198 (2014): 261–269.

24. Ibid., 267.

25. See Jean Aitchison, *Words in the Mind: An Introduction to the Mental Lexicon* (Malden, MA: Wiley-Blackwell, 2012). In what follows, I draw from Chaps. 1–2, 5, 7, 15, and 17.

26. The word *over* covers four full pages in *Webster's Collegiate Dictionary*. Among the myriad uses: over the goal line, falling over, boiling over, turning over, getting one's point over, winning someone over, running over-time, sleeping over, the day is over, read something over, do over, fly over, rule over, talk over dinner, talk over the phone, over there, argue over money, over heat, left over, overpower, get over an illness.

27. Lloyd, *The Ambivalences of Rationality*, 3–6.

28. See Olson, *The World on Paper*, 58–59, and Ong, *Orality and Literacy*, 125–29.

29. See Ong, *Orality and Literacy*, 117–129.

30. Ong, *The Presence of the Word*, 63.

31. Ibid., 64–65.

32. John Locke, *An Essay Concerning Human Understanding*, ed. Kenneth Winkler (Indianapolis, IN: Hackett, 1996), 46.

33. Ong, *The Presence of the Word*, 74–76.

34. Olson, *The World on Paper*, Chap. 8.

35. Ibid., 163–166.

36. Ibid., 166–173.

37. Ibid., 173–178.

38. *Discoveries and Opinions of Galileo*, trans. Stillman Drake (New York: Doubleday Anchor, 1957), 237–238.

39. Maasten Van Dyck and Albrecht Heeffer, "Script and Symbolic Writing in Mathematics and Natural Philosophy," *Foundations of Science* 19, no. 1 (March 2014): 1–10. Mathematical symbolism enabled reasoning about the full range of mechanical movements and their relations—position, velocity, force, acceleration, momentum—which strained geometrical analysis.

40. Ibid., 7.

41. Jacob Klein, *Greek Mathematical Thought and the Origin of Algebra*, trans. Eva Brann (New York, Dover Books, 1968), 161–185.

42. See Christopher Pincock, *Mathematics and Scientific Representation* (Oxford University Press, 2012).

43. In Homer, *phuō* usually refers to plant life, with a specific meaning of bringing forth shoots, and earth is commonly called *phusizoos*, that which gives forth life (*Odyssey*, 11.301).

44. Descartes, *The Philosophical Writings of Descartes* I, 19–20; Kant, *Philosophy of Material Nature*, trans. James W. Ellington (Indianapolis, IN: Hackett, 1985), 6. Descartes' thought was not restricted to deductive principles to the exclusion of experience. For Descartes, although the laws of nature are deduced necessarily from God's immutability, their truth is *confirmed* by experiment. See Steven M. Nadler, "Deduction, Confirmation, and the Laws of Nature in Descartes' *Principia Philosophiae*," *Journal of the History of Philosophy* 28, no. 3 (1990): 359–383.

45. Isaac Newton, *Mathematical Principles of Natural Philosophy* (Berkeley, CA: University of California Press, 1960), xvii.

46. *Descartes: Philosophical Letters*, trans. Anthony Kenny (Minneapolis, MN: University of Minnesota Press, 1981), 94.

47. *Meditations* V (*Philosophical Writings of Descartes* II, 48–49). It may be that the *Meditations* is not primarily about the separability of mind and body, but simply the radical distinctness of thought and extension. See Marleen Rozemond, "Descartes' Case for Dualism," *Journal of the History of Philosophy* 33, no. 1 (1995): 29–63. Thought and extension are principal attributes of mental and physical substance, and substance is the base of its "modes." Individual bodies are modes of the principal attribute of extension. A substance has only one principal attribute, defining its essence and bearing its modes. So, *res extensa* should not be called "body" but the core defining element of individual bodies. In other words, body can be nothing other than extension. This scheme allows the treatment of all bodies as subject to the singular analysis of mathematical relations, thus supplanting the Aristotelian view of qualitative differences among bodies, and justifying the reductive mechanism of the new physics of nature.

48. Blake D. Dutton, "Indifference, Necessity, and Descartes' Derivation of the Laws of Motion." *Journal of the History of Philosophy* 34, no. 2 (1996): 193–212.

49. Along these lines, the turn to the *cogito* in Descartes is not simply a matter of inward reflection but a radical withdrawal from both outside experiences *and* internal thoughts that are the effects of past experiences and influences. Such is the mark of

indifference (*Philosophical Writings of Descartes* II, 41) to all possible occurrences in the world and in the mind, which is what underwrites the method of radical doubt. See James Dodd, "The Philosophical Significance of Hope," *Review of Metaphysics* 58, no.1, (2004): 130–142.

50. *Discourse* VI (*Philosophical Writings of Descartes* I, 142–143).

51. Francis Bacon, *The Philosophical Works of Francis Bacon*, trans. Robert L. Ellis and James Spedding, ed. John M. Robinson (London: Routledge, 1905), 27.

52. Immanuel Kant, *Critique of Pure Reason*, trans. Werner S. Pluhar, (Indianapolis, IN: Hackett, 1996), B xiii.

53. See Geoffrey Gortham, Benjamin Hill, and Edward Slowik, eds., *The Language of Nature: Reassessing the Mathematization of Natural Philosophy in the Seventeenth Century* (Minneapolis, MN: University of Minnesota Press, 2016).

54. Descartes, *Philosophical Writings of Descartes* I, 13–16. Kant, *Critique of Pure Reason*, B 153–155.

55. See Rosa Antognazza, *Leibniz: A Very Short Introduction* (Oxford University Press, 2016), Chap. 2.

56. *Hegel's Philosophy of Mind: Part Three of the Encyclopaedia of the Philosophical Sciences*, trans. William Wallace and A.V. Miller (Oxford University Press, 1971), 179–240.

57. Ibid., 216.

58. Ibid., 218.

59. The 4E model of cognition argues that standard physiological accounts have simply moved from mind-body dualism to brain-body and brain-environment dualism.

60. Linell, *The Written Language Bias in Linguistics*, 86.

61. Ibid., 111–112.

62. Ibid., 120.

63. Ibid., 88–89.

64. In what follows, I draw from Olson, *The World on Paper*, 179–189 and Chaps. 10–11.

65. Ibid., 261.

66. I am drawing material from my essay, "Can We Drop the Subject? Heidegger, Selfhood, and the History of a Modern Word," in *Horizons of Authenticity in Phenomenology, Existentialism, and Moral Psychology*, eds. Hans Pedersen and Megan Altman (London: Springer, 2015), 13–30. The discussion is rather technical, so some readers may want to skip it.

67. Martin Heidegger, *What Is a Thing?* trans. W. B. Barton, Jr. and Vera Deutsch (Chicago, IL: Henry Regnery Co., 1967), 98–106.

68. Ibid., 90ff.

69. For an account of how dematerialized thought experiments and imagination figured in the science of mechanics, see Domenico Bertoloni Meli, "Patterns of Transformation in Seventeenth-Century Mechanics," *The Monist* 93, no. 4 (2010): 580–597.

70. In Aristotle, there is an important distinction between *hupokeimenon* and *ousia*, with the former usually pertaining to predication and the latter to being. Yet this distinction was not a separation along the lines of the modern subject-object split.

Being, for Aristotle, is a "fused" concept where the existential and predication functions of the "is" are two sides of the same coin. See Rick Van Brennekom, "Aristotle and the Copula," *Journal of the History of Philosophy* 24, no. 1 (1986): 1–18.

71. With respect to the mathematical, Heidegger insists that number is not its source, but a consequence of the original meaning of the Greek *mathēsis*, or presuppositions required for learning (Heidegger, *What Is a Thing?* 70ff.). Descartes bears this out in Rule IV of *Rules for the Direction of the Mind* (*Philosophical Works of Descartes* I, 15–20). There *mathesis universalis* is not universal mathematics but a general universal method of grounding thought by deduction from the intellect's natural capacity for measuring order (as set out in the *Meditations*). Descartes knew of the Greek sense of *mathēsis* as a process of learning (connected with Platonic recollection). And he took mathematics per se to be simply the purest instance of *mathesis universalis*. See Frederick Van Pitte, "The Dating of Rule IV-B in Descartes' *Regulae ad directionem ingenui*," *Journal of the History of Philosophy* 29, no. 3 (1991): 375–395.

72. George Berkeley, *Siris* (London: Innys and Hitch, 1744), para. 292. For a general analysis, see Michael Ayers, "Ideas and Objective Being," in *The Cambridge History of Seventeenth Century Philosophy*, Vol. 2, eds. Daniel Garber and Michael Ayers. (Cambridge: Cambridge University Press, 1998), 1062–1107.

73. See under "objective."

74. William Hamilton, who edited the collected works of Thomas Reid (first edition in 1846), provided extensive notes to Reid's texts, and one note gives a detailed account of the reversal of meaning between *subjectum* and *objectum*. In scholastic philosophy, he says, "a material thing, say a horse, *qua* existing was said to have *subjective* being out[side] of the mind; *qua* conceived or known, it was said to have *objective* being in the mind." See *The Works of Thomas Reid*, Vol. 2, ed. William Hamilton (New York: Elibron Classics, 2005), 806–809.

75. Heidegger, *What Is a Thing?* 103, 106.

76. *Philosophical Works of Descartes* II, 50.

77. Objection 2 in the third set of objections: *Philosophical Works of Descartes* II, 122–124.

78. Formal reality can apply to the mind, however, in the sense of an idea's actual presence in the mind, as distinct from the objective reality of an idea, namely what the mind grasps when it sees distinctions, particularly in clear and distinct ideas—where "clear" means being *present* and accessible to an attentive mind, and "distinct" means being clear plus being sharply marked off from other ideas so as to contain only what is clear (*Philosophical Works of Descartes* I, 206–207).

79. David Hume, *A Treatise of Human Nature*, eds. David Fate Norton and Mary J. Norton (Oxford: Clarendon Press, 2000), I.4.3.

80. Kant, *Critique of Pure Reason*, B 131, B 203.

81. Although the phrase "thinking subject" occurs frequently in *Critique of Pure Reason*, Kant also deploys earlier connotations of the subject as the substantive base of properties or the reference of predication (i.e., *subjectum* understood ontologically or logically). So, Kant actually works with three senses of the subject: cognitive, ontological, and logical. It should be noted that Kant critiques theories that move from the "I think" to a substantive self (A 348–351). The error of rational psychology is

taking the cognitive unity of consciousness as "an intuition of the [thinking] subject as an object" and illicitly applying the category of substance to this supposed object (B 421). For Kant in this case, the thinking subject is a precondition for thinking objects, not itself an object of thinking. Indeed, the transcendental cognitive subject is a "logical subject," not a "real subject" (A 350)—note all three senses of the subject used here. Despite such manifold uses, Kant's emphasis on the *thinking* subject seems to have cemented this denotation for philosophy afterward.

82. See Olson, *The World on Paper*, 187–191, 265–269.
83. Ibid., 269.
84. Ibid., 190.
85. See Paul Ricoeur, *The Rule of Metaphor: The Creation of Meaning in Language*, trans. Robert Czerny (New York: Routledge, 2003), Chap. 1.
86. See Stefan Forrester, "Theories of Metaphor in Seventeenth and Eighteenth-Century British Philosophy," *Literature Compass* 7, no. 8 (2010): 610–625.
87. See Francisco Varela et al., *The Embodied Mind: Cognitive Science and Human Experience* (Cambridge, MA: MIT Press, 1991).
88. If people are first asked to make a hand movement, such as reaching to grasp something, they are more readily able to comprehend a metaphorical notion like grasping a concept. See Benjamin K. Bergen, *Louder Than Words: The New Science of How the Mind Makes Meaning* (New York: Basic Books, 2012), Chap. 9.
89. Olson, *The World on Paper*, 88–89.
90. A classic work in this regard is George Lakoff and Mark Johnson, *Metaphors We Live By* (Chicago, IL: The University of Chicago Press, 2003); see also their *Philosophy in the Flesh: The Embodied Mind and Its Challenge to Western Thought* (New York: Basic Books, 1999); and Ricoeur, *The Rule of Metaphor*.
91. Lakoff and Johnson, *Metaphors We Live By*, 271–272.
92. What follows is drawn from *Metaphors We Live By*, Chaps. 1–4, 6–7, and 10.
93. See Zoltán Kövecses, *Where Metaphors Come from: Reconsidering Context in Metaphor* (Oxford: Oxford University Press, 2015).
94. Lakoff and Johnson, *Metaphors We Live By*, 126.
95. Some of what follows is taken from my *Nietzsche's Life Sentence: Coming to Terms with Eternal Recurrence* (New York: Routledge, 1995), 92–95.
96. Note the ironic departure from *factum*, in that scientific facts require reflection and sophisticated vocabularies, rather than mere actions and deeds.
97. See "White Mythology," in *Margins of Philosophy*, trans. Alan Bass (Chicago, IL: University of Chicago Press, 1982).
98. Aristotle dismissed metaphor from reasoning and definition (*Posterior Analytics* 97b37ff.).
99. See Stephen Halliwell, *Aristotle's Poetics* (Chicago, IL: University of Chicago Press, 1998), 349.
100. See Olson, *The World on Paper*, 189–190.
101. See Christiane Sourvinou-Inwood, *Tragedy and Athenian Religion* (Lanham, MD: Lexington Books, 2003).
102. See Ellen Dissanayake, *What Is Art For?* (Seattle, WA: University of Washington Press, 1988).

103. See Olson, *The World on Paper*, 28–33.

104. *Dialogue Concerning the Two Chief World Systems*, trans. Stillman Drake (New York: Modern Library, 2001), 120–121.

105. Ong, *Orality and Literacy*, 14–15, 81–82.

106. *Nicomachean Ethics* 1139a11.

107. *Physics* 199a15–17.

108. For reflections on the disclosive materiality of language, see Rasmus Gahrn-Andersen, "But Language Too Is Material!" *Phenomenology and the Cognitive Sciences* DOI: 10.1007/s11097-017-9545-8 (October 2017) and Karenleigh A. Overmann, "Concepts and How They Got That Way," *Phenomenology and the Cognitive Sciences* DOI: 10.007/s11097-017-9545-8 (October 2017). See also Ian Ravenscrift, "Engaging the World: Writing, Imagination, and Enactivism," *Philosophy and Literature* 41, no. 1 (April, 2017): 45–54.

109. A pluralistic account of literacy is also required. There are different types of writing, with different purposes, measures, and expectations of readers. Hyperliteracy is distinctive in its cultural and historical impact but it operates in the midst of a variety of written formats: academic texts (scientific articles, history books), novels, poems, plays, screenplays, biographies, autobiographies, memoirs, satires, magazines, self-help and how-to books, letters, emails, tweets, notes, annotations, directions, graffiti, train schedules, shopping lists, and so on.

110. The work of Marshall McLuhan pioneered reflection on the effects of new media on literate cultures, which presaged the kinds of questions raised by digital technologies. See Andrey Miroshnichenko, "Extrapolating on McLuhan: How Media Environments of the Given, the Represented, and the Induced Shape and Reshape Our Sensorium," *Philosophies* 1, no. 3 (2016), 170–189, and Robert K. Logan, "The Alphabet Revisited, McLuhan Reversals and Complexity Theory," *Philosophies* 2, no. 1 (2017), 1–8.

111. See Christian Vandendorpe, *From Papyrus to Hypertext: Toward the Universal Digital Library*, trans. Phyllis Aronoff and Howard Scott (Urbana, IL: University of Illinois Press, 2009).

112. See Laurence Scott, *The Four-Dimensional Human: Ways of Being in the Digital World* (London: Heinemann, 2015).

113. For research on the degree to which falsehood has been effective in new media, see Soroush Vosoughi et al., "The Spread of True and False News Online," *Science* 359, no. 6380 (March 2018), 1146–1151.

Glossary

affective attunement:
Interpretive disclosure of how things matter in terms of existential import; an evaluative disposition concerning how the world serves or blocks human interests; exhibited in moods and emotions that are neither objective descriptions nor purely subjective occasions having no bearing on how the world is. Fear, for example, can be an appropriate interpretation of real threats.

affordance:
An ecological concept referring to correlated possibilities-for-action, intertwined affiliations between an organism and its environment, which cannot be understood in terms of the environment or the action alone. The ground is an affordance for walking; a tool is an affordance for making something.

contravention:
A negative or disorienting effect on an immersed experience, which brings exposited attention to the meaning of the experience, objective conditions in the environment, and subjective elements relating to the experience. Contravention is exhibited in breakdowns, resistance, obstacles, mistakes, absence, lack, danger, disorder, and unfamiliar occurrences.

correlational scope:
Networks of relationships that figure in the meaning or nature of things and activities, usually in a recessed and tacit manner. Writing on a whiteboard in class, for example, carries a wide set of connections involving physical, productive, environmental, social, aspirational, pedagogical, and historical elements that are all implicated in the supposedly simple act of using a marker. Correlational scope means that piecemeal analyses cannot be the last word.

differential fitness:
A characterization of language that indicates (1) the normal way in which natural language usage fits the social and environing world in non-reflective occasions of working speech, and (2) the semiotic difference between words and their references. Fitness shows the world-disclosive power of language and the differential element shows how language can retain its disclosive power apart from immediate experience, especially regarding past and future references. Differentiation also allows the recursive and relational factors that figure in cognition.

ecstatic dwelling:
Immersed absorption in a practice that is "there" in the environment, not a subject-object relation of an interior consciousness connecting with an external world.

embodiment:
The necessary bodily element in human experience, not understood as a physical object but rather the meaning-laden engagement of bodying-forth in the world. The role of gesture and sound in speech is a prime example.

enactive interpretation:
The ongoing execution of a perspective on the world, such as the procedures and findings of factual description or the normative assessment of human behavior.

environing-world:
The meaning-laden involvement with one's surroundings and how that shapes the social and personal worlds.

existential naturalism:
Attention to the primacy of meaning-laden existence that we already find ourselves in before reflection, that we are born into, and that comes naturally to us in everyday life.

exposition:
Focused attention on specific aspects of the world, its meaning, and our experience of it, which follows from the contravention of an immersed activity.

factical life:
The concrete embeddedness and engagement in meaningful activities that mark pre-reflective existence, which is understood on its own terms rather

than abstract formal constructions; for instance, actually caring for a child, not the intentional relation of consciousness and its objects.

hyper-literacy:
The kind of literacy characterizing academic disciplines such as philosophy and science, as distinct from ordinary reading and writing skills.

immanence:
The presumption that the common-sense world in which we find ourselves before philosophical reflection is the primary reality, that no advanced reflective knowledge can be divorced from this first world. Immanence in this sense is not a philosophical "position" because it is the ineliminable condition that precedes, and makes possible, any philosophical posit.

immersion:
Pre-reflective absorbed experience that is not perceived as a conscious "self" connecting with external conditions of action; it is the actual *doing* without reflective attention.

indicative concepts and analysis:
Reflective attention that simply points *to* immersed, factical experience on its own terms, without reducing it to expositional analysis or abstract categories.

interpretation:
The circular condition wherein no inquiry can start from scratch because it is animated by modes of meaning and understanding that are already in place before inquiry. A hermeneutical approach acknowledges the circle and operates on three levels: (1) explicating what is implicit in an already animated inquiry, (2) selecting from among different perspectives what is appropriate for an inquiry, and (3) enactive interpretation that explores possibilities of disclosure from a given perspective.

intimation:
The tacit familiarity and background comprehension implicit in an engagement with the world, a "peripheral" understanding that operates directly *in* the engagement rather than more reflective cognition by way of explicit beliefs or descriptions.

lived world:
The meaningful world in which we dwell before reflection and objectification, the enactments of factical life having personal, social, and environmental characteristics.

personal-world:
The sphere of personal selfhood expressed in first-person language; it cannot be separated from the social and environing world, which is why introspection cannot be the first-order site of selfhood.

pluralism:
Refers to the plurality of truth, which can be located in various domains—science, art, history, ethics, politics, practical life, technology—where no one domain can reductively ground other domains.

presentation/representation:
Presentation refers to immediate disclosive occasions that are prior to representational relations between the mind and the world.

projection:
An ecological condition wherein one is caught up in, or cast into circumstances not of one's making or choosing, which therefore cannot be grounded in individual selfhood. Projection can be passive (being born and raised), active (choosing to be measured by established norms, such as getting married), and middle-voiced blends such as being educated.

proto-phenomenology:
Phenomenological description of the "first world" of factical life, *as* lived in concrete terms, which means that even some versions of phenomenology that emphasize cognition, transcendental conditions, or abstract notions such as intentional consciousness are missing something more original.

recursion:
The capacity of language to work with and on itself, creating lexical modifications, insertions, combinations, and relations that are liberated from normal constraints of extant spatial and temporal conditions. Time extension, analytical constructions, and verbal associations are recursive functions that make higher order thinking possible, such as causal explanation, recollection, prediction, scientific analysis, and literature.

reification:
The capacity of exposition to construct discrete "entities" or frame specific conditions marked off from other entities, conditions, and relations. Object designation is not the only form of reification; concentrated focus can construct references such as "mind" and "body," "percepts" and "concepts."

scaffolding:
The generative function of affordances that support, enable, and further human behavior, practical abilities, and intelligence. Upbringing, social relations, and instrumentation are examples of scaffolding effects, which show that human selfhood must be understood as a dynamically extended and ecological condition.

social-world:
That part of the lived world that involves social relations and practices, which are constitutive of human selfhood, or the personal-world. Social involvements exhibit ecstatic immersion, which therefore are not a mere aggregation of individual selves and do not require inferential steps to assign mentality to others.

temporality:
Prior to objective measures of quantified time, as in clock-time, lived temporality involves imprecise moments and spans of experience (I can't talk now; See you later; Is it time for lunch?). As opposed to discrete zones of past, present, and future, which are defined apart from each other, temporality is an inter-looping dynamic with a figure-eight structure, where past, present, and future are intertwined as recollection, attention, and anticipation. Here the "absences" of past and future have a "presence."

Bibliography

Aitchison, Jean. *Words in the Mind: An Introduction to the Mental Lexicon*. Malden, MA: Wiley-Blackwell, 2012.

Annoni, Marco. "What Lexicography Reveals about Cultural Objects." *Semiotica* 198 (2014): 261–269.

Antognazza, Rosa. *Leibniz: A Very Short Introduction*. Oxford: Oxford University Press, 2016.

Arendt, Hannah. *The Human Condition*. Chicago: University of Chicago Press, 1958.

Ariso, José María. "Learning to Believe: Challenges in Children's Acquisition of a World-Picture in Wittgenstein's *On Certainty*." *Studies in Philosophy of Education* 34, no. 3 (May 2015): 311–325.

Ayers, Michael. "Ideas and Objective Being." *The Cambridge History of Seventeenth Century Philosophy*, Vol. 2, edited by Daniel Garber and Michael Ayers, 1062–1107. Cambridge: Cambridge University Press, 1998.

Bacon, Francis. *The Philosophical Works of Francis Bacon*. Translated by Robert L. Ellis and James Spedding. Edited by John M. Robinson. London: Routledge, 1905.

Baddeley Alan. "Working Memory and Language: An Overview." *Journal of Communication Disorders* 36 (2003): 189–208.

Baker, Mark C. *The Atoms of Language*. New York: Basic Books, 2001.

Bakker, Egbert. "Storytelling in the Future: Truth, Time, and Tense in Homeric Epic." *Written Voices, Spoken Signs: Tradition, Performance, and the Epic Text*, edited by Egbert Bakker and Ahuvia Kahane, 11–36. Cambridge, MA: Harvard University Press, 1997.

———. "Discourse and Performance: Involvement, Visualization and 'Presence' in Homeric Poetry." *Classical Antiquity* 12, no. 1 (April 1993): 1–29.

Bar, Moshe. "The Proactive Brain: Memory for Predictions." *Philosophical Transactions: Biology and Philosophy* 364, no. 1521 (May 2009): 1235–1243.

Bargh, John A. "Bypassing the Will: Toward Demystifying the Nonconscious Control of Social Behavior." *The New Unconscious*, edited by Ran R. Hassin, James S. Uleman, and John A. Bargh, 37–58. Oxford: Oxford University Press, 2005.

Bargh, John A. and Erin L. Williams. "The Automaticity of Social Life." *Current Directions in Psychological Science* 15, no. 1 (February 2006): 1–4.

Barinaga, Marcia. "New Insights into How Babies Learn Language." *Science* 277, no. 5326 (August 1997): 641.

Bartsch, Karen and Henry M. Wellman. *Children Talk about the Mind*. Oxford: Oxford University Press, 1995.

Battezzato, Luigi. "Techniques of Reading and Textual Layout in Ancient Greek Texts." *The Cambridge Classical Journal* 55 (January 2009): 1–23.

Baz, Avner. "On Going (and Getting) Nowhere with Our Words: New Skepticism about the Philosophical Method of Cases." *Philosophical Psychology* 29, no. 1 (January 2016): 64–83.

Benson, Janette B. and Marshall H. Haith, eds. *Language, Memory, and Cognition in Infancy and Early Childhood*. New York: Academic Press, 2009.

Benzaquén, Adriana S. *Encounters with Wild Children: Temptation and Disappointment in the Study of Human Nature*. Montreal: McGill-Queen's University Press, 2006.

Bergen, Benjamin K. *Louder Than Words: The New Science of How the Mind Makes Meaning*. New York: Basic Books, 2012.

Berkeley, George. *Siris*. London: Innys and Hitch, 1744.

Bickerton, Derek. *Language and Species*. Chicago, IL: University of Chicago Press, 1990.

Bloom-Feshbach, Jonathan and Sally Bloom-Feshbach, eds. *The Psychology of Separation and Loss*. San Francisco, CA: Jossey-Bass Publishers, 1987.

Boelen, Bernard J. *Personal Maturity: The Existential Dimension*. New York: Seabury, 1978.

Borge, Steffen. "Talking to Infants: A Gricean Perspective." *American Philosophical Quarterly* 50, no. 4 (October 2013): 423–428.

Boucher, Jill. "The Prerequisites for Language Acquisition." *Language and Thought*, edited by Peter Carruthers and Jill Boucher, 55–75. Cambridge: Cambridge University Press, 1998.

Boyd, Brian. "The Evolution of Stories: From Mimesis to Language, from Fact to Fiction." *Wiley Inter-Disciplinary Reviews: Cognitive Science* 9, no. 1 (January/February 2018): 1–16.

Bredlau, Susan. "On Perception and Trust: Merleau-Ponty and the Emotional Significance of Our Relations with Others." *Continental Philosophy Review* DOI: 10.1007/s11007-016-9367-3 (May 2016).

Brownell, Celia A. "Early Developments in Joint Action." *The Review of Philosophy and Psychology* 2, no. 2 (June 2011): 193–211.

Bruner, Jerome. *Acts of Meaning*. Cambridge, MA: Harvard University Press, 1990.

———. *Child's Talk: Learning to Use Language*. New York: Norton, 1983.

Bulle, Natalie. "Slow and Fast Thinking, Historical-Cultural Psychology and Major Trends of Modern Epistemology: Unveiling a Fundamental Convergence." *Mind and Society* 13, no. 1 (June 2014): 149–166.

Burkert, Walter. *Savage Energies: Lessons of Myth and Ritual in Ancient Greece*. Translated by Peter Bing. Chicago, IL: University of Chicago Press, 2001.
———. *Greek Religion*. Translated by John Raffan. Cambridge, MA: Harvard University Press, 1985.
Butterfield, David. "Neo-Latin." *A Companion to the Latin Language*, edited by James Clackson, Chap. 25. Malden, MA: Wiley-Blackwell, 2011.
Cambron-Goulet, Mathilde. "The Criticism—and the Practice—of Literacy in the Ancient Philosophical Tradition." *Mnemosyne: Supplements* 335. Leiden, The Netherlands: Brill, 2012, 201–226.
Carpenter, Malinda et al. "Social Cognition, Joint Attention, and Communicative Competence from 9 to 15 Months of Age." *Monographs of the Society for Research in Child Development* 63, no. 4 (December 1998): 1–133.
Casey, Edward S. *Remembering: A Phenomenological Study*. Indianapolis, IN: Indiana University Press, 2009.
Cassirer, Ernst. *The Philosophy of Symbolic Forms*, Volume 2: *Mythical Thought*. Translated by Ralph Manheim. New Haven, CT: Yale University Press, 1955.
———. *Language and Myth*. Translated by Susan K. Langer. New York: Dover Books, 1953.
Chemero, Anthony. *Radical Embodied Cognitive Science*. Cambridge, MA: MIT Press, 2009.
Christakis, Erika. "How the New Preschool Is Crushing Kids." *The Atlantic* 377, no. 1 (January–February 2016).
Clark, Andy. "Magic Words: How Language Augments Human Computation." *Language and Thought*, edited by Peter Carruthers and Jill Boucher, 162–183. Cambridge: Cambridge University Press, 1998.
Clark, Eve V. *First Language Acquisition*. Cambridge: Cambridge University Press, 2003.
———. "Pragmatics in Acquisition." *Journal of Child Language* 41, Supplement 1 (July 2014): 105–116.
Clark, Herbert H. *Using Language*. Cambridge: Cambridge University Press, 1996.
Colonessi, Cristina et al. "The Relation between Pointing and Language Development: A Meta-Analysis." *Developmental Review* 30, no. 4 (December 2010): 352–366.
Consentino, Erica. "Self in Time and Language." *Consciousness and Cognition* 20, no. 3 (2011): 777–783.
Corbalis, Michael C. *The Recursive Mind: The Origins of Human Language, Thought, and Civilization*. Princeton, NJ: Princeton University Press, 2011.
Coulmas, Florian. *The Writing Systems of the World*. Cambridge, MA: Basil Blackwell, 1989.
Culbertson, Carolyn. "My Language Which Is Not My Own: Heidegger and Derrida on the Ambiguity of Linguistic Life." *Southwest Philosophy Review* 32, no. 2 (July 2016): 115–136.
Cunningham, Hugh. *Children and Childhood in Western Society Since 1500*. New York: Routledge, 2005.

Dahlstrom, Daniel O. "Towards an Explanation of Language." *Proceedings of the American Catholic Philosophical Association* 84 (2011): 33–46.
Daniels, Harry. "Mediation: An Expansion of the Socio-Cultural Gaze." *History of the Human Sciences* 28, no. 2 (2015): 34–50.
Dehaene-Lambertz, Ghislaine et al. "Nature and Nurture in Language Acquisition: Anatomical and Functional Brain-Imaging in Infants." *Trends in Neurosciences* 29, no. 7 (July 2006): 367–373.
Derrida, Jacques. *Dissemination*. Translated by Barbara Johnson. Chicago, IL: University of Chicago Press, 1981.
———. *Of Grammatology*. Translated by Gayatri C. Spivak. Baltimore, MD: Johns Hopkins University Press, 1976.
———. *Margins of Philosophy*. Translated by Alan Bass. Chicago, IL: University of Chicago Press, 1982.
———. *Monolingualism of the Other: Or the Prosthesis of Origin*. Translated by Patrick Mensah. Stanford, CA: Stanford University Press, 1998.
Descartes, René. *Philosophical Letters*. Translated by Anthony Kenny. Minneapolis, MN: University of Minnesota Press, 1981.
———. *The Philosophical Writings of Descartes* I. Translated by John Cottingham, Robert Stoothoff, and Dugald Murdoch. Cambridge: Cambridge University Press, 1985.
Detienne, Marcel. *The Masters of Truth in Ancient Greece*. Translated by Janet Lloyd. New York: Zone Books, 1996.
Dewey, John. *The Philosophy of John Dewey*. Edited by J.J. McDermott. Chicago, IL: University of Chicago Press, 1981.
Dissanayake, Ellen. *What Is Art For?* Seattle, WA: University of Washington Press, 1988.
Donald, Merlin. *Origins of the Modern Mind*. Cambridge, MA: Harvard University Press, 1991.
Dow, James M. "Mindreading, Mindsharing, and the Origins of Self-Consciousness." *Philosophical Topics* 40, no. 2 (Fall 2012): 39–70.
Duane, Anna Mae, ed. *The Children's Table: Childhood Studies and the Humanities*. Athens, GA: University of Georgia Press, 2013.
Dutton, Blake D. "Indifference, Necessity, and Descartes' Laws of Motion." *Journal of the History of Philosophy* 34, no.2 (1996): 193–212.
Eacott, Madeline J. "Memory for the Events of Early Childhood." *Current Directions in Psychological Science* 8, no. 2 (April 1999): 46–49.
Ebbesen, Sten. *Greek-Latin Philosophical Interaction*. New York: Routledge, 2016.
Ehrich, John F. "Vygotskian Inner Speech and the Reading Process." *Australian Journal of Educational and Developmental Psychology* 6 (2006): 12–25.
Eisenberg, Nancy and Janet Strayer, eds. *Empathy and Its development*. Cambridge: Cambridge University Press, 1987.
Engelland, Chad. *Ostension: Word Learning and the Embodied Mind*. Cambridge, MA: MIT Press, 2014.
English, Andrea R. *Discontinuity in Learning: Dewey, Herbart, and Education as Transformation*. Cambridge: Cambridge University Press, 2013.

Estany, Anna and Sergio Martinez. "Scaffolding and Affordances as Integrative Concepts in the Cognitive Sciences." *Philosophical Psychology* 27, no. 1 (February 2014): 98–111.
Esteve-Gilbert, Núria and Pilar Prieto. "Infants Temporally Coordinate Gesture-Speech Combinations before They Produce Their First Words." *Speech Communication* 57 (2014): 301–316.
Evans, Vyvyan. *The Language Myth: Why Language Is Not an Instinct*. Cambridge: Cambridge University Press, 2014.
Evans, Angela D. and Kang Lee. "Emergence of Lying in Very Young Children." *Developmental Psychology* 49, no. 10 (2013): 1958–1963.
Falcon, Andrea. *Aristotle and the Science of Nature: Unity without Uniformity*. Cambridge: Cambridge University Press, 2005.
Fernández, Manuel et al. "Re-Conceptualizing 'Scaffolding' and the Zone of Proximal Development in the Context of Symmetrical Collaborative Learning." *Journal of Classroom Interaction* 50, no. 1 (2015): 54–72.
Fernyhough, Charles. "Getting Vygotskian about Theory of Mind: Mediation, Dialogue, and the Development of Social Understanding." *Developmental Review* 28, no. 2 (June 2008): 225–262.
Ferrari, G. R. F. "Logos." *Classical Papers* (Department of Classics, University of California at Berkeley, 1997).
Fögen, Thorsten. "Latin as a Technical and Scientific Language." *A Companion to the Latin Language*, edited by James Clackson, Chap. 25. Malden, MA: Wiley-Blackwell, 2011.
Ford, Andrew. "From Letters to Literature: Reading the 'Song Culture' of Classical Greece." *Written Texts and the Rise of Literate Culture in Ancient Greece*, edited by Harvey Yunus, 15–37. Cambridge: Cambridge University Press, 2003.
Forrester, Stefan. "Theories of Metaphor in Seventeenth and Eighteenth-Century British Philosophy." *Literature Compass* 7, no. 8 (2010): 610–625.
Fridland, Ellen and Richard Moore. "Imitation Reconsidered." *Philosophical Psychology* 28, no. 6 (2015): 856–880.
Fulkerson, Matthew. *The First Sense: A Philosophical Study of Human Touch*. Cambridge, MA: MIT Press, 2014.
Galileo, Galilei. *Dialogue Concerning the Two Chief World Systems*. Translated by Stillman Drake. New York: Modern Library, 2001.
———. *Discoveries and Opinions of Galileo*. Translated by Stillman Drake. New York: Doubleday Anchor, 1957.
Gallagher, Shaun and Andrew Meltzoff. "The Earliest Sense of Self and Others: Merleau-Ponty and Recent Development Studies." *Philosophical Psychology* 9, no. 2 (1996): 211–233.
Gargarin, Michael. *Writing Greek Law*. Cambridge: Cambridge University Press, 2008.
Genberg, Arthur M and Vittorio Gallese. "Action-Based Language: A Theory of Language Acquisition, Comprehension, and Production." *Cortex* 48 (2012): 905–922.
Genesee, Fred. *Learning through Two Languages: Studies in Immersion and Bilingual Education*. Belmont, CA: Wadsworth, 1987.

Gentili, Bruno. *Poetry and Its Public in Ancient Greece: From Homer to the Fifth Century*. Translated by A. Thomas Cole. Baltimore, MD: Johns Hopkins University Press, 1988.

Gerrans, Philip and David Sander. "Feeling the Future: Prospects for a Theory of Implicit Prospection." *Biology and Philosophy* 29, no. 5 (September 2014): 699–710.

Gibson, Eleanor J. *An Odyssey in Learning and Perception*. Cambridge, MA: MIT Press, 1994.

Gill, Christopher. "Plato on Falsehood—Not Fiction." *Lies and Fictions in the Ancient World*, edited by Christopher Gill and T. P. Wiseman, 38–87. Austin, TX: University of Texas Press, 1993.

Goody, Jack and Ian Watt. "The Consequences of Literacy." *Comparative Studies in Society and History* 5, no. 3 (April, 1963): 304–345.

Gopnick, Alison, Andrew N. Meltzoff, and Patricia K. Kuhl. *The Scientist in the Crib: Minds, Brains, and How Children Learn*. New York: William Morrow, 1999.

Gortham, Geoffrey, Benjamin Hill, and Edward Slowik, eds. *The Language of Nature: Reassessing the Mathematization of Natural Philosophy in the Seventeenth Century*. Minneapolis, MN: University of Minnesota Press, 2016.

Gosetti-Ferencei, Jennifer Anna. "The Mimetic Dimension: Literature between Neuroscience and Phenomenology." *British Journal of Aesthetics* 54, no. 4 (October 2014): 425–448.

Goswami, Usha. "The Basic Processes in Reading: Insights from Neuroscience." *The Cambridge Handbook of Literacy*, edited by David R. Olsen and Nancy Torrance, 134–151. Cambridge: Cambridge University Press, 2009.

Gould, John. "On Making Sense of Greek Religion." *Greek Religion and Society*, edited by P. E. Easterling and J. V. Muir, 1–33. Cambridge: Cambridge University Press, 1985.

Grainger, Jonathan and Thomas Hannagan. "What Is Special about Orthographic Processing?" *Written Language and Literacy* 17, no. 2 (2014): 225–252.

Gregory, Maughn and David Granger. "John Dewey on Philosophy and Childhood." *Education and Culture* 28, no. 2 (2012): 1–25.

Griffin, Jasper. *Homer on Life and Death*. Oxford: Oxford University Press, 1980.

Hadot, Pierre. *What Is Ancient Philosophy?* Translated by Michael Chase. Cambridge, MA: Belknap Press, 2002.

Halliwell, Stephen. *The Aesthetics of Mimesis*. Princeton, NJ: Princeton University Press, 2002.

Hannan, Sarah. "Why Childhood Is Bad for Children." *Journal of Applied Philosophy* 35, S1 (February 2018): 11–28.

Harris, William V. *Ancient Literacy*. Cambridge, MA: Harvard University Press, 1991.

Harris, Paul L. et al. "'I Don't Know': Children's Early Talk about Knowledge." *Mind and Language* 32, no. 3 (June 2017): 283–307.

Harris, Roy. *The Linguistics of History*. Edinburgh: Edinburgh University Press, 2004.

———. *Rethinking Writing*. New York: Continuum, 2000.

Hart, Betty and Todd R. Risely. "The Early Catastrophe: The 30 Million Word Gap by Age 3." *American Educator* 27, no. 1 (Spring 2003): 4–9.

———. *Meaningful Differences in the Everyday Experience of Young American Children*. Baltimore, MD: Brookes Publishing Co., 1995.

Haskins, Ekaterina V. "'Mimesis' between Poetics and Rhetoric: Performance Culture and Civic Education in Plato, Isocrates, and Aristotle." *Rhetoric Society Quarterly* 30, no. 3 (Summer 2000): 7–33.

Hatab, Lawrence J. "Can We Drop the Subject? Heidegger, Selfhood, and the History of a Modern Word." *Horizons of Authenticity in Phenomenology, Existentialism, and Moral Psychology*, edited by Hans Pedersen and Megan Altman, 13–30. London: Springer, 2015.

———. "Dasein, the Early Years: Heideggerian Reflections on Childhood." *International Philosophical Quarterly* 54, no. 4 (December 2014): 379–391.

———. *Ethics and Finitude: Heideggerian Contributions to Moral Philosophy*. Lanham, MD: Rowman & Littlefield, 2000.

———. *Myth and Philosophy: A Contest of Truths*. Chicago, IL: Open Court, 1990.

———. *A Nietzschean Defense of Democracy: An Experiment in Postmodern Politics*. Chicago, IL: Open Court, 1995.

———. *Nietzsche's Life Sentence: Coming to Terms with Eternal Recurrence*. New York: Routledge, 2005.

———. "*Phainomenon* and *Logos* in Aristotle's Ethics." *Phenomenology and Virtue Ethics*, edited by Kevin Hermberg and Paul Gyllenhammer, 9–28. London: Bloomsbury, 2013.

———. "The Point of Language in Heidegger's Thinking: A Call for the Retrieval of Formal Indication." *Gatherings: The Heidegger Circle Annual* 6 (2016): 1–22.

———. "Tragic Values in Homer and Sophocles," *Logoi and Muthoi: Further Philosophical Essays in Greek Literature*, edited by William Wians, Chap. 6. Albany, NY: SUNY Press, 2018.

Havelock, Eric A. *The Muse Learns to Write: Reflections on Orality and Literacy from Antiquity to the Present*. New Haven, CT: Yale University Press, 1986.

———. *Preface to Plato*. Cambridge, MA: Belknap Press, 1963.

Heath, John. *The Talking Greeks: Speech, Animals, and the Other in Homer, Aeschylus, and Plato*. Cambridge: Cambridge University Press, 2005.

Hegel, G. W. F. *Hegel's Philosophy of Mind: Part Three of the Encyclopaedia of the Philosophical Sciences*. Translated by William Wallace and A. V. Miller. Oxford: Oxford University Press, 1971.

Heidegger, Martin. *Off the Beaten Track*. Translated by Julian Young and Kenneth Haynes. Cambridge: Cambridge University Press, 2002.

———. *On the Way to Language*. Translated by Peter D. Hertz. New York: HarperCollins, 1982.

———. *Poetry, Language, Thought*. Translated by Albert Hofstadter. New York: HarperCollins, 1971.

———. *What Is a Thing?* Translated by B. Barton, Jr. and Vera Deutsch. Chicago, IL: Henry Regnery Co., 1967.

Henning, Boris. "Cartesian *Conscientia.*" *British Journal for the History of Philosophy* 15, no. 3 (August 2007): 455–485.

Hobbs, Valerie. "Looking Again at Clarity in Philosophy: Writing as a Shaper and Sharpener of Thought." *Philosophy* 90, no. 1 (January 2015); 135–142.

Horst, Jessica S. et al. "Get the Story Straight: Contextual Repetition Promotes Word Learning from Storybooks." *Frontiers in Psychology* 2, no. 17 (February 2011): 1–11.

Hume, David. *A Treatise of Human Nature*, edited by David Fate Norton and Mary J. Norton. Oxford: Clarendon Press, 2000.

Hyland, Drew. *Finitude and Transcendence in the Platonic Dialogues.* Albany, NY: SUNY Press, 1995.

Ibbotson, Paul and Michael Tomasello. "Evidence Rebuts Chomsky's Theory of Language Learning." *Scientific American* 315, no. 5 (November 2016).

Inkpin, Andrew. *Disclosing the World: On the Phenomenology of Language.* Cambridge, MA: MIT Press, 2016.

Irwin, Brian A. "An Enactivist Account of Abstract Words: Lessons from Merleau-Ponty." *Phenomenology and the Cognitive Sciences* 16, no. 1 (2017): 133–153.

Jackendoff, Ray S. *The Architecture of the Language Faculty.* Cambridge, MA: MIT Press, 1996.

———. "How Language Helps Us Think." *Pragmatics and Cognition* 4, no. 1 (1996): 1–34.

James I. Porter, "Language as a System in Ancient Rhetoric and Grammar." *A Companion to the Ancient Greek Language*, edited by Egbert J. Bakker, chap. 34. Malden, MA: Wiley-Blackwell, 2010.

Janko, Richard. "From Gabii and Gordian to Eretria and Methone: The Rise of the Greek Alphabet." *Bulletin of the Institute of Classical Studies* 58, no. 1 (June 2015): 1–32.

Jeremiah, Edward T. *The Emergence of Reflexivity in Greek Language and Thought: From Homer to Plato and Beyond.* Boston, MA: Brill, 2012.

Johnston, Sarah Iles. "The Greek Mythic Story World." *Arethusa* 48, no. 3 (Fall 2015): 283–311.

———. "Narrating Myths: Story and Belief in Ancient Greece." *Arethusa* 48, no. 2 (Spring 2015): 173–218.

Jsewijen, J. I. and D. Sacré, "The Ultimate Effort to Save Latin as a Means of International Communication." *History of European Ideas* 16, no. 1–3 (1993): 51–66.

Kagan, Jerome and Sharon Lamb, eds. *The Emergence of Morality in Young Children.* Chicago: University of Chicago Press, 1987.

Kahn, Charles H. *The Verb "Be" in Ancient Greek.* Indianapolis, IN: Hackett, 2003.

———. "Writing Philosophy: Prose and Poetry from Thales to Plato." *Written Texts and the Rise of Literate Culture in Ancient Greece*, edited by Harvey Yunus, 139–161. Cambridge: Cambridge University Press, 2003.

Kant, Immanuel. *Critique of Pure Reason.* Translated by Werner S. Pluhar. Indianapolis, IN: Hackett, 1996.

———. *Philosophy of Material Nature.* Translated by James W. Ellington. Indianapolis, IN: Hackett, 1985.

Keller, Helen. *The Story of My Life.* New York: Bantam 1998.

———. *The World I Live In*. New York: NYRB Classics, 2004.
Kennedy, David. "Parent, Child, Alterity, Dialogue." *Philosophy Today* 45, no. 1 (Spring 2001): 33–42.
Kirkham, Julie et al. "Concurrent and Longitudinal Relationships between Development in Graphic Language and Symbolic Play Domains from the Fourth to the Fifth Year." *Infant and Child Development* 22, no. 3 (June 2013): 297–319.
Klein, Jacob. *Greek Mathematical Thought and the Origin of Algebra*. Translated by Eva Brann. New York: Dover Books, 1968.
Klein, Stanley B. and Shaun Nichols. "Memory and the Sense of Personal Identity." *Mind* 121, no. 483 (July 2012): 677–702.
Koch, Sabine et al., eds. *Body Memory, Metaphor, and Movement*. Amsterdam: John Benjamins, 2012.
Kövecses, Zoltán. *Where Metaphors Come From: Reconsidering Context in Metaphor*. Oxford: Oxford University Press, 2015.
Kramsch, Claire, ed. *Language Acquisition and Language Socialization: Ecological Perspectives*. New York: Continuum, 2002.
Lakoff, George and Mark Johnson. *Metaphors We Live By*. Chicago, IL: The University of Chicago Press, 2003.
———. *Philosophy in the Flesh: The Embodied Mind and Its Challenge to Western Thought*. New York: Basic Books, 1999.
Landes, Donald A. "Language Development: Paradoxical Trajectories in Merleau-Ponty, Simonden, and Bergson." *Phenomenology and the Cognitive Sciences* 16, no. 4 (September 2017): 597–607.
Langfur, Stephen. "Cogitor Ergo Sum: The Origin of Self-Awareness in Dyadic Interaction." *Human Studies* (December 2018): 1–26. DOI: 10.1007/s10746-018-09487-y.
———. "The You-I Event: On the Genesis of Self-Awareness." *Phenomenology and the Cognitive Sciences* 12, no. 4 (December 2013): 769–790.
Law, Vivian. *The History of Linguistics in Europe: From Plato to 1600*. Cambridge: Cambridge University Press, 2003.
Ledbetter, Grace M. *Poetics before Plato: Interpretation and Authority in Early Greek Theories of Poetry*. Princeton, NJ: Princeton University Press, 2002.
Leder, Drew. *The Absent Body*. Chicago: University of Chicago Press, 1990.
Leonhardt, Jürgen. *Latin: Story of a World Language*. Translated by Kenneth Kronenberg. Cambridge, MA: Belknap Press, 2013.
Levinson, Stephen C. "Language and Mind: Let's Get the Issues Straight!" *Language in Mind*, edited by Susan Goldin-Meadow and Dedre Gentner, 25–46. Cambridge, MA: MIT Press, 2003.
Lincoln, Bruce. *Theorizing Myth*. Chicago: University of Chicago Press, 1999.
Linell, Per. *The Written Language Bias in Linguistics: Its Nature, Origins, and Transformations*. New York: Routledge, 2005.
Lloyd, G. E. R. *The Ambivalences of Rationality: Ancient and Modern Cross-Cultural Explorations*. Cambridge: Cambridge University Press, 2018.
———. "Literacy in Greek and Chinese Science." *Written Texts and the Rise of Literate Culture in Ancient Greece*, edited by Harvey Yunus, 122–138. Cambridge: Cambridge University Press, 2003.

———. *Magic, Reason, and Experience*. Cambridge: Cambridge University Press, 1979.

Locke, John. *An Essay Concerning Human Understanding*. Edited by Kenneth Winkler. Indianapolis, IN: Hackett, 1996.

Logan, Robert K. "The Alphabet Revisited, McLuhan Reversals and Complexity Theory." *Philosophies* 2, no. 1 (2017): 1–8.

Long, Christopher P. *Aristotle on the Nature of Truth*. Cambridge: Cambridge University Press, 2011.

Lord, Albert Bates. *Epic Singers and Oral Tradition*. Ithaca, NY: Cornell University Press, 1991.

Lum, Jarrad A. G. et al. "Procedural and Declarative Memory in Children with and without Specific Language Impairment." *International Journal of Language and Communication Disorders* 45, no. 1 (2010): 96–107.

Luria, Alexander R. *The Role of Speech in the Regulation of Normal and Abnormal Behavior*. New York: Liveright Publishing Co., 1961.

Lyotard, Jean François. *Why Philosophize?* Translated by Andrew Brown. London: Polity Press, 2013.

Magrini, James M. "When Praxis Breaks Down: What Heidegger's Phenomenology Contributes to Understanding Miscues and Learning in Reading." *Analysis and Metaphysics* 12 (2013): 25–46.

Mampe, Birgit et al. "Newborns' Cry Melody Is Shaped by Their Native Language." *Current Biology* 19, no. 23 (December 2009): 1994–97.

Manetti, Giovanni. *Theories of the Sign in Classical Antiquity*. Translated by Christine Richardson. Indianapolis, IN: Indiana University Press, 1993.

Marincola, John. "Herodotus and Poetry of the Past." *The Cambridge Companion to Herodotus*, edited by Carolyn Dewald and John Marincola, 13–28. Cambridge: Cambridge University Press, 2006.

Marrou, H. I. *A History of Education in Antiquity*. Translated by George Lamb. Madison, WI: The University of Wisconsin Press, 1956.

Martin, Richard. *The Language of Heroes*. Ithaca, NY: Cornell University Press, 1989.

———. "The 'Myth before the Myth Began.'" *Writing Down the Myths*, edited by Joseph F. Nagy. Turnhout, Belgium: Brepols, 2013.

Mavrogenes, Nancy A. "Reading in Ancient Greece." *Journal of Reading* 23, no. 8 (May 1980): 691–97.

McCutcheon, R.W. "Silent Reading and Antiquity and the Future History of the Book." *Book History* 18 (2015): 1–32.

McGuirk, James. "Phenomenological Considerations of Habit: Reason, Knowing, and Self-Presence in Habitual Action." *Phenomenology and Mind* 6 (2014): 112–121.

McLuhan, Marshall. *The Gutenberg Galaxy: The Making of Typographic Man*. Toronto: University of Toronto Press, 1962.

McNeill, David. *Gesture and Thought*. Chicago: University of Chicago Press, 2005.

Meli, Domenico Bertoloni. "Patterns of Transformation in Seventeenth-Century Mechanics." *The Monist* 93, no. 4 (2010): 580–597.

Meltzoff, Andrew and M. Keith Moore. "Imitation of Facial and Manual Gestures by Human Neonates." *Science* 198 (1977): 75–78.

———. "Newborn Infants Imitate Adult Facial Gestures." *Child Development* 54 (1983): 702–709.
Meltzoff, Andrew and Rebecca Williamson. "Imitation: Social, Cognitive, and Theoretical Perspectives." *Oxford Handbook of Developmental Psychology*, Vol. 1, edited by P. R. Zelazo, 651–682. Oxford: Oxford University Press, 2013.
Merleau-Ponty, Maurice. *Child Psychology and Pedagogy: The Sorbonne Lectures 1949–1952*. Translated by Talia Welsh. Evanston, IL: Northwestern University Press, 2010.
———. *Texts and Dialogues: On Philosophy, Politics, and Culture*. Edited by Hugh J. Silverman and J. Barry Jr. Translated by Forest Williams. Atlantic Highlands, NJ: Humanities Press, 1996.
———. *The Visible and the Invisible*. Edited by Claude Lefort. Translated by Alphonso Lingis. Evanston, IL: Northwestern University Press, 1968.
Mintz, Steven. "Why the History of Childhood Matters." *The Journal of the History of Childhood and Youth* 5, no. 1 (Winter 2002): 15–28.
Miroshnichenko, Andrey. "Extrapolating on McLuhan: How Media Environments of the Given, the Represented, and the Induced Shape and Reshape Our Sensorium." *Philosophies* 1, no. 3 (2016): 170–189.
Monzalvo, Karla and Ghislaine Dehaene-Lambertz. "How Reading Acquisition Changes Children's Spoken Language Network." *Brain and Language* 127 (December 2013): 356–365.
Moore, Chris and Philip Dunham, eds. *Joint Attention: Its Origins and Role in Development*. New York: Psychology Press, 2015.
Morgan, T. J. "Literate Education in Classical Athens." *The Classical Quarterly* 49, no. 1 (1999): 46–61.
Morgen, Kathryn A. *Myth and Philosophy from the Pre-Socratics to Plato*. Cambridge: Cambridge University Press, 2000.
Morin, Alain. "Possible Links between Self-awareness and Inner Speech." *Journal of Consciousness Studies* 12, no. 4–5 (2005): 115–134.
Morris, David. "Rethinking Development." *Phenomenology and the Cognitive Sciences* 16, no. 4 (September 2017): 565–569.
Mosedale, Frederick E. "Meditations on the Origin of Philosophy." *Philosophical Investigations* 40, no. 4 (October 2017): 370–395.
Nadler, Steven M. "Deduction, Confirmation, and the Laws of Nature in Descartes' *Principia Philosophiae*." *Journal of the History of Philosophy* 28, no. 3 (1990): 359–383.
Neal, David T. et al. "Habits—A Repeat Performance." *Current Directions in Psychological Science* 15, no. 4 (August 2006): 198–202.
Nelson, Katherine. *Language in Cognitive Development: The Emergence of the Mediated Mind*. Cambridge: Cambridge University Press, 1996.
———. "Emergence of Autobiographical Memory at Age 4." *Human Development* 35, no. 3 (1992): 172–77.
———. "The Psychological and Social Origins of Autobiographical Memory." *Psychological Science* 4, no. 1 (January 1993): 7–14.
———. *Young Minds in Social Worlds: Experience, Meaning, and Memory*. Cambridge, MA: Harvard University Press, 2007.

Netz, Reviel. *The Shaping of Deduction in Greek Mathematics*. Cambridge: Cambridge University Press, 1999.

Newton, Isaac. *Mathematical Principles of Natural Philosophy*. Berkeley, CA: University of California Press, 1960.

Nordmeyer, Ann E. and Michael Frank. "The Role of Context in Young Children's Comprehension of Negation." *Journal of Memory and Language* 77 (November 2014): 26–39.

Oakes, Lisa M. "Using Habituation of Looking Time to Assess Mental Processes in Infancy." *Journal of Cognition and Development* 11, no. 3 (2010): 255–268.

Ober, Josiah. *Political Dissent in Classical Athens*. Princeton, NJ: Princeton University Press, 1998.

Olson, David R. "Literacy, Rationality, and Logic: The Historical and Developmental Origins of Logical Discourse." *Written Language and Literacy* 15, no. 2 (2012): 153–164.

———. *The World on Paper: The Conceptual and Cognitive Implications of Writing and Reading*, Cambridge: Cambridge University Press, 1994.

Olson, David R. and Keith Oatley. "The Quotation Theory of Writing." *Written Communication* 31, no. 1 (2014): 4–26.

Ong, Walter J. "Before Textuality: Orality and Interpretation." *Oral Tradition* 3, no. 3 (1988): 259–269.

———. *Orality and Literacy: The Technologizing of the Word*. New York: Routledge, 2002.

———. *The Presence of the Word: Some Prolegomena for Cultural and Religious History*. New Haven, CT: Yale University Press, 1967.

———. "Writing Is a Technology That Restructures Thought." *The Written Word: Literacy in Transition*, edited by Gerd Baumann, 23–50. Oxford: Oxford University Press, 1986.

Padel, Ruth. *In and Out of the Mind: Greek Images of the Tragic Self*. Princeton, NJ: Princeton University Press, 1992.

Parry, Adam, ed. *The Making of Homeric Verse: The Collected Papers of Milman Parry*. Oxford: Clarendon Press, 1971.

Pattamadilok, Chotiga et al. "Auditory Word Serial Recall Benefits from Orthographic Dissimilarity." *Language and Speech* 53, no. 3 (2010): 321–334.

———. "On-Line Orthographic Influences on Spoken Language in a Semantic Task." *Journal of Cognitive Neuroscience* 21, no. 1 (January 2009): 167–179.

———. "Unattentive Speech Processing Is Influenced by Orthographic Knowledge: Evidence from Mismatch Negativity." *Brain and Language* 137 (October 2014): 103–111.

Piaget, Jean. *Sociological Studies*. Edited by Leslie Smith. New York: Routledge, 1995.

Pinker, Steven. *The Language Instinct*. London: Penguin, 1994.

Podolsky, Andrey I. "Zone of Proximal Development." *Encyclopedia of the Sciences of Learning*, edited by Norbert M. Seel, 3485–3487. New York: Springer, 2012.

Powell, Barry P. *Homer and the Origin of the Greek Alphabet*. Cambridge: Cambridge University Press, 1996.

———. *Writing: Theory and History of the Technology of Civilization*. Malden, MA: Wiley-Blackwell, 2012.

Pratt, Louise H. *Lying and Poetry from Homer to Pindar*. Ann Arbor, MI: University of Michigan Press, 1993.

Prier, Raymond A. *Thauma Idesthai: The Phenomenology of Sight and Appearance in Archaic Greek*. Gainesville, FL: Florida State University Press, 1989.

Provenzo, Eugene F. and Asterie Baker Provenzo, eds. *Encyclopedia of the Social and Cultural Foundations of Education*. Thousand Oaks, CA: Sage Publishing, 2009.

Radman, Zdravko, ed. *The Hand: An Organ of the Mind, What the Manual Tells the Mental*. Cambridge, MA: MIT Press, 2013.

Ravenscrift, Ian. "Engaging the World: Writing, Imagination, and Enactivism." *Philosophy and Literature* 41, no. 1 (April, 2017): 45–54.

Ready, Jonathan L. "The Textualization of Homeric Epic by Means of Dictation." *Transactions of the American Philological Association* 145, no. 1 (Spring 2015): 1–75.

Reid, Thomas. *The Works of Thomas Reid*, Vol. 2. Edited by William Hamilton. New York: Elibron Classics, 2005.

Ricoeur, Paul. *The Rule of Metaphor: The Creation of Meaning in Language*. Translated by Robert Czerny. New York: Routledge, 2003.

———. *Time and Narrative*, 3 volumes. Translated by Kathleen Blamey and David Pellauer. Chicago, IL: University of Chicago Press, 1984, 1985, 1988.

Roberts, Beth. "The Evolution of the Young Child's Concept of 'Word' as a Unit of Spoken and Written Language." *Reading Research Quarterly* 27, no. 2 (Spring 1992): 124–138.

Robinson, Elizabeth J. and Shiri Einav, eds. *Trust and Skepticism: Children's Selective Learning from Testimony*. New York: Psychology Press, 2014.

Rochat, Phillipe. "Five Levels of Self-Awareness as They Unfold Early in Life," *Consciousness and Cognition* 12, no. 4 (2003): 717–731.

Roniger, Scott. "Speech and Being in Aristotle's *Metaphysics*." *International Philosophical Quarterly* 57, no. 1 (March 2017): 31–41.

Roochnik, David. "Homeric Speech Acts: Word and Deed in the Epics." *The Classical Journal* 85, no. 4 (April–May 1990): 289–299.

Rozemond, Marleen. "Descartes' Case for Dualism." *Journal of the History of Philosophy* 33, no. 1 (1995): 29–63.

Rutter, Michael. *Genes and Behavior: Nature-Nurture Interplay Explained*. Malden, MA: Blackwell, 2006.

Sallis, John. *Being and Logos: Reading the Platonic Dialogues*. Bloomington, IN: Indiana University Press, 1996.

———. *Chorology: On Beginning in Plato's Timaeus*. Bloomington, IN: Indiana University Press, 1999.

Sameroff, Arnold. "A Unified Theory of Development: A Dialectic Integration of Nature-Nurture." *Child Development* 81, no. 1 (January/February 2010): 6–22.

Sandler, Wendy. "Viva la Différence: Sign Language and Spoken Language in Language Evolution." *Language and Cognition* 5, no. 2–3 (2013): 189–203.

Schietecatte, Inga et al. "Exploring the Nature of Joint Attention Impairment in Young Children with Autism Spectrum Disorder: Associated Social and Cognitive Skills." *Journal of Autism and Developmental Disorders* 42, no. 1 (January 2012): 1–12.

Schmidhauser, Andreas U. "The Birth of Grammar in Greece." *A Companion to the Ancient Greek Language*, edited by Egbert J. Bakker, Chap. 33. Malden, MA: Wiley-Blackwell, 2010.

Schöner, Gregor and Esther Thelan. "Using Dynamic Field Theory to Rethink Infant Habituation." *Psychological Review* 113, no. 2 (April 2006): 273–299.

Scott, Laurence. *The Four-Dimensional Human: Ways of Being in the Digital World*. London: Heinemann, 2015.

Seemann, Axel, ed. *Joint Attention: New Developments in Psychology, Philosophy of Mind, and Social Neuroscience*. Cambridge, MA: MIT Press, 2011.

Segal, Charles. *Singers, Heroes, and Gods in the* Odyssey. Ithaca, NY: Cornell University Press, 1994.

Segerdahl, Pär. "Humanizing Nonhumans: Ape Language Research as Critique of Metaphysics." *Language, Ethics and Animal Life: Wittgenstein and Beyond*, edited by Niklas Forsberg et al., Chap. 1. New York: Bloomsbury, 2012.

Sheets-Johnstone, Maxine. "From Movement to Dance." *Phenomenology and the Cognitive Sciences* 11, no. 1 (March 2012): 39–57.

———. "On the Origin, Nature, and Genesis of Habit." *Phenomenology and Mind* 6 (2014): 77–89.

Sider, Theodore. *Writing the Book of the World*. Oxford: Oxford University Press, 2011.

Simms, Eva-Marie. "Chiasm and Hyperdialectic: Re-conceptualizing Sensory Deprivation in Infancy. *Phenomenology and the Cognitive Sciences* 16, no. 4 (September 2017): 637–648.

———. *The Child in the World: Embodiment, Time, and Language in Early Childhood*. Detroit, MI: Wayne State University Press, 2008.

———. Children's Lived Space in the Inner City: Geographical and Political Aspects of the Psychology of Place." *The Humanistic Psychologist* 36, no. 1 (January 2008): 72–89.

Sini, Carlo. "Gesture and Word: The Practice of Philosophy and the Practice of Poetry." *Between Philosophy and Poetry: Writing Rhythm History*, edited by Massimo Verdiccio and Robert Burch, 15–25. New York: Continuum, 2002.

Slobin, Daniel I. "Language and Thought Online: Cognitive Consequences of Linguistic Relativity." *Language in Mind*, edited by Susan Goldin-Meadow and Dedre Gentner, 157–191. Cambridge, MA: MIT Press, 2003.

Smith, P. Christopher. *The Hermeneutics of Original Argument: Demonstration, Dialectic, Rhetoric*. Evanston, IL: Northwestern University Press, 1998.

———. "Orality and Writing: Plato's *Phaedrus* and the *Pharmakon* Revisited." *Between Philosophy and Poetry: Writing Rhythm History*, edited by Massimo Verdiccio and Robert Burch, 73–89. New York: Continuum, 2002.

Snell, Bruno. *The Discovery of the Mind*. Translated by T. G. Rosenmeyer. New York: Harper and Row, 1960.

Soffer, Gail. "Phenomenology with a Hammer: Theory or Practice." *Continental Philosophy Review* 32, no. 4 (October 1999): 379–393.

Sourvinou-Inwood, Christiane. *Tragedy and Athenian Religion*. Lanham, MD: Lexington Books, 2003.

Sparrow, Tom and Adam Hutchinson. *A History of Habit: From Aristotle to Bourdieu*. Lanham, MD: Lexington Books, 2014.

Spelke, Elizabeth S. "What Makes Us Smart? Core Knowledge and Natural Language." *Language in Mind*, edited by Susan Goldin-Meadow and Dedre Gentner, 277–311. Cambridge, MA: MIT Press, 2003.

Stafford, Emma. *Worshipping Virtues: Personification and the Divine in Ancient Greece*. Swansea: Duckworth, 2001.

Steglich-Petersen, Asbjørn and John Michael. "Why Desire Reasoning Is Developmentally prior to Belief Reasoning." *Mind and Language* 30, no. 5 (November 2015): 526–549.

Stern, Daniel N. *The First Relationship: Infant and Mother*. Cambridge, MA: Harvard University Press, 2004.

———. *The Interpersonal World of the Infant*. New York: Basic Books, 2000.

———. *The Interpersonal World of the Infant: A View from Psychoanalysis and Developmental Psychology*. New York: Basic Books, 1985.

Storey, Robert. *Mimesis and the Human Animal: On the Biogenetic Foundations of Literary Representation*. Evanston, IL: Northwestern University Press, 1996.

Suggate, Sebastian P. et al. "Incidental Vocabulary Acquisition from Stories: Second and Fourth Graders Learn More from Listening than Reading." *First Language* 33, no. 6 (2013): 551–571.

Svenbro, Jesper. "The Interior Voice: On the Invention of Silent Reading." *Nothing to Do with Dionysos? Athenian Drama in Its Social Context*, edited by John J. Winkler and Froma I. Zeitlin, 366–384. Princeton, NJ: Princeton University Press, 1990.

———. *Phrasikleia: An Anthropology of Reading in Ancient Greece*. Translated by Janet Lloyd. Ithaca, NY: Cornell University Press, 1993.

Tabery, James. *Beyond Versus: The Struggle to Understand the Interaction of Nature and Nurture*. Cambridge, MA: MIT Press, 2014.

Talero, Maria. "Merleau-Ponty and the Bodily Subject of Learning." *International Philosophical Quarterly* 46, no. 2 (June 2006): 191–203.

Taylor, Charles. *The Language Animal: The Full Shape of the Human Linguistic Capacity*. Cambridge, MA: Belknap Press, 2016.

Taylor, Talbot J. "Calibrating the Child for Language: Meredith Williams on a Wittgensteinian Approach to Language Socialization." *Language Sciences* 40 (November 2013): 308–320.

Tesar, Marek et al. "Forever Young: Childhoods, Fairy Tales and Philosophy." *Global Studies of Childhood* 6, no. 2 (2016): 222–233.

Thomas, R. Murray. *Comparing Theories of Child Development*. Belmont, CA: Wadsworth, 2000.

Thomas, Rosalind. *Literacy and Orality in Ancient Greece*. Cambridge: Cambridge University Press, 1992.

Tolchinsky, Liliana. "The Configuration of Literacy as a Domain of Knowledge." *The Cambridge Handbook of Literacy*, edited by David R. Olsen and Nancy Torrance, 468–486. Cambridge: Cambridge University Press, 2009.

Tomasello, Michael. *The Cultural Origins of Human Communication*. Cambridge, MA: Harvard University Press, 1999.

———. *Constructing a Language: A Usage-Based Theory of Language Acquisition*. Cambridge, MA: Harvard University Press, 2003.

———. "The Key Is Social Cognition." *Language in Mind: Advances in the Study of Language and Thought*, edited by Dedre Gentner and Susan Goldin-Meadow, 47–57. Cambridge, MA: MIT Press, 2003.

———. *Origins of Human Communication*. Cambridge, MA: MIT Press, 2008.

Trevarthen, Colwyn. "What Is It Like to Be a Person Who Knows Nothing? Defining the Active Intersubjective Mind of a Newborn Human Being." *Infant and Child Development* 20 (2011): 119–135.

Turiel, Elliot et al. "Morality: Its Structure, Function, and Vagaries." *The Emergence of Morality in Young Children*, edited by Jerome Kagan and Sharon Lamb, Chap. 4. Chicago: University of Chicago Press, 1987.

Van Brennekom, Rick. "Aristotle and the Copula." *Journal of the History of Philosophy* 24, no. 1 (1986): 1–18.

Van Dyck, Maasten and Albrecht Heeffer. "Script and Symbolic Writing in Mathematics and Natural Philosophy." *Foundations of Science* 19, no. 1 (March 2014): 1–10.

Van Pitte, Frederick. "The Dating of Rule IV-B in Descartes' *Regulae ad directionem ingenui*." *Journal of the History of Philosophy* 29, no. 3 (1991): 375–395.

Vandendorpe, Christian. *From Papyrus to Hypertext*. Translated by Phyllis Aronoff and Howard Scott. Urbana, IL: University of Illinois Press, 2009.

Varela, Francisco et al. *The Embodied Mind: Cognitive Science and Human Experience*. Cambridge, MA: MIT Press, 1991.

Vatri, Alessandro. "The Physiology of Ancient Greek Reading." *The Classical Quarterly* 62, no. 2 (December 2012): 633–647.

Verducci, Susan. "Narratives in Ethics of Education." *Studies in Philosophy and Education* 33, no. 6 (November 2014): 575–585.

Vernant, Jean-Pierre. *Myth and Thought among the Greeks*. Translated by Janet Lloyd. New York: Zone Books, 2006.

———. *Myth and Society in Ancient Greece*. Translated by Janet Lloyd. New York: Zone Books, 1990.

Versnel, H. S. *Coping with the Gods: Wayward Readings in Greek Theology*. Leiden: Brill, 2011.

Vetlesen, Arne J. *Perception, Empathy, and Judgment: An Inquiry into the Preconditions of Moral Performance*. University Park, PA: Pennsylvania State University Press, 1994.

Vosoughi, Soroush et al. "The Spread of True and False News Online." *Science* 359, no. 6380 (March 2018): 1146–1151.

Vouloumanos, Athena and Suzanne Curtin. "Foundational Tuning: How Infants' Attention to Speech Predicts Language Development." *Cognitive Science* 38, no. 8 (2014): 1675–1686.

Vygotsky, Lev. *Thought and Language*. Translated by Alex Kozulin. Cambridge, MA: MIT Press, 1986.

Walton, Douglas. *The New Dialectic: Conversational Contexts of Argument*. Toronto, Canada: University of Toronto Press, 1998.

———. *The Place of Emotion in Argument*. University Park, PA: Penn State University Press, 1992.

Weisberg, Deena S. and Alison Gopnik. "Pretense, Counterfactuals, and Bayesian Causal Models: Why What Is Not Real Really Matters." *Cognitive Science* 37, no. 7 (August, 2013): 1368–1381.

Welsh, Talia. *The Child as Natural Phenomenologist: Primal and Primary Experience in Merleau-Ponty's Psychology*. Evanston, IL: Northwestern University Press, 2013.

———. "Do Neonates Display Innate Self-Awareness? Why Neonatal Imitation Fails to Provide Sufficient Grounds for Innate Self- and Other-Awareness." *Philosophical Psychology* 19, no. 2 (April 2006): 221–238.

White, E. Jayne. "Bringing Dialogism to Bear in the Early Years." *International Journal of Early Childhood* 47, no. 2 (August 2015): 213–216.

Whitney, Shiloh. "Affects, Images, and Childlike Perception: Self-Other Difference in Merleau-Ponty's Sorbonne Lectures." *Phaenex* 7, no. 2 (Fall/Winter 2012): 185–211.

Williams, Meredith. "The Significance of Learning in Wittgenstein's Later Philosophy." *Canadian Journal of Philosophy* 24, no. 2 (June 1994): 173–204.

Winsler, Adam et al. "The Role of Private Speech in the Transition from Collaborative to Independent Task Performance in Young Children." *Early Childhood Research Quarterly* 12 (1997): 57–79.

Wise, Jennifer. *Dionysus Writes: The Invention of Theatre in Ancient Greece*. Ithaca, NY: Cornell University Press, 1998.

Wolf, Maryanne. *Proust and the Squid: The Story and Science of the Reading Brain*. New York: HarperCollins, 2007.

Woolf, Greg. "Ancient Literacy?" *Bulletin of the Institute of Classical Studies* 58, no. 2 (December 2015): 31–42.

Wu, Zhen and Julie Gros-Louis. "Infants' Prelinguistic Communicative Acts and Maternal Responses: Relations to Linguistic Development." *First Language* 34, no. 1 (2014): 72–90.

Yapko, Michael. *Suggestions of Abuse*. New York: Simon & Schuster, 2009.

Yousef, Nancy. "Savage or Solitary: The Wild Child and Rousseau's Man of Nature." *Journal of the History of Ideas* 62, no. 2 (April 2001): 245–263.

Yu, Jiyuan. "The Language of Being: Between Aristotle and Chinese Philosophy." *International Philosophical Quarterly* 39, no. 4 (December 1999): 439–454.

Yunus, Harvey. "Writing for Reading: Thucydides, Plato, and the Emergence of the Critical Reader" *Written Texts and the Rise of Literate Culture in Ancient Greece*, edited by Harvey Yunus, Chap. 9. Cambridge: Cambridge University Press, 2003.

Zinchenko, Vladimir P. "Should the 'Postulate of Directness' Be Overcome?" *History of the Human Sciences* 28, no. 2 (2015): 51–71.

Index

Achilles, 190, 229n19
affective attunement, 31, 281
affordance, 15, 26–27, 281
Aithchison, Jean, 275n25
alphabet/alphabetic script, 155, 160;
  and conceptualization in Greek
  thought, 199; and elemental thinking,
  198–99; and learning to read,
  156–57; and the objectification of
  language, 156, 164
ancient Greece, 160–64; agonistic
  character of, 189, 203; education in,
  185n68; indigenous development
  of writing in, 160; and mimetic
  education, 175–76; oral poetry in,
  161–64; originally an oral culture, 160
animism, 86–87
Annoni, Marco, 275nn23–24
Antognazza, Rosa, 277n55
Arendt, Hannah, 91
Ariso, José María, 100n90
Aristotle, 57–58, 97n28, 146n34,
  146n49, 150n102, 173, 178,
  184n58, 185n74, 193, 232n79; and
  abstraction, 201; on being, 220–21,
  277n70; and *energeia*, 274n5; and
  logic, 223–25; and *logos*, 229n29;
  on mathematics, 252; and myth,
  229n24; on nature, 250–51; on
  phusis and *technē*, 266–67; and
  propositional truth, 218–19; and
  rhetoric, 226; and writing, 206, 209,
  233n92
Ayers, Michael, 278n72

Bacon, Francis, 249, 251
Baker, Mark C., 102n126
Bakker, Egbert J., 183n32, 183n35
Bar, Moshe, 101n111
Bargh, John A., 96n15, 100n93
Barinaga, Marcia, 101n122
Battezzato, Luigi, 231n54
Baz, Avner, 145n24
Benzaquén, Adriana S., 144n8
Bergen, Benjamin K., 186n82, 279n88
Berkeley, George, 256
Bickerton, Derek, 150n104
Boelen, Bernard, 95n2, 96n16,
  98n22, 97n30, 98n51, 99n67,
  99n75, 100n95, 100n97, 100n100,
  101n105, 148n63, 149n93,
  150n106
Boyd, Brian, 149n91
Bredlau, Susan, 98n55
Brownell, Celia A., 97n45
Bruner, Jerome, 97n38, 102n123,
  144n10, 145n30, 146nn31–33,
  146nn35–37, 146nn40–41

Burkert, Walter, 228n6, 228n8, 229n17
Butterfield, David, 274n7

Cambron-Goulet, Matilda, 232n74
Casey, Edward S., 148n78
Cassirer, Ernst, 183n40, 228n7
causality, 33–34
Chemero, Anthony, 148n69
childhood: and affective attunement, 86–88; development, 3–4; and ecstatic dwelling, 61–64; and embodiment, 91–93; and the environing-world, 79–86; and ethical development, 73–79; habit and know-how in, 82–84; history of, 58; and imitation, 66–67; immersion and contravention in, 63–64, 81–82; and individuation, 69–73, 76–77, 88; and joint attention, 67–69; and locomotion, 80–81; nature and nurture in, 65–66; and the personal-social-world, 64–73; phenomenology of, 58–59; and play, 84–86; pre-verbal period, 93–94; and projection, 88–89; proto-phenomenology and, 56–58, 59–61; and separation anxiety, 72–73; temporality and history in, 90–91; traditional philosophy and, 55–56; traditional theories of, 61–62; and wonder, 62–63
Christianity, 237
Clark, Andy, 147n51, 148n66, 149n80
Clark, Eve V., 102n126, 107, 144n6, 145n17, 145n29, 148n65, 148n73
common sense ontology, 11
communication, 36, 124–25
consciousness, 124, 147n56
contravention, 16–17, 281
Corbalis, Michael C., 184n64
correlational scope, 32, 281
Coulmas, Florian, 181n3, 181n5, 181n8, 184n62, 185n72
Culbertson, Carolyn, 233n81
Cunningham, Hugh, 95n5

Dahlstrom, Daniel O., 144n11
Daniels, Harry, 147n52
Dante, 240
Derrida, Jacques, 180n1, 185n75, 232nn77–79, 232n81, 271; challenge to his theory of phono-centrism, 213; complicity with Plato, 216–17; and the deconstructive critique of Plato on writing, 213–17; on metaphor, 263; phenomenological critique of, 213–17
Descartes, René, 9, 55, 147n56, 248, 250–51, 255, 257, 276n44, 276n47, 276n49, 278n71, 278n78
Detienne, Marcel, 183n33, 194, 230n32, 231n60
Dewey, John, 21
dictionaries, 245–47; differential fitness, 43–44, 49, 137–40, 282
digital media, 269–72; and democratization, 271–72; and non-literate disclosure, 269; and pace, 270–71; and threats to truthfulness, 271–72; and virtuality, 270
disclosure, 30–33
Dissanayake, Ellen, 279n102
Dow, James M., 97n40
Dunn, Judy, 99n72
Dutton, Blake, 276n48
dwelling, 10, 13, 30; and ecstatic experience, 14

Ebbesen, Sten, 274n4
ecstatic experience, 14, 282
Edwards, Carolyn Pope., 99n73
Ehrlich, John F., 184n54
embodiment, 29–30, 282; and child development, 91–93; and cognition, 34–35; and 4E model, 35
empathy, 24–25, 77–79
enactive interpretation, 33, 39, 50, 52, 85–86, 282
Engelland, Chad, 147m57, 148n70
English, Andrea R., 96n20

environing-world, 15–22, 282; as ecological, 15; meaning and value in, 22; and science, 21–22
existential naturalism, 12, 282
exposition, 15–20, 282; and contravention, 16–17; in language acquisition, 138–39; and science, 18; scope and importance of, 19–20
Evans, Vyvyan, 144n4

factical experience, 11, 282
Falcon, Andrea, 230n42
feral children, 105
Ferrari, G. R. F., 229n29
Field, Tiffany, 101n119
finitude, 16–17
Fögen, Thorsten, 274n4
Ford, Andrew, 184n58, 231n66
Forrester, Stefan, 279n86
4E model of cognition, 128–29, 277n59
freedom, 28
Fulkerson, Matthew, 101n118

Gahrn-Andersen, Rasmus, 280n108
Galileo, 249, 255, 266
Genesee, Fred, 145n19
Gentili, Bruno, 183n29
Gibson, Eleanor J., 101n116
Gill, Christopher, 232n72
Goody, Jack, 151
Gorgias, 197
Gosetti-Ferencei, Jennifer Anna, 186n81
Goswami, Usha, 181n10
Gould, John, 228n11
Griffin, Jasper, 228n16

Hadot, Pierre, 237
Halliwell, Stephen, 230n36, 279n99
Hamilton, William, 278n74
Hannan, Sarah, 95n8
Harris, Roy, 184n58, 186n80
Harris, William V., 231n64
Haskins, Ekaterina V., 230n38

Havelock, Eric, 151, 181n6, 182n22, 184n55, 184n59, 185n67, 228n3, 230n48, 233n87
Heath, John, 229n28
Hegel, G.W.F.: on alphabetic writing, 253; on recognition, 23
Heidegger, Martin, 181n1, 183n44, 278n71; on subjectivity and objectivity, 255–57
history, 28–29; and language acquisition, 136–37
Hobbes, Thomas, 257
Hobbs, Valerie, 185n66
Homeric poetry, 161–64; Achilles in, 190; and the divine, 163; and the heroic ideal, 190–91; as a lived world, 162–63; memory and truth in, 162–63; and mortality, 190–91; and non-centralized selfhood, 191–92; Odysseus in, 191; originally an oral tradition, 161; and proto-phenomenology, 192; reflexive character of, 163–64; world-forming character of, 161–62; the world in, 190–92
Husserl, Edmund, 53n2
Hyland, Drew, 230n33
hyper-literacy, 226–27, 244–45, 283

immersion, 15–16, 283; bidirectional relation to exposition, 19, 37; and presentation, 20
imitation, 66–67
indicative concepts, 13–14, 283
individuation and socialization, 25, 69–73, 88, 117–21
Inkpin, Andrew, iiin1
interpretation, 32–33, 90, 283; beginning with language acquisition, 106
intimation, 31–32, 283
Irwin, Brian A., 185n70

Jackendoff, Ray, 147n49, 147n51
Jerimiha, Edward T., 229n23

Johnston, Sarah Isles, 228n9
joint attention, 67–69, 126–27

Kahn, Charles, 230n43, 233n89
Kant, Immanuel, 55, 251, 252, 255; and subjectivity, 257–58, 278n81
Keller, Helen, 36, 46, 118, 122–23, 146n42
Kennedy, David, 96n26
Kierkegaard, Søren, 258
Klein, Jacob, 276n41
know-how, 21
Kövecses, Zoltán, 279n93

Laing, Kathryn E., 102n124
Landes, Donald A., 101n113
Langfur, Stephen, 98n53, 146n48
language, 9–10, 35–47; as differential fitness, 43–44; and embodiment, 42–43; and illocution, 242–43; and the literal-metaphorical distinction, 260–65; and the lived world, 37–40; and memory, 40; and the mind-body question, 124; as more than its lexical elements, 107; and the personal-social-environing-world, 38–40; phenomenological priority of, 36–38, 105–7, 108; and presentation, 10, 41; and representation, 9–10, 39–42, 49; and temporality, 40; and thought, 44–47
language acquisition, 4–5; and babbling, 130; as the beginning of self-awareness, 118–19, 122–23; challenge to traditional theories of, 108–14; and differential fitness, 137–40; early comprehension and norms in, 108–14; ecological conditions for, 106–7; and embodied enactment, 127–29; and the environing-world, 125–31; gesture and sound in, 129–31; and history, 136–37; as immersed dwelling, 107–14; and individual development, 117–21; and joint attention, 126–27;
as meaning-laden enactment, 108–11; and memory, 132–33; and narrative, 134–36; as a personal-social-world, 115–25; philosophical implications of, 121–25; pre-verbal capacities for, 104–7; and projection, 131; social origins of, 115–17; stages of, 107–8; and symbols, 139–40; and temporality, 131–34; and truth, 140–42; and words as focal indications, 112–14
Latin, 237–41; and the translation of Greek philosophy, 238–39. *See also* Neo-Latin/learned Latin
Law, Vivian, 185n74, 274n6
Ledbetter, Grace M., 183n36
Leder, Drew, 147n55
Leibniz, G.W., 252
Leonhardt, Jürgen, 274n7
Levinson, Stephen C., 148n74
Lincoln, Bruce, 229n26
Linell, Per, 181n3, 277nn60–63
literacy/writing/reading, 5–7, 143; and the alphabet, 155–56; and authorship, 166, 241–42; bias toward in traditional research, 153; can exhibit ecstatic immersion, 154, 156, 179–80; central features of, 155–56; and decontextualized abstraction, 168–70, 175–76; degrees of, 155; derived from oral language, 179, 235–36; and the difference between a text and its meaning, 167–68; different types of writing, 280n109; and digital media, 269–72; and disengaged prose, 172; and education, 244; elements of, 164–79; and the emphasis on literal, descriptive language, 242; and the explication of language, 153, 158–59; and the exposition of speech, 156; as extended cognition, 180; and figuration, 252–53; and the generation of philosophical questions, 153–54;

gradual dissociation from oral language in post-Roman periods, 241–44; and the Greek discovery of abstract concepts, 199–201; learning of, 156–60; and logical reasoning, 168–69; and mentality, 167–68, 170, 243–44; and modern science, 249–52; necessary but not sufficient condition for the development of Greek philosophy, 203–5; and the objectification of nature, 249–52; and the objectified explication of language, 241–43; and the openness of interpretation, 177–78; and philosophy, 6–7, 151–52, 203–5, 198–201; phonics *vs.* whole language, 182n20; and a post-literate world, 265–72; and progress, 267–68; and recursion, 174, 236; and reflective skills, 173–74, 208–9; and reification, 236; and the regulation of language, 176–77; and the regulation of life, 244–45; and representation, 165, 178–79, 253–54; and silent reading, 202–3; spatialization in, 165; and temporality, 160; unnatural character of, 157–58; value of, 154, 179–80, 265–67; and virtual worlds, 179–80; visual character of, 164; and visual processing, 157, 158–59
literate discoveries in Greek philosophy, 217–26; logic, 222–25; propositional truth, 217–19; substantial being, 219–22
lived world, 1–2, 10–13, 283
Lloyd, G.E.R., 229n30, 231n63, 233n84, 234n102, 275n27
Locke, John, 248
Logan, Robert K., 280n110
logic, 234n96
logos, 187, 193–94, 218–19, 229n29
Long, Christopher P., 234n97
Luria, Alexander R., 145n27
Lyotard, Jean François, 96n17

Manetti, Giovanni, 230n49
Marincola, John, 184n57
Marrou, H.I., 183n28
Martin, Richard P., 229nn26–27
mathematics, 198, 204, 249–50; and figuration, 249–50; and *mathēsis*, 278n71; and mechanics, 276n39; and the modern conception of nature, 249–52
Mavrogenes, Nancy A., 231n53
McDowell, John, 144n7
McGuirk, James, 100n89
McLuhan, Marshall, 151, 280n110
Medieval thought, 237, 239
Meli, Domenico Bertoloni, 277n69
memory, 28
Merleau-Ponty, Maurice, 29, 34–35, 70, 95n2, 99n66, 100n88, 100n104, 148n60
metaphor, 35; and human thinking, 260–62
mind-body question, 124
Miroshnichenko, Andrey, 280n110
Morgan, Kathryn A., 232n76
Morin, Alain, 146n44
Morris, David, 95n10
Mosedale, Frederick E., 145n24
muthos, 187, 193, 229n27
myth, ancient Greek, 188–92; ambiguity of, 194–95; as culture-forming, 188–89; as a lived world, 188; and mortality, 189; pluralistic character of, 188–89; and the sacred, 188; and sense-making, 193–94

naturalism, 33–34, 250
natural language, 35–36, 103; as support for proto-phenomenology, 103–4
nature: in ancient and modern thought, 250–52
nature and nurture, 65–66, 104–5
Nelson, Katherine, 57, 67, 83, 95nn11–13, 96nn21–22, 96n25, 96n27, 97n33, 97n35, 97n44, 99n82,

100n91, 100n96, 100nn98–99, 101nn111–12, 143n2, 144n12, 145n18, 145n22, 145n24, 145n28, 146n39, 148n61, 149n79, 149nn81–84, 149n86, 149nn88–89, 150nn95–99, 181n9, 181n11
Neo-Latin/learned Latin: and the passage from oral/natural language to literate and technical formats, 239–41
Netz, Reviel, 230n40
Newton, Isaac, 250–51

Oakes, Lisa M., 96n18
Ober, Josiah, 231n62
Odysseus, 163–64, 191, 192, 196, 233n83
Oedipus, 196
Olson, David R., 184n44, 184nn50–52, 234n101, 241–43, 254, 275nn10–20, 275n28, 275nn34–35, 277nn64–65, 279nn82–84, 279n89, 279n100, 280n103
Ong, Walter, 151, 154, 181nn38–39, 181nn41–42, 184n49, 184n53, 184n61, 185n71, 185n73, 185n77, 228n3, 230nn45–46, 232nn80–81, 234nn98–99, 240, 275nn7–8, 275n21, 275nn29–31, 275n33, 280n105
orality/oral language, 5–6; aural character of, 164; elements of, 164–79; and embodiment, 166–67; as a literate construction, 152; and lived context, 168–70; and lived narrative, 175; and mimetic immediacy in early Greek culture, 263–65; and poetic engagement, 170–72; as precondition for literacy, 157; and presentation, 178; primary and secondary, 204; and rhetoric, 225–26; temporal character of, 165; and traditionalism, 176
ousia, 221, 233n88
Overmann, Karenleigh A., 280n108

Padel, Ruth, 229n21
Parmenides, 221, 224, 234n94
Parry, Milman, 161
philosophy: its advent in ancient Greece, 192–93; as critique of oral poetry in ancient Greece, 160–61, 187, 194; as hyper-literacy, 226–27; and literacy, 6–7, 187, 198–201; Medieval, 237; Modern, 9–10, 12, 18, 44, 237, 248
phusis, 250, 276n43
physicalism, 52
Piaget, Jean, 60, 66, 86–87
Pinock, Christopher, 276n42
Pinker, Steven, 101n121
place and space, 29–30
Plato, 146n49, 172, 173, 271, 185n74, 193, 234n93; and abstraction, 200–201; on being, 219–20; his critique of oral poetry, 195–98, 263–64; his critique of writing, 206–11; on language in the *Seventh Letter* and the *Cratylus*, 209–11; and *mimēsis*, 197–98, 215; and rhetoric, 225–26; and writing, 205–11; writing and philosophy in, 211–12
pluralism, 32–33, 50–52, 268, 284
Pound, Ezra, 172
Powell, Barry P., 181n5, 181n7, 182n25
Pratt, Louise H., 233n82
presentation, 10, 47–49, 284
personal-world, 14–15, 284
presumption of immanence, 11–13, 283
Prier, Raymond A., 185n79, 230n36, 232n81
print, 245–49; and the development of science, 247; and dictionaries, 245–47; and the individual reader, 247–48; and the objectification of language, 245; and the standardization of language, 245–47
proto-phenomenology, 1–2, 9–10, 284; and appearance, 10–11; and being, 221–22; and the borderlands of philosophy, 272–73; and causality, 33–34; and child development, 3–4;

and language, 2–3, 35–38; and language acquisition, 4–5, 143; and naturalism, 11–12; scope of, 21–22; and a summary of Volumes I and II, 272–74; and world, 14
projection, 26–27, 284

Ravenschrift, Ian, 280n108
reading. *See* literacy/writing/reading
Ready, Jonathan L., 183n27
recursion, 174, 236, 284
reification, 17, 236, 284
Ricoeur, Paul, 149n90, 279n85
representation, 9–10, 20–21, 100n99, 253–54
Robb, Kevin, 182n21, 183n26, 185nn68–69, 232n68, 232n71, 232n73
Roberts, Beth, 181n14
Rochat, Phillipe, 98n52, 101n117
Roniger, Scott, 234n95
Roochnik, David, 229n20
Rozemond, Marleen, 276n47
Rutter, Michael, 96n23

Sallis, John, 230n33
Sameroff, Arnold, 96n23
Sandler, Wendy, 181n2
scaffolding, 27, 285
Scott, Lawrence, 28n112
scriptio continua, 201–3
second nature, 19
Segal, Charles, 183n29, 228n12, 230n39
Segerdahl, Pär, 145n21
Sheets-Johnstone, Maxine, 97n43, 100nn92, 100n94
Sider, Theodore, 235
sign language, 180n2
Simms, Eva M., 95n6, 99nn80, 99n84, 149n85, 149n87
Sini, Carlo, 231n51
skepticism, 121–22, 125
Smith, P. Christopher, 228n4
Snell, Bruno, 229n30, 230n44
social-world, 22–25, 285

Socrates, 175–76, 192–93, 196; in the *Meno*, 232n69; and the search for definition, 199–200
Soffer, Gail, 96n17
Sourvinou-Inwood, Christiane, 279n101
Spelke, Elizabeth S., 148n62
Stafford, Emma, 228n10
Stern, Daniel N., 95n7, 96n24, 97n38, 101n106
Storey, Robert, 148n58
subject-object binary, 9–10, 22, 254–60; different senses of subjectivity and objectivity, 258–59; and the Latin terms *subjectum* and *objectum*, 255–57; and subjectivism, 259
sumbolon, 150n100
Svenbro, Jesper, 231n52, 231n54, 231n56, 232n17

Tabery, James, 96n23
Talero, Maria, 100n88
Taylor, Charles, iiin1
temporality, 27–28, 30, 285; and language acquisition, 131–34
Thomas, R. Murray, 95n3
Thomas, Rosalind, 183n26, 231n58, 231n64
Thucydides, 172
Tolchinsky, Liliana, 181n15
Tomasello, Michael, 97n42, 144n3, 145n6, 147n57, 148nn59–60, 148n72, 148n76
Trevarthen, Colwyn, 98n48
Trump, Donald, 150n107
trust, 48–49, 71, 140
truth, 47–52; as appropriate disclosure, 51; and differential fitness, 49; in early childhood, 140–42; and falsehood in Greek culture, 217–18; as fitting discourse, 49; and pluralism, 50–52; presentational, 47–49; settings of, 50–52; and trust, 48–49, 140

Uher, Jana, 3n39

Van Brennekom, Rick, 278n70
Vandendorpe, Christian, 231n57, 280n111
Vatri, Alessandro, 231n55
Verducci, Susan, 99n72
Vernantt, Jean-Pierre, 228n8, 231n61
Versnel, H.S., 229n31
Vetlesen, Arne J., 99n78
Vygotsky, Lev, 84, 96n15, 118–20

Welsh, Talia, 94n2, 98n50
White, E. Jayne, 98n54
Whitney, Shiloh, 98n50
Williams, Meredith, 94n2

Wise, Jennifer, 183n42, 184n43, 184n45
Wittgenstein, Ludwig, 146n46
Wolf, Maryanne, 158, 181n16, 183n37, 185n76
Woolf, Greg, 230n40
writing. *See* literacy/writing/reading

Yapko, Michael, 99n68
Yousef, Nancy, 144n9
Yu, Jiyuan, 233n91
Yunus, Harvey, 184n47

Zinchenko, Vladimir, 147n53

About the Author

Lawrence J. Hatab is Louis I. Jaffe Professor of Philosophy and Eminent Scholar Emeritus at Old Dominion University. He is the author of *Nietzsche's On the Genealogy of Morality* (2008), *Nietzsche's Life Sentence: Coming to Terms With Eternal Recurrence* (2005), *Ethics and Finitude: Heideggerian Contributions to Moral Philosophy* (2000), *A Nietzschean Defense of Democracy: An Experiment in Postmodern Politics* (1995), and *Myth and Philosophy: A Contest of Truths* (1990).

www.ingramcontent.com/pod-product-compliance
Lightning Source LLC
Chambersburg PA
CBHW050857300426
44111CB00010B/1284